There Is No Place for Us

"This is a tremendous achievement in reporting, in narration, in emotional and intellectual understanding. Brian Goldstone's book will stand with J. Anthony Lukas's *Common Ground* and other works that tell the story of our country by telling the stories of our fellow citizens."

—James Fallows,
author of *Our Towns*

"*There Is No Place for Us* is at once a profound reckoning with housing inequality and an intimate, never-pathologizing account of people working themselves to death in their struggle to secure a home—proving the lie of American meritocracy in the process. It is an urgent indictment of the narrow definition of homelessness that leaves millions of people in jeopardy and disguises the true extent of the crisis that capitalism has created. Above all, it is a deeply researched, meticulously reported, and care-filled book."

—Christina Sharpe,
author of *Ordinary Notes*

"Brian Goldstone's blistering investigation into the true scope of America's ballooning homelessness crisis beautifully depicts the tenacity and heart of several vulnerable families struggling to survive in a system that refuses to help them—or even to acknowledge them at all."

—Roxanna Asgarian,
author of *We Were Once a Family*

"As Brian Goldstone illustrates in this beautifully written work of heartbreaking journalism, even a grinding cycle of full-time, low-wage work doesn't guarantee a roof over your head once you clock out. Hidden homelessness is a nationwide epidemic, and *There Is No Place for Us* shows how rapidly gentrifying cities like Atlanta are becoming epicenters of the crisis. Within these pages, people whose lives and labor have long been invisible are given the space to tell their stories—and to remind the reader that any one of us could end up in their shoes unless something changes on a structural level, and fast."

—Kim Kelly,
author of *Fight Like Hell*

"Since unhoused people showed up on America's street corners in the 1980s, mass homelessness has been a public crisis. Yet official data hides the reality, dominant myths blame the victims, and the numbers of unhoused people continue to grow. Brian Goldstone understands we cannot address this crisis until we experience the very human reality of the second-class citizenship that exists for people who have no place to call their own. To read this book is to know, like those who fought Jim Crow before us, that none of us can enjoy the freedom this nation promises until we guarantee an equal right to a place to be."

—Jonathan Wilson-Hartgrove,
author of *Strangers at My Door*

"*There Is No Place for Us* is a crucial, masterful book that will change the national conversation about homelessness. Brian Goldstone gives us a wrenching chronicle of what happens when the fact of a home cannot be taken for granted. Poignant and infuriating, his book reveals the tragic myths embedded in the stories we tell ourselves about working hard in America."

—Rachel Aviv,
author of *Strangers to Ourselves*

"A model of ethical journalism . . . [Goldstone] trains an empathetic eye on families that are struggling in an increasingly gentrified city that prizes property above people. . . . Make a place for this book alongside Jane Jacobs' classic *Death and Life of Great American Cities*."

—*Kirkus Reviews*

"Harrowing . . . Goldstone weaves a richly detailed narrative of his subjects' increasingly desperate struggles. . . . It's a gripping, high-stakes account of America's housing emergency."

—*Publishers Weekly*

There Is No Place for Us

There Is No Place for Us

WORKING

AND

HOMELESS

IN

AMERICA

Brian Goldstone

CROWN
NEW YORK

CROWN

An imprint of the Crown Publishing Group
A division of Penguin Random House LLC.
1745 Broadway,
New York, NY 10019
crownpublishing.com
penguinrandomhouse.com

Library of Congress Cataloging-in-Publication Data
Names: Goldstone, Brian, author.
Title: There is no place for us: working and homeless in America / Brian Goldstone.
Description: New York: Crown, [2025] | Includes bibliographical references and index.
    Identifiers: LCCN 2024029738 (print) | LCCN 2024029739 (ebook) |
    ISBN 9780593237144 (hardcover) | ISBN 9780593237168 (paperback) |
    ISBN 9780593237151 (ebook)
Subjects: LCSH: Homelessness—United States.
Classification: LCC HV4505 .G66 2025 (print) | LCC HV4505 (ebook) |
    DDC 362.5/920973—dc23/eng/20250108
LC record available at https://lccn.loc.gov/2024029738
LC ebook record available at https://lccn.loc.gov/2024029739

Hardcover ISBN 978-0-593-23714-4
Ebook ISBN 978-0-593-23715-1

Manufactured in the United States of America on acid-free paper

Editor: Amanda Cook | Editorial assistant: Katie Berry | Production editor: Terry Deal
Text designer: Aubrey Khan | Production manager: Heather Williamson
Copy editor: Elisabeth Magnus | Proofreaders: Lorie Young, Daina Penikas,
and Sophie Garcia-Cubas Assemat | Indexer: Stephen Callahan
Publicist: Penny Simon and Mary Moates | Marketer: Mason Eng

Map by Nick Springer, copyright © 2024 Springer Cartographics

9 8 7 6 5 4 3 2 1

First Edition

The authorized representative in the EU for product safety and compliance is
Penguin Random House Ireland, Morrison Chambers, 32 Nassau Street,
Dublin D02 YH68, Ireland, https://eu-contact.penguin.ie.

For Elaine

| CONTENTS |

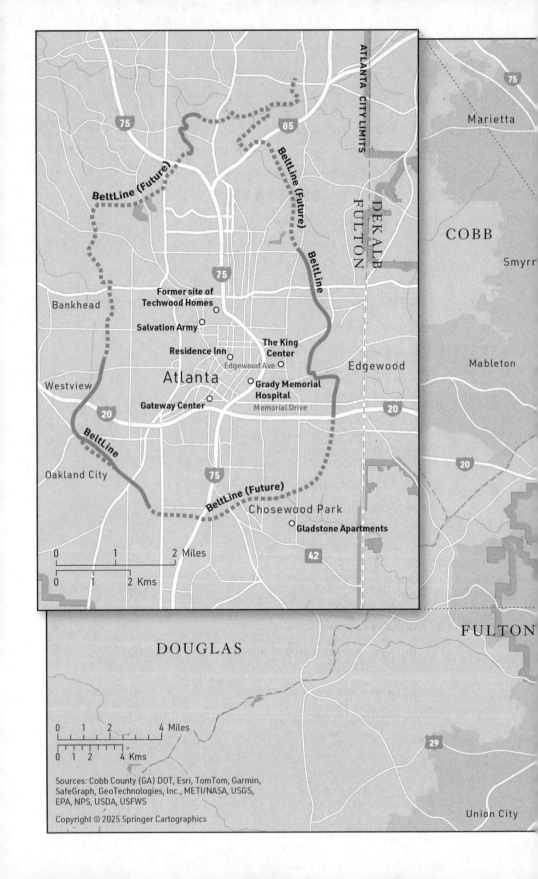

Marietta

75

ATLANTA CITY LIMITS

85

BeltLine (Future)

BeltLine (Future)

BeltLine (Future)

BeltLine

COBB

Smyrr

DEKALB
FULTON

Bankhead

Former site of
Techwood Homes

Salvation Army

Residence Inn

The King
Center

Edgewood Ave

Mableton

Atlanta

Westview

Grady Memorial
Hospital

Edgewood

20

20

20

BeltLine

Gateway Center

Memorial Drive

Oakland City

75

BeltLine (Future)

Chosewood Park

Gladstone Apartments

42

0   1   2 Miles

0   1   2 Kms

DOUGLAS

FULTON

0   1   2   4 Miles

0   1   2   4 Kms

29

Sources: Cobb County (GA) DOT, Esri, TomTom, Garmin,
SafeGraph, GeoTechnologies, Inc., METI/NASA, USGS,
EPA, NPS, USDA, USFWS

Union City

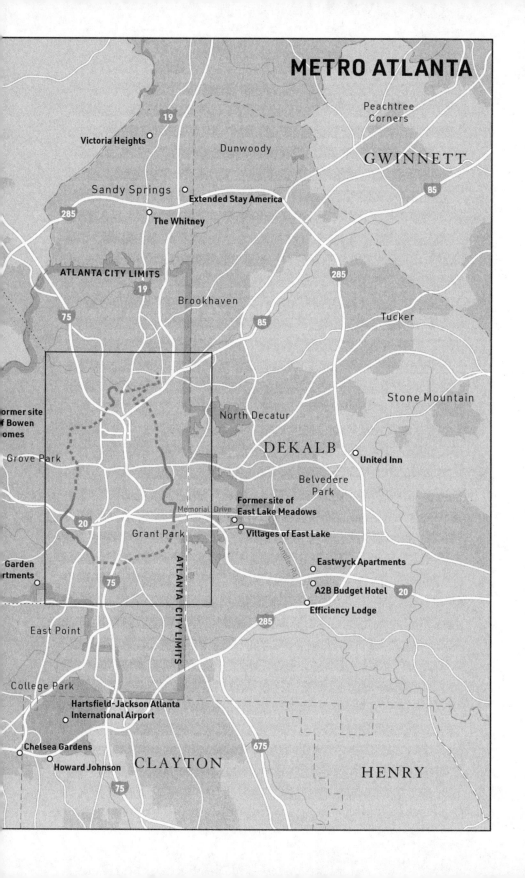

METRO ATLANTA

Peachtree Corners

Dunwoody

GWINNETT

19

Victoria Heights

Sandy Springs

Extended Stay America

285

The Whitney

85

ATLANTA CITY LIMITS

19

Brookhaven

85

Tucker

285

Stone Mountain

former site
f Bowen
omes

North Decatur

Grove Park

DEKALB

United Inn

Belvedere
Park

Memorial Drive

Former site of
East Lake Meadows

20

Grant Park

Villages of East Lake

Candler Rd

Garden
rtments

Eastwyck Apartments

75

A2B Budget Hotel

20

ATLANTA CITY LIMITS

Efficiency Lodge

East Point

285

College Park

Hartsfield-Jackson Atlanta
International Airport

Chelsea Gardens

675

Howard Johnson

CLAYTON

HENRY

75

| THE FAMILIES |

■ BRITTANY ("BRITT") WILKINSON

Desiree—daughter

Kyrie—son

Aaliyah—sister

Devin—brother

Josiah—brother

Cassandra ("Cass")—mother

Alonzo—father

Javon—Desiree and Kyrie's father

Trisha—aunt

Kimi—aunt

Theresa—grandmother

Granny—great-grandmother

Big Mama—great-great-grandmother

■ MAURICE AND NATALIA TAYLOR

Shantel—daughter

Anthony—son

Matthew—son

Aaron—cousin and children's godfather

■ KARA THOMPSON

Grace—daughter

Nathaniel—son

Jermaine—son

Joshua—son

Darius—Grace's father

Isaiah—Jermaine's father

■ MICHELLE SIMMONS

DJ—son

Danielle—daughter

Skye—daughter

Jacob—Skye's father

Daniel—DJ and Danielle's father

Regina—aunt

■ CELESTE WALKER

Nyah—daughter

Jalen—son

Micah—son

Caleb—grandson

| AUTHOR'S NOTE |

This is a work of nonfiction. Events and dialogue were witnessed firsthand or reconstructed on the basis of primary documents, published accounts, and extensive interviews with sources present at the time. My reporting also draws from government records, background interviews, and many hours of audio and video recordings. The names of the five main families have been changed to protect their privacy. No other facts, names, or identifying information have been altered. For more detail, see "Sources and Methods" in the notes section (page 371).

INTRODUCTION

By the time I met Cokethia Goodman and her children, they had been homeless for three months. Their ordeal began on an afternoon in August 2018, when Cokethia discovered a terse letter from her landlord in the mailbox. The home she had been renting over the past year was in a quiet Atlanta neighborhood, within walking distance of a playground and her kids' schools. But the area was gentrifying, and their landlord had decided it was time to cash out on her investment. The property would be sold; the family's lease would not be renewed. Unable to find another affordable apartment nearby, they relocated to a dilapidated rental in Forest Park, on the city's outer periphery. The rent was $50 more per month. After just two weeks in the house, Cokethia heard a scream from the kitchen: her twelve-year-old son had been washing dishes when, reaching his hand into the soapy water, he got a painful electric shock. Code enforcement arrived and, discovering exposed wiring in the basement, immediately condemned the home. The family moved into a squalid extended-stay hotel, until the weekly rent proved too expensive. There was nowhere left to go.

When Cokethia shared her story with me, she was still in a state of disbelief. It wasn't just the circumstances that had deprived her family of housing. It was the fact that they had become homeless despite her full-time job as a home health aide—a point Cokethia returned to again and again, as if unable to wrap her mind around it. Like many of us, she had been taught to believe that homelessness and a job were mutually exclusive: that if she worked hard enough and stayed on top of her responsibilities, if she clocked enough hours, she could avoid such a fate. And yet here she was, dressed in bright blue medical scrubs and checking her phone to see if any shelter beds had opened up. "I grew up in this city," she told me. "I graduated from high school in this city. Through my job, I've been taking care of men and women in this city. And now my kids and I are *homeless*? How does that even happen?"

I recounted the family's plight in an article for *The New Republic* in 2019. But their story wouldn't let me go. Was their predicament a bizarre anomaly, an exception to the rule? Or was their experience representative of a larger trend? If that was the case, then why did it seem so out of sync with our prevailing assumptions about homelessness? As I continued to research and write about housing insecurity, I realized that the problem was much bigger than this particular family or even this particular city. I started seeing it everywhere. In Northern California, I visited "safe parking lots" full of working families living in their cars and minivans. I talked to a shelter director who explained that more than half of the people his organization served were employed in low-wage jobs.

One freezing January morning, at an encampment in midtown Atlanta, I met a woman in her late forties. Wearing slacks and a dark blazer, she was often mistaken for a case manager. But in fact she lived in one of the tents. Over breakfast at a Chick-fil-A around the corner, she pointed to a garbage dumpster behind the restaurant, where a garden hose was peeking out. Each day at dawn, she told me, she left her tent and used the hose to shower, praying no men were nearby. Then she went to work at a call center.

There were others: people who had worked their entire lives and, now disabled, were on the street because of paltry government support (or none at all); the man outside the food pantry who had just landed a second job in the meat department at Kroger, living with his wife and kids at a Super 8; the young Uber driver who did airport runs during the day and slept in the same car at night. And soon there were the families whose journeys I have sought to document in this book.

■

THE *WORKING HOMELESS:* the term seems counterintuitive, an oxymoron. In a country where hard work and determination are supposed to lead to success—or at least stability—there is something scandalous about the very concept. Popular media and scholarly accounts alike often depict unhoused people as lacking, almost by definition, not only homes but jobs; the view that these men and women are "unconnected to the world of work," as sociologist Peter Rossi argued in his seminal 1989 book *Down and Out in America,* has persisted into the present day. Yet a growing number of Americans confront a starkly different reality. Besieged by a combination of skyrocketing rents, low wages, and inadequate tenant protections, they are becoming the new face of homelessness in the United States: people whose paychecks are not enough to keep a roof over their heads.

Today there isn't a single state, metropolitan area, or county in the United States where a full-time worker earning the local minimum wage can afford a two-bedroom apartment. Currently, 11.4 million low-income households are classified as "severely cost burdened," spending, on average, an astounding 78 percent of their earnings on rent alone. But strikingly, it's in the nation's richest, most rapidly developing cities—the ones "doing well"—that the threat of homelessness has become particularly acute. New York, whose economy soared over the last three decades, has watched its shelter population more than triple. Washington, D.C., boasts some of the country's highest median incomes; it also has one of the greatest per capita homeless rates. Seattle is close behind. In Austin and Phoenix, Denver and Nashville, the pattern is similar. Unemployment is at a record low; corporate profits have surged; the signs of growth are everywhere. Yet the delivery drivers, daycare workers, supermarket cashiers, and home health aides who help sustain our cities are being relentlessly priced out of them—and often out of housing altogether. Unlike earlier periods of widespread immiseration, such as the recession of 2008, what we're seeing today is an emergency born less of poverty than prosperity. Families are not "falling" into homelessness. They're being pushed.

Atlanta, the third-fastest-growing metropolitan area in the country, is a case in point. For much of the past century, the city has been shaped by a strategic partnership between its Black political leadership and white business elites that prioritizes stability and growth above all else. *Resurgens,* the city motto, has been seen to refer not only to Atlanta's rise from the ashes after the Civil War but to a perpetual process of commerce-driven renewal. Fashioning Atlanta into an economic powerhouse has always been an aspiration for city leaders, and in recent decades they have achieved this goal. Home Depot, Coca-Cola, Delta Airlines, and UPS are some of the many Fortune 500 companies now headquartered there. Often referred to as the "Silicon Valley of the South," the city has become a leading technology hub—Google, Microsoft, and Amazon all have outposts—and it has also emerged as a key center for healthcare and life sciences, transportation and logistics. Then there's the entertainment industry: these days, more movies and TV series are being shot in Atlanta, or "Y'allywood," than in California. The area's population surge has been equally dramatic, nearly doubling since 1990—and showing no sign of slowing down.

But by far the most startling transformation has been the remaking of the city's physical landscape. For decades, Atlanta typified the "poor in the core" phenomenon seen in many postindustrial urban areas, the result of deliberate disinvestment and the flight of white residents to surrounding suburbs. This began to change with Atlanta's hosting of the 1996 Olympic Games, which coincided with a concerted campaign to draw a more affluent demographic to the city proper. Tax incentives and other public subsidies were mobilized to entice developers and real estate capital to build and invest within city limits. Twenty years later, whole swaths of Atlanta had been changed beyond recognition. The place was shinier, trendier—and much wealthier. For anyone who had associated the city solely with traffic-clogged highways or fortress-like convention hotels in an otherwise desolate downtown, the makeover was shocking. The ultimate signifier of this "new Atlanta" was the BeltLine, a twenty-two-mile mixed-use trail built on a former railway. The multibillion-dollar megaproject was hailed as one of the most ambitious urban redevelopment projects in the nation.

As in other cities where such engineered renewal was underway, Atlanta's development boom was presented as advantageous for everyone. Under the guise of "smart growth" and "New Urbanism," the promise of a more beautiful, environmentally sustainable city—with abundant jobs, improved schools, and upgraded infrastructure—was sold to new and old residents alike. In mayoral speeches and community engagement meetings, the message was consistent: Atlantans of all stripes would benefit from their revitalized city.

Today, all the amenities are there, but the city's renaissance has exacted a heavy toll on its low-income residents. Between 2010 and 2023, median rents soared by 76 percent, and the metro area lost a staggering sixty thousand apartments renting for $1,250 or less. The problem is not so much a lack of new housing as the kind of housing that is being built. Over the past decade, 94 percent of the tens of thousands of apartments added to the city's rental market have been luxury units, featuring resort-style swimming pools, coworking spaces, pickleball courts, and onsite dog parks. Atlanta is no longer "poor in the core."

But attend a yoga class or visit a new craft brewery, and chances are somebody's affordable housing complex was torn down to make way for it. A city that was 67 percent Black in the early 1990s is now 47 percent Black. Many families have been pushed to Atlanta's outer edges, far from their jobs and public transit and other services—but where rents are still absurdly high. According to the most recent studies, there are now more than 159,000 low-income households in Atlanta spending more than half of their earnings on rent, living in grossly substandard conditions, or both. Indeed, what has emerged in recent years is a kind of dystopian rejoinder to the claim—famously put forward by the urbanist Richard Florida in his book *The Rise of the Creative Class*—that the future of America's cities would stand or fall on their capacity to attract a wealthier, more educated and "vibrant" demographic. Well, cities like Atlanta have, and scores of families are suffering the consequences.

A similar interplay of growth and displacement, development and deprivation can be found in many American cities. In these places, a low-wage job is homelessness waiting to happen. The slightest setback or unanticipated expense—minor car trouble, disrupted childcare, a brief illness—can be disastrous. Outrageous housing costs would be less painful if incomes were rising at a comparable rate. But since 1985, rent prices nationwide have exceeded income gains by 325 percent. Some fifty-three million Americans, or almost half of the country's workers between the ages of eighteen and sixty-four, hold jobs that pay a median hourly wage of $10.22, which amounts to a mere $21,000 a year—below the poverty line for a family of three. If you're disabled and receive Supplemental Security Income (SSI), which is capped at $943 a month, it's even worse: the national average rent now amounts to 142 percent of this form of fixed income. In Atlanta, the "housing wage" needed to afford a modest two-bedroom apartment is $29.87 an hour. (Georgia's minimum wage is $7.25 an hour.) In Boston, a tenant earning the local minimum wage would have to log 141 hours a week to afford the same apartment; in San Francisco, it's 160 hours. Confronted with the bleak arithmetic of stagnant incomes and out-of-control housing expenses, people cut back wherever possible. Eventually they've cut all they can.

These families find themselves trapped in a sort of shadow realm, languishing in their cars, the overcrowded apartments of friends and relatives, and hyperexploitative extended-stay hotels and rooming houses. How many people are caught in this nightmare? It's a hard question to answer. Counting the homeless has always been politically charged: government officials have a clear stake in keeping the numbers as low as possible. One way they've done this is to define homelessness ever more narrowly. Each January, when a battalion of volunteers, service providers, and public employees fan out across the country to conduct the federal homeless census, only those defined as "literally homeless"—people staying in shelters and on the street—are tallied. Everyone else is rendered doubly invisible: at once hidden from sight and omitted from the reported statistics.

Not only are those who fall outside this narrow definition denied vital assistance, but as the census figures make their way into the media, the true scale and nature of the phenomenon are obscured. It's an alarming thought: as bad as the official numbers are—in 2023, the limited annual count showed the largest nationwide increase on record—the reality is far worse. Recent research reveals that the actual number of those experiencing homelessness in the United States, factoring in those living in cars or hotel rooms or doubled up with other people, is at least *six times* larger than the official figure. Driving around the nation's richest cities, we see the sprawling tent encampments, we see the makeshift dwellings on sidewalks and under overpasses. But those are just the most visible manifestations of a far more pervasive crisis.

This is a book about what we're not seeing. It follows five families in Atlanta desperate to secure a home. Maurice and Natalia make a fresh start in the city after being priced out of D.C. but now find themselves at the mercy of a cutthroat rental market, living paycheck to paycheck. Kara dreams of starting her own cleaning business while mopping floors at a public hospital. Michelle is in school to become a social worker, even as she struggles to raise her own three kids. Britt's roots in Atlanta go back five generations; she believes a long-awaited housing voucher will give her a foothold in her increasingly unrecognizable city. Celeste is a person of a thousand talents, savvy and unflappable, but a cancer diagnosis and a predatory housing system prove overwhelming even for her. Some of these families are isolated and on their own; others rely on an extensive network of friends and relatives. All are part of the country's low-wage labor force. All are renters. And all are Black— as are 93 percent of homeless families in Atlanta, the cradle of the civil rights movement.

It used to be that owning a home was held up as the ultimate goal, a reward for diligent effort and perseverance. Now simply *having* a home has become elusive for many. The myth that hard work will lead to stability has been shattered, revealing a stark disconnect between the story America tells about itself and the reality of deepening precarity. We need a new narrative, a new perspective on a nation whose citizens toil in vain for one of the most basic human necessities. The reach of homelessness is expanding. As it pulls more and more people into its grip, we might wonder: Who gets to feel secure in this country? And who are the casualties of our prosperity?

PART ONE

Equilibrium

1

Britt scrutinized her face in the bathroom mirror, hoping she looked less tired than she felt. Sleep had been hard to come by since she began working the closing shift at Low Country, a "new Southern cuisine" restaurant at Hartsfield-Jackson International Airport. Some nights, after a grinding hour-plus commute from the airport back to her great-grandmother's apartment in Atlanta's East Lake neighborhood, she managed to crawl into bed beside her two-year-old son, Kyrie, and four-year-old daughter, Desiree, without waking them. Last night she was not so lucky: Kyrie stirred and Britt was up with him until well past midnight. No sooner had they finally drifted off than Britt's phone alarm sounded, and it was all she could do to get the kids dressed and fed by six o'clock, when their daycare van arrived. Now, seven hours later, she massaged cocoa butter moisturizer onto her cheeks and forehead. *Good enough,* she thought with a sigh.

"Britt!" her great-grandmother bellowed over a television commercial. "Don't forget to tidy up my living room before you leave!" Britt examined herself one last time. She hadn't been able to wash her line-cook uniform between the previous night's shift and the one she would be starting shortly, but the stains weren't too noticeable.

For five months, Britt and her kids had been living out of several oversized tote bags in a corner of the apartment's compact living room, next to the pullout sofa bed they shared. An ironclad rule at Granny's apartment was that you pick up after yourself, and as Britt rushed to fold their clothes and blankets, she tried to arrange everything as neatly as possible. She had never asked Granny for a closet or dresser drawer in which to keep these items, in part because it seemed like there wasn't any room to spare—the older woman had a propensity to squirrel away whatever toy or child's sweater or pajama set she thought could be handed down to the family's newest members—but mostly because she needed to believe that their stay at her apartment was only temporary. For her part, Granny made it clear in her own loving but not particularly subtle way that she was in no need of roommates. Britt described it to a friend as a "don't get too comfortable" situation.

After reassembling the sofa bed and arranging its cushions, Britt hurried into the kitchen to finish preparing the kids' dinner for later: chicken tenders, rice, green peas, and Pillsbury Crescent Rolls. She glanced at Granny, perched in her rocking chair a few feet away from the TV. Britt often marveled at the disconnect between this kindly arthritic woman, who passed the hours glued to *Judge Mathis* or Tyler Perry's Madea movies while clutching her large-print Bible, and the stories she'd grown up hearing about her. Britt's favorite photo of Granny from her younger years showed a scowling, self-professed hustler outside Butler's Shoes in downtown Atlanta, sporting an all-white Levi's denim suit with a smart red bow tie. These days the sole vestige of Granny's former self was her fierce independence, which a recent diagnosis of Alzheimer's had done little to diminish.

"Girl, it's almost one-thirty. Shouldn't you be on your way?" Britt hadn't noticed her mom, Cass—short for Cassandra—enter the apartment. As always, the forty-three-year-old had a brusque, tightly coiled energy. She greeted Granny with a quick kiss on the top of her head.

"I'm making food for Des and Kyrie," Britt replied. "If you could just throw it in the microwave when they get back—"

Cass cut her off. "What? You think I can't put together some nuggets for my grandchildren?" She said this playfully, if a bit defensively. For a brief moment Britt stared at her, as if there was a lot she could say in response. "You get going and let me handle this," Cass said.

At the front door, beside Granny's "wall of fame," where dozens of pictures taken at graduations and proms and athletic events had been assembled, Britt put on a thin, stylish camouflage-print jacket. "Where's your coat at?" Cass yelled from the kitchen. "You know how cold it is? Why don't you step out on that patio and find out."

"Oh, she thinks she too cute for a *puffy* jacket," Granny teased.

"Well, her ass is gonna freeze," Cass said. The two women laughed. Britt, grinning, said, "Yeah, yeah," and shut the door behind her.

Outside, Britt headed toward the bus stop on Glenwood Avenue. She had been walking this route since she was a toddler. Granny's apartment building was a stone's throw from the public housing project where Britt had spent the first few years of her life. Five generations of the family had lived together at East Lake Meadows. That had not been the plan. When Granny's mother—"Big Mama," as everyone called her—landed a job at an Atlanta printing factory in 1961, her hope was to eventually purchase her own house. But this was before the Fair Housing Act was signed into law. A century of housing discrimination ensured that the path to homeownership remained closed to the majority of Black Americans. Unlike some of her white co-workers, who were approved for low-interest mortgages and able to move to the nearby suburbs, Big Mama and her progeny were confined to Atlanta's renter class—spending ten years at an apartment at 949 Washington Street, located in the predominantly Black Peoplestown neighborhood, before relocating to East Lake Meadows in the early seventies.

In the public imagination, the 650-unit complex known as "Little Vietnam" was rampant with crime and violence, but Britt's family spoke about it differently, as a place where people managed to forge a community despite living in terrible conditions. And the conditions *were* abysmal. Government neglect had plagued the project from the very beginning. Then, in the early nineties, Atlanta real estate titan Tom Cousins purchased the historic but derelict East Lake Golf Club, which bordered the housing project. Instead of advocating for the city to renovate the complex, he began calling for its demolition: his goal was to "rehabilitate" the neighborhood surrounding the golf course. Soon the complex was razed.

By 2001, when Britt was eight, the area had its first grocery store, a charter school, and The Villages of East Lake, a privately owned apartment complex built on the former site of East Lake Meadows. Cousins's revived golf club became the annual host of the prestigious PGA TOUR Championship. The neighborhood's rapid change was celebrated in media reports across the country, but not everyone benefited from it: because of strict eligibility requirements and the limited number of apartments set aside for low-income households, a mere 15 percent of the families residing at East Lake Meadows before its demolition were able to move into the new development. Granny and Big Mama, who died shortly after settling into her unit at the Villages, were among this select group. Cass and her kids were forced to go elsewhere.

A cold February wind cut through Britt's outfit as she raced to catch the bus on Glenwood that would take her to MARTA's Edgewood-Candler Park station and, from there, after transferring at Five Points, to the domestic terminal at Hartsfield-Jackson. As Britt rounded the corner, she saw that her bus was already approaching. She had to sprint to catch it.

It was only when she boarded the Gold line train at Five Points that Britt allowed herself to relax. She put in her earbuds and closed her eyes. The gentle opening notes of "Be Blessed" by Yolanda Adams—first an unadorned piano, then the deep, resonant tones of a gospel organ—began to settle her nerves. Prone to minor panic attacks, Britt had come up with strategies to stave off such episodes. Although she didn't consider herself religious, listening to this song had a way of grounding her. It was as if Adams were an older, wiser friend, perfectly aware of Britt's traumas and regrets but steadfast in the conviction that she need not be defined by them.

> I want you to be blessed, don't live life in distress
> Just let go, let God, He'll work it out for you
> I pray that your soul will be blessed
> Forever in His hands, for you deserve His best, no less.

Britt played the song twice and, when it ended, realized there was only one stop left before she arrived at the airport. As she had already done a number of times that day, she checked her email. She wasn't expecting to see the message she'd been waiting for, but she still felt a pang of disappointment when it wasn't there.

Securing a home for her children, Britt believed, hinged on a long-anticipated email from the Atlanta Housing Authority (AHA). Two years earlier, in January of 2015, she'd been excited to hear that AHA was about to open its Housing Choice Voucher Program to new applicants. These "Section 8" vouchers, as they were popularly known, had an almost mythical status among her relatives and friends: voucher holders paid no more than 30 percent of their income on rent to a private landlord, with federal funds covering the rest. Yet acquiring a voucher was no easy task. Although the program had become the nation's primary means of offering housing support to low-income families, the money allocated by Congress was woefully inadequate. Some social safety net programs, such as Medicaid and food stamps, provided benefits to everyone who met the eligibility criteria. Not so with housing aid. Roughly fourteen million poor renter households who qualified for housing assistance would never receive it. But everyone in Britt's world knew at least one co-worker or cousin's friend who had gotten a voucher. For these lucky few, the support could be life-changing—lifting the strain of constant financial instability, of having to choose between paying the rent or the electric bill.

In the weeks before AHA opened its application portal, voucher fever seemed to grip the city. The excitement was understandable: it had been fourteen years since low-income Atlantans could apply for a voucher. On the radio and local news shows, officials from AHA explained the process. Over the course of seven days, from January sixth to the thirteenth, those wishing to apply would need to do so online, after which a computerized system would select a given number of names at random. Those who were chosen would feel like they'd won the lottery.

The odds were far worse in other places. In 2010, a crowd of thirty thousand gathered outside the housing authority office in East Point, a city southwest of Atlanta, when it was announced that voucher applications would be handed out; the small municipality had a total of 455 housing vouchers. A year later, in Dallas, several people were trampled as thousands of residents rushed the doors at Jesse Owens Memorial Complex, where applications were going to be distributed on a first-come, first-served basis. Prior to this stampede, the line of applicants, many of whom had camped out the night before, stretched over a mile long.

Britt had filled out the application on her phone. It was the morning the AHA portal went live, and she had to decide whether to include the kids' father, Javon, on the lease. Their relationship had been up and down since Desiree's birth, but for the last year they'd been staying together at his mother's house on the West Side and things were going well: they were both working—he was a mechanic; she had two part-time jobs, one at Chick-fil-A and the other with SecurAmerica—and they hoped to get their own place before their second child arrived. Even Javon's mother wasn't sure that he should be a "co-head of household."

"You crazy?" she said to Britt one day. "These men ain't shit." Britt said nothing in response. She was proud of belonging to a long line of strong, industrious women who could get by without a man. "The females in this family will do anything to put food on the table," her mom liked to joke, "except sell our bodies." But it annoyed Britt that Javon's mother would project her own experiences with men, her own heartaches and resentments, onto her son. Still, the comment nagged at her, and she decided at the last minute to leave his name off the application. It turned out to be the right call. That summer, a few months after Kyrie was born, a trivial disagreement escalated to shouting and cursing, and then, for the first time, Javon hit her. In tears, she threatened to call the police; he pulled out a handgun. She'd had no idea he owned a gun. Britt resolved never to live with him again.

When the application window closed on January 13, 113,000 people had applied for a housing voucher. Britt was one of 10,000 to win a spot on the waiting list. In Atlanta, as in other cities across the country, it was not uncommon for families to spend years waiting to actually receive their voucher. In larger cities, the wait could be a decade or more. Still, Britt considered it a miracle. She told herself that "delay is not denial," that the wait could turn out to be a blessing. And besides, as with getting onto the waiting list, names were selected off the list at random—which meant there was a possibility she wouldn't be waiting long at all.

She began incessantly checking and rechecking her email, fantasizing about her future apartment. She imagined birthday parties for the kids and family gatherings at Thanksgiving. She decorated each room in her mind; it would be modern but cozy, she decided, extremely chill. She browsed the aisles of furniture stores, determining which coffee table went best with her favorite couch, which nightstand with her favorite bed frame. She wondered what life would be like: maybe she'd coach cheerleading or gymnastics—Desiree was already following in Britt's footsteps—or get more involved at the children's school, as her own mom had been. Or perhaps she'd go back to school herself. She could start to date again; she'd have a *my place* to go back to at the end of the night, no longer ashamed to be staying in Granny's living room.

Desiree and Kyrie had their own hopes for the new place. But gradually they stopped asking Britt how much longer the wait would be.

BRITT WAS EMBARRASSED to admit it, but walking through the airport en route to work always gave her a little thrill. Something about the frenetic atmosphere, the important-looking people coming from every corner of the planet and speaking languages she'd never heard, made her aware that she was living in a big, exciting city. It didn't matter that she was headed to a dead-end job in the Concourse A food court. The ambient bustle of this massive airport, the busiest in the world, was strangely energizing.

Britt loved the new Atlanta. She loved the fashionable bars and converted warehouses, the reclaimed parks and green spaces. She had no time for the cranky *I liked it better then* sentiment voiced by her older relatives. When she met up with friends at Ponce City Market, she barely registered the fact that Cass used to work there filing police reports before the hulking, half-abandoned City Hall East building was repurposed as a BeltLine-adjacent food and retail complex modeled on New York's Chelsea Market. When she spotted sparkling new apartments near the city-owned vacant land once occupied by Bowen Homes, the public housing project where she and her family had lived after leaving East Lake Meadows, she was neither bitter nor nostalgic. She just wanted to move into one of those units herself.

And yet, without the voucher, she knew it was impossible. Although her job at Low Country was the highest-paying position she'd ever had, her hourly wage was not nearly enough to afford an apartment in the city. The median rent for a one-bedroom unit had leaped to $1,600 a month—this despite a building frenzy that had resulted in an enormous increase in Atlanta's rental housing stock—and most landlords required that prospective tenants earn three times the monthly rent, which translated to $4,800 a month for a median-rent unit. Working full-time, Britt was grossing $1,920 a month. But she was undeterred. She and Atlanta had grown up alongside each other. It was the only place she'd known. The city was as much hers as anyone's.

"C'mon, let's go," said her shift manager by way of greeting as Britt clocked in. It was only ten minutes past three, and the food court was nearly empty, but the older woman had a habit of saying these sorts of things; it seemed to Britt that she was kinder than she let on, that she was merely performing the role of a gruff manager. Through a window where aluminum trays of sausage gravy and green beans and cheese grits were being passed into the serving area, Britt saw that Nikita, a friend from high school who'd helped her get this job, was already busy cooking. She joined Nikita in the kitchen and gave her a hug from behind. "What about me?" said Lewis, who worked next to them on the line. Britt and Nikita shook their heads, laughing. He'd nicknamed them the "twerk sisters," since the two friends, hidden from customers, started moving whenever anything like a dance song came on. But the trio had an efficient system, and tonight, like most nights, the hours flew by: Lewis on the grill and fryer, Britt on salads, and Nikita on the chicken and salmon. Apart from sporadic unannounced visits from the restaurant's finicky owner, a celebrity chef whose wall-sized portrait hung next to the register, or the rare shift when Britt was called up front to take orders, the work itself wasn't too bad.

During her dinner break, Britt carried a plate of food to a nearby gate and sat facing the window, watching the planes take off. She had a running list of places she wanted to take her kids: Tampa, where her brother, Josiah, was on a football scholarship at the University of South Florida; Wisconsin, where her incarcerated father and his family lived; the Mall of America in Minnesota, where they would ride the famous indoor roller coaster they had seen on the Travel Channel. She thought about the first time she had flown on an airplane as a teenager. Through a youth program at the Urban League, a national civil rights and urban advocacy organization, she and three other girls had entered a competition to come up with their own clothing brand. Britt's idea—2nd2None—won the girls and their mentor an all-expenses-paid trip to Boston. She remembered how surreal it felt, during the Young Entrepreneur Convention, to have so many successful businesspeople remarking on her intelligence, her creativity, her potential.

As closing time approached, Britt completed her cleaning checklist with intense focus. It was crucial that she make it to the Edgewood-Candler Park station before the last bus departed at eleven-thirty. Missing the bus, which had happened on a few occasions, meant calling Granny—who would then have to drag Kyrie and Desiree out of bed and wrangle them into her ailing Chevy Lumina. It also meant standing alone in a deserted parking lot until they arrived, her sense of vulnerability heightened since TSA agents had confiscated her mace on her first day at the airport.

She clocked out at eleven sharp and began power walking toward the airport MARTA station. She passed through a dimly lit corridor where the art exhibit *Zimbabwe Sculpture: A Tradition in Stone* was on permanent view, and then ascended a steep escalator to the smiling visage of Atlanta's mayor, Kasim Reed, welcoming visitors to the city. In the massive atrium beside the baggage claim, metal gates covered the fronts of shops and restaurants, a grand piano sat unplayed, and a cadre of custodial staff was quietly scrubbing the place clean. Some nights, Britt's mother could be found among them, polishing the floors and wiping down seats and tables until the early morning. Like many of the sixty-three thousand people who worked at Hartsfield-Jackson, Cass's employer was not the airport itself but a private contractor, and for the last year they had offered her a maximum of twenty-nine hours a week; at thirty, she would have been eligible for health insurance and other benefits. Britt saw the toll this job was taking on Cass. When their shifts overlapped, she brought her mom dinner from Low Country, hoping to cheer her up.

The train hadn't yet appeared when Britt reached the platform, so she took out her phone and checked her inbox. And after two years of waiting, there it was: an email from Atlanta Housing Authority.

T he psychiatric ward was unusually quiet as Kara Thompson
pushed her cleaning cart down a deserted hallway. She had been
on the clock for nearly sixteen hours, but even now, with the sun beginning to rise and her double shift finally winding down, she felt vigorous
and alert. The first-trimester waves of nausea that had assailed her in
recent weeks were mercifully receding. Earlier, in the basement cafeteria, a group of male co-workers on the janitorial staff had been complaining about their aching muscles. Kara told them that she had
trained herself to ignore such discomfort; if it was up to her, she said,
she would have taken on not just two but three shifts in a row. They
chuckled, assuming she was kidding. She laughed along with them.
What she thought, however, was *I could outwork every single one of you.*

Kara had been cleaning the thirteenth floor of Grady Memorial
Hospital for more than a year. Initially she had balked at being assigned
to this particular floor. The mammoth safety-net hospital was infamous
for its chaotic environment, but even by those standards the inpatient
ward of Grady's psychiatric unit—which treated about fifteen thousand poor and indigent Atlanta residents annually—was regarded as a
place to be avoided at all costs.

Her first impression of the crowded unit, passing through an airport-
style metal detector, seemed to confirm the rumors she'd heard. But the
twenty-nine-year-old came to relish the idea of working in a setting

that others couldn't handle. Many patients on the ward defied her expectations. A surprising number of them, she discovered, weren't suffering from some mysterious illness but were simply beaten down by
life. Kara could see herself in these men and women, and during the
course of wiping down their rooms or scrubbing the unit's common
spaces she went out of her way to try to lift their spirits: bringing them
snacks, showing them pictures of her three kids, praying with them.
Cut off from her family and with few friends to speak of, she led a
solitary, isolated existence. Beyond occasionally attending church, these
interactions with patients and co-workers made up the sum of her social life.

Kara only wished that she were afforded the same basic benefits and
protections as other Grady employees. A decade earlier, when the hospital was privatized amid a vast restructuring to keep it afloat, positions
like Kara's were outsourced to a for-profit company. While the pay was
slightly more than she had been making at Captain D's, where she'd
quit after her arm was badly scalded by the deep fryer, Kara remained
without health insurance and was reluctant to ever call in sick for fear
of losing precious income, or even the job itself.

At 6:00 a.m., Kara double-checked to make sure that her final tasks
had been completed and then hurried down to the employee parking lot. After a sleepless, highly caffeinated night inside the hospital's
fluorescent-lit corridors, stepping out into a fresh morning produced
a disorienting sensation. She kept walking, trying to shake it off. She
figured that if she left promptly, and if there wasn't too much traffic
on Interstate 20 heading east, she would be able to get her two older
children to school on time.

But minutes later, as she settled in behind the wheel of her Honda
Pilot, something powerful overcame her: a total, unadulterated exhaustion. The dam holding back several days of fatigue abruptly burst. She
felt an almost irrepressible urge to close her eyes, but she willed them to
stay open; the overnight babysitter she'd been forced to hire when her
supervisor moved her to the graveyard shift had sent her a text message,
saying the kids were dressed and ready. Kara took a long sip of lukewarm iced tea and turned the key in the ignition. Before pulling out of

the lot, she hesitated. She rarely wore a seatbelt these days, finding it uncomfortable, but now she put it on.

She'd driven this route hundreds of times: Left onto Jesse Hill Jr. Drive. Left onto Capitol Avenue. Ease onto the highway. She switched on the radio, V103, "The People's Station," and turned the volume up loud. She rolled down all four windows. Cold air blasted through the SUV, providing the jolt she'd hoped for.

"You got this, Kara," she said out loud. Soon she would be turning off the highway, toward the babysitter's home in Lithonia, a small working-class suburb about twenty miles southeast of downtown Atlanta. Just a couple of miles to go. If only she could rest for a moment.

The crash was like a bomb detonating. When Kara next opened her eyes, she found herself wedged, immobile, between the steering wheel and driver's-side door, which was jutting inward. Her vehicle was upside down.

She tried to move her head, to look around, but she couldn't. There was shouting, the sound of distant sirens. Then a pair of hands was reaching through the window, yanking aside a deflating airbag, attempting to free her. She managed to unbuckle her seatbelt, noticing, in the process, that the Honda's tan upholstery was covered in blood. Tiny shards of glass were embedded along the length of her arm. After being pulled from the vehicle, she passed out.

She woke up in the back of an ambulance. She asked the paramedic leaning over her where they were going. "Grady Hospital," he replied.

THREE HOURS LATER, Kara sat upright in an ER examination room, waiting to be discharged. She had been lucky. No other cars had been involved in the accident, which had taken place on a quiet residential road, and her injuries, astonishingly, were relatively minor: a concussion, cuts on her arm and head requiring stitches, and a sharp, throbbing pain in her lower back and neck. When she mentioned to the attending doctor that she was pregnant, he ordered an ultrasound. But everything looked normal; there was no evident cause for concern.

Kara, still in a daze, muttered that guardian angels must have been looking out for her.

During the ultrasound, as a gloved technician squirted cold blue gel onto her stomach, Kara had thought about her first pregnancy in 2005, when she was in high school. For weeks, the shy freshman had kept it a secret from her parents, from her younger sister, even from the handsome eighteen-year-old whose unexpected—and fleeting—attention had gotten her into the situation. She wore baggy sweatshirts to hide the growing swell of her belly. A part of her believed that if nobody else found out, that if she could continue to deny its reality, then the whole ordeal would just end.

But concealing the pregnancy eventually became impossible. Her parents were incensed, demanding to know how she could have done such a thing, how she could have been so stupid. They seemed less appalled at Kara's sinful behavior—although they berated her for that too—than embarrassed that her baby would be born out of wedlock. Her father, a hot-tempered heavy drinker who subsisted on disability benefits in the wake of a construction accident, was quick to dictate a solution. She would get an abortion. Her mother agreed that going through with the birth was out of the question.

Kara didn't know what to think or what she wanted. At school, panicking, she confided in her Spanish teacher. The older woman, a devout Christian, pleaded with her not to terminate the pregnancy. Explaining in graphic detail what the procedure involved, she told Kara that abortion was murder, plain and simple. If need be, her teacher added, she would raise the child herself.

Her parents were resolute, however, and it wasn't long before Kara and her mother were in the waiting room of a women's health clinic near their home in Decatur. The experience had a dreamlike quality. After her mother signed a form providing the parental consent required for minors, Kara was led to a cubicle for a state-mandated counseling session—the result of a recently passed law in Georgia. Over the next hour, she was informed of the medical risks associated with abortion, as well as its potential "detrimental psychological effects." She was given the gestational age of the fetus she was carrying, told that the baby's father was liable for child support, and handed a booklet that included information about fetal pain, a list of agencies offering alternatives to abortion, and pictures showing the development of the fetus in two-week increments. Finally, she read and signed a document stating that she consented "freely and without coercion" to the procedure she'd be undergoing—by which point she was desperate to get it over with. The new law, though, made patients wait twenty-four hours before receiving an abortion. She and her mom had to come back the following day.

When Kara returned to school, she overheard students gossiping about the abortion—one group of girls began calling her "baby killer"— and she grew convinced that even teachers and staff were looking at her funny or whispering behind her back. Aside from her Spanish teacher, who cried and embraced the fifteen-year-old, nobody asked her how she was doing. She became withdrawn, by turns angry and humiliated, resentful and ashamed, and she had trouble focusing on assignments. As the year wore on, a suspicion gradually hardened into certainty: she was on her own.

It was around this time that her relentless work ethic began to emerge. Kara found a job as a cashier at McDonald's. She requested as many shifts outside of school hours as possible, grateful not only for the money but for the excuse to be out of the house. The more she worked, the less she cared about the pursuits that preoccupied her teenage peers. She had sensed, since elementary school, that she would never be outgoing or attractive or stylish enough to win the popularity game, but now, from her new vantage point, these things appeared small and insignificant. Each affirming word, every gesture of validation from a manager or fellow employee, was stored away for later—for lonely lunches in the cafeteria, for the tense silences that pervaded her family's apartment. It occurred to her that she was good at her job: she was punctual, was adept at multitasking, and was regularly complimented on her customer service skills. Clocking in, she was able to disengage from the parts of herself that felt inadequate; here, instead, was a Kara who was confident and charming, whose jokes made people laugh. There was even talk of promotion to a managerial position if she stuck around.

And yet, seeing co-workers in their thirties and forties who toiled constantly and still couldn't make ends meet, she feared getting trapped at the fast-food franchise. So she decided, at the beginning of her junior year, to take a drastic step: she dropped out of school to join Job Corps, the nation's largest vocational program for low-income young adults. Launched in 1964 as part of the federal War on Poverty, the program offered eligible students free tuition and, crucially for Kara, covered her room and board at its campus in Brunswick, Georgia. But it turned out to be plagued with problems—a series of scathing government audits would document widespread mismanagement, safety issues, and a persistent failure to "demonstrate beneficial job training outcomes"—and she soon left for a job with Walden Security, using the money she'd saved to rent a studio apartment. For four years, while living alone, she worked at an array of retail stores and restaurants. It was a difficult period for her, and she came to regret having dropped out of school. When she heard about a Georgia-based online program called James Madison High School, she spent more than $1,000 to enroll, slowly earning credits toward a diploma during meal breaks and between shifts. At her graduation ceremony, held at Cobb Energy Centre in northwest Atlanta, no family or friends were there to see her walk across the stage.

Any lingering thought of reconciling with her parents vanished with the birth of her daughter, Grace, in 2011, when Kara was twenty-two. They seemed at once disappointed and unsurprised. "Where's the father?" they asked. If she later struggled with the burden of having another mouth to feed, they told her, she should remember that she'd brought this on herself. "Don't expect us to pay for your irresponsible choices," they said, just as they had when she was younger.

Yet there was no judgment they could direct at Kara that she hadn't already leveled at herself. She hated how a craving for physical intimacy led her to flings with men who were interested in little more than hooking up. Each subsequent pregnancy—three years after Grace came Nathaniel, followed by Jermaine four years later—brought a new ferocity of self-reproach, even as the children gave her life direction. The kids became her world. "It wasn't about me anymore," she recalled. "It was about: What do I need to do to provide for these children? What kind of future are they going to have?"

The car accident occurred five weeks after Kara found out that she was pregnant again. She'd wept when she saw the positive test. She considered herself a strong person, but the prospect of giving birth to a fourth child while her youngest was still an infant pushed her to the edge of despair. She wondered if her parents had been right. Despite a punishing work schedule, she was barely scraping by. There was no margin, no room for contingencies.

Before Grace was born, she'd had a clear vision of the sort of mom she wanted to be: the kind who delighted in her kids, who played hide-and-go-seek with them, who celebrated their little milestones—first words, first steps—and encouraged their particular talents. Seven years and three children later, that mother had appeared only intermittently, flickering in and out; with the addition of another baby, she might vanish altogether. Kara rarely saw the children, the bulk of whose daily lives comprised a patchwork of daycares, after-school programs, and babysitters. A fourth sibling meant that Grace, Nathaniel, and Jermaine would get even less of her. A capacity for playfulness and affection, patience and tenderness—she'd come to realize that these were finite resources, and that she was close to depletion. So despondent was Kara that, in the days leading up to the car crash, she'd thought about ending the pregnancy.

Now, waiting to be discharged at Grady, she was no longer contemplating this course of action. The paramedic had told her that, considering the damage to her vehicle, he had expected her injuries to be severe, even life-threatening. Yet both she and the baby had been spared. She told herself that God must have had a reason for protecting them. And so, sitting in the ER, remembering God's promise not to burden his people with more than they could bear, she resolved to embrace the pregnancy in much the same way that she had her three previous ones: as an unasked-for gift.

JOSHUA THOMPSON WAS BORN at Atlanta Medical Center in November 2018. In the hours after the delivery, Kara held him close to her chest, skin to skin, awed by the fact of his physical existence. She had wondered, as her due date approached, whether she had grown habituated to the experience of childbirth, and she'd worried that her emotional bond with the newborn might be dulled as a result. But the opposite was true: from the moment the nurse handed him to her, she felt a deep connection with her son. She was alive to his scent, his breathing, the warm softness of his skin. Alone in a dimly lit private room, time seemed suspended. Her other children were with a babysitter. There was nowhere she had to rush off to, nobody she needed to be with except for him.

She couldn't stop kissing him. They had already been through so much together, she told him. "You're a strong one," she whispered.

The empty sleeper chair beside her bed was a reminder of Joshua's absent father. She had met him at a grocery store, where he'd flirted with her and asked her out. Their subsequent tryst turned out to be a one-night stand. Later, when she tried calling him to tell him about the pregnancy, his number had been disconnected. She had no other means of reaching him.

Kara was hurt but took the rejection in stride. Of the four times she'd given birth, only Jermaine's dad, Isaiah, had been with her during the delivery. That he had rushed from his job at The Cheesecake Factory in Alpharetta, an hour's drive from the hospital, in order to be present at the birth meant a great deal to her. For several months, he had been giving her money for food and gas, and to her surprise he had expressed interest in eventually moving in with her and the children. But he also had a mean streak, especially when he was using. Not long after Jermaine was born, Isaiah busted Kara's lip and left her face bruised and swollen, before being jailed on felony drug and domestic violence charges. Kara hadn't seen or heard from him since.

The room she now shared with Joshua was devoid of all this. There was a lightness that Kara would later describe as "lovely." When her thoughts drifted to the world outside, they landed on what awaited her. She pictured a happy reunion with her other kids ("Good luck, Mommy!" Grace had called when she'd dropped them off). She couldn't wait for them to meet their baby brother. And then there was the job she'd be starting soon. Five days earlier, just prior to going into labor, she had successfully interviewed for a full-time EKG tech position at Grady. Not only would her hourly wage increase but she would only occasionally be expected to work graveyard shifts. This meant she'd no longer be handing over a chunk of her paycheck to the overnight sitter. "Your supervisor spoke very highly of you," the woman from human resources had told her after offering her the job.

Her mind turned to her two-bedroom apartment on Oakwood Manor. With its bare walls and half-unpacked boxes, the place still had a temporary feel to it, even though they had been there for several months. She decided that she was ready to settle in. She would begin with her own bedroom. It would be a proper nursery, with a rocker and changing table, and with Joshua's and Jermaine's cribs positioned on either side of her bed. She would put paintings on the wall and hang mobiles above the boys' cribs.

Sometime that afternoon, as a sliver of sunlight came through a narrow gap where the blackout curtains met, Kara noticed that Joshua had dozed off. She rang the nurse, who gently placed the baby in a bassinet next to his mother. Then Kara herself fell into a deep, contented sleep.

"Baby, wake up."

Maurice Taylor gently nudged his wife's shoulder. The thirty-six-year-old didn't need an alarm after a lifetime of rising before dawn, but Natalia, who was in no way a morning person, depended on him to ensure she wouldn't be late for work. The digital clock on the couple's bedside table read 5:15. Outside it was pitch black; the only light in the room was the pallid incandescent glow from a nearby parking lot. "Okay," Natalia said. "I'm getting up." Then she rolled over and sank into her pillow. "Give me another minute," she mumbled.

Maurice slipped on a pair of Adidas slides and shuffled into the kitchen. As he quietly brewed a pot of coffee, careful not to wake the kids, he heard the shower begin to run. It never occurred to him, on these weekend mornings when Natalia needed to be at the call center by seven, to stay asleep. This was the rhythm of the life he and Natalia had built together: During the week, in addition to seeing Anthony and Shantel off to school, Natalia helped Maurice make it to work on time, and he'd been doing the same for Natalia since her 11:00 a.m. to 7:00 p.m. schedule at State Farm was expanded to include early Saturday shifts. Natalia's job, though less physically demanding than his, had proven equally exhausting because of her bus commute from Sandy Springs to Dunwoody. Maurice, who worked as a full-time "service adviser" at Enterprise Rent-A-Car, where he earned $11.50 an hour, was able to walk to the office on Roswell Road. They were conscious of the irony that Maurice serviced cars for a living but couldn't afford to buy one himself.

Before long, Natalia entered the kitchen in her bathrobe. Maurice handed her a cup of coffee, flavored with the caramel creamer they both liked. "Thanks, Buddha," she said with a smile and then went to get dressed.

Maurice switched on SportsCenter, the volume turned low. He was eager to revisit the highlights from the Washington Wizards' game the night before. Although he and his family had left D.C. five years earlier, Maurice remained loyal to the teams of his hometown. Sports had always been important to him. His first love was basketball, but because of his size—he wasn't just taller but also thicker and more muscular than most of his peers—he'd defaulted to football in high school, alternating between fullback and defensive lineman. It was this pursuit that had helped him to survive his adolescence, and to avoid the fates of others he'd grown up with in the southeast corner of D.C.

After Natalia left for the State Farm office, Maurice started prepping breakfast for the kids, who would soon be out of bed. He mixed batter to put in an old cast-iron waffle maker and put bacon in a pan to fry. He had learned to cook watching his mother and grandmother in the kitchen. Those were the years before everything had fallen apart. He was ten when his grandmother passed away, and seventeen when his mom, who'd raised three children by herself while working as a printer at the Department of the Treasury ("I make a million bucks a day," she would joke), died from breast cancer. He and his younger siblings found themselves living alone in the house where she had spent their final days, a house that she'd been so proud to own. Maurice did the best he could to take on the responsibilities of a parent, but soon the inevitable occurred: his brother and sister became wards of the state (unlike Maurice, they were still minors), and the house went into foreclosure. He rarely allowed himself to think back on this period.

But he remembered the feeling of waking up, as a child, to the smell of a home-cooked meal, and preparing breakfast for his kids offered a chance to continue that tradition. It was also his way of delivering on a promise he'd made to himself shortly before Shantel was born: that he would be present for his children in a way his own father had never been. He helped get Shantel down for naps and, after playing Rock, Paper, Scissors with Natalia to determine whose turn it was, had no problem changing diapers. When they switched to formula, Maurice bottle-fed Shantel in the middle of the night, holding her to his chest. As the kids grew older—Shantel was now eleven and Anthony was eight—he made it a point to carve out time with them. Especially Anthony. He'd been born with alopecia and a pigmentation disorder, and his classmates sometimes mocked him for his pale skin and patchy hair and eyebrows. He had also been diagnosed with autism spectrum disorder, which made his social life at school even more challenging. Anthony seemed to relish these times with his dad—their "adventures," as he called them.

That afternoon, Natalia arrived home to a familiar scene: Anthony and Shantel were watching a movie while Maurice dozed on the couch beside them. The apartment was spotless. Earlier, after they'd finished eating breakfast, Maurice and the kids had tackled the kitchen together, followed by the living and dining room. Then Maurice had smoked a couple of cigarettes on the balcony while the children straightened up the bedroom they shared, enticed by the reward of video games. Coming home to a clean apartment meant a lot to Natalia; she called it her love language. She noticed that the back and front windows had been opened to let in fresh air, a gesture she appreciated.

At dinnertime she had an idea. She suggested that she and Maurice take a bottle of wine and some of the pork kebabs he'd just grilled down to a manmade lake in the middle of the complex. The exorbitant cost of hiring a babysitter made going out a rare luxury for the couple, so they had to settle for humbler, more spontaneous dates. They could rush back if the kids needed them.

They threw together a small picnic basket and walked to a gazebo situated on a patch of grass near the lake, not far from the leasing office. It was getting dark, the warm spring air starting to turn chilly. They poured themselves glasses of Pinot Grigio. Gesturing at the landscape, Maurice gave a toast. "To this place," he said. Suddenly, out of a Bluetooth speaker Maurice had grabbed before leaving, came the opening track of their favorite Scarface album, *The Fix*. Natalia shook her head and grinned. It had been fourteen years since they had first listened to the album, parked outside Natalia's apartment in a sedan Maurice had borrowed from his cousin. Then, as now, he beamed as Natalia rapped along with the explicit lyrics. She still knew every word.

THEY HAD MOVED to Atlanta on December 31, 2013, laughing at the corny symbolism of starting a new life in a new city on this particular date. Their rented Zipcar was a cocoon of optimism. During the ten-hour drive from D.C., Shantel and Anthony enumerated in fantastic detail all that they expected to do and see in this place they'd never even visited. Two months earlier, when Natalia learned that the real estate firm she worked for was opening an office in Atlanta, she and Maurice jumped at the chance to relocate. Everything they knew about the city—its centrality to the civil rights movement, its prestigious historically Black colleges and universities, its reputation for Black achievement in business and media and music—led them to believe that it was a place where they could "thrive, not just survive," as Maurice put it.

The area they ended up in, however, was hardly the "Black Mecca" they had envisioned. PROMOVE, a company that assisted corporate clients in securing housing for their employees, found them an apartment in Sandy Springs, a short bus ride to the office park where she'd be working. After their first few days in the neighborhood, Maurice and Natalia wondered if they had stumbled into a cosmic prank: they'd thought they were putting down roots in the birthplace of Dr. King and had landed instead in a majority-white epicenter of suburban sprawl. They hadn't realized that much of Atlanta was actually a six-million-person expanse of suburbs located beyond the city proper. Born of white flight in the 1960s and '70s, many of these communities, especially the northern cities and counties, had been defined early on by their staunch segregationism (two spokesmen for Sandy Springs promised in 1965 to "build up a city separate from Atlanta and your Negroes and forbid any

Negroes to buy, or own, or live within our limits"). This eventually gave rise to a "politics of suburban secession:" a refusal on the part of wealthy residents to see their tax dollars redistributed or their enclaves invaded by the problems—and people—of the city. It was from these reliably Red suburbs that Newt Gingrich had famously launched his "Republican revolution," but now places like Sandy Springs were evolving in subtle ways. They were becoming less homogenous, both racially and politically. Still, it was a universe away from anywhere Natalia or Maurice had ever lived.

But they soon began to see why the area was attracting so many people from around the country: the relative quiet, the safety, the abundance of parks and proximity to the Chattahoochee River, the excellent public schools. For Natalia and Maurice, this suburban existence was increasingly, and unexpectedly, appealing. Even the bland big-box shopping centers started to grow on them; since they'd lived in an urban food desert, nothing seemed more solidly middle class than Chili's and Barnes & Noble and Bed Bath & Beyond.

By the time Maurice was hired on at Enterprise—before his interview, he had done research on the company, and the hiring manager was surprised to hear that Maurice knew things about Enterprise that even he didn't—he and Natalia felt that they were exactly where they were supposed to be. Their only real frustration was the apartment, which looked nice enough on the outside but turned out to be old and musty. Just prior to the deadline to renew their lease, Maurice overheard a group of neighbors talking about a condo owner at Victoria Heights, an adjacent complex, who was looking for a long-term tenant. She had recently purchased a house and wanted to keep the condo as an investment. Maurice asked them for her contact information. About six weeks later, the family was settling into a remodeled two-bedroom, two-bath unit. Natalia had managed to negotiate their rent down to the same amount—$950 a month, not including utilities—they'd been spending at the older complex.

The years that followed passed in a kind of contented monotony. Natalia was able to find a slightly better-paying job at State Farm, and soon Maurice had been with Enterprise long enough to qualify for health insurance and paid time off. Although their work schedules could be grueling and they had difficulty making friends, they grew closer with the kids. There were trips to Six Flags Over Georgia and other excursions; there were Friday night dinners at Hibachi Grill, the children's favorite restaurant. There was Maurice's thirty-fifth birthday in 2017, the year before, when Natalia surprised him with a fancy lunch, then told him to close his eyes in the Uber and took him to Jeju Sauna Home of Wellbeing in Duluth. Some of their happiest moments took place when Maurice's cousin Aaron—and Teddy, Aaron's Pomeranian—visited from D.C.: dance parties in the living room, an influx of new toys (Tayo the Little Bus for Anthony, Monster High figures for Shantel), salon outings with Natalia, and alcohol-fueled conversations that lasted well into the morning.

As for the condo, it was ideal for them. Not only was it close to work and school, but it was affordable as well. Maurice and Natalia were able to save a little money each month, which they planned on putting toward their first car; whatever else suburban Atlanta had going for it, public transportation was notoriously limited. The condo's sole drawback was its lack of a third bedroom. There was another baby on the way, and Shantel made no secret of her desire to have her own space.

But the unit was well maintained, and there was a playground outside, and even Shantel had to concede that it was the best place they'd ever lived. So determined were Maurice and Natalia to be exemplary tenants that they were always careful to send their rent check a couple of days early. They feared doing anything that could jeopardize their arrangement. Once they even went so far as to pay two months' rent in advance, and Summer, their landlord, an affable lawyer in her early forties, had to gently tell them that this wasn't necessary, that there was no reason to worry.

| 4 |

Michelle was in the zone. After a shaky start involving a mishap with the candied yams, she had recovered quickly, and now the parade of dishes appeared one by one: collards and potato salad, creamed corn and mac 'n' cheese, honey-baked ham and cornbread dressing. It was late afternoon on December 24. While all holiday meals were taken seriously in her family, Michelle had been raised to believe that Christmas Eve dinner was a matter of particular gravity. She took a bite of dressing. She was under no illusions that it would have passed muster with her late grandmother, whose own cornbread dressing ("not 'stuffing,'" she'd indignantly point out) was legendary. But it tasted pretty damn good.

There were 436 front doors at Eastwyck Village, the apartment complex where Michelle lived with her fiancé and three children, but only one of them had been decorated to resemble a wrapped Christmas present. In Michelle's household, the Christmas season began early—on the evening of Thanksgiving, to be precise, right after the dinner dishes had been washed and put away. That's when the family lugged their six-foot-tall artificial tree out of a storage closet, put on the Temptations' holiday album, and set about filling their three-bedroom unit with each and every yuletide item they had accumulated over the years. Battery-operated candles. A snowflake-adorned tablecloth. Giant red bows and plastic candy canes and strings of lights. Many of these decorations were remnants of Michelle's childhood, evoking memories of performing in church pageants or the rare carefree moment with her mother, who struggled with addiction and would disappear for long stretches of time. When she was young, Michelle's proudest accomplishment was learning how to unwrap and meticulously rewrap her gifts in the days leading up to Christmas morning, in order to take a peek without the adults finding out.

Michelle had recently turned forty but looked a decade younger, dressed in stonewashed skinny jeans, unblemished Nikes, a Santa hat, and, in defiance of the vexingly warm Atlanta winter, a thick green sweatshirt. She had given birth to Skye, now napping in the master bedroom, almost two years earlier. The previous Christmas had been a special one: it was their first with Skye, and thus their first as the fully formed family that Jacob, Skye's father, had promised Michelle and her two teenage children when they moved in together. She hoped this Christmas would feel the same, despite an argument earlier that morning with her thirteen-year-old daughter, Danielle, and the fact that Jacob had been distant and irritable lately. She thought it might be about his job. He was employed as a handyman at their complex, and he hated being called away at random hours to address the problems that were constantly arising. But when she asked him what was wrong, he told her he was fine. Michelle tried to put it out of her mind.

Satisfied with her progress in the kitchen, she went to check on Skye and, seeing that she was still asleep, started tidying up the apartment. Normally Michelle would have been doing schoolwork during Skye's nap. After spending most of her adult life in low-paying daycare jobs, she and Jacob had decided, right before Skye was born, that it was time to be more ambitious. "I thought, 'If it's not too late to have a baby,'" Michelle said, "'then maybe it's not too late for a career change.'" She enrolled in the associate degree Health and Human Services program at Ultimate Medical Academy, an online university based in Florida. Her plan was to become a social worker; she'd once watched a news report about the prevalence of elder abuse and neglect, and it was addressing this problem, specifically, that motivated her. Jacob was supportive. They agreed that, for the foreseeable future, Michelle would be a student and stay-at-home mom while Jacob would serve as the family's main breadwinner, their income supplemented by the minimal student loans Michelle had taken out. It had been twenty-two years since she'd graduated from high school, and she liked being back in the "classroom," as she jokingly referred to the folding table where her laptop sat. But like her high school self, she was also grateful for the holiday break.

"Hello?" Michelle stood outside the closed bedroom doors of her two older children, trying to make herself heard without waking Skye. "Are my kids going to be helping me at all today?"

There was no response from Danielle, who had been giving Michelle the silent treatment for the last several hours. Before long, though, the other door opened, and DJ emerged with a sigh. The fourteen-year-old did not appreciate being called away from his latest art project, a graphic novel loosely based on Tite Kubo's manga series *Bleach*. Tall and slender with a deep baritone that belied his age, DJ was sensitive and precocious—the kind of teenager who liked "ethereal music"; who asserted that he was not a "loner" but rather "socially selective"; who made a careful distinction between "friends" and people he called "associates." The latter might be willing to listen to what you were going through, but only the former would initiate such conversations, would show a genuine interest in how you were doing. He claimed he had no friends, just lots of associates.

Michelle told DJ to set the dining room table, which he proceeded to rush through, looking irritated. Michelle was intent on coaxing him into a better mood. "Don't Stop 'Til You Get Enough" was playing on a portable stereo near the stove, and when DJ entered the kitchen to fetch utensils, Michelle sidled up beside him, bumping her hips against his. Michelle's dance moves were a surefire way of getting DJ and Danielle to laugh. At midnight on their birthdays, she had a tradition of bursting into their rooms and turning on the lights. Ignoring their pleas to let them go back to sleep, she would belt out Stevie Wonder's "Happy Birthday" and pull them out of bed. They would invariably relent and dance with her. And that's what DJ, smiling his big electric smile, finally did there in the kitchen, mother and son enjoying a dance party all their own.

NIGHT HAD FALLEN by the time Jacob returned home. Michelle was putting the final touches on dinner while DJ played with Skye on the living room carpet. The room was illuminated by candles and colored lights. When DJ heard Jacob coming up the stairway, he and Skye hurriedly hid behind a window curtain, and Jacob cried out in mock surprise as they jumped out at him. He was holding a box from Piccadilly containing a red velvet cake, Michelle's favorite. "Wait a sec, let me put this down," he said, carefully placing the box on a side table. Then he scooped his daughter up and started tickling her. Skye squealed with laughter.

Jacob and Michelle had first met each other in the seventh grade, when they were students at Ronald E. McNair Middle School in DeKalb County—the same school Danielle now attended. They became fast friends and, a couple of years later, dated briefly, but they lost touch after graduating from high school in 1996. Michelle moved to Opelika, Alabama, a town near Auburn University where her mother had relocated, and she eventually began a relationship with a family acquaintance named Daniel, who worked at an auto body shop. Convinced she had found her "soulmate," as she put it, she married him, and had a son and daughter a mere fifteen months apart. But with children came a new relationship dynamic, and even though they both had jobs, the burden of parenting fell primarily on Michelle. Daniel complained that she was giving him nothing but the scraps of her energy and attention. He grew possessive of her, erupting in anger if she so much as smiled at another man. She sought to rationalize this behavior as an expression of his fierce love for her. But gradually he turned physically violent. The first time he hit her, he apologized profusely and promised it would never happen again. But it did happen again, and again. His apologies became less emphatic, and it no longer seemed to bother him that the kids witnessed the abuse.

One evening in the winter of 2013, while Daniel was out with friends, Michelle bundled the kids into her car and drove to Atlanta, arriving at her aunt's house in the middle of the night. It was totally unplanned; all Michelle knew was that she needed to leave immediately. They had only the clothes and personal items that Michelle had been able to hastily pack. DJ and Danielle, who were ten and nine at the time, were in shock, having had to leave everything—their home, their friends, their elementary school, and above all their father—so abruptly. But they saw that Michelle was afraid, and this made them afraid. She just kept saying that they were going to be all right.

Over the next year, Michelle rebuffed Daniel's entreaties, alternately contrite and threatening, that she return to Alabama with their children. At times she wondered if she'd made the right choice: it was a challenge to start over in Atlanta as a single parent. She had already lost the grandmother who'd raised her, and when her mom passed away shortly after she left Daniel, she felt unmoored. She still had her mother's oldest sister, Regina, who was severely disabled and lived with an elderly brother, and Michelle was grateful to her aunt for allowing her and the kids to stay with them. But old conflicts were soon rekindled. It wasn't long before Michelle realized that Regina wanted her out.

By the time she secured an apartment and landed a job at a daycare center in Decatur, she was effectively on her own. She grew closer and closer to DJ and Danielle, "holding onto them for dear life." Later, she had three silver puzzle-piece necklaces custom-made with their names engraved on them; each necklace held a medallion that, when put together with the others, formed a single heart. The kids learned how to cook and clean and do laundry, and on weekends Michelle often took them bowling. She did her best to hide the residual pain of her marriage to Daniel, trying to create a peaceful, playful environment for the children.

In early 2015 she reconnected with Jacob, who was still living nearby and recovering from his own breakup. For Michelle, he was a breath of fresh air. Where Daniel was brooding and intense, Jacob was funny and charismatic, with the physique of a bouncer: barrel-chested with a shiny bald head, a beard, and thick, tattooed forearms. He made it clear that he was interested not simply in being with Michelle but in getting to know her kids as well, and although DJ and Danielle were initially skeptical—"We weren't really feeling him at first," DJ said—he slowly earned their trust. As his relationship with Michelle became serious, Jacob began to treat Danielle and DJ as though they were his own children, referring to them as his son and daughter—which was significant to them since Daniel no longer called, not even on birthdays and holidays. A photo taken about a year after Skye was born showed Jacob, Michelle, and the three kids in matching red and white T-shirts with the midtown Atlanta skyline lit up behind them. Across the picture, in bright cursive, was scrawled "It's All About Family."

"OKAY, Y'ALL, LET'S EAT," said Michelle, carrying a platter of greens into the apartment's small dining area. Jacob, DJ, and Skye were already seated around the table, but Danielle had yet to appear. It had been like this for much of the school year: Danielle isolating herself in her room for hours on end, making it known to everyone that she was not to be disturbed—except by Skye, toward whom she was unfailingly affectionate. Some days, after school, she and DJ rode the bus to South DeKalb Mall; sometimes she hung out with two neighbors her age at Eastwyck's decaying playground, sitting idly on the swings while gossiping or discussing music and movies. But mostly she stayed in her room. She made Dubsmash videos and practiced dance moves in front of her full-length mirror, and she scrolled incessantly through her social media feeds, nursing the manifold insecurities that middle school had unleashed with a vengeance. Yet Michelle took comfort in the fact that Danielle still confided in her and DJ. It wasn't uncommon for Danielle to lay her head in Michelle's lap as they watched TV, or for her to pull Michelle aside and vent about her latest friendship drama, leading off with "Mom, don't repeat this to anybody, but . . ."

"It's time to eat," Michelle said more loudly in the direction of

Danielle's bedroom, her frustration obvious. Her tone conveyed that the night could take a turn for the worse. But Danielle, as if sensing that her mother's patience had reached its limit, seemed content when she joined them. "This looks incredible," she said of the elaborate spread covering nearly every inch of the dining table.

After dessert, when the last piece of red velvet cake had been polished off, the five of them lingered at the table, blissfully full. Typically there was enough left over for lunch the following day, but this year it appeared unlikely; even Skye, whose pickiness drove Michelle nuts, had devoured her food. As they ate, Jacob and Michelle had regaled the kids with tales from their own childhood Christmases, most of them involving a crazy relative or some harmless mischief they'd succeeded in getting away with. Danielle and DJ loved these stories, including the ones they had already heard and could more or less recount verbatim. Every couple of minutes they broke into fits of laughter.

At some point it was decided that their postdinner activity would consist of assembling an exceptionally large gingerbread house. Shopping for presents at T.J. Maxx in late November, Michelle had thrown a kit into her cart at the last minute, thinking it might make for a fun diversion during the break. Now Danielle was clearing the coffee table and laying out paper towels to catch any crumbs. The family spent the next hour putting the house together, a task made a good deal slower by Skye's increasingly brazen attempts to snag a gumdrop or a dollop of icing. It was only when she drifted off on the couch that they managed to finish building the house. They gazed at their lopsided creation, mocking its shoddy construction.

As the evening was winding down, Michelle had a sudden impulse to end the night with a word of prayer. It was Christmas Eve, and she was feeling unsettled. All night, Jacob had been sweet with the children and, as always, was quick to tell her how much he enjoyed her cooking. Yet she could have sworn he had been avoiding eye contact with her. "Hold on," she said, extending her hands. Jacob had been about to turn on the television, and DJ and Danielle were ready to retreat to their bedrooms. But the three of them reluctantly joined Michelle, forming a little circle.

| 5 |

On a chilly Saturday just after the new year, Efficiency Lodge was coming to life. Children finished breakfast and raced their bikes and scooters through the narrow parking lot. Grandmothers pushing strollers made their way to the closest bus stop, in need of diapers and groceries. A young woman carrying two industrial-size garbage bags full of dirty clothes squeezed herself through a hole in the razor-wire fence surrounding the property—a shortcut to the laundromat in a neighboring shopping plaza. And three hard-looking men in their early twenties tried to hide their late-morning blunt from Lisa, the hotel manager, who passed them with a grin and told them not to be acting stupid.

Lisa stopped in front of the room of a single middle-aged woman. "Hey, darlin', you got my rent?" she asked in a thick southern drawl as the door opened a crack. The woman explained that the assistant manager, who'd been in charge while Lisa was away on vacation, had told her she could have a couple of extra days to get the money together. "Nope, that ain't right," Lisa said. "I'll need the full amount by three o'clock." The woman muttered something, but Lisa was already moving on to the next room. "Sorry, sweetie," Lisa said loudly over her shoulder. "The bitch is back."

When Lisa finished making her rounds on the front side of the extended-stay hotel, she proceeded to the back. At some point, the nickname "Buckhead"—a wealthy enclave located north of downtown

Atlanta—had been given to the front of the property, where the office (and directly above it, Lisa's own room) was located. Residents had dubbed the dingier, less surveilled rear side "Bankhead," after a neighborhood on the city's West Side. A group of boys on bicycles nearly plowed into Lisa as she rounded the corner. "Good morning, Ms. Lisa!" they yelled in unison. "Mornin'," she replied. "Y'all watch where you're riding."

She noticed that one of the older boys had a Black & Mild tucked behind his ear. "Hey, get your ass over here," she commanded him. She swept her dyed-brown hair off her forehead, her gray roots showing underneath. "What's that?" She pointed to the boy's ear.

"Nothin'," he said meekly.

"Well, I'll let you in on a little secret," Lisa said. "Not only does that stuff stunt your growth but it'll make your teeth yellow like mine. So yellow that they'll fall out. And you ain't gonna be able to kiss no girls, you know why?"

"Why?"

"Cuz you gonna smell like a damn ashtray."

His friends giggled. As they rode away, Lisa told an eight-year-old named Mason to stay behind. She had a special fondness for the boy. His mother, Christina, was raising six small children on her own, surviving on food stamps, child support, and whatever else she could scrounge up. Mason couldn't remember a time when they hadn't lived at the hotel; his family's three-hundred-square-foot room was the only home he'd known. Lisa, seeing that he was unable to zip his threadbare winter jacket, pulled him closer. She flipped his collar back and checked the label, figuring he'd need one at least two sizes bigger. "Tell your mama I'm gonna find you a new coat," she said.

Lisa had started off as a desk clerk but got promoted after the previous manager refused to reside onsite any longer, fed up with the conditions. Efficiency Lodge sat on a notorious three-and-a-half-mile stretch of Candler Road running from Memorial Drive to Interstate 285. Just north of the intersection of Candler and Memorial were stylish cafés, a women's liberal arts college, and Craftsman bungalows shaded by a lush tree canopy. South of Memorial there was scarcely any greenery at all. This was the Candler Road name-dropped in lyrics by Gucci Mane, Yung Mal (who would be charged with murder after a shooting near the hotel), and 21 Savage: a long, pockmarked thoroughfare comprising block after block of dialysis clinics, liquor stores, pawnshops, payday lenders, hair-braiding salons, plasma donation centers, twenty-four-hour daycares, storefront churches, and ramshackle motels. Like much of DeKalb County, the neighborhoods around Efficiency had been hit hard by the recession of 2008. The result was foreclosed homes, shuttered businesses, and deteriorating infrastructure. But whereas other parts of the county soon rebounded, inaugurating a surge of new development, Candler Road and its environs remained stuck in a period of decline.

Increasingly in Atlanta, there were two kinds of poor Black neighborhoods: those where property values were rising and investors were buying up land, waiting for the inevitable transformation, and those like the area around Efficiency, where people usually ended up after being pushed out of the gentrifying neighborhoods. These spaces, hollowed out by what the geographer Ruth Wilson Gilmore has referred to as "organized abandonment," did not simply coexist alongside newly or soon-to-be gentrified segments of the city. They were actively *generated* by them. Although they appeared worlds apart, these areas were intimately connected, like a balloon squeezed at one end. Candler Road was not a deviation from the booming new Atlanta but another by-product of it. One did not exist without the other.

Her morning rounds now completed, Lisa returned to the office and found Celeste Walker waiting to pay her rent. "Always on time," Lisa said. "If everyone was like you, my job would be a hell of a lot easier." She unlocked the office's inner door and walked around to the front desk, facing Celeste from behind a thick pane of bulletproof glass.

"Well," Celeste replied playfully, sliding her cash under the metal slot, "you let me know when you're ready to bring me on as an assistant manager."

Five weeks earlier, after a sleepless night in her cherry-red Dodge Durango, Celeste had tried to get a room at the Efficiency Lodge in Forest Park—the chain had eleven locations in Atlanta—but she arrived too late: somebody had just snagged the last room. The manager suggested that Celeste try the Efficiency on Candler Road; since the hotel didn't accept reservations, the best approach, she said, was to inquire in person. Twenty minutes later, Celeste arrived at the extended-stay, parking near a door with OFFICE stenciled in fading block letters over it and a small sign reading SMILE, YOU'RE ON CAMERA pasted to the adjoining window. It was almost seven, and the woman who greeted her was preparing to leave. Before Celeste could get the words out, Lisa gruffly said she had no rooms available. Her only empty unit had been vacated that morning, and she couldn't rent it out until it had been cleaned. "It ain't pretty," she said.

Celeste was unfazed. What if she cleaned the room herself? she asked. Lisa looked at her more closely, and then she sighed. The rate, she said, was $257 a week, due each Saturday by noon. "And if that's too much for you," she added, preempting a common complaint, "you're more than welcome to go to one of the other places around here." There were nearly a dozen extended-stays in the vicinity, but Lisa knew as well as Celeste that Efficiency was the cheapest. Gulf American Inns across the street, for instance, cost twice as much, as Celeste had discovered that afternoon while calling around to budget hotels. The place was booked solid. "No, ma'am, that'll be fine," said Celeste. "I'll take it." She and her children—Micah was six, Jalen was fourteen, and Nyah was sixteen—spent the next few hours scrubbing the filthy room and kitchenette from top to bottom. The following afternoon, Lisa stopped by to check on them and, shocked that their room was spotless, remarked not entirely in jest that Celeste should come work for her.

Now, in the office, Lisa gestured toward her assistant, who was outside smoking a cigarette. Her low opinion of the younger woman was hardly a secret. "Believe me," she said. "I'd hire you if I could." Confident and articulate, Celeste had a way of making herself indispensable wherever she went. She carried herself with an air of invulnerability, which might have been off-putting were it not for her charm and sense of humor. Lisa liked her. And the feeling was mutual: Lisa reminded Celeste of her mom, who was "ghetto white," as Celeste put it, and had a similar "sweet but don't fuck with me" demeanor. Born and raised in Cabbagetown, back when the Atlanta neighborhood was still poor and working class, Lisa had worked for more than two decades as a bartender and, before that, as a waitress at Waffle House. She had now been at Efficiency for nine years. "I've been down that road myself," she'd told Celeste, referring to the financial insecurity experienced by most of the hotel's residents. "I wasn't given no silver spoon." The only reason she had a place to live, she'd said, was because her job included free accommodations.

"All right, girl," said Celeste, turning to leave the office. "Just promise you won't forget about me."

THE PATH TO EFFICIENCY had been a harrowing one for Celeste. Eight months earlier, in May of 2018, she had just picked up Micah and Nyah from a friend's apartment when her phone rang. It was a muggy afternoon, and she was worn out after a long day at the warehouse where she worked as a parts inspector for Novem, a company that produced high-end car interiors. The man on the other end was yelling hysterically. It took her a moment to register what he was saying.

"Hello? Ma'am? You need to get over here! Please!"

"What? Who is this? I think you got the wrong number."

"Naw, man, this your neighbor, Ketchup! Your house is on fire! You better get here right away!" He hung up.

Celeste's adrenaline started to surge. Jalen, who was thirteen at the time and enrolled in an after-school program, would have been home by then. The fifteen-minute drive to East Point, where the squat two-bedroom house she'd been renting for the past year was located, was the longest of her life. As she pushed the Durango to more than a hundred miles per hour on Interstate 75, she dialed 911; if any officers saw her speeding, she frantically told the dispatcher, it was because her home was on fire and she had no way of reaching her son, who was there alone. She gave the dispatcher her address and begged her to call the fire department. Finally she turned onto Westover Drive and found the cul-de-sac blocked off. She jumped out and began sprinting toward her house but was quickly intercepted by a group of firefighters.

"My child's in that house!" she screamed, struggling to free herself. She saw that the house's frame was already charred and smoldering.

"We can't let you inside," said one of the men. "But I can assure you that nobody was in there." Soon a school bus pulled up to the barricaded road and Jalen stepped off. The buses had been running behind schedule.

As the firefighters finished up, a Red Cross volunteer arrived and gave Celeste a prepaid debit card to cover food and toiletries and several nights at a hotel. Beyond that, the only things the family had with them were the kids' backpacks, Celeste's phone, and three hampers full of dirty clothes: that morning, before school, Celeste had asked Jalen to load up her trunk with the laundry, since their washing machine had stopped working. It occurred to Celeste, while they drove to a Howard Johnson hotel near the airport in stunned silence, that she had never gotten around to purchasing renters' insurance.

The following day, the four of them returned to the house, hoping to retrieve some other belongings. Celeste and Nyah stepped cautiously inside the entryway, but they could go no farther. It was clear that whatever hadn't been destroyed by the flames had been water-damaged by the firehoses. Later that afternoon, Celeste posted on Facebook. "God we need you more than ever right now. Our house burned down and we've lost everything."

Investigators determined that the fire was the result of arson: a neighbor's camera had caught someone approaching the house moments before it went up in flames. Watching the footage, Celeste recognized a man she had briefly dated. When she broke up with him, he had begun sending menacing text messages—she'd dismissed his threats as the rants of a "mentally disturbed" individual—and she had subsequently blocked his number. Police arrested him shortly after the fire.

Two or three days passed before it dawned on Celeste that she and her children no longer had a place to live. When the Red Cross funds ran out, she started dipping into her savings to pay for their hotel room. Compounding her anxiety was the less-than-sympathetic response from her supervisor at work. In the wake of the fire, the woman told Celeste that she could take two days off—unpaid—to get her bearings, but that any additional time away would not be approved. The house had burned down on a Monday night, and she told Celeste that if she wasn't there on Thursday morning, she might as well look for another job. Celeste was forced to choose between searching for a new home or continuing to earn a paycheck.

It was a brutal calculus: she knew that getting into an apartment or house on such short notice would involve countless phone calls and emails during business hours, but she was also aware that without a job it would be impossible to pay for whatever she found. She chose to prioritize the housing search, returning to the staffing agency that had gotten her the job at Novem and requesting that she be placed with a different company. She was soon hired on at ProLogistix as a "picker/packer" in their Decatur warehouse. She began dropping the kids off at school and working until one o'clock, then driving around Atlanta to check out apartments the rest of the day. Yet finding a place that fell within her budget proved even more challenging than she had expected. Their house on Westover Drive had been riddled with structural and cosmetic problems, but at $850 a month, not including utilities, she could at least afford it. Now such properties were being bought, renovated, and either sold or rented for considerably more nearly everywhere in the city. A fundraiser organized by her cousin brought in $360, but it became obvious that remaining at the Howard Johnson would not be feasible.

That summer, Celeste contacted pretty much everyone in her wide social network who she thought might have a living room floor or a spare couple of couches where her family could sleep. She called in favors from friends whose kids she'd babysat free of charge or whose taxes she'd helped prepare; she offered to cook and clean their apartments in exchange for a place to crash. Many nights, lying uncomfortably on the floor beside Micah, Nyah, and Jalen, she flipped through photos and videos from the home they'd lost. There was a selfie of her and Micah cuddling in her bed, the five-year-old clad in his favorite Spiderman pajamas—which, to Micah's dismay, hadn't made it into the hampers they'd taken with them. There was a picture of Celeste and some friends gathered in the dining room, with the full dinnerware set she'd gotten for her birthday laid out in front of them. And there was a video she'd taken on the morning they awoke to a yard covered in snow, a rare occurrence in Atlanta. "Check it out, y'all, this is our front yard," she had narrated in a whisper, as if worried the spell could break. In the distance, Micah was building a snowman. "We have our own private winter wonderland right outside our house."

By late August, Celeste had exhausted her list of potential places to stay. She swallowed her pride and asked her ex's mom, Micah's grandmother, to fly the boys down to Tampa to live with her for a brief period. Their relationship had long been strained, and the older woman implied that Celeste was to blame for the hardships she and the kids were experiencing, yet she agreed to take them. The boys would be away for seven weeks, causing them to miss almost two months of the new school year. In an attempt to save money, Celeste and Nyah slept in the car for much of this time.

Not long after Jalen and Micah left, Celeste came across a promising apartment listing. It was $175 more per month than their previous rental, and it was considerably smaller, but it was in the same school district, and when she visited the complex it appeared relatively secure and well maintained. An affable leasing agent said they could move in as soon as they were approved. Celeste paid the $50 application fee and told Nyah the good news. Later that week, however, she received a call from the agent, whose tone had changed. He said she had been rejected because of the recent eviction on her record. "No," she said, "that's a mistake. There hasn't been any eviction."

She was wrong. Back in May, in the immediate aftermath of the fire, Celeste had reached out to her landlord about the prospect of relocating to a different property. Her home was owned and managed by The Prager Group, an Atlanta-based real estate investment, management, and private equity firm. Founded in 2009 during the foreclosure crisis, it was "set up to capitalize on the opportunity to acquire single family homes at historically low prices" and to "rent out and operate them with an institutional discipline that generates a cash flow stream ranging between 4 percent and 6 percent per year," according to its website. Its portfolio included roughly three thousand rental properties worth more than $350 million. A Prager representative had told Celeste that in order to break her lease and get her $850 security deposit back, she would first be required to pay not only the current month's rent—the house had burned down on the seventh of May—but an additional month as well. Celeste had hung up in disgust.

Now, after speaking with the leasing agent, Celeste realized what had happened following her earlier call with Prager. She immediately drove to East Point and parked outside the vacant house on Westover Drive. In the mailbox of the still-charred home was an eviction notice with her name on it. An identical form had been affixed to the front door. The sheriff who had carried out this "tack and mail" delivery of the dispossessory notice—Georgia is among the states where tenants do not have to be notified of an eviction in person—wrote at the bottom of the document that it was "served to fire damaged property." Celeste then drove to the Fulton County courthouse, where a clerk told her that when she'd failed to file a response to the notice within seven days, a default judgment had been handed down in favor of the landlord. She had been evicted, without her knowledge, from a home that had been destroyed and deemed uninhabitable. In the long run, she realized, the eviction could prove more devastating than the fire itself. The stain on her rental history, this "Scarlet E," could haunt her for years to come.

The final blow came toward the end of November. In a last-ditch effort, Celeste had posted about their predicament in a six-thousand-member Facebook group called "In Need of Housing in GA." An acquaintance saw it and told Celeste that she knew of an Atlanta family who would soon be moving and were looking for someone to sublet their apartment. Celeste jumped at the opportunity. Within days, she was meeting with the property manager at Pavilion Place on Cleveland Avenue. They had a friendly rapport, and the man was willing to overlook her recent eviction if Celeste could pay cash, up front, for the two months remaining on the lease. They moved into the spacious second-floor unit on November 2 with their only items of furniture: a couple of air mattresses, a floor lamp, a card table, and some folding chairs. Still,

they were thrilled. Celeste finally had her boys back and she felt optimistic that the manager would agree to start a new lease in her own
name when the current one expired.

Then on Monday, November 19, three days before Thanksgiving,
Celeste's godson stopped by the apartment in the early evening to hang
out with Nyah. Accompanying him was a friend named Souleymane.
Not long after arriving, while Celeste was straightening up and Jalen
and Micah were watching a movie at the kitchen table, Souleymane
started showing off a pistol he'd recently bought. He handed it to her
godson and, in doing so, fired off a shot. It went through the floor, striking a fourteen-year-old girl who lived in the unit below. She was dead
by the time the paramedics came. She had also been eight months
pregnant.

When the property manager showed up, he was sympathetic; although Souleymane would later be arrested, it was obvious that the
shooting was a bizarre and tragic accident. Nevertheless, he couldn't
allow them to remain in the apartment. He told them that they would
need to be out by the end of the week. He returned the money Celeste
had given him.

She used it to pay for a month at Efficiency Lodge.

ONE EVENING DURING her first week at the hotel, Celeste had just
finished cooking dinner when there was a tap on her window, which
she'd slid open to allow in fresh air. "Yo, that smells *nice,*" a man named
Kodak said as she turned around. She recognized him from the night
before. He and a few friends had been standing in the breezeway near
her room, laughing and carrying on; it had been almost 2:00 a.m., and
Celeste and the kids needed to be up early. Micah was the only one
asleep. Nyah, who'd heard rumors about the men—they were part of a
larger crew of drug dealers—pleaded with her mom not to say anything. But Celeste snapped. She opened the door and went off on the
group, explaining that if others were too scared to confront them, she

certainly wasn't. Her profanity-laced tirade did the trick. The men moved elsewhere.

"Sorry we were so loud last night," said Kodak. He then took out a twenty-dollar bill and offered it to her in exchange for a plate of food. She laughed and said he could have it for free, but he insisted that she take the money. Kodak's reaction when he started eating sparked an idea. Celeste had always dreamed of opening her own restaurant—she even had a name for it, Passion Foods. At the hotel, it was not uncommon for a resident's room to double as a place of commerce: in addition to drugs and sex, you could buy pretty much anything. One older man peddled an assortment of bottom-shelf liquors and tepid beers, while his downstairs neighbor sold a hodgepodge of everyday necessities, from batteries and cigarette lighters to Drano and deodorant. By the following weekend, a rudimentary version of Passion Foods was operating out of Room 147.

Celeste's eatery quickly distinguished itself. For $10, plus 50¢ for a can of soda, you could get a large serving of whatever dish she happened to be preparing that day: shrimp fettuccine alfredo, "fully loaded nachos," steak fried rice, turkey chili. In a neighborhood devoid of fresh meat and produce and where Dairy Queen, Taco Bell, and a Shell gas station were the sole dining options within walking distance, Celeste's meals were a revelation. Having drastically underestimated the demand for such offerings—on the first Saturday, she made a mere four servings, which sold out immediately—she had begun capping her output at ten servings per lunch or dinner; depending on the dish, each order yielded between $4 and $7 in profit. Although she'd only been doing this for a month, she already had a routine: On Fridays after leaving work (she was now a full-time employee at ProLogistix), she would drive to the Walmart Supercenter on Gresham Road, where she bought the items she'd need that weekend. She woke up early to prep the meals. If a dish required the crockpot, she started cooking it the night before.

After paying her rent and chatting with Lisa, Celeste hurried back to her room. She had about an hour to finish cooking. When she returned, a woman was standing outside her door. Since the food was first come, first served, people tended to hover in anticipation. "It'll be ready in a little bit," Celeste said. The woman asked her what was on the menu. "Smashed potatoes with a side of salmon," Celeste replied. Topped with butter, melted cheese, and a seasoned mix of ground turkey, beef, and pork, the potato dish was one of her favorites—though preparing it in the cramped confines of her room's kitchenette, equipped with only a microwave, a toaster, and two rusted coil burners, was no small feat.

But cooking brought her pleasure, and over the next hour she bantered with her customers through the window while churning out one plate after another. Nobody would have guessed that she'd been feeling unwell lately, with sharp abdominal pain and a loss of appetite. She assumed it was the stress of the last several months catching up with her. Outwardly, however, she seemed as invincible as ever. Among the hotel's residents, word had spread that, along with her cooking prowess, Celeste was someone who could solve any problem that might arise, be it a legal matter or figuring out how to sign up for WIC or Medicaid. "Ask Ms. Celeste" had become a standard response to a range of questions.

"Thanks, hon," Celeste said to a short, heavy-set man named Robert, the last person to be served, as Jalen tucked the bills he'd been handed into a tattered envelope. With Jalen's help, lunch had gone remarkably well. Now it was his turn to eat: Celeste had set aside a healthy portion for her children.

She grabbed a bottle of blue Powerade and walked outside, leaving behind a pile of dirty dishes that she and Nyah would tackle later. In lieu of a place to rest—Lisa had recently banned furniture on the walkways, though many residents ignored the rule—Celeste climbed onto the hood of her Durango and sat facing the parking lot. As on most weekends when it wasn't raining, the asphalt expanse was thrumming with activity. Kids on bikes or playing freeze tag darted this way and that, while their parents, bundled up against the cold, stood in clusters around parked cars, chatting and sipping drinks. A few of the cars had music drifting out of their open windows. Taking in the scene, Celeste wondered where all these people would be if extended-stays like Effi-

ciency did not exist. It was a frightening thought. She had been surprised to learn from Ms. Abigail, a social worker at Micah's elementary
school, that the school system classified students living at hotels and motels as homeless. From which it followed, Celeste reasoned, that these
places were functioning as homeless shelters, albeit expensive ones.

Earlier that week, Ms. Abigail had given Celeste a twenty-five-
dollar gas card and the county's "Homeless Resource List," a four-page
directory of churches, nonprofits, and government agencies that provided support to homeless families and individuals. She'd apologized
for not being able to offer more. "But please," she said, "try the numbers on the list." Celeste thanked her but was reluctant to go that route;
she couldn't bring herself to accept that this label, this category, might
apply to her own family. The list was still folded in the back seat of the
Durango, alongside a stack of other forms.

PART TWO

Storm

| 6 |

On the first night in her new home, Britt was giddy with relief. She kept walking around the bare apartment, opening cabinets, running her fingers along the freshly painted yellow walls. The furniture she'd ordered had not yet arrived, and Desiree and Kyrie were passed out on an air mattress in the gray-carpeted living room. They'd been so excited earlier, eagerly pushing past her as she opened the front door, causing her to laugh out loud. How many times had she visualized that exact moment? And now here they were.

After two years spent on the Housing Choice Voucher waiting list, it seemed incredible that the three of them finally had a place of their own: a spacious two-bedroom unit at QLS Gardens Apartments in southwest Atlanta. No more waking up achy and tired on Granny's old pullout sofa; no more worrying that they had worn out their welcome and would need to find somewhere else to stay. Even the apartment's less-than-appealing aspects, such as the stale, unpleasant odor coming from the kitchen, could not dampen Britt's spirit. She lit a vanilla-scented candle to mask the smell.

With the voucher, Britt was required to spend only 30 percent of her income on rent, which came out to just under $600 a month. She was aware of her good fortune. Although the "30 percent rule"—the idea that housing costs, including utilities, shouldn't exceed 30 percent of household income—had become conventional wisdom among policymakers and personal finance gurus, the vast majority of low-income tenants in Atlanta were handing over the bulk of their paychecks to landlords. If not for the voucher, Britt would have joined the ranks of the severely cost burdened: most apartments in the city, even ones located in rough neighborhoods, would have cost her 80 or 90 percent of her monthly earnings.

Freed from the uncertainty of how she would make ends meet, she bought a used Hyundai sedan and threw herself into the task of creating a homey and comfortable apartment. She focused especially on Desiree and Kyrie's bedroom. She bought toy bins and bookcases and Disney character blankets for their beds, hoping it would help them sleep alone. But having never slept in a separate bed from Britt, much less a separate room, they had difficulty adjusting. Most nights one or both of them wound up under the covers with her.

Britt understood how the kids were feeling. She, too, found it daunting to be living in their own place. Staying on top of utility bills and maintenance requests, paying her $310 car note, ensuring that the apartment remained stocked with food and household essentials—these responsibilities were suddenly hers alone. It took some getting used to, but gradually she hit her stride. A former cheerleader who could be mistaken, on her days off, for a college athlete—she usually wore leggings, running shoes, and a fashionable hoodie—Britt felt herself becoming the sort of parent, the sort of *person,* she'd always imagined herself to be. She organized birthday parties for the kids: a Little Mermaid extravaganza for Desiree, a fish broil for Kyrie when he turned three. ("What can I say," Britt said with a laugh, "the kid loves seafood.") She hosted dinner-and-movie nights with her friends, a few of whom, the ones without a place of their own, ended up staying over. Britt had leaned on others during challenging times, and now it was her turn to offer support. In her social and familial world, it was taken for granted that there were seasons of need and seasons of abundance, when you responded to others' needs. If she caught herself feeling frustrated at these intermittent intrusions into her personal space, she tried to remember what it had felt like to be on the other side.

So Britt didn't hesitate to say yes when her cousin Steve, who had recently gotten out of prison, asked if he could stay with her for a while. Like many men and women attempting to rebuild their lives after a period of incarceration, the twenty-three-year-old had confronted a harsh reality upon release: his prospects of securing not only a job but a place to live were exceedingly grim. In Atlanta and across the country, systematic discrimination against formerly incarcerated men and women made them ten times more likely to experience homelessness than the general public—often leading to a revolving door of further arrests, imprisonment, and housing precarity. But to Britt, Steve was not a "convicted felon." He was a family member, a kid she'd played with as a child and, later, a classmate at Booker T. Washington High School. She had fond memories of the two of them hanging out at family barbecues; Steve was always getting into trouble even then, but she had a soft spot for him. She couldn't imagine turning him away.

As their first year in the apartment drew to a close, life for Britt and the kids had settled into a predictable rhythm previously unknown to them. Their weeks had been filled with all the "normal stuff," as Britt called it, that to her mind signified what a sane, undramatic existence should look and feel like. Desiree was attending kindergarten at an elementary school not far from the complex, and Kyrie was enrolled in a local daycare program. On weekends, the enclosed patio outside their ground-floor unit became a bonus play area for the kids, and sometimes, if Britt had to work, they spent the day with their great-aunt Trisha, who lived nearby with her own adult children. As for Britt, she realized that her bouts of anxiety had grown much less frequent since moving into the apartment. When she was tired, it was now a good tired, not the kind she had become so accustomed to.

But this new normalcy was short-lived. On a morning in early spring, Britt went to the rental office to inquire about renewing her lease. After she gave the young woman on duty her name and apartment number, a manager appeared and said that they were unable to offer her a renewal. Britt forced herself to stay calm. "Is there any particular reason?" she asked. The manager told her that a man had been spotted entering and leaving her unit repeatedly over the course of a few weeks—her front door lay within sight of the office—adding that people with "criminal backgrounds" were not allowed to reside on the property. Britt betrayed no emotion. She just nodded, said "Okay, whatever," and walked out. Steve had left nearly a month earlier to stay with a new girlfriend, and Britt suspected that her next-door neighbor, who was "always up in everyone's business, always sayin' shit," as Britt put it, was the one who had told the office about his history.

BRITT WAS BLINDSIDED by the news. She compared it to the feeling of dating someone for an extended period of time, thinking the relationship was going well, and then abruptly getting dumped. But her initial anger and disappointment quickly gave way to resignation. She compiled a mental catalog of everything she wouldn't miss at QLS: its location on a "high-crime, low-everything else" portion of Campbellton Road; the lack of parks and playgrounds for Desiree and Kyrie; the slow, often shoddy maintenance work. Telling herself that she had settled for a less-than-ideal arrangement—she'd jumped at the chance to rent the unit after hearing about it through her aunt, and it was the only place she'd applied for—Britt took solace in the fact that she still had her voucher. A nicer apartment no doubt awaited them.

Her confidence was such that she let several days pass before starting to look for a new place. When she finally began the search in earnest, scrolling through Zillow and Craigslist and Apartments.com, an unsettling pattern emerged: she'd see a listing that looked promising, but at the bottom of the page it would say "No Section 8" or "Vouchers Not Accepted." Moreover, her voucher had come with strict parameters as to the cost and size and location of the unit she could rent. It had to be situated within the city limits of Atlanta, which meant that apartments in some of the more affordable suburbs of Dekalb, Clayton, and Fulton County were out of bounds. And because she had two kids, the apartment needed to have at least two bedrooms. Even if she wanted to make do with a studio or one-bedroom, sacrificing privacy for the chance to live in a better neighborhood or complex, she couldn't.

Britt consulted the list of landlords and property management companies given to her by AHA. One by one she crossed each of them off. Those who answered the phone or bothered replying to her emails informed her that they were no longer taking vouchers, or had no two-bedroom units, or had raised their rents beyond what the voucher would cover. Others had no vacancies at all for the foreseeable future.

The ease with which she had been able to secure her apartment at QLS was starting to seem like a fluke. The problem, she realized, wasn't that her rental applications were getting rejected. It was that there were no places where she could even apply. She remembered her elation the day she'd won the voucher lottery and, two years later, her relief at having made it off the waiting list. Now, with their move-out date fast approaching, she felt only dread.

Finding a place to live had not been so difficult for older members of Britt's family. By the 1970s, when her mother, aunts, and grandmother moved into Capitol Homes, and her great-grandmother and great-great-grandmother settled at East Lake Meadows, affordable apartments were relatively plentiful, though their conditions often left much to be desired. This was the tail end of a golden era in public housing, one that had begun just a couple of miles from Capitol Homes in the 1930s.

Techwood Homes, the nation's first public housing project, was situated in downtown Atlanta between Georgia Tech and what would later become the Coca-Cola headquarters. Conceived at the height of the Great Depression under the auspices of the Public Works Administration (PWA), the project was a shining example of New Deal Progressivism. Secretary of the Interior Harold Ickes, who directed the PWA, had traveled to Atlanta in 1934 to break ground on the development. "We have met here today to do something that has never before been done in this country," he said in a nationally broadcast radio speech, praising Atlanta for being a "pioneer" in the endeavor to create "low-cost housing projects available to people in the lowest-income classes at rents that will be within their ability to pay." The plan was not without its adversaries—Atlanta's real estate industry bitterly denounced public housing as a "socialistic" danger to private enterprise—but it was generally considered a godsend for the city. "Uncle Sam Uses Atlanta as

His Housing Laboratory," declared a local front-page story, observing that "the most advanced attack yet made on the housing problems in the United States is planned in this southern capital."

Yet these "bright, cheerful buildings," as President Franklin D. Roosevelt referred to Atlanta's new public housing, were intended only for some Americans. Despite government rhetoric to the contrary, it was almost exclusively for upwardly mobile working-class families, the majority of them white: tenants who were "lower class in income but middle class in values or aspirations," in the words of one scholar. Techwood was typical in this respect. Although the slum neighborhood cleared to make way for Techwood had been multiracial, the new housing project was a segregated, whites-only community. (A separate project for Black families called University Homes was built on the city's West Side, but most residents displaced from the former slum had incomes that were too meager to qualify.) Those accepted into public housing, meanwhile, enjoyed enviable conditions and the most up-to-date modern appliances. Tenants at Techwood even had their own orchestra and newspaper. The high quality of life in Techwood's garden-style red-brick apartments was later recalled fondly by early residents, including Truett Cathy, who would go on to found Chick-fil-A. As late as 1968, Techwood could still be described as a "large, beautiful" place that had "matured and improved as an integral part of central Atlanta."

By the 1970s, the racial and economic composition of public housing had undergone a drastic shift. Over the previous two decades, white families had been steadily leaving projects like Techwood for the suburbs, where they could take advantage of federally subsidized low-interest mortgages largely denied to minority families. A result was that when whites-only projects were finally desegregated in the late 1960s, these buildings had a large number of vacant apartments: the demand for such units among white families had dramatically diminished. This, combined with growing pressure to loosen eligibility requirements, led local housing authorities to begin accepting more and more low-income applicants. Before long, the nation's projects were majority-Black. White flight made it possible for families like Britt's to find housing.

It was at this point that politicians started to gut funding for the projects. Beginning with President Richard Nixon, who referred to these complexes as "monstrous, depressing places," successive administrations went on to decimate the government's budget for low-income housing. "We're getting out of the housing business. Period," said a top U.S. Department of Housing and Urban Development official in 1985. With no money for maintenance, repairs, and other basic services, America's housing projects rapidly deteriorated. The federal government had created the very conditions that were later pointed to as evidence of the "failure" of public housing.

In 1994, the year Britt was born, Atlanta undertook a second great experiment in public housing: demolishing it. The city had been selected to host the 1996 Summer Olympic Games, and the prevailing view, promoted by boosters and reporters alike, was that Atlanta was at last achieving the "world-class" status it had long craved. Housing projects like Techwood, Capitol Homes, and East Lake Meadows, where Cass and her newborn moved in with Granny and Big Mama, threatened to undermine this image. Techwood's downtown location and proximity to the future Olympic Village made it a particular embarrassment and liability. An assistant to the president of Georgia Tech called it a "cesspool"; *The Washington Post* described Techwood as "infested with crack dealers." For Atlanta's political and business elite, eliminating the spectacle of "Olympic Games meet Southern Slum," as another newspaper put it, became an urgent necessity.

Atlanta Housing Authority embarked on an ambitious campaign to dismantle the city's public housing. Democratic mayor Bill Campbell appointed Renée Glover, a former Wall Street lawyer, to serve as the CEO of the agency. Under her leadership, AHA showed little interest in refurbishing Atlanta's dilapidated projects, where a remarkable 13 percent of the city's population (and 40 percent of schoolchildren) were living—a greater proportion than in any other American city. Rather, the agency rebranded itself as a "diversified real estate company" and took on the new mission of creating entire communities "from the ground up," as Glover put it—which meant tearing down public housing complexes, giving eligible families vouchers, and enlisting private developers to build, own, and manage mixed-income communities where the projects had once stood.

But AHA's innovations didn't stop there. Inspired by efforts at the federal level to move people from "welfare to work," AHA became the first housing authority in the country to impose a strict work requirement on its beneficiaries. These measures, declared an admiring column in *The Atlanta Journal-Constitution,* had turned the city's housing authority into a "conservative's dream." When Glover described her approach as revolutionary, she wasn't exaggerating. The Atlanta Model, as it came to be known, was soon adopted as the blueprint for redevelopment in Chicago, Miami, and a number of other major cities.

For more than thirty years, business leaders and real estate developers had sought to remake the downtown areas where the public housing developments were situated. One notorious plan put forward by Central Atlanta Progress, a powerful business group, had called for the construction of a moat—the term used was *water feature*—to separate the projects from a proposed residential zone composed of townhomes and upscale apartment towers. Seizing the opportunity presented by the Olympics, Glover's AHA would ultimately succeed where previous attempts to reinvent the neighborhood had faltered. Together with an aggressive effort to rid Atlanta of its unsheltered population (among other draconian measures, one-way bus tickets out of town were given to homeless men and women on the condition that they not return), the bulldozing of Techwood in 1995 became emblematic of the city's new urban landscape. Glover proudly pointed to the estimated $1 billion of private investment that poured into the area after the demolition. This feat of revitalization was accomplished by removing not just the crumbling buildings but the families who lived in them. At Centennial Place, the lauded apartment community that replaced Techwood, only seventy-eight of its nine hundred units would be occupied by former residents.

In the winter of 2011, Atlanta's final remaining housing projects were dynamited. Much of the media coverage of this watershed period, influenced by AHA's well-funded public relations machine, presented a before-and-after narrative of urban blight miraculously giving way to

urban renaissance. The first city in the country to embrace public housing became the first to do away with it altogether.

But another sea change had taken place more quietly: the Housing
Choice Voucher program was now the primary form of housing assistance in the country. Three decades earlier, a task force appointed by
President Ronald Reagan had concluded that housing the poor should
be left to the "genius" of the free market. "Rental housing is an important component of the nation's housing stock," a HUD report noted in
1981, "and with limited exceptions the private market is successfully
addressing this need." To the extent that government involvement was
still required, it should be limited to moving as many people into the
private market as possible.

For a booming city like Atlanta, the voucher program was portrayed
as a win-win. The inner-city neighborhoods where sprawling housing
projects used to stand could be handed over to private developers and
investors, enabling a "civic rebirth." And poor working families who at
one time would have qualified for a public housing unit could use their
voucher to move into homes owned by private landlords. Everyone
would benefit from this new arrangement.

So why, Britt wondered, would no one accept her voucher?

BRITT AND THE KIDS had to move out of their apartment in late
May. It was Britt's twenty-fourth birthday. The offers from friends and
family to take her out that night did not extend to helping her pack and
transport her belongings, so the day was shaping up to be a long one. As
she filled several oversized tote bags with whatever linens and stuffed
animals and kitchen items she could squeeze into them, Desiree and
Kyrie watched videos on her phone. Although it was a weekday, she'd
decided to keep the children with her; this slowed her down, but it was
comforting to have them nearby. Earlier, and not for the first time, Britt
had tried to explain why they were leaving. She said the apartment
didn't belong to them, and that the people who owned it wanted it back.

Still, her son and daughter didn't seem to grasp that they would no longer be living there.

When Britt mentioned to the kids that the three of them would be
going to Aunt Trisha's place, she assured them—without really believ-
ing it—that it would be just for a few nights. Her aunt had been less
than thrilled to open her already-crowded home to them, but Britt
had few options. She couldn't bring herself to go back to her great-
grandmother's apartment. And her grandmother, Theresa, was anxious enough about allowing Cass to sleep on her couch, fearful of
violating the terms of her lease and risking eviction.

The same went for Britt's younger sister, Aaliyah, who lived with
her boyfriend and his brother in a small one-bedroom unit. The more
people in the apartment, the more suspicion it aroused, and while
Aaliyah had made it clear that Britt and the kids could stay there if all
else failed, the last thing she needed was to give their landlord an excuse
to put them out. Given what had happened to Britt, Aaliyah was especially on edge; only Trisha, who was accustomed to relatives coming
and going on a regular basis, seemed unconcerned about upsetting her
landlord. Aaliyah had, however, agreed to store some of Britt's bigger
pieces of furniture, including her bed frame, which Aaliyah was happy
to take after months of sleeping on a mattress on the floor. Everything
else—Britt's side table and bookcases, the TV stand, Desiree's bed—
would be left beside the dumpster for neighbors to pick through. She
hadn't been able to sell these items online, and getting rid of them was
cheaper and easier than renting a moving van and storage unit. Emptying each room, Britt felt like she was dismantling the life she had finally
managed to build.

Even as she packed and loaded her car and trudged back and forth
between the dumpster and the apartment, Britt had one thing on her
mind: finding a new place to live. Every ten minutes or so, she took her
phone from the kids and checked to see if any property managers had
returned her calls or if any new listings had been posted. She was convinced that the day would bring encouraging news. It was her birthday,
after all.

The week before, Britt had been informed by an AHA caseworker that she had sixty days to secure another lease—after that, she would lose her voucher. Reading the email, she recalled the mandatory orientation meeting she'd attended after first receiving the voucher. In a room packed with dozens of other new recipients, Britt listened as an AHA staff member went through the program's byzantine rules and requirements, including the sixty-day deadline. One woman raised her hand and asked if anybody from AHA would be assisting them in their search. The answer was no, this was *their* responsibility. "We're not gonna be holding your hand," Britt recalled one staff member saying. She had bristled at the woman's tone; to her, it implied that if someone couldn't rent a place within the allotted time frame, then they were to blame, like the person wasn't trying. But Britt and the other new voucher holders were optimistic the night of the orientation. Everyone assumed there'd be plenty of places to choose from. This confidence seemed borne out by how quickly Britt had landed the unit at QLS. Now that she was preparing to return her keys and facing a deadline once again, a different reality had set in.

The weeks after moving were exhausting. She was increasingly desperate as her efforts to find an apartment became a full-time job—on top of her actual full-time job. She had left Low Country back in June to work at a Chick-fil-A on the Georgia Tech campus. Though it paid $2 less per hour, she didn't have to commute to the airport or arrange nightly childcare for Desiree and Kyrie. But the 9:00 a.m. to 6:00 p.m. shifts left room for little else, so her housing search was limited to thirty-minute meal breaks and scouring the internet when she got home. Except "home" was now Aunt Trisha's cramped and noisy duplex, where it was impossible to concentrate.

Britt decided to cut back her work schedule—enough to allow her to take a more aggressive and proactive approach to seeking out landlords, but not so much that she could be penalized for failing to meet the AHA's stringent work requirement. She began driving around the city for hours at a time, looking for rent signs on the lawns of single-family homes and visiting leasing offices that hadn't responded to her calls and emails. Leasing agents were friendly and apologetic when they told her that vouchers were not accepted at their properties. Before long, Britt realized that whole areas of Atlanta were off limits to people with vouchers. As each day of apartment hunting blurred into the next, she could feel the life draining out of her. She lost track of the number of places she'd inquired about.

One afternoon, Britt spotted an ad that had just been posted. Knowing how crucial it was to jump on it right away, she merely skimmed the brief description and glanced at the low-resolution pictures. The house appeared run-down, the sort of dwelling she would never have considered a couple of months earlier. But near the end of a long list of rental requirements were the words "Government Vouchers Accepted," followed by a number for "serious inquiries only."

A man answered the phone and quickly punctured Britt's hopes. The line about the voucher had been mistakenly left in from when he'd last listed the home. "I've got nothing against folks with vouchers," he said amiably. "It just doesn't make sense anymore."

This had become a common refrain among Atlanta landlords and their counterparts around the country. They complained about the extra property inspections and administrative hassle that came with the voucher program, and they believed that accepting vouchers would hinder their ability to raise rents at will: if they wanted to charge more, they would need to get approval from the housing authority. Blatant prejudice was also a factor. There was a widely held assumption that "Section 8" tenants were, by virtue of needing the subsidy, less responsible or financially capable than other tenants, and many landlords simply did not want to deal with "those people." When the voucher program was first introduced, lobbyists for the real estate industry enthusiastically championed the idea. Unlike public housing, vouchers were not seen as a threat to their business model. But they vigorously fought attempts to mandate participation in the program; they wanted to accept vouchers only when it was in their best interests to do so. Vouchers were supposed to deconcentrate poverty and enable greater socioeconomic mobility for recipients. In reality, families with vouchers were often able to find homes only in poor, underserved neighborhoods where landlords had a clear financial incentive to rent to them.

And as these neighborhoods gentrified and began attracting wealthier renters, even this incentive disappeared. The "hotter" the local rental market, the less likely it was that vouchers would be accepted. In Atlanta, as in other booming cities where apartment vacancies were at an all-time low and rents in the private market were soaring, voucher holders suddenly found themselves competing for fewer and fewer eligible units. Many voucher-accepting landlords saw that they could extract greater profits from unassisted tenants.

Before hanging up, the man wished Britt luck in her search.

IN EARLY JULY, Britt requested an extension from her AHA caseworker and was given an additional thirty days. She prayed for a last-minute miracle. But she didn't get one. She wasn't alone: that year, AHA issued 1,674 new housing vouchers; 1,055 expired before they could be used. If Britt hoped to receive another voucher, she would need to start the entire process over again.

Kara dialed her landlord's number. It went straight to voicemail.

"Um, Mr. Dejene, this is Ms. Thompson again. We still don't have hot water and it's been over a week. You said the guy was coming, but nobody's been out here. I'm getting really sick and tired of this. Please call me right away."

Kara had just returned home from work and, as she'd done the day before, and the day before that, had walked immediately to the bathroom sink to see if the water heater had been fixed. Maybe the repairman had been there while she was at the hospital? After she'd let the tap run for about five minutes, though, it remained cold. She'd cursed and picked up her phone.

She yearned for a hot shower. Although Kara was enjoying her new position as an EKG tech, she hated how she felt at the end of her shift: grimy and germ-ridden. Her kids had learned not to bother her until she'd removed her scrubs and rinsed herself clean. But this had proved difficult over the past week. No matter how vigorously she scoured her skin with a washcloth and then doused herself with cups of stove-heated water, she still felt unclean.

Since Joshua's birth Kara had been running on fumes, waking to feed her infant son in the middle of the night and rarely sleeping for more than a few hours. Her plans for a proper nursery had quickly dissolved, and her rental home still had a provisional feel to it: unpacked boxes, barren walls. She had recently financed a used Toyota Avalon to replace the totaled Pilot—buying another vehicle, she'd realized, was necessary if she wanted to keep her job and avoid having to find a new daycare for the kids—but because of her low credit score, the interest rate was a punishing 17 percent. She was now paying $150 more per month than she'd been paying for the Pilot. She had no room in her life for anything else to go wrong.

She could have dealt with three or four days without hot water. But not a week, or two weeks, or however long this was going to drag on. The time and effort required to hand-wash the breakfast and dinner dishes, or to heat up pot after pot of water in order to bathe the children, was time and effort she couldn't spare. Yet she had never neglected to keep the kids "looking decent," as she put it. She felt gratified when strangers commented on their appearance and good behavior. Walking down sidewalks or through grocery stores, the family resembled a mother duck and her dutiful ducklings, the two older boys—hair neatly cropped and sporting matching outfits, usually crisp polo shirts and khaki pants—kept in line by Grace, a miniature version of Kara: head held high, hair braided, wearing a brightly colored dress with a vaguely African print. Kara's desire to project competence and respectability was in direct proportion to the judgment she had faced, above all from her parents. No matter how long it took her to bathe the kids, she was determined to keep them meticulously clean.

Having dealt with her share of slumlords in the past, Kara had been grateful to discover, when they moved into the baby-blue house on Oakwood nine months earlier, that the place was in relatively good shape. The landlord seemed pleasant enough. Now she assumed that Dejene was showing his true colors. She didn't hear back from him that evening, which was no surprise, but two days later a plumber finally showed up and, after inspecting the water heater, said it was badly corroded and needed to be replaced. Most gas water heaters, he explained, had a life span of eight to twelve years. Her heater had been manufactured in 1996, making it twenty-three years old. He said he'd tell Dejene that a new one needed to be installed.

With each passing day after the plumber left, Kara grew convinced that Dejene had no intention of replacing the water heater. Her exasperation turned into a hard, seething anger. The disrespect was so familiar. At work, she could feel the germs and perspiration accumulating on her body from one shift to the next. *God, I smell like shit,* she thought. Unable to get fully clean, she tried to avoid standing close to people. Yet physical proximity with patients was inescapable. She imagined them holding their noses whenever she was in the room.

After a month without hot water, Kara began calling lawyers and local media outlets, trying to alert them to her plight. Nobody followed up with her. In Atlanta, other families were facing far worse. Georgia, among the most landlord-friendly states in the country, was one of only three that did not require property owners to guarantee the habitability of apartments they rented out. Skyrocketing rents were not translating into better conditions—on the contrary, exorbitant rent hikes were occurring at places that, in many cases, were barely livable. Rats and overflowing sewage, leaking ceilings, black mold, exposed electrical wiring: these were endemic in complexes occupied by the city's poorest families. Their only recourse was to contact code enforcement. But nothing prevented landlords from evicting tenants for reporting hazardous conditions; here, too, Georgia was one of the few states that did not prohibit "retaliatory evictions." As a result, tenants frequently had to choose between becoming homeless or enduring substandard housing. And landlords were well aware that if one family decided to leave, there were plenty of others willing to take their place.

"Fuck this," Kara said to herself. Dejene, she had concluded, was taking advantage of her powerlessness. Impulsively, unable to sleep one night, she called him in a rage and left another message saying that she wouldn't be giving him another penny until a new water heater was installed. For all Kara knew, Dejene had blocked her number and would never even hear it. Eventually, however, his response arrived: an eviction notice. This only strengthened Kara's resolve. No way was she

going to pay her rent. She welcomed the opportunity to air her grievances before a judge.

On the morning of May 7, after driving Grace and Nathaniel to
school and then Jermaine and Joshua to daycare, Kara parked outside
the DeKalb County courthouse. She was wearing her hospital scrubs.
Though she had taken the day off, she hoped to distinguish herself
from other people in the courtroom at risk of losing their homes. She
wanted to show the judge that she was a "skilled working person," as
she put it, not "some deadbeat." She came armed with a printout of text
messages meant to demonstrate Dejene's deliberate negligence.

When her case was called, Kara noticed that, as in the overwhelming majority of eviction hearings nationwide, her landlord had retained
an attorney. She was representing herself. The judge, Phyllis Williams,
who had a genial but no-nonsense manner, began by addressing Kara.
Was it true, the judge asked, that Kara had failed to pay her monthly
rent of $1,200?

Kara was flustered. She had prepared a speech detailing what she
and her children had been going through, and what the plumber had
told her, and what she saw as Dejene's callous disregard. The judge's
question threw her off. "Yes, that's true," she said. "But please, can I
explain?" She began to mount her defense but quickly became self-
conscious. She could tell the judge was unmoved by her story. Even to
her own ears, the whole thing sounded much less scandalous than it had
felt at the time.

Judge Williams ruled in favor of Dejene. In many other states, tenants could withhold rent until repairs were made. Not in Georgia. The
money judgment awarded to Dejene, in the amount of her unpaid rent
plus court fees; the "writ of possession," which was to be enforced
within thirty days—Kara barely registered the judge's words. The next
case was called, and Kara, suddenly queasy, ran to the nearest bathroom.

Afterward, she spotted Dejene in the hallway. He was sitting on a
bench beside his lawyer. Before the landlord could react, Kara charged
toward him, stomping on his foot. Sheriff's deputies intervened. They
said she'd be arrested if she didn't immediately leave the premises.

"Y'ALL NEVER BEEN TO THE OCEAN." Kara was driving south on Interstate 75. She kept her voice down so as not to wake Jermaine and Joshua. "Trust me," she said. "You're gonna love it."

Grace and Nathaniel hung on her every word. Kara had been trying to get them excited for what she was calling their "summer vacation," and it was working. Their moods tended to mirror hers. When Kara was happy, they were happy; when Kara was angry or withdrawn, as she had been in the frantic aftermath of the eviction hearing, scrambling to return her rent-to-own furniture and move their other things to a storage unit, they became angry and withdrawn. The children were most definitely happy now. She'd considered telling them the truth about this trip to Florida—that it wasn't just a vacation, that the five of them were probably going to stay there permanently—but she thought it better to tell them later, once they had all settled in.

A month and a half earlier, in late March, Kara had received a message on Facebook from Darius, Grace's father. It had been more than a year since she'd heard from him. As with the other men who passed in and out of Kara's life, communication with Darius had always been on his terms, when he was ready to reply to a long-unanswered DM or send along his new phone number after a previous one had been disconnected. They had met at Job Corps; he was finishing a Certified Nurse Assistant program just as she was beginning it. The first time she talked to the stocky, dreadlocked twenty-two-year-old, she was struck less by his looks than by his intelligence. He offered to help her with a difficult class assignment, and later he invited her to an off-campus party some of his friends were throwing. It was a "real date," she said, her first brush with genuine romance. That night, at her urging, Darius wore a condom, but he took it off while they were having sex.

Soon Kara was pregnant. Darius encouraged her to get an abortion, but Kara described her ordeal in high school and told him she would never go that route again. Darius returned to Vero Beach, where his family lived, before Grace was born. He promised to send money, which, for the first year of Grace's life, he did sporadically. Then she stopped hearing from him. Struggling financially on her own, she began the process of obtaining child support. But Georgia's Division of Child Support Services was unable to locate Darius, making it impossible to conduct a paternity test. After a brief, unannounced visit from Darius when Grace was almost two, Kara chose to let things be. She decided it was better to guilt him into sending money than to see him arrested for failing to make payments—and ruin any chance of having him in their daughter's life.

Her first impulse when she saw Darius's Facebook message was to delete it. She was annoyed at its casual tone ("hey how are u") and the fact that he hadn't acknowledged how long it had been since she'd last heard from him. But they ended up talking on the phone that night. She found it comforting to hear his voice. He was playful and flirtatious, and he validated her anger at the situation with the hot water heater. "I'd be pissed too," he said. Later, when she called him crying outside the courthouse and told him about her eviction and near arrest, his response surprised her. He said that Kara and the kids could come stay with him for a while. Darius had made a similar offer during his visit years earlier—when she'd had only one child, not four—but Kara hadn't taken him seriously. This time, compelled by a vision of starting over in Vero Beach, she suppressed her skepticism.

It was already dark when Kara pulled up to the address Darius had given her—a buffet-style restaurant where he'd recently started working. He had the night off and was waiting for them in the parking lot. He hugged Kara as she got out of the car. "Where's my baby at?" he said, looking at Grace. The nine-year-old stood stiffly beside her mother. She seemed unsure what to do or say. She had no memory of ever having met this man. "Ah, she just gettin' to know you," Kara said. He moved on to Nathaniel and Jermaine, giving them high fives, and said, "Wassup, big man" to the baby, tickling his leg. Darius bought them dinner. The last person who'd paid for anything was Isaiah, Jermaine's father, before he went to jail on drug and domestic violence charges. Darius held Kara's hand under the table. They had dessert and then followed Darius to his apartment, which was actually a lone bedroom in a large rooming house—a detail he had neglected to share with Kara.

Not wanting to appear ungrateful, she hid her disappointment. As the six of them crammed into his room, he assured Kara that a separate bedroom was scheduled to be vacated soon. She could have it while she searched for a rental of her own.

The next day was close to perfect. After breakfast, Darius left for work and Kara drove to her first appointment. Before leaving Atlanta, she'd had an idea: she would start a cleaning company in Florida. The money she earned would supplement her income from the healthcare job she hoped to eventually find. She'd christened her company Kara's In & Out Cleaning Service and had ordered business cards, which she planned on putting in neighbors' mailboxes. She even had a big decal made for the side of her car. Finally, she'd posted ads on Yelp and Craigslist and Angie's List. During the journey down to Vero Beach, she got her first call from a potential client, a woman who lived alone. They agreed to meet at her condo.

Kara was nervous, worried that having the kids with her might scare the woman off. But when they arrived at the condo they were warmly received. The woman, a Jewish retiree in poor health, listened intently as Kara explained the circumstances that had led her and the children to relocate from Atlanta, fudging only one fact: she claimed that she had already purchased the supplies she'd need for her new business. The woman hired her for an initial cleaning. If it went well, the woman said, she'd recommend Kara to her friends.

Kara was overjoyed. Some people, she thought, would have been astonished by this stroke of luck. But not her. When one door closed, God always opened another. That night, they went with Darius to a get-together at a relative's house. The adults grilled outside and smoked weed while the kids watched TV in the den. For Kara, the evening felt like a celebration.

They returned to the rooming house around midnight. Kara guided a half-asleep Grace, Nathaniel, and Jermaine toward the front porch. They were trailed by Darius, who was carrying Joshua in his car seat.

"Who are *you*?"

In the darkness, Kara hadn't noticed the young woman sitting on the front porch. Although Darius had sworn he wasn't seeing anyone, the woman's tone of voice told Kara everything she needed to know. "Who the hell are *you*?" Kara said. Within seconds the two were trading blows. When the woman, whose name was Tamara, sprayed mace in the direction of Kara's face, Kara began choking her, letting go only when Darius pulled her off.

"Stop!" he pleaded. "She's pregnant!"

The kids were hysterical. Kara grabbed Joshua's car seat and marched back to her Toyota. Darius and the children were behind her.

"Bitch, you outta your mind!" Darius yelled at his girlfriend. He buckled the children in and got into the driver's seat. As he was about to pull away, Tamara opened Kara's door and plunged a fork into her shoulder.

Darius drove Kara to the emergency room. Over the next several hours, sitting in the waiting area, Darius begged her to hear him out. She just shook her head. She'd made up her mind the moment Tamara confronted her.

She felt utterly humiliated. How could she have convinced herself that Darius would become the person she wanted him to be? The whole plan—moving to Vero Beach, living with Darius, starting a cleaning business—now seemed ludicrous. And she realized that, deep down, she had expected it to go this way. Perhaps that was why, instead of quitting her job at the hospital, she had merely taken a week off, unpaid. And why she'd kept the kids enrolled in their subsidized daycare program.

By the time Kara was discharged from the ER, the sun was almost up. She told Darius to find his own ride home and began the ten-hour drive back to Atlanta.

KARA TORE A PIECE OF PAPER out of Grace's notebook and wrote EXPENSES across the top of it. Since returning from Florida two weeks earlier, she'd been renting a room at United Inn, an extended-stay on Memorial Drive. It was $380 a week, or double that if you were paying by the day. She detested the mold-and-roach-plagued room, with its filthy carpet, broken stove, and, beyond their door, the open drug dealing and prostitution. But it was the cheapest she could find with availability. Kara missed her rental on Oakwood, where, if she had a hard time sleeping, she could go into the garage, sit in her old thread-bare recliner, and process her thoughts. Sometimes she improvised gospel songs—she'd sung in the church choir when she was young—and other times she rolled a blunt to calm her nerves. Some nights she did both. Now all she had was a stained loveseat, which faced the bed where her children had finally drifted off.

She'd been trying not to think about the bigger picture. Anything beyond the tasks immediately in front of her—going to work, keeping the kids clean and fed, making sure her car stayed in working order—felt too daunting to contemplate. But now she was nearly broke, and the question of how they'd get by over the coming weeks—or however long it would take to secure a place to live—had become impossible to avoid. She made a list of her current monthly expenses. After she added up her car payment and insurance, the cost of gas, her cellphone bill, the hotel rent, and the cost of the storage unit that contained most of her family's belongings, the total came to $2,320. There was also the $50 "family fee" she was required to pay the state of Georgia for the children's daycare, as well as any food that wasn't covered by her food stamps—a quick dinner at Little Caesars in lieu of cooking, the occasional Blueberry Heaven at Smoothie King. But she was trying to get the daycare fee waived, and they could forgo eating out for the foreseeable future, so she left these off. Then she considered her monthly earnings after taxes: roughly $1,900, depending on the number of overtime hours she picked up. She closed her eyes; she had a throbbing headache. Her car, phone, and storage unit were essential. The hotel room was not.

The next morning, in the employee parking lot outside Grady Hospital, she did an internet search for family homeless shelters. She had no idea how to go about getting into such a place or how to choose between them. She clicked on the first result, a place called Drake House. She then tapped a banner on the nonprofit's homepage. It read, "If you're experiencing homelessness and in need of assistance, click here." She was directed to two pages of questions meant to determine her eligibility. She took her time answering them. When she clicked "submit," a new window appeared. "Thank you. Your form was successfully submitted. Based on the information given, our services are not a match for your needs." She stared at the screen.

She then tried City of Refuge, whose Eden Village program—"low-barrier assessment bridge housing for single mothers with children"—seemed to be exactly what she was looking for. The program's FAQ page noted that walk-ins were not accepted. Those seeking admission needed to call to inquire about available space.

Kara dialed the number. It rang and rang. "The mailbox is full and cannot accept any messages at this time. Goodbye."

After submitting a "Request for Help" form on the Our House website and emailing Hope Atlanta, Kara left detailed voice messages with the Salvation Army, Solomon's Temple, and Decatur Cooperative Ministry. Her shift would be starting soon, and she had yet to actually speak to anyone.

She tried one last place: My Sister's House, run by Atlanta Mission, a Christian organization. It was the largest women and children's shelter in the city. The Google reviews were scary. "This place needs to be inspected by the health department ASAP," read one. "The rooms for mother and children has rat feces mold problems and other health issues that could be a problem to a young person's health." The review was accompanied by photos of the shelter's squalid conditions. Another woman had written: "If you can choose any other shelter please DON'T go here. . . . They will make you quit your job to comply with the rules of the program. It's very stressful. Go somewhere that'll let you work, save, and get back on your feet."

Kara was dubious about the complaint. Why would a homeless shelter not allow people to work? It made no sense. But when she went to the website, it appeared that this was indeed the case. The shelter's admissions policy explicitly barred residents from working outside jobs so that they could attend mandatory classes on parenting and financial literacy and spiritual growth. The idea of potentially sacrificing her job to take a class on money management seemed preposterous to Kara.

Financial literacy? What kind of "financial literacy" would make it easier to afford $380 a week rent on a $12-an-hour wage?

But it was a moot point. When she dialed the number for My Sister's House, her call went straight to a recording explaining that the shelter was at full capacity. Those seeking assistance, the message added, should call 211, the United Way helpline. She dialed the number. A pleasant "community connection specialist" asked Kara what resources she was looking for. "Okay," the woman said after a quick search. "Do you have a pen?" She gave her the number for My Sister's House. Kara thanked her and hung up.

She was late for work. Kara gathered her things and rushed into the hospital, thinking that she might hear back soon from some of the other shelters. But only one responded that day. An email informed her that, unfortunately, there was not sufficient space for a family of five.

THE FOLLOWING NIGHT was their first sleeping in the car. Kara drove to pick up the kids and took them to McDonald's for dinner, allowing them to linger with their Happy Meal toys. It was there that she told them about her plan for the night. It would be fun, she said, but she needed them to be extra, extra helpful, and to do an especially good job listening. They said they would, but Kara knew they didn't understand what they were agreeing to.

Outside the restaurant, Kara got the kids loaded into their usual spots: Joshua and Jermaine in their car seats with Nathaniel squeezed between them, and Grace in the front passenger seat. She gave the boys her phone to keep them occupied, and then, for the next hour or so, she drove around looking for a place to park. She wanted a location that was secluded but not *too* secluded, that was safe but not so nice that their presence could arouse concern about a "suspicious" vehicle. It was disorienting, this peculiar search. The Atlanta she had been born and raised in suddenly felt unfamiliar, forbidding.

Merging onto the interstate, Kara headed south, into the farthest reaches of Fulton County. Ultimately, she settled on a well-lit parking

lot in front of a Walmart Supercenter. She circled the lot to make sure
no security guards were patrolling. In many states, including Georgia,
there were ordinances that made sleeping and living in your car risky.
All day, a scene had been playing out in her mind. Someone calling the
cops. A tap on her window while they slept; the beam of a flashlight
shining through. Then, finally, a Division of Family and Children Services caseworker arriving to take her kids away. For Kara, it was the
most terrifying scenario imaginable. Her fear was not unfounded: in
recent years, approximately 20 percent of child removals in Georgia
were due to "inadequate housing."

The night seemed to go on forever. It was one thing, Kara discovered, for an adult to hunker down until the morning in a cramped Toyota sedan. It was quite another for a parent to do this with four kids,
the youngest still nursing. It was so hot that she had to run the car's
air-conditioner for much of the time, wasting precious gas. By eleven
o'clock there were only a handful of other vehicles in the parking lot.
Forcing herself to stay awake, Kara maintained a weary vigilance.

Her lavender work scrubs were laid out neatly in the trunk, and she
tried not to think about how exhausted she would feel the next day. At
one point well before dawn, Nathaniel needed to use the bathroom, so
Kara guided him to some nearby bushes. Afterward, sleep was hopeless
for the family. Kara kept snapping at Jermaine to quiet down. In the
front seat, Grace held her infant brother Joshua close to her chest, trying to console him. Kara recalled the discomfort of long nights spent in
her own mother's car as a young girl, after escaping her father's drunken
abuse. Kara dreaded what her children would remember as adults.

The next night they were back in the Walmart parking lot. On the
third night, Kara was buying gas at a QuikTrip when the attendant
casually asked her how she was doing. She said she was fine. She started
to walk away, but then, sensing a sincerity about the man, she returned
to the register. She told him the truth. She described what the last several weeks had been like, and how frightening it had been to pass the
night in a parking lot, wondering if someone might try to hurt them or
if the police would show up. He shook his head. He said he was sorry.

The attendant told Kara that she was welcome to park her car in front of the gas station. He would be there all night, he said, and he could keep an eye on them. Kara almost broke down crying. These were the first compassionate words she had heard in months.

After feeding Joshua, she fetched the kids' pajamas and a bag of toiletries from the trunk. She led her children to the station's bathroom, where they changed and brushed their teeth and scrubbed their hands and faces. It was dark when they exited the minimart. Kara was scheduled to be at the hospital at ten the following morning. She yearned for sleep. She told herself this was only temporary. She would get paid soon; they could go back to the hotel; she would figure out a way to get them into their own place again. They just had to make it through a few more nights.

Her car was waiting for them under a column of glaring fluorescent lights, bright as day.

8

The running faucet did little to dull the sound of Celeste's violent retching. It was four o'clock in the morning, and she had been hunched over the toilet for almost an hour. Her stomach had long since emptied, causing her to dry-heave. The air in the mildew-stained bathroom, cut off from the window AC unit in the bedroom, was rancid and warm. She craved coolness but was determined not to wake her children; a few days earlier, Micah had begun crying when he saw his mom vomiting. The lock on the bathroom door was broken, so she kept it closed with an outstretched foot.

For four months, Celeste had cycled between emergency rooms at three different hospitals, desperate to get a handle on the vague but persistent symptoms that were afflicting her. It had started with the strange pains in her abdomen and pelvis and lower back. She also experienced a loss of appetite and discomfort while urinating. Initially, she dismissed these symptoms as a by-product of stress or the physical toll of her warehouse job. But as they worsened she grew concerned.

Her emergency room visits followed a pattern: She would suppress her worry until she panicked and rushed to the hospital, where she would sit for hours in a crowded, chaotic waiting area and then submit to a cursory examination. There were varying and contradictory diagnoses—gastroenteritis, a urinary tract infection, an upper respiratory infection, muscular strain—and there was the instruction, at the end of each visit, to follow up with her primary care provider if her condition did not improve. Like many patients on Medicaid, however, she had no primary care provider.

Celeste was unsure how to present herself so that nurses and physicians would take her seriously. Was she being too assertive? Or too passive? Did she sound too knowledgeable or not knowledgeable enough? She implored the doctors examining her to review her medical records, which she was able to access via an online portal, but these pleas went unheeded. Without them saying it, she sensed that the medical staff saw her as overreacting. Celeste thought this was absurd, since going to the ER meant missing work and losing vital income. After one such demoralizing encounter, she wondered aloud to a friend whether somebody else, exhibiting an identical set of symptoms—say, a well-dressed white guy with private insurance—might elicit a different response.

This cycle came to an end only when a blood test at Northside Hospital revealed anemia so severe that Celeste was urgently referred to a specialist. Her subsequent appointment with Dr. Simbo Aduloju marked a turning point in her ordeal. Aduloju reviewed the entirety of her medical records and, in addition to treating the anemia with intravenous iron, ordered a battery of tests and scans. The results came back a few days later. She sat across from the doctor with a nurse at her side. Celeste was told that she had ovarian and breast cancer. It appeared to be at an early stage, having not yet spread to other parts of her body. Celeste broke into tears. "I know this is very difficult news," the nurse said softly, offering her hand. "No, it's not that," Celeste said. "They made me feel like I was insane." That evening, when she returned to Efficiency Lodge, she was so weak that she couldn't get out of her car. Travis, a young handyman who lived and worked at the hotel, had to carry Celeste to her room.

Now, lying prostrate on the bathroom floor, Celeste was three weeks into what was expected to be at least four months of chemotherapy. Her hair had started falling out, and the medicine she'd been prescribed to ease the ferocious nausea seemed to be having little effect.

Celeste washed her face, turned off the faucet, and quietly returned to the bedroom. Her T-shirt was drenched with sweat. She tiptoed across the hotel room's brittle gray carpet, careful not to bump into a plastic storage tower holding assorted toiletries, and then she propped herself up in bed using several oversized pillows and stuffed animals. Her kids, barely visible in the predawn light, were fast asleep. Micah and Nyah were on an old air mattress, and Jalen was beside her in the bed. On the wall facing her was a large poster of a rock-strewn coastline, its waters glimmering in a resplendent sunset.

Celeste watched Nyah sleep. The sixteen-year-old, who had dropped out of school not long after the fire, was street smart and conscientious, with a maturity well beyond her years. But she also harbored an anger and insecurity that Celeste couldn't fully grasp. Her daughter had been in some vicious fights over the years and had very few friends or acquaintances; she hated her appearance, to the point where she refused to have her photo taken. Perhaps because of this, she allowed herself to get involved with young men who treated her poorly. Her boyfriend, Keyondre, had recently been arrested for murder and armed robbery, and before going to jail he'd asked his best friend, Mike, a weed and coke dealer, to look out for Nyah. Lately the two of them had been spending a great deal of time together, often alone and late at night. Celeste was worried. She knew how these situations tended to play out.

Depleted, Celeste closed her eyes and rested her head on a pillow. But it was too late to try to sleep. She had to be at Gateway Center, Atlanta's primary hub for homeless services, in just over an hour.

WHEN CELESTE HAD first arrived at Efficiency, she'd had a plan to make her family's stay at the hotel as brief as possible. It wouldn't be easy to get a place with the eviction from the burned-down house on her record, but one property management company had given her a glimmer of hope: they'd told Celeste they would consider renting to her if she paid her outstanding debt—a total of $2,100, including legal fees—to The Prager Group, the real estate company that had evicted her. They said it was her only shot at being approved.

The financial challenges of going this route were steep, requiring her to chip away at the debt while simultaneously paying her rent at the hotel and keeping up with her other monthly expenses. But Celeste believed she could do it. *If we're gonna get out of here,* she thought, *I'll just have to work my ass off.*

Her cancer diagnosis derailed that plan. Since beginning chemo, she was barely able to go to work—and to the disappointment of her customers, the makeshift restaurant she'd been operating out of her room was on indefinite hiatus. She considered applying for SSI, but then she got an earful about the application process from a fellow patient in Dr. Aduloju's waiting room. It was not uncommon, she was told, to wait a year or longer for approval, during which time applicants were discouraged from holding a job—otherwise, you could disprove your own claim. "How's someone supposed to survive that long with no money coming in?" the woman said. Later, Celeste learned that high initial denial rates often forced applicants to hire an attorney. Even a cancer diagnosis was no guarantee of approval. And the reward for those tenacious enough to see the process through to the end? Disability benefits that didn't begin to cover basic living expenses. She put the idea out of her head.

It was during this period that she began to see Efficiency in a new light. On a Sunday morning a few months earlier, Lisa had knocked on Celeste's door and practically begged her to help with a cleaning job; Lisa's assistant manager had abruptly quit, and a newly vacated room was, as Celeste would soon discover, "torn to shit." If the compensation for Celeste's labor—$50 off her rent for that month—struck her as somewhat meager, she was grateful that Lisa had finally taken her up on her offer to work.

But as she spent more time around Lisa and gained an inside view of how the hotel was run, Celeste began to see something capricious, even vindictive, about her behavior. Lisa was always reminding the hotel's residents that their comparatively inexpensive rooms were scarce commodities—"There are plenty of folks who will gladly take your place" was a constant refrain—and she wielded it like a weapon. Whether a family remained at Efficiency or was forced to leave often turned not on their capacity to pay but on their ability to stay in Lisa's good graces. Celeste saw one resident evicted for "disrespecting the manager," and another for calling the corporate number to report unsafe conditions. That Lisa's volatility stemmed in part from a worsening meth habit was an open secret, as was her practice of allowing a select group of residents to slide on their rent if they supplied her with drugs or got high with her.

For Celeste, the predatory conditions at Efficiency were finally, fully revealed the week that the DeKalb County Board of Health was going to be visiting the property. Lisa knew that a handful of rooms were likely to raise alarms if randomly inspected, so she hired Celeste and another resident to clean them. Lisa was concerned that a low safety score could get her fired. In July of the previous year, county officials had discovered more than three hundred code violations at the extended-stay, and the most recent Board of Health visit had found, in the words of the inspector, "trash, garbage, and debris throughout grounds . . . soil on walls and ceiling . . . dog feces on ground" and "dead German roaches in rooms 208, 250, 248."

One of the rooms Celeste was told to clean belonged to Ms. Debbie, a frail, soft-spoken woman in her late sixties who had been living at the hotel for three years. "At first it looked like the surfaces were covered in dust," Celeste said, "but as I got closer I saw that it was mold. It was *everywhere*." Standing there, she remembered that Ms. Debbie suffered from frequent asthma attacks and had needed to be rushed to the hospital on several occasions. Now she understood why. Although Lisa, after frequent complaints from Ms. Debbie, was perfectly aware of the rampant mold, she had no intention of eradicating it. Instead, she instructed Celeste to "spruce up" the room by painting over any mold-damaged areas.

Celeste thought about going to a different hotel, but her illness kept her from working overtime, so she couldn't afford it. Other residents had their own reasons for staying put. Some were dependent on the support that they received from their neighbors: rides to work, last-minute childcare. Some had long ago arranged with their children's school to have the bus pick them up there in the morning. Some, based on prior experience, knew that the conditions were no better elsewhere. If Efficiency was awful, at least it was familiar.

And besides, Celeste concluded, going to another hotel wouldn't solve her problem: she'd still be stuck in the "hotel trap," as many referred to it. It was a business model that, like payday loans or rent-to-own schemes, preyed on the desperation of those with nowhere else to turn. Unable to lease an apartment, whether because of bad credit or a prior eviction or the sheer unaffordability of most places, families were compelled to pay excessive rates for accommodations that offered none of the security or clear tenancy rights of formal housing. The extended-stays were not simply filling a gap in the city's housing landscape. They were actively exploiting that gap. As more and more people found themselves pushed out of the rental market, hotels like Efficiency—where a mold-infested room could devour the entirety of a family's income, making it impossible to save enough money for a security deposit and first month's rent at a real apartment—had grown ubiquitous.

At Efficiency, Celeste had yet to meet a single person without a "plan" to leave soon. Even residents like Ms. Debbie, who had been at the hotel for years, scraping by on her Social Security checks and a part-time job at a discount store, seemed unable to acknowledge the intractability of their situations. At worst, if money was tight, families were forced to move between hotels, their car (if they had a car), a friend or relative's floor, an emergency shelter, or sometimes even the street. At best, they were trapped at Efficiency, caught in a semipermanent state of limbo. In this respect, the hotel motto looming behind Lisa's desk, "Stay a Nite or Stay Forever," was less an invitation than a threat.

GATEWAY CENTER, located in downtown Atlanta, was a four-story, 110,000-square-foot former jail only a short walk from the gold-domed state capitol. The surrounding blocks were crammed with institutions (the Department of Community Supervision, the Municipal Court, the Division of Family and Children Services) charged with overseeing the urban poor and the businesses—bail bondsmen, private probation companies—that profited off them. When homeless men and women were arrested for panhandling, sleeping on a sidewalk, public urination, or any other violation of the city's "quality of life" ordinances, they were taken to Gateway's next-door neighbor, the Atlanta City Detention Center. It was not uncommon for people to be shuttled back and forth between these two facilities, occasionally ending up in the ER at Grady Hospital, which was also nearby.

In addition to offering beds to 350-plus men through its residential programs, Gateway served as the main entry point for Atlanta's Continuum of Care—an initiative mandated by HUD to streamline coordination among local agencies and nonprofits. Most American cities had their own version of Gateway: a central place where homeless people in need of services could access them. In practice, this entailed funneling unhoused families and individuals into a crowded building where scarce resources were distributed in a triage-like manner.

When Celeste parked her vehicle down the street from Gateway at 6:00 a.m., a long line was snaking down the sidewalk outside of the building. She'd been told that since homeless assessments were conducted on a first-come, first-served basis, people often began lining up in the middle of the night. Still, she was surprised to find such a large crowd already gathered. The doors wouldn't be opening for another two hours. Celeste joined the queue, stepping gingerly around handcarts and baby strollers and small clusters of men and women wrapped in blankets, their belongings stacked beside them on the concrete. Having forced herself to eat a lukewarm Cup Noodles for breakfast, she felt woozy—and a little frightened too. A noticeably unwell man was cursing loudly and harassing another person nearby. She considered leaving but decided to stick it out, clutching a manila folder filled with documents while trying to avoid making eye contact with those around her.

Six weeks earlier, when Celeste started her cancer treatment, any notion of securing long-term housing on her own had quickly vanished—and with it her resistance to seeking outside assistance. A fear of getting trapped indefinitely at Efficiency now outweighed the embarrassment of pleading for help; pride and dignity were luxuries she could no longer afford. And so, one morning during a work break, she'd gone out to her Durango and fished out the Homeless Resource List given to her by the social worker at Micah's school. Some phone numbers on the list were disconnected; others prompted her to leave a voicemail. But she was able to get through to a few service providers, and each of them, after Celeste described what she was looking for— help finding a landlord who would rent to her despite the eviction, and maybe some financial support to cover a security deposit—told her the same thing: To receive such aid, she'd first need to undergo an assessment through Gateway's "coordinated entry" system. And it had to be done in person.

Celeste told Mason's mom, Christina, her neighbor a couple of doors down, that she was planning on going to Gateway soon. "Good luck with *that*," the mother of six scoffed. Her own trek out to Gateway had been fruitless. Celeste thought: *Yeah, well, you're not me*. If anyone could navigate this system, it was her. She wasn't going to be undone by a little paperwork.

It was almost nine-thirty when she finally entered the building. The interior was spacious and clean, if not quite welcoming. An airport-style metal detector opened onto an intake counter, a security guard station, and a few dozen chairs, occupied by people dozing or staring ahead or attempting to console their crying baby while waiting for their name to be called. In a corner of the lobby, alongside a clinic operated by Mercy Care, a community health center, a hallway led to public showers and a clothing bank; in the opposite corner, there was a large room that, on the coldest nights of winter, was used as a warming center for kids and their mothers. (Since 2013, Gateway's overnight facilities had been designated exclusively for men, but women with children were permitted to sleep in this glass-enclosed space—with no furnishings, no privacy—whenever outside temperatures fell below freezing.) Celeste checked in at the counter, located an unoccupied chair, and waited another hour and a half to be seen.

A petite caseworker conducted Celeste's assessment in a bare, windowless office. As the woman settled in behind a computer, Celeste placed a stack of documents on her desk—hotel receipts, a police report from the arson, paystubs—and then launched into the story of how she

and her kids had ended up without a home, which she'd been rehears-
ing in her head all morning. Adept at code-switching, she spoke in a
clipped, professional manner—what she thought of as her "talking to
white people voice." The caseworker politely stopped her. In order to
determine how best to assist her, she said, it was important that she first
ask Celeste a series of questions. "Oh, of course. No problem," Celeste
replied.

After a scripted preamble in which the woman explained that only
"yes," "no," or one-word answers were acceptable and that any question
could be skipped or refused, the assessment began. How many months
had it been since Celeste had lived in permanent stable housing? Had
she ever been diagnosed with a behavioral health disorder? What about
HIV or AIDS? Since becoming homeless, had she been arrested? Or
tried to harm herself in any way? Or been beaten up? How often did
she drink or use drugs? Did she ever exchange sex for money? Or share
needles with others?

Celeste was perplexed. She wondered how all this was relevant to
her situation. At one point, she gravely mentioned the cancer diagnosis;
at another, she interjected to insist that she wasn't lazy, that she had
been working nonstop since she was a teenager. The caseworker tapped
away at her keyboard. And where was she living now? the woman
asked. Celeste told her about the extended-stay.

The assessment was over in a matter of minutes. The caseworker
looked up and sighed. The purpose of these questions, she said, was
to figure out who most urgently needed help. Based on the answers
Celeste provided, it was clear that her vulnerability score, as the woman
called it, would be very low—too low to qualify for housing assistance.
The score had been calculated using the Vulnerability Index—Service
Prioritization Decision Assistance Tool, or the VI-SPDAT. Created in
2013 by OrgCode Consulting, the VI-SPDAT was quickly adopted nationwide, as local communities sought to meet a new federal regulation
that made funding for homeless services contingent on the implementation of a standardized intake and assessment process. The stated objective of the VI-SPDAT was to identify homeless individuals who were
most at risk of dying or being sent to a jail or hospital, and to parcel out

limited resources accordingly. In cities and counties across the United States, this technical-sounding survey had become a key instrument in efforts to address homelessness: a mechanism for determining who would—and would not—be eligible for support.

"But what about the cancer?" Celeste asked, her tone changing. It felt demeaning to have to ask such a question. She had begun to realize that all the things she had been so proud of, such as her work ethic, were making it more, not less, likely that she would leave Gateway empty-handed. "Doesn't that count for anything?"

"Yes," the caseworker said, seeming to choose her words carefully. The illness did make Celeste more at risk. The real obstacle, however, was that she and her children did not fit the criteria for "literal home-lessness" as set out by HUD. "In order to get housing aid," she contin-ued, "you have to be considered literally homeless, which means you're in a shelter or on the street. Unfortunately, other circumstances don't qualify."

Celeste's predicament was increasingly common. The existing sup-port system ignored scores of homeless families who did not fit the gov-ernment's definition of "homeless." Advocacy groups had been fighting to expand the definition, refuting the myth that families with children living in extended-stays and doubled-up arrangements were somehow less vulnerable than other homeless populations; they argued that these conditions could be just as detrimental to a child's education, mental and physical health, and long-term development. Indeed, the U.S. De-partment of Education counted as homeless anyone who lacked "a fixed, regular, and adequate nighttime residence"—which explicitly in-cluded those in hotels, motels, and living temporarily with others. That year, 2019, the Department of Education reported 35,538 homeless chil-dren and youth enrolled in Georgia public schools, an increase of 34 percent from a decade earlier. But the state's HUD-administered total—not only for children and youth but Georgia's entire homeless population—was 10,433. Politicians cited the smaller number when discussing homelessness in the state, claiming it was on the decline. This figure also helped determine the amount of money allocated to homeless services the following year. Meanwhile, the parents of those

35,538 students were caught between two parallel definitions. At their child's school, they were considered homeless. At places like Gateway, they were not.

"So let me get this straight," Celeste said. "If I want y'all's help getting a home for me and my kids, I need to be considered—what did you call it—literally homeless?"

"Yes, that's correct."

"And to be considered literally homeless, we've gotta be in a shelter?"

"That's right. Or somewhere not meant for human habitation."

"All right then," Celeste said. "So how do we get into a shelter?"

The caseworker took a deep breath. "You said your son recently turned fifteen?"

"Yes."

"I hate to say it, but I don't know of any family shelters that allow boys over the age of thirteen. Usually older boys have to go to a men's shelter."

"No way," Celeste said. "Absolutely not. I'm not going to let my family be separated."

"I wish I had more to offer," the woman said. "I'm sorry."

When Celeste left the building, the line outside Gateway was just as long as it had been that morning.

Maurice groaned as he cracked open the freezer. "Dammit," he hissed, and then said in a louder voice, "Talia, the stuff in here is already defrosting. You want me to reach out to Summer?" Natalia was in bed with Matthew, their new baby boy. The refrigerator had stopped working the day before, so Maurice had moved as many things as possible to the freezer, which also now appeared to be broken. During the four years they'd lived at the condo, they had avoided bothering their landlord with any but the most urgent requests—despite Summer's friendly demeanor, they had a fear of being seen as "difficult"—yet there was no way they could repair the appliance on their own. "It's all right," Natalia called back. "I'll handle it." She heard the front door close behind Maurice as he hurried to get Anthony and Shantel to school.

Only three days remained before Natalia's maternity leave was set to end. The thought of going back to work filled her with dread; she had no idea how she would function. A month earlier, struggling to adjust to life with a newborn, she and Maurice had been awakened in the middle of the night to shocking news: Maurice's forty-four-year-old cousin, Aaron, who was also the children's godfather and the couple's most cherished friend and confidant, had just passed away. They had known that Aaron was HIV positive but not that he had recently been diagnosed with hepatocellular carcinoma, an aggressive form of liver cancer prevalent among people with HIV.

In the four weeks since his death, Maurice and Natalia had been in a kind of stupor, unable to fully register, much less properly mourn, this sudden loss. Natalia reread one of her final exchanges with Aaron, when she told him that their son's full name would be Matthew Aaron Taylor. "Awwww," Aaron replied with a crying face emoji. When Aaron had noticed, prior to Matthew's birth, that hardly anything on their Amazon baby registry had been purchased, he surprised them by buying every last item. Now the bottle warmer and Pack 'n Play and swaddling blankets were reminders that he was gone.

Natalia picked up her phone to text Summer. She described what was wrong with the refrigerator and conveyed the urgency of getting it fixed: she'd had a baby in late January, she explained, and was dependent on the refrigerator to keep her breast milk from going bad. "OMG, congrats!!" came the reply. "I didn't even realize you were pregnant!" She promised to send someone over. Natalia thanked her. And then, a couple of minutes later, Summer added that there was one other matter they needed to discuss.

Acknowledging that it was "probably the last thing" Natalia wanted to hear, Summer wrote: "Remember I mentioned the possibility of selling the condo?" Natalia recalled nothing of the sort. In fact, she was certain that the subject had never come up. There had been talk of a rent increase in the future, but no indication that Summer was thinking about selling the unit. "Well," her landlord wrote, "I've decided to put it on the market." The ideal time to list it, she added, was the beginning of summer, and she asked if the family could be out by the first week of June—in just over sixty days.

Natalia was too caught off guard to protest. Matthew had started howling. She simply typed, "Yes, that should be fine."

NATALIA RESISTED THE URGE to call Maurice right away. She decided to wait until they could be alone and, as they had done after the devastating news from Aaron's sister, figure out how and when to tell the kids.

During their fourteen years together, the couple had seen many highs and lows. Their relationship had begun at Beltway Plaza Mall in Prince George's County, just outside of D.C. It was an October night in 2004, and Maurice was working as a security guard, patrolling the mall's lower level, when he spotted Natalia walking briskly toward one of the exits. He ran to catch up.

"Excuse me," he said. She ignored him and kept going. He noticed her uniform and guessed that she had just gotten off work at the Target next door. "Miss!" he said forcefully. "The mall is closed."

"I always cut through the mall," she said.

"You can't be doing that anymore."

"Look," she said, finally stopping. She glared at him. "It's almost midnight. I'm tired. I've got class in the morning. And you talkin' about I can't walk through the damn mall?"

"That's correct," Maurice responded.

"Seriously? I live right behind the mall. I guess you want me to walk all the way around the parking lot."

"You live at Springhill Lake?" he asked, skeptical. The apartment complex had a reputation.

"Yes. I do." There was a pause as they stared at each other.

"Well," he said more tentatively, "will you be okay walking back there?" He added: "I can go with you if you want."

"I'm good," she said. "I just want to get home." She pushed open the glass door and left without looking back.

Natalia's irritation at Maurice had subsided by the following evening. Later, relating the story to friends, Maurice would swear that he wasn't waiting around for her. But he did seem to materialize rather suddenly when she came through the entrance.

Their brief strolls from one end of the mall to the other became a nightly ritual. They kept it light, friendly, not flirtatious; they talked about Natalia's courses at Bowie State, the historically Black university where she was a junior, and Maurice's desire to go to college. They discovered a mutual love of horror films, and Maurice was impressed that her taste in music—UGK, Master P, Goodie Mob, and yes, Scarface—was remarkably similar to his own.

Soon, however, they started lingering at the exit, and then they found themselves walking aimlessly for hours, lost in conversation. Maurice divulged things about his life that he never discussed with anyone. Natalia, in turn, recounted a turbulent childhood: Her father was a functioning addict and her mother was a nonfunctioning one. She'd been raised primarily by strict, Catholic grandparents. She mentioned the death of her ten-month-old baby brother, Eric, when she was eight. Maurice asked if this was her most painful memory as a kid. She said it wasn't even in the top five.

Natalia was unlike anyone Maurice had ever met. Creative and self-assured, she was an avid reader with a deep, private spirituality—given to astrology and crystals and dream interpretation. Maurice was more pragmatic and direct. Yet they clicked. As for physical attraction, it was there for each of them, but it wasn't until Maurice took her out for the first time that another side of Natalia revealed itself. He'd been accustomed to seeing her in high-water khakis, a Target polo shirt, and what in D.C. was referred to as a "Southeast ponytail" (once described as the hair equivalent of "a frayed paintbrush secured with an industrial rubber band"). He was dumbstruck when he picked her up; she'd done a bit of modeling on the side, and it was evident. "You didn't know I'm like Superman," she said. Although their times together were enjoyable, their bond increasingly intense, Natalia had firm boundaries and was hesitant to get too romantically involved. She wanted to be sure that Maurice was solid, dependable. Only then did she invite him up to her apartment after a date. The next morning, after he left, Natalia told her roommate that this one was for real. "He's the yin to my yang," she said.

Shantel was conceived that first night at her apartment. When Natalia found out she was pregnant, she was scared to tell Maurice, worried he'd leave her. But he was elated at the news. A few months prior to Natalia's due date, as they were preparing to go to work, Maurice told her that they should get married. "Shut up, you playin'," Natalia said, continuing to brush her hair. He walked across the room, took hold of her wrist, and looked her in the eyes. "I'm not joking," he said. "We should get married." Natalia laughed. "So . . . I guess this is the proposal?"

It was, and she accepted. Their engagement, though, lasted more than three years. Maurice had agreed that they should hold off on a wedding until they could build up savings, but Natalia had other reasons for delaying. Since she was young, she had dreamed of working in fashion. With a sewing machine given to her by her grandparents, she'd designed special outfits for her Barbie dolls; more recently, she'd modeled for a friend's clothing line, and she was majoring in marketing with the hope of landing a job in the industry. When she pictured what such a life might look like, she thought about a loft apartment she'd once seen above an Urban Outfitters in Chinatown, after leaving a nearby club. The loft's oversized windows, its towering ceilings, and its exposed brick interior were all visible from the sidewalk. She stood transfixed by this vision of sophistication. It left a mark on her, and she caught herself returning to it whenever Maurice raised the question of setting a wedding date, as if these futures were incompatible. She felt no ambivalence toward Maurice himself. Her uncertainty concerned a more abstract image of marriage and domesticity. But getting pregnant again, when Shantel was three, convinced Natalia to embrace her new reality. She told Maurice that she was ready.

Their wedding, a low-key, somewhat perfunctory affair, took place at the D.C. Superior Court's Marriage Bureau. Money was tight, and Natalia was pregnant again, so they had little energy for a grand production. Yet a surprise awaited them afterward. Aaron was among the handful of attendees at the civil ceremony. Maurice had always spoken highly of him to Natalia, and when Natalia finally met him she understood why. Aaron insisted on throwing Natalia a baby shower—as a single gay man, he joked that this was the closest he'd come to having a kid of his own—and he was overjoyed when Maurice and Natalia asked him to be Shantel's godfather. Realizing, in the days leading up to the wedding, that there was no reception planned, Aaron took it upon himself to organize one. The newlyweds were shocked when they arrived at Aaron's apartment on M Street and found a large gathering of friends and relatives, one of whom was videotaping the event. "How are you feeling right now?" he asked Maurice, who was smiling giddily. Dance music blared around them. "I feel good," Maurice replied. "I feel real good. I feel like singing. I feel like skipping."

The next two and a half years proved difficult, however, as it became apparent that remaining in the city of their birth was no longer feasible. D.C. was changing before their eyes, and particular blocks, then entire streets and neighborhoods, were being transfigured. The change was so abrupt that it seemed, at times, as if they had gone to bed in one city and woken up in a completely different one.

This was not just their impression. A study from the National Community Reinvestment Coalition found that between 2000 and 2013, D.C. saw a staggering 202 percent increase of white, mostly affluent newcomers, skyrocketing housing costs, and the displacement of more than twenty thousand Black residents. Even with their combined income from Maurice's security guard position and the receptionist job that Natalia had recently landed, they knew that getting priced out of the city was a real possibility. Several family members had already packed up and moved: to South Carolina, to Tennessee, to Virginia. In departing for the South, these relatives were part of a larger wave of Black Americans who, seeking livelihoods that had grown unattainable in the urban North, were relocating to the very states their grandparents had fled during the Jim Crow era. It was a new Great Migration, a reversal of the previous mass exodus.

Maurice and Natalia slowly accepted that they too had little choice but to leave. Natalia would later pinpoint the moment she realized that their days in D.C. were numbered. She was riding the bus not far from their apartment on Livingston Road, an area still relatively untouched by the redevelopment craze, when she observed two white women jogging on the sidewalk. Her fellow passengers saw them as well. "We were all staring at the women," she recalled. "You would have thought we'd seen a ghost. And then this older guy was like, 'Well, I guess we need to start looking for another place to live.'"

AT THE DINNER TABLE THAT EVENING, Natalia, still reeling from Summer's text, tried to conceal her anxiety. She was especially concerned about Shantel, who had been shaken by the death of her "goddaddy," as she lovingly referred to Aaron. Shantel had compiled all the photos from Aaron's visits into a video slideshow, which she continued to watch again and again. Her parents wondered if she should see a therapist, and one of Natalia's initial worries, upon getting the news from Summer, was that their impending move—coming just before Shantel's twelfth birthday—might further deepen her daughter's distress.

It was almost eleven when the kids finally fell asleep. Natalia and Maurice retreated to their bedroom, a private realm where they could curse and sometimes cry or argue freely. Their tumultuous upbringings had led to a tacit agreement between the two of them: that they would insulate their children, to the extent possible, from their own fears and disappointments. They believed it to be the parent's role to project confidence, to appear unbreakable. In the bedroom they could let their guard down.

As Matthew dozed in his crib a few feet away, Natalia handed Maurice her phone. He read the text exchange twice, then a third time, shaking his head. It became clear to him, in that moment, that this place where they had spent the last four years did not belong to them, had *never* belonged to them—that what they'd thought of as their home was, to its owner, merely a source of potential profit, an asset to be sold when the timing was right.

What stung, he and Natalia realized as they processed the news, wasn't so much losing the condo itself. It was recognizing how little control they had. They'd done everything they were supposed to do: they'd kept the unit clean, they'd never been late on their rent. Yet here they were. This involuntary move, unlike a court-ordered eviction, had no spectacle tied to it: no armed deputy showing up, no belongings piled on the curb. There was nothing to argue before a judge. Summer was asking them to leave a month before their lease was up, but she had also given them the required sixty-day notice. It was all perfectly legal. Nevertheless, with that one brief sentence—"I've decided to put it on the market"—something significant had been ripped from them.

They agreed that since Natalia hadn't yet returned to work, she would start the process of looking for an apartment right away. They also devised a plan for how they would present the move to Anthony and Shantel: they would frame it as an exciting change, an opportunity to get that third bedroom they had been begging for—maybe even a swimming pool.

The next morning, Natalia set up her laptop at the dining table. She created a Word document to keep track of prospective rentals. Though still in a twilight zone of sleeplessness, grief, and constant nursing, she forced herself to focus on the task at hand. Browsing apartment listings, she was struck, first of all, by the large quantity of new, amenity-stacked complexes in the area—which was hardly surprising, given the construction up and down Roswell Road—and, second, by how expensive everything seemed to be. It was as if, while they were living at the condo, the ground had shifted under their feet.

And in many ways, it had: like Atlanta's "revitalized" urban core, suburbs such as Sandy Springs were in the midst of their own development boom. Two major projects typified the alterations underway in the metro area's northern quadrant. City Springs, in downtown Sandy Springs, was a fourteen-acre, $230-million "modern city center" that included a performing arts venue, restaurants, and a farmers' market; Gateway (no relation to the homeless services site) was a 122,000-square-foot "multi-use retail, dining, and living centerpiece" that had been completed in 2016. It had involved the demolition of four older complexes, displacing an estimated three thousand residents, most of them lower-income families with children. These poorer tenants were being pushed out in favor of wealthier (and whiter) ones. Dan Immergluck, a professor of urban studies at Georgia State University, called this "a classic example of displace-and-replace suburban redevelopment." The irony was not lost on Maurice and Natalia: having fled gentrification in D.C., they were now falling prey to it in Atlanta. Over the past six years, rents in Sandy Springs had increased by 39 percent, while the number of apartments that lower-income families could afford had dropped by a whopping 1,700. Later, Natalia remarked: "I think we may have jumped from the frying pan into the fire."

Sitting at her computer now, Natalia found plenty of apartments nearby, ranging from modest to more upscale units. Soon she had assembled a list of a half-dozen places that met their criteria. The problem, she realized, was the cost of applying for them. Atlanta's red-hot rental market had enabled landlords not only to raise rents but to begin tacking on exorbitant application and "administrative" fees—which had to be paid up front and were nonrefundable, even if you were rejected. A handful of states, like Washington and Minnesota, had put a legal limit on the fees a landlord could charge, stipulating that they not exceed the cost of running a background check. Georgia was among the states where there was no such limit.

Natalia was aghast at what some of the properties on her list were charging: between $50 and $75, per adult, plus another $100 to $150 in administrative fees. One complex was charging a nonrefundable administrative fee of $200 in addition to $75 per adult for the application itself—meaning it would cost Maurice and Natalia $350 simply to *apply* for an apartment. *This is unreal,* Natalia thought. Why would they be demanding this extra money? She answered her own question: *Because they can.* It occurred to her that a landlord could encourage one prospective renter after another to apply, reject them for any reason whatsoever, and still pocket hundreds of dollars. She wondered how many people had been denied after paying fees they couldn't afford.

The frugal thing to do, clearly, was to narrow the list down to one or two places. This would save them money on application fees—and money was definitely a concern, particularly since they'd just dipped into their savings to buy their first car. Atlanta's underfunded mass transit system consistently ranked among the worst in the country, and after years of trying to get by on public transportation, Maurice and Natalia had finally accepted the fact that they needed their own vehicle. For Maurice, the final straw came when Natalia started going into labor and the family had to wait for more than forty-five minutes for their Lyft ride to show up. "I was about to have a heart attack," Maurice said. He found a used Camry the following week. They had budgeted for the purchase, but after the down payment, monthly car note, and insurance—along with all the additional expenses a third child entailed—their financial cushion had grown a good deal smaller.

Yet as they considered their next step, they both felt that time was more scarce than money. Between Natalia returning to State Farm and Maurice's already-demanding work schedule, sixty days were going to fly by. What if they applied for only a couple of apartments but it took weeks for them to hear back? Or what if, after being approved, they saw the place in person and discovered it wasn't right for them? They were clear about their biggest priority: that the transition be smooth for the kids. So after calling to confirm that the units were still available, they decided to bite the bullet and apply for several apartments at once. Casting a wide net, they reasoned, would improve their chances of securing a place to live before the clock ran down.

THE REJECTIONS CAME SWIFTLY. Some property managers offered no explanation for why the family had been denied, emailing only a generic form letter. Those that did provide a reason cited Natalia and Maurice's credit scores.

In hindsight, they felt foolish for not having thought of it. From their perspective, they had been strong applicants. They had good jobs and no criminal background, and they'd had a spotless rental history for nearly a decade. They hadn't imagined that their credit scores, lowered over time by overdue hospital and student loan and credit card bills, would pose such a significant barrier to renting an apartment.

But this, too, was a feature of the changing housing landscape. In D.C., where they had rented from individual landlords who owned only a handful of properties, their credit scores had never been an issue. Nor had the scores come up when they'd signed a lease for their first apartment in Sandy Springs. Later, during conversations with Summer about them moving into the condo, she made no mention of their credit—she was more interested in receiving letters of reference from their prior landlords and seeing proof of income. But as large corporate landlords and property management companies came to dominate

competitive rental markets like Atlanta's, there was a growing demand for faster, more streamlined and automated methods of vetting
applicants—methods that would ensure higher profit margins by better
predicting and eliminating risk. Credit scores, which since the mid-
nineties had been a key tool in establishing interest rates for mortgage
applicants, had come to drive the tenant screening process as well.

The National Consumer Law Center and other advocacy groups
had denounced this trend. They pointed to the opaque, underregulated,
notoriously error-prone nature of America's credit scoring system; they
drew attention to the well-documented ways that, far from being unbi-
ased or "objective," these algorithmic models at once reflected and
served to perpetuate racial and economic inequality. These groups also
bemoaned the fact that consistent rent and utility payments over a period of several years had no positive impact on someone's credit score,
while missing even one rent payment could trigger an eviction filing
and cause your score to plummet, often irreparably. But these organizations were largely powerless in the face of the credit lobby, which had
succeeded in making a three-digit number the decisive factor in Americans' quest for housing.

With about four weeks left before they needed to be out of their
apartment, Maurice and Natalia still hadn't been approved anywhere.
But one leasing agent had given them a useful tip, encouraging them to
reach out to a company called Liberty Rent. Launched in 2014, the
Nevada-based service was among several "cosigning companies" that
had sprung up in the wake of the Great Recession as more and more
people faced homelessness due to evictions and bad credit. The premise
was straightforward: for a fee, Liberty guaranteed leases for tenants
whose applications would otherwise be denied. Natalia and Maurice
saw it as a godsend, and after filling out the company's online application, they were quickly approved. (Not everyone with poor credit was
eligible; the company had developed its own "risk profile" to ascertain
which applicants would be the safest bets.) Yet it turned out there were
two drawbacks to using Liberty as a cosigner. There was the company's
nonrefundable fee of one month's rent, in addition to everything else
the client remained responsible for paying—security deposit, applica-

tion fees, monthly rent, and so forth. And, more worryingly, they had to choose an apartment complex that worked directly with Liberty. In Sandy Springs, there were only two: The Harrison and The Whitney. Both were marketed as luxury properties and cost far more than the family could afford.

Around this time, as they debated how best to proceed, one of Maurice's co-workers suggested that they check out apartments in his neighborhood, in southwest Atlanta. "It's more 'hood than Sandy Springs," he said, "but it's less expensive." He gave Maurice the names of a few complexes to check out, and later, when Natalia looked them up, she scrolled to the section where ratings for nearby public schools were listed. Two out of ten, one out of ten—the ratings were abysmal. She had an immediate, visceral reaction. She could live with a long commute; she could deal with the prospect of resettling in a rougher, unfamiliar area of the city. But she wasn't willing to sacrifice her children's education. Anthony, with his recent autism diagnosis, was especially in need of support. The Individualized Education Program they'd devised in consultation with his teachers and principal was working well for the third grader. "It seems cruel," she told Maurice, "to force him to start over in one of these other schools. Why would we do that?" Although the apartments his co-worker had mentioned were less expensive, they weren't *that much* less expensive.

Maurice agreed. He had no desire to uproot the kids. But neither did he want to live beyond their means. Natalia, he felt, was downplaying the danger of going with Liberty. Things had been getting tense between the two of them. Aaron's death, a harried trip to D.C. to attend the funeral, the baby, the stress, the exhaustion, the lack of time to seek out other options: it had their minds all twisted.

ON THE FIRST SATURDAY IN JUNE, Maurice and Natalia and their three children moved into their new home at The Whitney, located down the road from the condo they had just vacated. Rents at The Whitney, a 309-unit complex built in 1968, were slightly lower than those at The Harrison, but a three-bedroom was still way too much. So, despite Maurice and Natalia's earlier assurances to Shantel and Anthony that they'd be getting their own rooms, they ended up with a two-bedroom unit. "At least it's bigger," observed Natalia. The apartment was nice enough, with fresh paint and stainless steel appliances, and outside there was a pool and playground. But "luxurious" it was not. Their rent was $1,450 a month. This was $500 a month—or $6,000 a year—more than they had been paying Summer. Between Liberty's fee of $1,450, a $175 application and administrative fee, the first month's rent, a $1,450 security deposit, and the cost of renting a moving truck, the family's savings were basically wiped out by the time they received their keys.

Maurice had put up a fight, but now, like his wife, he was doing his best to appear upbeat about the decision to move there. He went out of his way to tell Natalia how much he liked the place, voicing every bit of optimism he could muster. It was in this spirit of graciousness that, when he opened a kitchen cabinet and discovered three dead cockroaches surrounded by pepper-sized droppings, he kept it to himself. He hastily scooped up the roaches with a piece of cardboard and deposited them in a trash bag.

On a humid morning in mid-July, Michelle was pushing Skye in her stroller through their apartment complex when she spotted Mr. Davis, Jacob's supervisor, talking to another tenant. Mr. Davis, an older, gregarious man in charge of maintenance at Eastwyck Village, had always greeted Michelle and her children warmly. As he saw Michelle approaching, however, his expression darkened. He told her that he was sorry for what had happened to Jacob.

Since Christmas, Michelle had felt in her gut that something was amiss. Jacob was still playful and ebullient, taking DJ and Danielle bowling or to a Georgia Tech football game one weekend, to Dave & Buster's the next. With Skye, who had turned two in March, he was as affectionate as ever. Yet Michelle thought he seemed jittery, not fully present. She noticed that his phone now had a passcode on its lock screen and that he'd begun to keep it with him at all times, even in the bathroom while showering. During the couple's date nights, always initiated by Jacob, he made it a point to be, in Michelle's words, "extra lovey-dovey," but she found herself withdrawing from him physically, refusing his advances. Jacob accused her of needlessly creating drama, of allowing her past "relationship issues" to distort her view of him.

Now Mr. Davis was telling her he hoped the family could find a way to stay in their apartment. Michelle said she had no idea what he was talking about. He just stared at her and then he said, "Wait, he hasn't told you?" Jacob, it turned out, had recently been fired after numerous days of failing to show up for work. Mr. Davis urged Michelle to go to the rental office as soon as possible.

Michelle's mind raced. When she and Jacob had decided to get a place together after Skye was born, he'd put himself in charge of their finances, insisting that Michelle concentrate on school and take care of their baby while he worked and paid the bills. As long as the lights stayed on and she had enough money for food and clothes and whatever else the kids needed, she didn't ask any questions. ("It was about his pride," Michelle said. "He wanted to be the head of the house. And honestly? That was fine with me.") Minutes later, in the office, she was handed a printout showing that it had been two months since their rent had been paid in full; she was also given copies of notices threatening eviction if this back rent was not paid immediately. The most recent notice had been left in their mailbox only a week earlier.

The next few days were a blur: the screaming matches, the sense of betrayal, the discovery that Jacob had somehow squandered the last of her student loan funds. It felt impossible to get a straight answer from him. Where had all the money gone? Where had he been when he was supposed to be at work? He said he'd kept the news about losing his job from Michelle because he hadn't wanted to worry her, and he seemed nonchalant about the unpaid rent, pointing out that it was his name, not hers, that was on the lease. "But it's *our* home!" she shouted. He claimed that he'd already been hired at a different maintenance company. "I'm handling it," he said. Later that week, Michelle was doing a load of laundry and discovered a plastic bag with cocaine residue in Jacob's pants pocket. When she confronted him, he brushed her off, glued to his phone. So she grabbed it and smashed it on the floor.

She now assumed that, in addition to whatever else Jacob had gotten involved in, he had been cheating on her. "You must think I'm a complete idiot," she retorted when he denied it. But Michelle figured she could deal with that later. A more urgent concern was keeping a roof over their heads. In his softer moments, Jacob expressed a desire to regain her trust. "I want to make things right," he said. "Just tell me what to do and I'll do it."

It was obvious that in order to stay in their apartment they needed money—and they needed it fast. Frantic to gain control of the situation, Michelle began searching for temp jobs that would allow her to work at night while Jacob and the kids were home asleep. One day, as she browsed the "gigs" section on Craigslist, an ad caught her attention. The TV series *Divorce Court* had relocated from Los Angeles to Atlanta and was looking for "REAL COUPLES on the verge of BREAKING UP."

> Are you DONE and ready to call it quits?
>
> Do you suspect your spouse or long-term partner of CHEATING?
>
> Is your spouse's behavior TEARING your family apart?

Michelle chuckled bitterly at the casting call's relevance. She was about to move on when she noticed the compensation for those willing to appear on the show: $1,100 per couple, or $550 each. Their rent was $1,300 a month. On a lark, she emailed the address listed in the ad, expecting nothing to come of it. The next morning, though, she received a response from one of the show's producers. He wanted to know how soon they could be available. When Michelle presented the idea to Jacob, he balked. Why on earth, he asked, would anyone air their personal issues on national television? But Michelle prevailed. She had no intention of exposing her "actual self," as she put it; the two of them would simply offer up "some reality show nonsense." It would just be for the money. She reminded Jacob that *he* was the one who'd gotten them into this mess and that he had not yet gotten them out of it.

On a sizzling morning at the end of August, a car arrived to take Michelle and Jacob to a soundstage at Tyler Perry Studios, located fourteen miles away on the old Fort McPherson army base. Despite the air conditioner running full blast, Michelle was sweating. Still, she maintained a sharp focus, making Jacob repeat back to her the plotline they'd prepared. "You'd better not screw this up for us," she warned.

The taping took place on a sleek, modern set that looked nothing like a traditional courtroom. For Michelle the whole experience was bizarre. She kept reminding herself that none of it was real—that the tanned, handsome bailiff (or "Bae-liff," as his adoring fans referred to him) was actually a fashion model, that the audience members were paid extras, and that the presiding judge, Lynn Toler, had one objective: to make each episode maximally entertaining. For his part, Jacob delivered an expert performance. He was funny, articulate, charismatic. He had impeccable comedic timing. Michelle was more subdued, with a deer-in-headlights look on her face. Three-quarters through the taping, the manic worry that had led her to pursue this farce abruptly gave way to an overpowering sadness—a genuine sadness, not performed, as if the emotions she'd been trying to keep at bay were spilling out all at once. In response to a question from the judge, she broke down sobbing. A producer later reassured her that the tears would play well in the heavily edited product.

Afterward, in the green room, as other couples hovered around a table stacked with fruit and pastries, Jacob approached Michelle with a big smile. "We did good!" he said, as if they were on the same team and had accomplished something together. "I think we nailed it." Michelle sneered and walked away. She went to look for the production assistant in charge of distributing payments. Far from grateful, she felt resentful that Jacob's deceit and irresponsibility had brought them to this point.

Having received her half of the payment, Michelle requested a separate car back to Decatur. She prayed that none of her friends or relatives—or, God forbid, her kids—would ever see the episode.

ON THE AFTERNOON OF September 9, 2019, DJ, Danielle, and about a dozen other students at McNair High School got off their bus in front of Eastwyck Village. It was a Monday, and the new school year had begun five weeks earlier. Danielle, a freshman, hung back at the gated entrance with a group of acquaintances as DJ made his way into the sprawling complex. A fellow tenth grader was headed in the same direction.

"Oh shit," the boy said. "Looks like somebody's gettin' put out." He pointed to an unruly mound of household objects some distance away. "Wow, that's messed up," DJ said. Then, as they drew closer to the pile, DJ saw his mom sitting alone on a nearby stoop, and in the jumble of mattresses and electrical appliances, he suddenly recognized specific items: his family's sofa, his blue bedspread, Danielle's sticker-covered wall mirror.

Michelle appeared shell-shocked. She barely glanced at DJ as he came and stood beside her. Finally, in response to a question he hadn't asked—he hadn't said anything at all—Michelle muttered, "You should talk to *him*." Her words were laced with vitriol.

She'd made no attempt during the past month and a half to shield DJ and Danielle from the discord between her and Jacob. On the contrary, she'd sought to draw them into her anger. She'd told them about the bag of coke and Jacob getting fired; she'd shared her suspicion that their stepdad was cheating on her and had asked if they'd seen or heard him speaking to any other women. The conflict had become so all-consuming that Michelle and Jacob seemed oblivious to how the start of school was going for their children. DJ was fiercely loyal to Michelle, but he wasn't interested in taking sides. He felt that he'd already lost his biological father, the man whose name he bore (the "D" in DJ stood for Daniel) but who hadn't so much as called or texted him on his last two birthdays. He wasn't prepared to lose Jacob too.

DJ looked up and saw Jacob chatting with a few other guys, smoking a cigarette. One of the men chuckled. They could have been talking about last night's game or their plans for the weekend. DJ took off his backpack and sat next to his mom. Skye was in her stroller, absorbed in a CoComelon video. Finally, Michelle turned to DJ. "I can't believe this," she said.

That night, Jacob got the five of them a room at the Days Inn on Candler Road. There had been a ferocious debate over what to do with their belongings. Michelle was not only livid that Jacob, who must have known that an eviction was imminent, had given her no advance warning, allowing her to be caught unawares when the deputy showed up with a crew of movers. She was also angry that he had done nothing to prepare for it. He claimed, implausibly, that he'd put his portion of the *Divorce Court* money toward paying down their rent balance, leading him to assume that they could stay in the apartment—and leaving him, he said, with insufficient funds to rent a storage unit and moving truck. He wanted Michelle to use her own share of the *Divorce Court* payment to store their things. But with limited funds and no sense of how long they'd need to be at a hotel, she was reluctant to do this. In the end, as it was getting dark, a neighbor drove them to Days Inn, and they were able to take only what they could squeeze into the car—everything else was left behind. They had a vague plan to return to Eastwyck the next morning. Maybe they could convince Jacob's mother, who lived nearby, to store a few pieces of furniture? But in the face of other pressures, they never got around to asking her.

Over the next few days, the tension between Michelle and Jacob continued to mount. One evening Michelle announced that she was going out for a while to clear her head, and when she came back a couple of hours later, she was clearly intoxicated. Soon, provoked by a snide remark about her inebriated state, she was mercilessly upbraiding Jacob, calling him names. "You're an asshole," she screamed at him. "You're a no-good piece of shit!"

DJ and Danielle took Skye outside. This wasn't the first time they'd seen Michelle drunk. In the wake of her mother's death in 2013, which coincided with her worsening abuse at the hands of their father, Daniel, Michelle had begun drinking to dull her pain. Sometimes she passed out. Sometimes the alcohol made her mean. But gradually, after she'd left Daniel, these episodes had grown more infrequent until they ceased entirely. Listening to their mom's slurred tirade, DJ and Danielle felt scared. They hoped it was an isolated incident, not the resumption of an old habit.

After an expensive week at the Days Inn, Jacob and Michelle decided to relocate to the A2B Budget Hotel down the road. An acquaintance of Michelle's, a woman named Mercedes, worked at the extended-stay hotel, and she'd put in a good word with her manager, who had offered Michelle a job at the front desk. Though leery about moving to A2B, whose conditions Mercedes had described in less-than-glowing terms, Michelle was grateful for the job's overnight hours and the discounted room rate. Jacob agreed that it was their best option.

When it came time to leave the Days Inn, however, Jacob informed Michelle that he wasn't going with them. He said he could no longer deal with her "negative attitude." He told Michelle that a friend of his had agreed to take him in. Promising to see the kids soon, he gave Skye a kiss—DJ and Danielle were already at school—and then he took off. Michelle later learned that the friend Jacob had gone to stay with was a young woman who used to work in the rental office at Eastwyck.

JACOB'S DEPARTURE HIT DJ especially hard. While Danielle continued to stay in touch with Jacob, sporadically texting him on the sly, her brother's sense of betrayal was intense, nearly as crushing as Michelle's. The fact that Jacob had referred to him as his son and said he loved him now seemed like a cruel joke. "It was like he was messing with our heads," DJ said. He felt ashamed that he'd ever trusted Jacob, that he had failed to see him for what he was. In the span of a single week, DJ realized, he and his mom and sisters had lost not just their apartment but the idea of family they'd so easily latched onto. He swore to himself that as an adult he would never be like Jacob or Daniel. He would never cheat or beat up a woman. He would be a different sort of man: the kind who stuck around.

Despite the circumstances that had brought them there, Michelle and the kids found their footing at the A2B. Each evening, after finishing the homework that Michelle insisted they not neglect, DJ and Danielle got Skye fed and bathed as Michelle went downstairs to begin her shift. In the morning, around a quarter to seven, they took Skye to Michelle before heading off for school.

Skye was sweet and affectionate. And she was a handful. She was in constant motion, squirming and wiggling and lunging, and while awake she required nonstop supervision. Unlike Eastwyck, where there'd been a playground, at the hotel there was nowhere for the two-year-old to burn off energy. Her older siblings took on the role of coparents during the ten to twelve hours when Michelle was working: they coaxed Skye into bed, comforted her if she had a nightmare, and got her dressed and made her breakfast. For her part, Michelle was too tired to be depressed. Even with the discounted room rate and food stamps she'd successfully applied for, she was living paycheck to paycheck. Saving enough to rent an apartment felt like a distant fantasy. But she'd made it through worse. At night, as she tried to keep up with her online course assignments while sitting at the front desk, she nurtured an image of one day becoming a social worker, having a career and the security that came with it.

Her friend and co-worker Mercedes hadn't exaggerated when she said the hotel could be a rough place. An around-the-clock security detail did little to deter the fights and petty robberies and kicked-in doors that brought DeKalb County police to the property on an almost daily basis. The four-story hotel resembled an enormous box dropped haphazardly onto a desolate field of concrete. Traffic noise from I-20, which ran parallel to A2B, was unceasing. But that was the least of it. The hotel was situated on a particularly bad stretch of Ember Drive, a side street off Candler Road. "Name a problem the community faces—poverty, blight, nuisance properties, gun violence, drugs, gangs, endangered children," observed an article on Ember Drive in *The Atlanta Journal-Constitution*. "This street has them all." People still talked about the shooting in 2015 of Thearon Lee Almond by a hotel security guard who wasn't supposed to be carrying a gun. In a lawsuit, Almond's family alleged that hotel employees had made no attempt to help as the unarmed man bled to death in the parking lot.

Michelle hated that the kids' school bus didn't pick them up at the hotel, forcing them to trek down Ember Drive and cross a dangerous intersection, but the teenagers saw it as a blessing. They were mortified to be living at A2B and feared their classmates would find out. Other "hotel kids," as they were called, were viciously teased. They might as well have been staying at a homeless shelter—the stigma was the same: such kids were perceived as dirty and foul-smelling, while their parents were derided as crackheads, hos, deadbeats. While DJ had long cultivated an aura of aloofness, Danielle tended to be more self-conscious about her social standing. But lately her brother had become sensitive to these slights as well.

DJ had begun dating a sophomore named Tyneria. She was his first girlfriend and, as he sheepishly confided to Danielle, the first girl he'd been in love with. He imagined her dumping him if she discovered where he lived. But his worry was unfounded. When he eventually divulged his secret, Tyneria told him that she, too, used to live at an extended-stay with her grandmother. She, too, had kept it hidden from her teachers, her classmates, even her closest friends.

TWO MONTHS AFTER arriving at A2B, about a week before Thanksgiving, Michelle and the kids were eating microwaved dinners on the floor of their room when Michelle's phone buzzed.

It was her boss. She said they were moving Michelle to the morning shift at a different location. Another employee had quit and they were in need of an immediate replacement. Michelle bristled at her boss's tone, which to her ears suggested not a request but a command, and said she wasn't sure if she could manage it. She explained that she had no childcare during the day and that the other hotel was at least an hour's bus ride away. It would take a little while for her to make arrangements.

The conversation devolved from there. It ended with Michelle abruptly hanging up and uttering an epithet at her phone. She shook her head, incredulous.

"I think I just got fired," she said. DJ and Danielle were silent.

"What are you gonna do?" Danielle finally asked.

"I have no idea," Michelle said.

Britt smiled through Thanksgiving dinner, trying to hide her despair. Three months had passed since her housing voucher had expired, and being back in Granny's apartment for the family gathering reminded Britt of how hopeful she'd felt when she had moved out. That optimism now seemed delusional, but she had spent the evening trying to push such thoughts away. On Instagram, she had posted a photo of Granny seated at the head of the table, framed by a border of pink hearts, and another of Desiree and Kyrie in the special outfits she had bought them for the occasion, set against a backdrop of pumpkins and orange leaves. "Happy Thanksgiving!" was emblazoned across the bottom.

At seventy-eight, Granny was still spry and strong-willed, but her Alzheimer's had begun to take a toll. She was increasingly irritable and forgetful; some of the dishes she had cooked earlier that day were missing basic ingredients. And everyone was surprised when Granny abruptly shooed them out as soon as dessert was finished. Five generations had been crammed into her small dining area, and apart from Kyrie, they made up what Britt's mother, Cass, referred to as a "tough-ass group of females." There were Granny's only child, Theresa, and Theresa's four daughters, Cass, Trisha, Veronika, and Kimi; there were also Trisha's adult daughter, Jada, and Britt and her two kids. (As on most holidays, Britt's siblings—Aaliyah, Devin, and Josiah—

were across town with their father, Eric, and his sprawling extended family.)

Although various boyfriends had appeared over the years, these women saw it as a point of pride that their ability to survive—or to have a good time—was not dependent on any man. Finishing off the smoked neck bones that Veronika had prepared for her, Granny had her family in stitches with stories from her wild youth. "Y'all don't know, I was a *menace to society,*" she said emphatically. Her great-great-grandchildren giggled along with the adults. Later, the table erupted when someone started teasing Theresa about her new hairstyle, saying it resembled a comb-over. "What, you tryin' to look like Trump?" Kimi asked. She was not only the youngest but also the feistiest of her sisters. Since Theresa had been in the throes of drug addiction during her pregnancy with Kimi, she hadn't been sure if her baby would make it, and a particular closeness had developed between the two of them. "Now that's just *mean,*" Theresa responded amid the laughter.

Britt enjoyed being with her family, but she missed having her own home to go back to at the end of the night. She knew they didn't judge her for her predicament, but she still found the whole ordeal—the non-renewal at QLS, losing her Section 8 assistance, practically begging people for a place to stay—deeply embarrassing. It didn't help that her aunt Trisha, who a month earlier had hinted that it was time for Britt and the kids to vacate their spot on her living room floor, had been avoiding Britt all evening. But Britt didn't blame her. She knew what it was like to be in her position.

Fortunately, Aaliyah had put aside her fear of getting evicted and had allowed her sister, niece, and nephew to crash at her place. She hadn't needed to tell Britt that it wasn't a long-term solution—that much was obvious. Cass, who had quit her janitor job at the airport and was now a housekeeper at Twelve Downtown, an upscale hotel near Centennial Olympic Park, had recently moved in with Aaliyah, as had her brother, Devin. Aaliyah's boyfriend was not shy about expressing his displeasure, making the living situation especially combustible. Cass was irritable and prone to outbursts. In the weeks they'd been there, even though Britt was contributing a substantial amount of money toward rent and utilities, she had tried to stay away from the apartment as much as possible. Meanwhile, when she wasn't working, she had continued to search in vain for a rental she could afford. Friends and relatives sometimes called with leads, but again and again these went nowhere.

Shortly after Thanksgiving, Yateshia Evans, an old family friend, called to let Britt know about an apartment that would soon be opening up. It hadn't yet been advertised, and Yateshia didn't have many details, so she encouraged Britt to reach out to a woman in the rental office named Cindy. "Just tell her I sent you," she said, "Cindy's like kin to me." Yateshia told her to call the following morning. Britt promised she would. She then asked what the complex was called.

"Gladstone," Yateshia answered. "When's the last time you went by there?"

Of course, Britt thought. She'd heard that a number of Yateshia's own family members—among them her daughter and grandkids, her brother, and her elderly mother—had moved to Gladstone Apartments a while back, made possible by some inside connection Yateshia had at the complex. Britt was less familiar with Gladstone than with the surrounding neighborhood, where her family had deep roots. There was the church she'd attended every Sunday and Wednesday growing up, Church of Atlanta Lighthouse, situated on the same forlorn stretch of Boulevard as the apartments, and a few blocks away, the rickety duplex where Cass had lived as a newborn with Theresa and Granny and Granny's mother. It had been ages since Britt was in the area, but in her memory it was a kind of no-man's-land, ghetto and run-down: vast abandoned industrial tracts alongside dilapidated houses and maybe the odd gas station or liquor store. The southeast neighborhood's most well-known landmark, the federal penitentiary, loomed ominously down the road, and Britt remembered that Englewood Manor, a large housing project, used to sit adjacent to Gladstone, their red-brick buildings almost indistinguishable. Englewood had long since been demolished, but in Britt's mental geography this neighborhood, like others from her early life, belonged to an Atlanta that she had little interest in returning to.

As if reading Britt's thoughts—or preempting misgivings she had heard before—Yateshia pointed out that the Gladstone units were cheap, "really cheap." The word rubbed Britt the wrong way. She was in need of a place that was affordable. But cheap? Even on the off chance that "cheap" was actually cheap (as opposed to *relatively* cheap), cheap was other things too. Cheap was busted security gates and shards of glass on decaying playgrounds. It was rats and leaking sewage. It was—to take an example from her childhood—your mother covering your body with her own in an empty bathtub while shots rang out. Britt knew she was in no position to be picky; beggars and choosers and all that. And her credit score, hovering around 500, threatened to consign her to "second-chance housing," which invariably meant second-*class* housing. Still, she wasn't ready to let go of another version of her future—the one she had begun to glimpse at QLS, the one she had been told awaited her since she was a middle schooler with straight A's. That future was anything but cheap.

When Yateshia called, Britt had just pulled up outside Aaliyah's apartment. She had grabbed dinner for everyone, a couple of big greasy bags of fast food. Now, as she walked through the front door, Kyrie ran to greet her, and Britt ended the call with what she hoped was an appreciative tone.

LATER THAT WEEK, after getting off work, Britt sat in her car and let out an exasperated sigh. She was parked near the downtown headquarters of Georgia Power, where she'd taken a part-time job as a security guard to supplement her pay at Chick-fil-A. With almost two hours to spare before the kids needed to be picked up from daycare, she had been browsing apartments online, hoping to stumble across a new listing within her budget. She found nothing. She considered trying to take a nap—sleep had been hard to come by lately—but she felt restless, overcaffeinated. Then Britt recalled her conversation with Yateshia and, without giving it much thought, headed toward Gladstone Apartments.

Driving south in the languid midafternoon traffic, she moved through Old Fourth Ward and Sweet Auburn before turning onto Hill Street and entering the leafy, largely residential neighborhood of Grant Park. Atlanta's zoo, which she had loved visiting on field trips as a child, was close by, and for her there was something comforting about these tree-lined streets. But whereas in the past an invisible border had seemed to separate Grant Park from poorer, predominantly Black communities such as Peoplestown, that line of demarcation had become much less pronounced. Only a mile or so from Gladstone, just past the spot where her grandmother's high school used to stand, Britt was stunned to discover The Beacon Atlanta, a nine-acre former industrial site that had been resurrected as an attractive dining and entertainment district. Making her way slowly around the repurposed warehouses, she spotted a chic salon, a cupcake café called Baker Dude, an enormous "Artist Cove," and, most appealingly, a Brazilian coffee-and-cocktail bar. This was not the place she remembered.

From Hill Street she turned left at McDonough, and there, in vivid reds and yellows and purples, she encountered a giant mural painted onto a cinderblock wall encircling the long-shuttered General Motors plant. The mural welcomed visitors to Chosewood Park.

Chosewood Park? Growing up, it had never occurred to Britt that the neighborhood where her family's church was located had a name, a distinct identity. People had simply referred to it as the South Side. As she continued up Boulevard, past Brite Bubbles laundromat and a deserted car wash and Carnicería y Tiendas El Progreso, she noticed that in some ways the area appeared unchanged. There were the vacant lots and the boarded-up, graffiti-covered dwellings. There was the corner store with a WE ACCEPT EBT banner hung across its barred windows.

But now she realized how green and densely forested the neighborhood was, the hilly terrain allowing unobstructed views of the city skyline. Even the nearby federal prison, which real estate agents had begun extolling for its "historic" Beaux Arts architectural style, seemed a bit less threatening than it once had. Most surprisingly, she noticed freshly remodeled homes up and down the street. Her favorite, a white Craftsman bungalow with a big front porch and a For Sale sign on the lawn, sat directly opposite Church of Atlanta Lighthouse. In 2017, the bungalow had been purchased for $5,000 from the estate of a recently deceased woman. The buyer, Recycled Investments, LLC, then sold it eight months later—in the same condition—to another shell company, Lazarus Investment Partners, LLC, for $99,000. By the time Britt slowed down to admire the renovated house, it was on the market for $425,000.

Economically depressed for decades, Chosewood Park, like other historically Black communities along the BeltLine, had seen a recent surge in land values, leading investors to descend on the neighborhood. These investors targeted older residents potentially unaware of what their homes were worth, bombarding them with unsolicited text messages, letters, and phone calls (a practice known as "dialing for dollars") and trying to convince them to sell—often for a fraction of the house's actual worth. The properties were then flipped, or refurbished and rented out, or left unoccupied until they could be sold again for maximum profit. (The seemingly abandoned house next to the one Britt liked was in fact owned by a Florida-based investment firm.) In Oakland City, on the West Side, property values were up 146 percent over the past three years; in Westview, they were up 176 percent. In Chosewood Park, property values had risen an astonishing 348 percent.

The skyrocketing land and property values; the emergence of new dining, entertainment, and retail destinations like The Beacon; the visual alterations to the built environment: these changes were the manifestations of a much larger social, economic, and spatial restructuring that had been taking place in Atlanta for over two decades. Speculators and homebuyers did not have to take it on faith that their assets in Chosewood Park would appreciate. They merely had to drive a few minutes up the road, into areas whose transformation was further along, to see what the neighborhood would soon look and feel like— and what it would soon be worth.

These revitalized blocks were not just scattered pockets of redevelopment amid an otherwise unchanged urban landscape. Atlanta as a whole had become a radically different city, and communities that weren't "in transition" or "on the rise" were now exceptions that proved the rule. In 1990, 27 percent of residents were college educated; three decades later, 56 percent had a college degree. During the same period, the city's Black population had declined by 20 percent, and there was a drastic drop in the number of families living below the poverty line— not because these families were bringing in more money, but because they had been priced out. Strikingly, the central city's median income now exceeded the suburbs', an inversion that would have been unthinkable a generation before. Low rents had become high; complaints about failing infrastructure had finally been heard, and funding had suddenly materialized. But by and large it was the newer, wealthier residents who benefited from these improvements. Many longtime residents were no longer around, casualties of gentrification in the sense defined by the LA Tenants Union: the "displacement and replacement of the poor for profit."

Several months earlier, around the time Britt was searching for a landlord who would accept her housing voucher, a study by the Federal Reserve Bank of Philadelphia had observed that Atlanta was the fourth-fastest gentrifying city in the country. The heavily publicized report was no surprise to most Atlantans; the evidence was everywhere. But why and how this remaking of the city had occurred, what exactly had propelled it, was less clear. In Atlanta, as in other cities, people tended to point to what they saw—beautified streets, homogenized architecture, stylish coffee shops replacing old storefronts—and then work backward to find an explanation. Did it come down to changing tastes? Individual preferences? Was it just the invisible hand waving a magic wand over a distressed neighborhood and changing it beyond recognition?

Gentrification, in Atlanta and elsewhere, *has* involved the refashioning of physical space, and of course the whole process could not unfold without the actions and decisions of individual businesses and residents ("urban pioneers," as they used to be called). But that's only part of the story. Gentrification is purposeful and produced. Before the gentrifiers arrive, a neighborhood first has to become gentrifiable. The conditions for transformation must be created.

In his book *Capital City,* Samuel Stein, a housing analyst and city planner, shows that gentrification is the third stage in a cycle of strategic investment, disinvestment, and reinvestment in a particular area. It is a highly orchestrated process, driven by the intertwined interests of real estate capital and urban policy. Why does a specific neighborhood gentrify? Because investors have identified a "rent gap," as geographer Neil Smith terms it. This gap represents the difference between the current value of land and the higher returns it *could* yield through some intervention, such as renovating a property, demolishing and constructing new buildings, or evicting old tenants and attracting different ones. The wider the rent gap, the stronger the incentive for investment. Factors such as proximity to green space, transportation, and other amenities may contribute to its emergence, but the primary drivers of the rent gap are shifts in urban policy and market demand. Urban planners—increasingly concerned with growth, and so beholden to the priorities of developers and investors—play a critical role not only in creating rent gaps where none previously existed but in helping landlords and property owners exploit them. In this way, gentrification becomes a political process as much as a social and economic one: an outcome of zoning changes and tax abatements, infrastructure upgrades and public-private partnerships.

In Atlanta, no single project has more profoundly reshaped the urban landscape than the BeltLine—arguably the greatest rent-gap generator in the city's history, and a prime example of planned gentrification. This transformative endeavor, winding through forty-five neighborhoods and redefining Atlanta's core, epitomizes the interplay between city governance, urban planning, and real estate interests. Originally conceived as a green mobility project that would connect residents and communities in the city, the twenty-two-mile network of trails and parks was quickly recast as a means of fundamentally altering Atlanta's character, to the tune of approximately $4.7 billion in projected costs. As a giant magnet for development, much of it publicly financed, the BeltLine has indeed enhanced the desirability—and consequently the value—of nearly everything in and around its path.

By the time Britt was looking at Gladstone, the Eastside Trail segment of the BeltLine, stretching from Piedmont Park to Reynoldstown, had already been completed, attracting scores of new restaurants, upscale townhomes and apartment complexes, boutique hotels, and enormous faux-public commercial "hubs" such as Ponce City Market and Krog Street Market. It had also intensified the pressures of displacement, pushing property values up and poorer residents out. A similar dynamic was unfolding along the Westside and Southside Trails—the latter of which, though still in the initial phases of construction, ran through a park adjacent to Gladstone.

In the Gladstone rental office, a smartly dressed woman who Britt assumed was Cindy was deep in conversation with an elderly female tenant. Not wanting to interrupt them, Britt hovered near the door, gazing out at the apartment complex through a bank of windows. Gladstone's garden-level units, spread over thirty acres in a mix of one- and two-story buildings, appeared to be in pretty good shape. The grass was cut, and the walkways were clear of weeds and trash. There was nothing remotely contemporary or fashionable about the place—old and worn-out was more like it—but the complex exuded a tidy, inviting calm.

The three-hundred-unit property had been built in 1949 and originally called Wellswood Apartments (after its owner, Leon W. Wells, who lived with his family on an adjoining piece of land) and over the following decades its most noticeable change was the racial and class makeup of the residents. The earliest tenants were employed at the nearby GM plant and other local factories; the majority of them were white and, judging by the rents they paid, lower middle class. Newspaper ads from the period hint at the clientele Mr. Wells hoped to attract: "Suburban Living in the Heart of Atlanta," declared one, while others boasted of "Dixie Living" and "Estate Living." But then in the late sixties, amid white flight, Chosewood Park underwent a drastic demographic shift, and by 1971, when the Englewood Manor housing project opened beside Wellswood, that transformation was complete. The two apartment communities seemed almost interchangeable—indeed, there was talk under Mayor Maynard Jackson of trying to convert Wellswood itself into public housing.

Meanwhile, the surrounding area continued to be hollowed out. As plants and factories disappeared, so did restaurants and grocery stores. The final nail in the coffin was the recession and foreclosure crisis of the late 2000s, which had a particularly devastating effect on this part of Atlanta. A disproportionate number of Black residents lost their homes, jobs, and businesses. Soon Englewood Manor was gone as well. But Gladstone Apartments, as it had been renamed by its latest owner, somehow survived it all, persisting as the sole multifamily complex in a neighborhood on the cusp of another reversal of fortune—likely its most dramatic yet.

"What can I do for you?" Cindy asked Britt when she was finished with the other woman.

Britt told her that Yateshia had suggested she stop by. "Oh, you're Cass's daughter," Cindy said brightly. "P mentioned that you were looking for an apartment." "P," which stood for pumpkin, was Yateshia's nickname as a teenager at East Lake Meadows, where Yateshia and Cindy had both grown up. They'd lost touch when the project was razed but had reconnected about twenty years later, after bumping into each other downtown. Their lives had taken different paths: Cindy was married to a real estate broker and had landed a salaried position with a property management company, whereas Yateshia had raised two daughters on her own, scraping by as a housecleaner. But their old bond remained, and Cindy, who had started running things at Gladstone, told Yateshia to holler at her if she knew of anyone looking to move.

Thus began a mutually beneficial arrangement. Yateshia was able to help various relatives and acquaintances secure apartments—so many that Gladstone gradually became home to a large percentage of people who'd once lived in public housing. And Cindy never had to worry about filling empty units, confident that her friend would only send her people who could keep up with their rent.

A one-bedroom, Cindy said, was scheduled to come available in early January. "Do you want me to set it aside for you?" she asked.

Although Britt had been determined to find a two-bedroom, she changed her mind when Cindy told her what the rent would be: $550 a month, not including utilities. It was just a little more than she'd been paying with her voucher. In Atlanta, you could still happen upon the odd landlord charging comparably low rents. But their properties tended to be filthy and crime-ridden, their units barely habitable. Truly affordable apartments in relatively good condition—and without months- or even years-long waiting lists—were all but extinct in the city. "Yeah, I'd really appreciate that," Britt replied. She dropped off a security deposit the following morning.

Britt was still riding high a few days later when she stopped at the Walmart on Cleveland Avenue. Before Thanksgiving, she had finished her Christmas shopping for the kids, putting their presents on layaway, and now the deadline to settle her bill had arrived. At the customer service counter, she was greeted by a young guy. "Did you not see the news?" he asked. Earlier in the week, Tyler Perry, the entertainment mogul, had spent over $400,000 paying off every item on layaway at that specific store, in addition to another local Walmart.

But the best gift was being able to move into her new apartment after the new year. At 542 square feet, the unit was even smaller than she expected, and it was lacking a dishwasher, a garbage disposal, and a washer-dryer hookup, among other things. She wasn't complaining, though. In lieu of a second bedroom, she had decided to put the children's mattresses in the living room. This didn't bother them in the slightest: on weekends, it allowed them to fall asleep watching movies. And Britt could retreat to her own bedroom, her humble oasis.

The apartment was nobody's idea of a dream home. But it was a home, and Britt had already been through enough to know how lucky she was to have found one.

12

Natalia removed her headset and quietly, almost inaudibly, began to cry. *Don't do this,* she berated herself. *Not now. Not again.*

It was a midweek afternoon in August, and Natalia was at her desk on the twentieth floor of the State Farm tower in Dunwoody. Attempting to steady herself, she focused her gaze on some of the personal objects that filled her cubicle. An anniversary card from Maurice. A photo of her and Maurice and the kids walking in a forest near their apartment. A large close-up picture of Matthew's chubby, smiling face. But it didn't work. She stood up and walked toward the bathroom, where she had sequestered herself numerous times over the past couple of months. As she made her way there, however, she became dizzy. She crouched down and pretended to tie the laces of her dress boots, in case anyone was watching her. Then her knees buckled. She fell to the floor, shaking and weeping uncontrollably.

"We should call 911," she heard someone say. A group of co-workers had returned from lunch and were huddled around her. Natalia's friend Breanna, one of several colleagues who'd thrown her a surprise baby shower in January, quickly intervened. She eased Natalia to her feet and, supporting her from behind with one hand on her back and another on her shoulder, gently guided her toward the "silent room": a small, dimly lit space where the call center's staff could collect themselves. "It's all right—you're all right," Breanna said softly once they were alone. "Remember those breathing exercises I was teaching you?" Natalia gave Breanna her phone and asked her to let Maurice know about the panic attack; usually Natalia FaceTimed with him during her crying episodes, as she referred to them, but she felt too shaky to talk. Soon her supervisor opened the door without knocking. "You almost done in here?" she asked, plainly annoyed. Natalia nodded yes, but her face conveyed a different message. "You know what?" her supervisor said. "Forget it. Just take the rest of the day off."

It had been like this since Natalia and her family moved to The Whitney. With little savings left, they found that they were now living from one paycheck to the next: a harsh reality for a couple who prided themselves on budgeting and saving and spending responsibly.

Natalia blamed herself for this state of affairs. During that frenetic sixty-day period when they were scrambling to find a place to live, spending hundreds of dollars on application fees and receiving rejection after rejection, her anxiety had gone into overdrive. She had been bent on making the transition as smooth as possible for the kids. If she had been more open to relocating to other parts of Atlanta, then maybe they wouldn't have needed to use Liberty Rent as a cosigner. They wouldn't have had to pay Liberty's fee of $1,450, and, most fatefully, they would not have been compelled to go with one of the two local complexes that worked with Liberty. Perhaps, in that case, they wouldn't be spending $500 more a month on rent than they'd been paying at Victoria Heights. And maybe they wouldn't have ended up in a "luxury" unit at The Whitney that was infested with cockroaches. The roaches were everywhere: in the bathtub and closets, on the headboard of Shantel's bed, in their kitchen cabinets. Forking over all that extra money for a place that was nice and well-maintained was one thing. It was another matter to spend it on an apartment where you needed to keep your baby off the carpet for fear that a pack of cockroaches might scurry by.

While Maurice had the same regrets, he was adamant that the choice to go with Liberty and The Whitney had been a joint decision, not Natalia's alone. Yet he was unable to reassure his wife in a way that she could hear. Her sadness, her apprehension about not only their fragile financial state but so much else, seemed impenetrable—and that's how Natalia was experiencing it as well. Sometimes, particularly at the office, she felt as if she were being buried alive. As a customer service rep at an insurance company, she knew that being screamed at by irate policyholders was part of the job. Now these attacks lingered long after the calls were finished. And yet she sensed that what she was going through could not be reduced to job stress or money issues. It wasn't simply about cockroaches or her chronic lack of sleep or even Aaron's passing. Painful moments from her childhood were resurfacing; old wounds she'd assumed were healed were opening up again.

She started seeing a therapist, a white woman in her fifties. Within minutes of the first appointment, Natalia knew it was a bad fit—"Her responses were awful," Natalia recalled—but she was the only nearby therapist who accepted her insurance. At the beginning of their fourth or fifth session, Natalia mentioned that Maurice was downstairs in the parking lot, and the woman asked if she could meet him. When Maurice appeared, the therapist proceeded to grill him. Her questions, peppered with stereotypes about Black men, were devoid of curiosity and implied that Maurice was somehow to blame. Later, in the car, they managed to laugh about the encounter. "My God, *that's* therapy?" Maurice asked. Natalia never went back.

Meanwhile, work was becoming more unmanageable, and the day of her panic attack turned out to be her last in the office for the next four months. Natalia was told by her boss that she couldn't return until she'd undergone a mental health evaluation. Although she accepted the directive—Natalia knew she was in the midst of something serious—it took her a few days to work up the resolve to seek out a psychiatrist. When she began calling around to providers within her insurance network, she was told that the earliest appointment she could get was a month away. (Such wait times for mental health treatment are hardly uncommon: one nationwide study found average waits of nearly ten weeks.) Unbeknownst to Natalia, this delay would prove disastrous for her family. But at the moment, she was, in her words, just "trying to make it through the day."

In mid-September, she showed up at the psychiatrist's office feeling wary after her experience with the therapist. Dr. Sandhu, however, was warm and empathetic. She listened intently as Natalia described in detail what the previous several months had been like. In stark contrast to her appointments with the therapist, Natalia didn't feel like she needed to present a competent, coherent version of herself. Dr. Sandhu seemed, as Natalia later put it, perfectly at ease with her patient's "mess." She diagnosed Natalia with severe postpartum depression and wrote her a prescription for Sertraline, an antidepressant. She also strongly recommended that Natalia go on short-term disability leave. "You need a break," she said. Her words nearly caused Natalia to burst into tears.

But the doctor had one stipulation. Earlier, Natalia had mentioned how raw and tired she felt from working four ten-hour shifts a week. Now Dr. Sandhu said she would only sign off on the paid leave if Natalia significantly cut her hours when she returned. "You're putting too much on yourself," Dr. Sandhu said. It didn't sound like an ultimatum. It seemed as if it was coming from a place of genuine care. Natalia agreed to the plan.

IN THE WEEKS PRECEDING and immediately following the panic attack, Natalia's attention, like Maurice's, had been scattered. Navigating the vicissitudes of severe anxiety and depression while continuing to manage a household with three children, one of them an infant, was demanding enough. But when Natalia finally went on short-term disability, the reality of their financial situation snapped back into view.

What they saw was alarming. "Paid leave" was not the arrangement they'd assumed it would be. They'd been under the impression that Natalia's monthly income would remain the same during the four months she'd be at home. But because Dr. Sandhu had required her to switch to part-time upon returning, Natalia discovered that she'd be earning *part-time* pay, or roughly half of her usual income, during her leave—minus an additional 30 percent, since her insurance only reimbursed up to 70 percent of monthly wages. And then there was the four-week gap when she was waiting to see a psychiatrist and, afterward, the two weeks she waited for her short-term disability benefit to be approved and processed: she received no pay for that period. These delays alone cost the couple $3,150 in expected earnings.

Their leaky boat was now sinking. This became brutally clear at the beginning of October, when most of their bills came due. The month before, already short on cash, Maurice had skipped their car note payment of $460. Still expecting Natalia's short-term disability benefit to pay her what she'd been making before, he planned on catching up once the benefit went into effect. Soon, however, they received a notice from their auto lender. Their Camry risked being repossessed if their account was not brought up to date immediately; in Georgia, as in many states, creditors could legally seize a vehicle after just one missed payment. Now, at the start of a new month, Maurice and Natalia had to figure out how to cover their expenses. The prospect of a repo was frightening to both of them: not only had Maurice been transferred recently to an Enterprise branch in Alpharetta, a twenty-minute drive from their apartment, but a repossession was certain to tank their already subpar credit. So, as they had done in September, they decided to make only partial payments on their other bills—electric and gas, Wi-Fi, their car insurance premium, their Verizon family plan, Natalia's student loan interest—while cutting back as much as they could on groceries and gas.

That left their rent, their largest monthly expense. Unable to pay the whole $1,450 until the second of Maurice's two paychecks was deposited in their bank account (his hourly wage earned him biweekly checks of roughly $950 each), Natalia left a message with the rental office, explaining the reason they would be a little late. She promised it wouldn't happen again. Maurice, determined to make up for the drop in their income, took on a second job. He began driving for Uber Eats, delivering food on weekends and after getting off work at Enterprise.

The family's rent was due on October 5. Five days later, they came home to see a dispossessory letter tacked to their front door. Summer, their previous landlord, had told them that if they were ever in need of additional time to pay their rent, they should let her know and she would work with them. They had never been forced to go that route—they'd never been late on their rent, not a single time—but they'd thought a similar understanding could be reached with their current landlord. Instead, without warning, an eviction had been e-filed against them with the Fulton County Magistrate Court.

What they didn't know was that the owner of The Whitney, though hidden behind a company called Roswell Road Partners, LLC, was in fact a private equity firm notorious for its aggressive eviction practices. Based in Nashville, Covenant Capital Group managed some $2 billion in real estate assets and owned more than fifteen thousand apartment units across the country. In Indianapolis, an investigation would later show that Covenant, under a variety of LLC names, had an eviction filing rate of 20 percent, more than three times the city's average; in Nashville, Covenant's reputation was so bad that a Change.org petition titled "Stop Putting Your Tenants on the Streets" was addressed to the firm. But Covenant's eviction activity, while extreme compared to small-scale "mom and pop" property owners, was very much in keeping with that of the newer, larger corporate landlords. Many of them were drawn to states, like Georgia, with weak tenant protections. Indeed, Atlanta—a "private equity strike zone," in the words of one researcher—had become an epicenter of Wall Street's incursion into the rental market. These real estate behemoths employed a stock set of tactics in attempting to "unlock value" from their acquisitions: hiking rents, skimping on maintenance and security and upkeep, slashing staffing costs, tacking on extra fees. Most startlingly, evictions were becoming increasingly automated. An algorithm could determine the course of action: if the rent was three days late, an eviction notice automatically went out, a late fee was tacked on, and the tenant was saddled with any court costs incurred by a filing. This allowed the new breed of mega-landlords to aggregate resources at scale—and to remove decisions involving rent collection and eviction from the messy realm of human interaction. All this was aimed at rapidly maximizing profits so investors could turn around and sell the property at a premium.

Maurice and Natalia had a week to "answer" the dispossessory notice if they wished to avert a default judgment. In the blank space beside *I state the following in response to Plaintiff's claim,* Natalia simply wrote: "Will pay." They received a court date of November 5, which gave them less than three weeks to come up with not just October's rent and the $150 late fee that had been added to it but November's rent as well. It seemed an impossible task.

On Facebook, Natalia alluded to this turn of events. "Your life literally can change overnight," she posted. For the first time ever, she found herself searching online for emergency rent support. She came across the Community Assistance Center (CAC), a nonprofit that, according to its website, prevented approximately 675 households in Sandy Springs and Dunwoody from being evicted annually. The organization had a rigorous screening process—they provided aid solely to people "experiencing a documentable crisis such as job loss, illness, or divorce"—but Natalia and Maurice were quickly approved. In court, the couple was able to give a representative from ZRS Management, The Whitney's property management company, two checks covering the entirety of what they owed: a onetime contribution from the CAC of $407 and a cashier's check for the remaining portion. The money was accepted. "Let's never do that again," Maurice said to Natalia as they walked away from the courthouse, shaken by how close they had come to losing their home.

Yet their financial situation continued to spiral. No matter how many extra hours he clocked for Uber Eats, Maurice couldn't seem to dig his family out of the hole they'd fallen into. Paying the two months of rent and staying caught up on their car note and insurance made it inevitable that they would fall behind on other obligations, like their light bill, and one day they awoke to an apartment without electricity. Reconnection required that their balance be paid in full, plus a fee. It wasn't long before the same process—disconnection, reconnection, fee—happened with their cellphone service.

This stress made Natalia's "season of healing and self-care," as Dr. Sandhu had put it, something of a perverse joke. When her paid leave began, Natalia had pulled Matthew out of daycare, unable to justify the expense. So he'd been at home with her the entire time: still being breastfed, still napping fitfully, still demanding her near-constant attention. Since Maurice was working later and later, the bulk of the parenting and household responsibilities fell on Natalia—even as she

was racked with guilt for having put her family in such a difficult position. If only she had better controlled her feelings, she thought. If only
she had managed to keep functioning at the call center. Aware of the
burden she was carrying, Maurice tried to downplay his own worry and
exhaustion. "I just had this mantra that we could handle whatever came
at us," he said later.

Natalia wondered if her medication was doing anything. She felt
worse than ever. One night, after the kids went to bed, she sat alone at
the kitchen table and drank an entire bottle of Chardonnay. She refilled
the wine bottle with water, hoping that Maurice wouldn't notice.

WHEN DECEMBER ARRIVED there was no money for Christmas
presents. Maurice and Natalia couldn't bring themselves to sign up for
Adopt-a-Family, a holiday gift drive administered by the CAC. But
their caseworker had also mentioned a Santa's Village where the kids
could pick out donated presents, and later in the month, once school
had concluded for the break, Natalia decided to take them there. Looking up the street address on the website of Empty Stocking Fund, which
ran the program, she saw that the organization's mission was to "bring
joy to the lives of disadvantaged children." Natalia felt a pang of re-
morse. Was that what her kids were now?

With Matthew snug in a baby carrier on Natalia's chest, she and
Anthony and Shantel boarded a MARTA train for downtown Atlanta
and then traveled by bus to a massive warehouse in the northwest part
of the city. It was freezing outside, and hundreds of families were in
line, waiting their turn. The warehouse was festooned with holiday
decorations: a North Pole on Jefferson Street. On Christmas morning,
in addition to a few gifts from their grandparents, the children unwrapped the toys and art supplies that they themselves had selected. To
Natalia and Maurice's relief, Anthony appeared oblivious to how unusual their Christmas had been. And if Shantel, at thirteen, was old
enough to discern that her parents were struggling, she was also old
enough to know not to ask questions.

The following month, less than a week before Natalia was due back at State Farm, she was stepping out of the shower when she heard a knock at the front door. She quickly threw on some clothes and checked on Matthew, who was fast asleep. At the door was one of The Whitney's maintenance workers and a woman from the rental office. "Oh, sorry," the man said, peering past Natalia into the interior of the apartment. He seemed nervous. "I guess we have the wrong unit."

About thirty minutes passed, and then there was another, more forceful knock. It was a deputy from the Fulton County Marshal's Department. He was accompanied by a crew of movers. Only later—after their apartment had been emptied of their belongings; after Maurice eventually arrived home; after he had found a large storage unit for them to rent—did the two of them piece together what had happened. Back in November, the landlord had accepted their money, thus stopping an eviction from taking place. But according to the paperwork that the deputy gave them, the presiding judge had authorized an immediate writ of possession should Maurice and Natalia be even one day late in paying each subsequent month's rent. Somehow they had missed this crucial detail. They'd paid on time in December. But in January their rent was due on a Monday, and Maurice was set to be paid on Friday. By then their landlord had notified the marshal's office.

They never told Shantel and Anthony the real reason why, after picking them up from school that afternoon in January, the five of them drove not back to their apartment but to a room at Extended Stay America. Maurice said it was a burst water pipe that had forced them to leave.

| 13 |

DJ bolted upright, his heart racing. A nightmare had startled him awake. Woozy and disoriented, it took him a minute to get his bearings. He felt around for his phone and checked the time: almost 10:00 a.m. A sharp January chill suffused the storage room where he and his mom and sisters had been secretly staying for the past four nights.

On the floor next to him, Skye was asleep on a thin cushion of bath towels. Frightened by the howl of sirens just after dawn, the two-year-old had finally drifted off to a video of "Wheels on the Bus" a few hours earlier. She was nestled beside Danielle, who was also dozing, her head covered in a tightly drawn hoodie and propped up on a backpack full of clothes. Nearby was a heap of discarded cleaning supplies, water buckets, and random small appliances. There was no heat. There was a working bathroom, but because they were trying to remain undetected, they had showered only once in its dirty, curtainless tub.

DJ tried to go back to sleep, but it was futile: he was too sore and cold. He was also hungry, having last eaten at school the day before. He reached for the plastic bag that contained what was left of their groceries for the week. There was nothing inside except a quarter-loaf of bread.

He took out a piece of bread and ate it slowly. The night before, Michelle had told them that she'd be heading out early in the morning to earn some money. DJ and Danielle were skeptical but held their tongues. Michelle promised them lunch at Burger King. Since it was Saturday, DJ had nowhere to be. He lay back down on the floor and watched an action movie on his phone, awaiting his mom's return.

LESS THAN A MILE AWAY, Michelle was sitting cross-legged on a patch of brown frostbitten grass at Resthaven Garden of Memory. Everyone had regarded her grandmother, Shirley, as a kind of saint: a registered nurse blessed with a resplendent singing voice and an abiding selflessness that had earned her the honorific of "evangelist" at her church. In the fifteen years since she'd passed away, her plot at Resthaven had become for Michelle a sanctuary, a place to soak up what had always been her grandmother's calming presence.

But today was different. Michelle felt blank, detached. The drive and resourcefulness she'd summoned when Jacob left had steadily diminished in the seven weeks since losing her job at A2B. Lacking childcare for Skye, she was unable to get a day job, and even if it had been logistically possible to leave Skye with DJ and Danielle while working a graveyard shift somewhere else—which it wasn't, given how early the teenagers needed to begin their long walk to the bus stop—she knew it was unsafe for them to be at the hotel by themselves. And dangerous for her, too: walking alone at night down unlit Ember Drive was not, to her mind, something that any sane woman should do. She had submitted an application for Georgia's CAPS (Childcare and Parent Services) program, which provided low-income working families with scholarships to help pay for daycare, but she'd heard it could take a while to be approved. Until then, Michelle had needed a way to cover their no-longer-discounted weekly room rate of $275, due each Sunday at twelve noon.

Desperation, Michelle had told DJ and Danielle when they were younger, forces you to get creative. After putting what remained of her final paycheck toward a week at the hotel, she had to figure out how to cobble together rent through other means. She pawned a DVD player and some jewelry Jacob had given her, along with the laptop, still in perfect condition, that she had purchased for her online social work program. She decided that she could keep up with the coursework using her smartphone. Money borrowed from her aunt and a loan from a former co-worker helped cover a few additional weeks. She also began selling her plasma, earning between $40 and $50 for the roughly ninety minutes it took the "donation" center to siphon off as much as federal regulations allowed.

On a weekend in December, Jacob promised to watch the kids while Michelle worked as a ticket taker at an event downtown. A staffing agency had posted an ad on Facebook offering $15 an hour for the one-off job, and Michelle had jumped at it. Skye was eager to see her dad for the first time in months. But on the day of the event, after Michelle had already left, Jacob never showed—he never even answered his phone. Michelle had to return to the hotel. The next day, in need of more than $100 to avoid losing their room, Michelle and Skye rode the bus to a small convenience store where, according to another resident at A2B, you could sell your food stamps for 50¢ on the dollar. They simply swiped your EBT card, asked you to enter your PIN number, and handed you your cash. Michelle sold about $350 worth of stamps, nearly the entirety of her monthly allotment, for $175. And with that, her creativity had reached its limit.

As December wore on, keeping their room became more and more of a challenge. Michelle grew consumed with fear. And so, during the week before DJ and Danielle went on Christmas break, she put Skye in her stroller, bundled her up in blankets, and, holding a paper sign that read HOMELESS PLEASE HELP, stood for hours on end outside a local Big Lots and CVS. She would later describe the experience as the most degrading of her life. Fortunately, a combination of unusually cold weather and holiday goodwill seemed to make people generous. She prayed to God that no one would recognize her—nobody she'd graduated from high school with, or parishioners from her aunt's church, or any of her old neighbors from Eastwyck.

When men openly propositioned her, when they rolled down their car windows and, despite the presence of Skye, offered her money for an hour or two together, she found herself making calculations in her head. How many weeks could she pay for with that kind of money? Where would Skye be while these transactions were taking place? In the end, though, this was a line she couldn't bring herself to cross. Standing there with her daughter, holding her flimsy sign, she remembered what she had been doing almost exactly a year earlier: buying the kids' presents, building the gingerbread house with Jacob and the kids. "That's when I almost lost it," Michelle said. "I just kept repeating to myself, 'This too shall pass, this too shall pass.'"

Christmas came and went, and then New Year's. In mid-January, after missing a payment and with a lockout imminent, Michelle convinced one of the hotel workers to lend her the key to a storage room that she knew was never used. She and the kids slept on the filthy floor, trying to keep warm with the few blankets and bath towels they'd brought with them.

Now, at the cemetery, after four nights in the storage room, Michelle was out of money and out of ideas. She wondered if the most productive thing to do was go back to the hotel, make up some excuse to take Skye with her, and spend the rest of the day panhandling. Thinking such thoughts—deceiving DJ and Danielle, using sympathy for Skye to earn more money—while gazing at her grandmother's headstone felt shameful.

She was about to leave when an older woman approached her. The woman later said that Michelle looked anguished and that she'd mistaken the petite forty-one-year-old, dressed in skinny black jeans and a puffer jacket, for a teenager.

"You okay?" she asked Michelle.

Michelle hated that her current situation forced her to treat any expression of pity or compassion as an opportunity to plead for help. Yet, like many people who stopped outside the stores to give Michelle a couple of dollars or a MARTA pass, the woman apologetically explained, after hearing Michelle's story, that she didn't have much to give—she herself was struggling to make ends meet. She did, however, offer to call her friend Phillis, who ran their church's homeless outreach. "Yes, that would be great," Michelle said. The woman made the call, and together they waited for Phillis to arrive.

An hour later, Michelle was in Phillis's hatchback. They drove up and down the surrounding thoroughfares—Candler, Glenwood, Memorial, Columbia—searching for the most affordable extended-stay with an available room. Phillis's church, The Beloved Community, was located in a Black working-class neighborhood of Atlanta called Pittsburgh. On a threadbare budget, the church operated a food pantry and helped feed and clothe the men and women squatting in the area's empty investor-owned homes (some were paid to guard these properties). With the BeltLine slated to open nearby in the coming year, The Beloved Community was suddenly at risk of falling prey to the very "renewal" that, in adjacent neighborhoods, had displaced residents who were now reliant on the church for support. But there was an emergency fund for families in immediate need, and it was out of this reserve that Phillis said she could assist Michelle and her children.

Michelle had presumed that A2B was the least expensive extended-stay in the area. But it turned out that there was one place that occupied a rung below even A2B. By early afternoon Phillis was paying two weeks' rent, up front, for the family's room at Efficiency Lodge. After they retrieved their few belongings from Phillis's car, the manager, a friendly woman named Lisa, welcomed them to the hotel.

DJ HATED EFFICIENCY. His initial relief at being able to leave the storage room—"C'mon, grab your stuff," Michelle had said to her children, "this lady's gonna be helping us"—was already dissipating as Lisa checked them in behind the bulletproof glass. He hated the trash and little puddles of urine and discarded mini liquor bottles that dotted the hotel's walkways; he hated the middle-of-the-night shouting matches and bass-heavy music that prevented him from sleeping. He hated how the other guys his age, sitting in stairwells or on the trunks of cars, sized him up as he walked by, and how Michelle, discerning right away the sort of environment this was, demanded that he stay inside after school and on the weekends. And so he quickly came to hate, above all, their tiny room itself: the dorm-sized refrigerator that accommodated barely any food; the grease-encrusted stovetop whose burners had long ago ceased to function; the narrow sliver of tiled floor, situated between the dresser and the bed that his mom and two sisters shared, where at night he adjusted and readjusted his blankets in a fruitless attempt to get comfortable.

Already predisposed to solitude—at school he usually sat by himself during lunch, reading manga or sketching in his notebook—DJ turned increasingly inward. Like Danielle, he used his headphones to create a private world. He'd found a video-editing app that allowed him to construct elaborate collages out of music videos and anime and his own artwork, and he spent hours absorbed in this activity. Mostly it was a way of distracting himself from the heartache he was feeling. He and Tyrenia had split up after returning from winter break.

It was also painful to watch his mom suffer. DJ was aware that, if not for him, his mother and sisters could have been staying free of charge at a family shelter, where boys over the age of thirteen were prohibited. When Danielle soon accepted her friend Jaime's offer to live with her family for the rest of the semester, DJ wished that he, too, could ease Michelle's burden. He thought about dropping out of school to find a job. Walking past the drug dealers at the hotel, he imagined joining them, making quick cash and relieving the stress his mom was under. He saw the long list of nonprofits and social service agencies Phillis had told Michelle to contact, and he watched as his mom crossed off each one in turn, after being told that her family was ineligible for this or that assistance program or that the organization had run out of funds. In the months since Jacob left them, DJ had begun to relate to Michelle less as a child than as a peer or sibling. They had long, intimate conversations, and DJ marveled at the fact that, despite everything they'd been through, Michelle still stayed on top of her class assignments, hunched over her phone in bed as Skye dozed next to her.

But there was tension as well. Once, around dinnertime, DJ could tell that his mother had been drinking. When he criticized her for spending money on beer, she became belligerent and told him to mind his own business.

Michelle desired nothing more than to be working—both for financial stability and for her sanity. But a lack of childcare remained an insurmountable barrier. It had been nearly three months since she'd applied for CAPS and she still hadn't been approved: her online application continued to be marked as "pending." Multiple calls to the government department overseeing the program had not been returned. She scoured single-parent Facebook groups and Reddit pages about daycare scholarships, searching in vain for similar programs or another phone number for CAPS. She just wanted to talk to someone, anyone, to find out what was causing the delay and whether she could be doing anything to move the process along. But Michelle's predicament was not unusual in a state where the average cost of daycare had risen to roughly $800 a month. She couldn't begin to work until she had childcare, and—unless she received a CAPS scholarship—she couldn't afford childcare until she began to work.

In the meantime, every week at Efficiency was a down-to-the-wire struggle to keep their room. A counselor at Danielle's school insisted on paying for a week out of her own pocket when Danielle told her what was going on. Michelle was stunned by this unsolicited act of charity, but she was back in the same position the following week. Panicking, she again sold the bulk of her food stamps, which meant that they had very little food that month. But better for the kids to go hungry, she decided, than for them to be on the street. Phillis dropped off a food box from her church. When that ran out, Michelle traveled around the city looking for other food pantries.

Skye's already scrawny frame seemed to be growing thinner by the day, and the most filling meals of DJ's week came from the free lunches he got at school. Michelle herself ate little, causing her to pass out one day in the middle of yet another visit to the plasma center. For her, the only thing more scarce than food was rest. It was not uncommon for Skye to fall asleep at 10:00 p.m. and then wake up, fully alert, at 3:00 a.m.; sometimes she was still awake when DJ had to leave for school. And with no parks or playgrounds within walking distance, with nothing to jump or climb on, the hyperactive toddler had only Michelle's phone to keep her occupied. The blare of YouTube Kids videos in their room was unremitting: Michelle or DJ would turn down the volume, and Skye would crank it up again. "Baby Shark," Michelle thought, was going to be the end of them.

There was a time in the not-too-distant past when someone in Michelle's position could have received cash assistance to get them through a period of hardship. Contrary to popular belief, the majority of people on welfare in the 1980s and 1990s were not trapped in an endless "cycle of dependency" but rather used the aid to rebound from temporary misfortune: job loss, a family crisis. Extensive research showed that most women who turned to cash welfare used it as a lifeline, relying on it for only brief stretches of time. But in 1996, when President Bill Clinton made good on his famous pledge to "end welfare as we know it," that safety net was shredded. What replaced it was a program called Temporary Assistance for Needy Families. Unlike the old model, TANF gave states flexibility not only in how money was spent but in who would receive it. The program's poor design and draconian requirements—including stringent work mandates, random drug testing, school attendance monitoring, and severe penalties for noncompliance—meant that fewer and fewer families received help. In 1979, welfare benefits reached eighty-two out of every one hundred families with children in poverty. When TANF was first introduced, that number dropped to sixty-eight. By 2020, a mere twenty-one out of every one hundred impoverished families managed to access this resource.

That was on a *national* level. In Georgia, only five out of every one hundred families living below the poverty line received support through TANF in 2020, even though they were eligible for the assistance. It wasn't just a problem of chronic underfunding. It was that states were wasting, diverting, or simply refusing to spend the money they were given. In 2020, when Michelle found herself in dire need, only 10 percent of Georgia's TANF funds went toward cash assistance, whereas 60 percent was spent on the state's foster care and child welfare systems—an imbalance that reflected the state's willingness to spend money on separating children from their families but not on preventing the "neglect" or "inadequate housing" that led to that outcome.

$107 million remained unspent. It was little wonder, then, that many destitute parents in Atlanta, including Michelle, had never heard of the program.

On a morning in mid-February, after DJ left for school, Michelle got Skye dressed and told her, "We're 'bout to find out what's going on with this CAPS thing." It took them just under an hour to make their way to the Division of Family and Children Services office on Sams Street. The place was deserted. A small notice on the front door stated that all DFCS operations had been relocated to 2300 Parklake Drive—another hour away by bus. Undeterred, Michelle and Skye turned around and headed there. When they finally arrived at the new location, which occupied the bottom floor of a huge six-story government building, the waiting area was packed. It resembled a DMV, albeit one filled almost entirely with women and young children. A security guard asked Michelle what she was there for and then pointed her to a single empty chair. "She can sit on your lap," the man said, nodding at Skye.

Frustration permeated the room. Michelle looked around, wondering how many of these women were in her situation. At that point, she was still under the assumption that if you met all the eligibility requirements for daycare assistance, you would automatically receive it—that it was just a matter of waiting to be approved. But this was not the case. Funding for CAPS came primarily from a federal program created by the 1996 welfare reform bill, the Personal Responsibility and Work Opportunity Act. The idea was that former welfare recipients, most of them single parents, should not be impeded from entering the labor force because of a lack of childcare. Yet the program was set up not as an "entitlement," meaning anyone who was eligible for benefits or services could obtain them, but, like TANF or housing vouchers, as a block grant: a fixed amount of money that the federal government provided to states. As a general rule, block grants' funding for programs serving low-income Americans fell far short of meeting existing need— and this was especially true of the Child Care and Development Block Grant that funded CAPS. Nationwide, less than 17 percent of low-income families with children under the age of six managed to receive childcare subsidies. In Georgia, that figure was 7 percent.

There is an inherent dignity in work, the architects of welfare reform had piously declared. *Without a job, single mothers are incapable not only of escaping poverty but of realizing the blessing of self-sufficiency.* Never mind that most of the jobs available to these women paid poverty wages, came with no health insurance, and were at constant risk of being eliminated by companies' "restructuring strategies." Many women didn't have access to the childcare that would allow them to work such jobs. And it wasn't only parents who were in urgent need of safe, reliable childcare. Kids like Skye, stuck all day in the pressure cooker of a small hotel room, glued to their parents' phone and unable to run or play or be around other children, needed it just as badly.

State agencies, for their part, had devised both formal and informal methods of rationing scarce childcare assistance. The formal methods were numerous: narrowing eligibility requirements, establishing wait-lists, freezing intake, and imposing cumbersome rules on those already receiving subsidies. Less formal methods involved deliberately limiting outreach efforts, so that fewer families knew that scholarships were available.

But there was another informal method: driving applicants mad until they simply gave up. When at last it was Michelle's turn to approach the counter, her interaction with the DFCS employee took about forty seconds. Michelle said she was there to figure out why her CAPS application hadn't yet been approved.

"Did you apply on the website?" the woman asked. She seemed at once bored and irritated.

"I did," Michelle replied.

The woman said she had no information beyond what appeared on the online portal.

TOWARD THE END OF THE MONTH, in late February, Michelle saw a glimmer of hope. SoulShine, a high-end daycare and preschool whose mission was to "create a sustainable future through permaculture concepts," had advertised a teacher position in their two- and three-year-old Turtles classroom. The job seemed ideal. Located only a few miles from Efficiency in an affluent part of Decatur, the daycare center offered starting pay of $12 an hour. It was also on the bus line, and, unlike every other job she'd ever had, it was full-time with benefits. Most importantly, it could solve her childcare dilemma. At SoulShine, she reasoned, not only would Skye receive the highest quality of care, but—based on Michelle's past experience working at daycares—it would likely be at a heavily reduced employee rate. She spent hours composing a résumé and cover letter on her phone, and a week later she was invited to interview for the position. Michelle requested an afternoon time slot, when DJ would be free to watch Skye.

Michelle showed up to the interview wearing black slacks, a forest-green blouse, a black shawl, and low-heeled dress shoes, all of which she had purchased the day before at Roses, a discount clothing store near the hotel. She'd also paid to get her hair braided, allowing her to take off the headwrap she had been wearing to cover her neglected hair. As Michelle saw it, this wasn't a waste of money—it was an investment that could determine whether or not she landed the job. She felt confident for the first time in months.

A veteran teacher named Jackie gave Michelle a tour of the center. She emphasized the distinctive aspects of the "SoulShine ecosystem": the locally sourced farm-to-table food, the yoga and sign language instruction, the homesteading philosophy. Michelle was in awe of the place. During her interview with the assistant director, however, Michelle was calm and articulate. She could tell it was going well. Afterward, as Jackie walked her to the front door, Michelle casually asked if there were any open spots, at the moment, for the children of SoulShine teachers. "I think there are," Jackie replied. "But you do have to work here for a year before your kids can enroll." Michelle nodded, trying to hide her despair.

That evening Michelle logged into the CAPS portal. Her application was still pending. When SoulShine's assistant director left a message two days later offering her the position, Michelle never returned the call.

"No. No no *NO.*" Kara read the email a second time.

> Effective Monday, March 16, 2020, all Fulton County
> schools and administrative offices will be closed until
> further notice. This action is being taken in an effort to
> slow the rapidly spreading COVID-19 virus. . . . We
> recognize the hardship this decision places on many
> families but believe it is in the public's best interest. All
> school and district activities are canceled/postponed
> effective tomorrow, Friday, March 13, 2020.
>
> Students will be expected to complete online learning
> assignments and/or work packets as assigned by their
> classroom teachers.

Kara was leaving to pick up her kids when the announcement came
in. Fulton County schools, including the one Grace and Nathaniel attended, had in fact already been closed for the past two days, after a
district employee at Bear Creek Middle and Woodland Middle Schools
tested positive for the coronavirus—the sixth confirmed case in Georgia. Luckily the daycare that Joshua and Jermaine attended, which in
normal times functioned as an after-school program for her older kids,

had agreed to keep Grace and Nathaniel until their school reopened. But even the slightest deviation from her family's hard-won routine tended to rattle Kara. What in the world, she wondered, did a single infected employee in Fairburn have to do with an elementary school located forty minutes away? Why couldn't they simply "clean and disinfect every frequently-touched hard surface" (as the email put it) at Bear Creek and Woodland while letting the other schools stay open?

Since late February, when anxieties about the novel coronavirus took root, Kara had only faintly registered the risk it posed. Like Super Bowls and mass shootings and impeachment trials, the increasing likelihood of a pandemic hovered at the periphery of her attention: a vaguely ominous development with seemingly little direct relevance to her own life and circumstances. Fearful of getting sick, she did start washing her hands with greater frequency, and there was a cursory—and unsuccessful—attempt to stock up on hand sanitizer at Kroger, where the shelves containing such items were completely bare. But by and large the early concerns and controversies surrounding Covid—a growing panic about the acute shortage of tests, the uproar following President Trump's falsely reassuring remarks at the CDC in Atlanta—felt abstract to Kara, who was consumed by more immediate impediments to her family's well-being.

The words "closed until further notice" in the email from the school superintendent changed all that. What had been an inconvenience two days earlier—a last-minute scramble to make arrangements for Grace and Nathaniel—was suddenly escalating into a full-blown crisis. At KinderCare, the children's daycare center, there had been talk that week of a potential closure if area public school districts deemed it necessary to shut down. "Flattening the curve" was presented as a civic mandate. Kara saw the urgency of containing the virus, but now, as she drove to pick up the kids, her thoughts were on one thing only: How could she possibly manage with both the schools *and* daycares closed?

She had achieved a fragile equilibrium in recent months, after the eviction over the water heater and the humiliating trip to Florida. In December, she had lost her job at Grady Hospital for clocking in late too often ("*You* try living in your car with four kids," she'd wanted to tell her supervisor), but she had quickly found a new job as a home health aide with MCS Healthcare Staffing. The job's flexible hours and, depending on the client, higher hourly rate allowed her to secure a hotel room for longer stretches. Then, in early February, she had taken out a tax refund loan of $3,000, or roughly $2,800 after fees and interest, which she had planned on using to get her and the children into an apartment. When the fresh eviction caused her to be denied at two different complexes, however, she'd decided that instead of wasting money on application fees, she would put her tax refund toward the next best option: a larger, better-equipped hotel room. Between her friendly new client in Conyers and their room at HomeTowne Studios, an extended-stay on Jimmy Carter Boulevard, life was finally feeling steady. She was on guard against anything that might set her back again.

The scene at KinderCare when she arrived told Kara that she wasn't alone in her panic. A number of other parents were dreading the prospect of having their kids at home. How would they continue to work? How would they pay their rent and bills? An administrator told them that while the situation was evolving rapidly and no definitive decisions had yet been made, the families should prepare for a temporary closure. She added that she couldn't imagine the center staying closed for more than a week or so.

The next morning, Kara contacted her boss to ask if there was any way her children could accompany her to her client's house. The answer was a firm no.

For Celeste, the pandemic started at a Kentucky Fried Chicken three blocks from Efficiency. With her twice-monthly chemotherapy treatments leaving her body wrecked, the physical demands of her warehouse job had become too much to bear. Worried that any loss of income could jeopardize her ability to stay current with her car note and hotel room, she'd applied for a cashier position at KFC. The man who'd interviewed her, looking over her lengthy résumé, observed that she would be better suited for a management role. But Celeste demurred. Because of her health issues, she'd explained, she just needed a regular paycheck. She was hired on the spot.

Seven weeks later, as the country was locking down, Celeste awoke at 4:45 a.m. and opened the hot-pink composition book she had been using as a journal. "Yesterday," she wrote, "was definitely a hard day."

> *I went to clock in at KFC and my fingerprint wasn't recognized. I went to get a manager only to be informed that due to the coronavirus they were cutting back staff to a minimum. I felt devastated knowing what might happen without this money. They didn't even have the decency to call me before I got there.*

> *God, give me the strength to get through this test. I have a little bit of savings that will carry me for maybe a month and I know you say don't worry but I'm human and the nature of my flesh is to do so. God, you know my heart and I know you promised to never leave nor forsake me. So I'm just asking for you to give me the strength to make it through this.*

NATALIA REFUSED TO LET GO of Maurice's hand. "*Pleeease,* take me with you," she groaned. "Or at least trade places with me." Maurice chuckled at what had turned into something of a morning ritual between the two of them. "Believe me," he said. "I wish I could." He kissed the hand that was holding his. "One day at a time, right?"

They were sitting outside their room at Extended Stay America. Since it lacked a separate bedroom, the couple's Camry had come to serve as one of the only places where they could be alone. This had been true even before the pandemic, but now, in early April, thirteen days into a citywide stay-at-home order and four after the announcement that Georgia's schools would be staying closed for the remainder of the school year, these stolen moments in the parking lot had become a lifeline. Every morning before Maurice left for work—rental car companies were among the essential businesses permitted to keep their doors open—he and Natalia would carry their coffee mugs to the car and commence another daily "conference," as they referred to it. They would discuss their finances, or how the kids were holding up, or what they had dreamed the night before (Natalia was an avid dream interpreter), or merely listen to music in an effort to forget, for a little while, the tedium and fear that ruled their lives. For Natalia, whose only other opportunity to go outside consisted of the occasional grocery run at the Publix next door, each minute in the Camry was one to savor. And when it eventually came time for Maurice to leave, when delaying any longer would cause him to be late, Natalia forced herself to return to a room that seemed to be shrinking each day.

She had been back at State Farm for about a month when it was decided that the call center staff would begin operating remotely. But after picking up her equipment from the office, she realized that working out of their hotel room would be impossible. It wasn't just the cramped quarters and complete lack of privacy. Dependent on the hotel's public Wi-Fi, she had no secure wireless network to use, and then there was the more mundane obstacle of simply not having a large enough surface on which to fit two monitors, a mouse, and a keyboard. Natalia tried perching the monitors on their kitchenette's narrow bar counter and lunged to catch one of them as it nearly crashed to the floor.

"Where exactly are you?" asked her new supervisor on the phone when Natalia conveyed the practical constraints of her current living situation. Natalia said that she and her family were temporarily at a hotel, but the "hotel room" her boss had in mind, he later told her, was the kind he and his family typically stayed in—the sort that, at the very least, had a decently sized desk. Natalia took a picture and sent it to him. "He called me back and said, 'Oh, yep, I see what you mean.' I could tell he felt bad. I'm sure it looked like we were refugees." Sparing her the embarrassment of having to explain why she was at an extended-stay, he said that Natalia could go on unemployment for a month or two—to expedite the process, State Farm would file a claim on her behalf—until her circumstances changed or the office reopened, whichever came first.

This arrangement proved fortuitous, because Natalia couldn't fathom attempting to field calls from indignant policyholders for eight hours a day while simultaneously supervising her children's remote learning. Shantel's transition to virtual schooling had gone pretty smoothly: having early on claimed the hotel room's diminutive sofa, she'd managed to remain focused without too much prodding from her mom. She was always careful to position her borrowed Chromebook's screen so that her sixth-grade classmates wouldn't be able to tell where she was living.

Anthony was having more trouble. His special ed teacher did as much as she could to help, regularly adjusting his workload on Google Classroom and allowing him to forgo live online instruction, but ultimately it was Natalia who had the herculean challenge of ensuring that her neurodivergent nine-year-old completed his assignments. She felt miserably inadequate to the task. *You don't know what the hell you're doing* was constantly running through her head. One minute she would be absorbed in some math problem with Anthony, hunched beside him on one of the room's two queen beds, and the next Matthew would be emptying a box of cereal onto the faux hardwood floor. On more than a few occasions, she'd gone into the bathroom, shut the door, and hoped her kids couldn't hear her crying.

In many ways, then, Natalia experienced these early weeks of lockdown less as a rupture than as a continuation of the distress she had been feeling for much of the past year. In the months leading up to their eviction, she'd felt like she could crack at any time—and now, sequestered in a single stale room with three kids, she had even fewer moments to herself.

She was jealous of Maurice, who would often sneak out to the car after dark, smoke a bowl, and, reclining in the driver's seat, stare at the night sky through the parking lot's floodlit haze. Natalia took comfort in reading articles, particularly first-person accounts, about the difficulties others were facing. It helped her to remember that millions of people were also struggling to cope, that a communal "we" was also on the verge of going nuts. But then she would read a personal essay about sourdough starters or backyard camping or binged Netflix shows, and the limits of collective identification became brutally clear. She couldn't even open their hotel room window more than a couple of inches, and the sluggish internet connection made any effort to stream movies a frustrating endeavor.

But it wasn't just conditions inside that belied the popular notion of Covid as "the great equalizer." Maurice was acutely aware that his family's material survival depended on him continuing to go out and work. And yet, as the U.S. death toll surpassed ten thousand in early April, he grew increasingly afraid to leave. Although he and Natalia mostly avoided the topic, or made light of it when it came up, the possibility of Maurice bringing a lethal virus back to their room was terrifying. But they had no choice. For all the talk of essential workers' heroism and self-sacrifice, Maurice felt financially coerced into laboring under potentially deadly conditions—a feeling that became more intense when an older co-worker tested positive. It was obvious that only some people were being asked to assume such risk.

AT EFFICIENCY, residents started to engage in a kind of gallows humor. "What the Lord is trying to teach us," a now-unemployed housepainter named Greg solemnly intoned, "is that things can always get worse."

For those at the extended-stay, life was already economically precarious. The pandemic threatened to push them over the edge. Across the country, the ranks of the newly jobless had swelled to more than twenty-two million—the most dramatic spike in unemployment since the Great Depression, easily dwarfing the calamitous figures of the recession of the late 2000s. But the outlook at Efficiency was even bleaker. It was as if someone had flipped a switch, and suddenly the low-wage jobs that had provided these men and women with barely subsistence-level earnings prior to Covid—work in retail and custodial services, leisure and hospitality—had vanished. LeAnn, the latest hire at the front desk, estimated in mid-April that as many as eight out of every ten adults at the hotel had lost their incomes. She mentioned one striking example: Defriese, a forty-seven-year-old mother of four who had worked at McDonald's for eighteen years—first at the location near Grady, then at the Atlanta airport—had been abruptly laid off without a penny of severance pay.

Amid this pervasive hardship, desperate residents were compelled to reenter the workforce, scavenging in that narrow sliver of the labor market that had evaded the recent avalanche of job cuts. Of course many people, especially parents with young children, needed to hunker down at home. Mercifully, the federal CARES Act, signed into law at the end of March, not only added a supplementary stipend to the meager unemployment benefits offered by states but expanded eligibility to include gig workers, the self-employed, and others not typically covered by unemployment insurance. But the real hurdle—as those who'd applied, or had tried applying, for unemployment quickly found out—was not qualifying for the benefit but actually getting it.

A month into the pandemic, Georgia's unemployment system, unprepared and understaffed, seemed on the verge of collapse. In February 2020, the state's labor department had handled roughly 17,000 claims. By April, that number had rocketed to 716,000. Soon it climbed to 1.3 million. A government audit later revealed that during this period staffers received nine million phone calls; only 4 percent were answered. The result, in Georgia and a number of other states, was a process plagued with extreme delays and unjustified denials. Claimants who were approved had no way of knowing whether their initial payment would be arriving in two weeks or two months—and for tens of thousands, the wait turned out to be even longer than that. A resident who had finally gotten through to the unemployment office told a group of neighbors about her experience. "I said to the guy, 'Yeah, *I'm* cool with waiting. My bills, though? They ain't gonna wait. My son's stomach's not waiting. I need that money *now*.'"

And yet, with schools and daycare centers closed, parents found it difficult to seek out alternate sources of income. Childcare was in short supply, and it was here that Celeste—always the entrepreneur—saw an opportunity both to offer help and to make a little extra cash: namely, by running a makeshift daycare out of her room. She knew this was dangerous health-wise. At first, in the days after being laid off at KFC, Celeste had remained isolated, concerned that the cancer treatment put her at higher risk of severe illness, or worse. She applied for unemployment (five weeks later, she still hadn't been approved), stayed in her room, and wore the surgical mask she'd been given at her last chemo appointment. But maintaining the precautions became impractical. "Shelter in place" implied an environment that was private, contained, controllable—and life at Efficiency was anything but. It felt cruel to keep Micah and Jalen, who had recently turned fifteen, confined 24/7, so Celeste let them hang out with friends. Soon her door was open at all times, and bored neighbors were stopping by to chat. She was also running errands, winding up in cramped, poorly ventilated spaces—the corner store, the laundromat—where social distancing was nonexistent. Given these conditions, it seemed a small step to watching a bunch of kids.

Celeste told Jalen to get the word out. He liked engaging in these sorts of tasks: anything to break up the monotony. And besides, it gave him an excuse to neglect his schoolwork. Like his mother, Jalen was witty and outgoing, a natural extrovert. As a keen eavesdropper on hotel gossip, he knew who'd been arrested the night before, or who'd gotten Covid, or who the man upstairs had been sleeping with behind his girlfriend's back. "Yo, my mom wanted me to tell you she's doing babysitting now," he said to two young women smoking outside their rooms. Celeste had instructed him not to knock on anyone's door; at Efficiency, a closed door meant "do not disturb." Jalen grinned when he saw that the lady in room 120 had been less subtle in her request to be left alone. DON'T FUCKIN KNOCK!! PLEASE DONT KNOCK RIGHT NOW SLEEPING!! the paper taped to her door read.

On the front side of the hotel, after talking to several other parents, he came to a room whose occupants—a woman with a toddler, and a boy who appeared to be about his own age—Jalen had spotted only a couple of times. But Michelle's shades were drawn and her door was shut, so Jalen kept walking.

■

ACROSS TOWN, at Willy's Mexicana Grill on Caroline Street, Kara waited impatiently for two burritos, four soft tacos, and a queso dip. She was supposed to have picked up the order ten minutes earlier, but the restaurant was running behind. The girl at the counter promised it would be ready soon. Kara glanced out the window to make sure that her car was still there and her kids were still in it. Over a month had passed since her daycare had shut down, forcing her to stop working as a home health aide. For a little while, she had continued to live off her tax money, but those funds were almost depleted. If she wanted to keep their room at HomeTowne Studios and prevent her car from getting seized, she knew she would need to improvise. And so, after catching a news segment about the growing demand for food delivery workers, she had signed up to be a DoorDash driver. Her Toyota had already served as shelter for her family. Now it was her only means of earning money.

Before becoming a delivery driver, Kara thought the work would be relatively easy and straightforward. The teenagers who'd brought Papa Johns or Domino's to her door over the years had never seemed too frazzled. But driving for DoorDash was a different story. For eight to ten hours a day, including weekends, Kara was at the mercy of a taskmaster unlike any she'd encountered.

As a "dasher," her shifts began when she tapped a button on the company's app that searched for orders in the vicinity. When one came in, a screen offering her the job—and revealing the name of the restaurant, the deliver-by time, the total mileage involved, and the amount of money she'd be paid—would then appear. The pay rate for each delivery was determined by a mysterious algorithm, which DoorDash claimed accounted for time, distance, "effort," and a range of other factors, with the minimum pay of $2 per job. While drivers had the option of accepting or rejecting a particular job—they had about thirty seconds to decide—a dasher's overall performance metrics were based not only on customer ratings and on-time deliveries but on acceptance rates: dashers were penalized for trying to limit their deliveries to higher-paying or lower-distance jobs. Thus Kara frequently found herself accepting three- or four-dollar orders that required her to drive a total of ten miles, sometimes even farther. In Atlanta traffic, it could take a half hour or more to drive that distance.

What made this work especially brutal was the fact that DoorDash, like delivery apps such as Uber Eats, Grubhub, and Instacart, classified its drivers not as employees but as "independent contractors," allowing the company to circumvent labor laws that applied to all other businesses. Dashers were not entitled to a minimum wage, overtime and sick pay, health insurance, or workers' compensation for injuries on the job. Nor, crucially, were their work-related expenses reimbursed: drivers had to cover their own gas, cellphone use, and any necessary repairs to their vehicle. And they received pay only for *completed* orders, not cancelled ones or, more significantly, the often-lengthy periods of time between orders. All told, Kara figured that two weeks of dashing—two weeks of racing to deliver orders on time, struggling to keep the kids in check, dealing with an overheated engine, and nearly getting into a handful of accidents—had earned her approximately $600 after factoring in the cost of gas. That broke down to just over $6.50 an hour, or 75¢ less than the minimum wage.

By the time the Willy's order was ready, Kara was almost twenty minutes behind schedule. She'd been driving for three hours and had already been late on two orders. She hurried to her car with the insulated DoorDash bag and, opening the driver's door, noticed that one of the boys had spilled potato chips onto the floor of the back seat. "Nathaniel did it," Grace said. Her brother, seated between Jermaine and Joshua's car seats, was springing to pick up the chips. He looked afraid of what was coming. The more chaotic her life felt, the more fastidious Kara became. When she was angry, she would fix on a certain phrase or command and repeat it again and again, her voice rising. She started in on Nathaniel: "Get that stuff off my floor . . . get that stuff off my floor . . . get that stuff off my floor and *do not* smush it on my floor!" Nathaniel didn't burst into tears, but Jermaine did. "Stop it," Kara hissed. "Stop your crying before I lose my temper."

They drove to the delivery address in silence, Grace in the front seat and the three boys in the back. Since Kara needed her phone in order to use the DoorDash app, the children were unable to watch videos. They had to devise other ways to pass the hours. Nathaniel had his coloring book. Jermaine and Joshua played with plastic cubes and building blocks. Grace had a book of "brain games": crossword puzzles, mazes, and the like. The four of them napped, fussed, and napped some more. When Kara was in good spirits, she sang to the kids, making up lyrics as she went along. Recognizing that the smell of burgers and wings and pizzas was torture for them, she kept a supply of snacks and juice boxes on hand. But she also needed to avoid the delays created by bathroom stops, so Grace and Nathaniel (the younger boys were still in diapers) had been taught the art of discreetly peeing in an empty bottle beside the car.

A few times, while their mom walked an order to a customer's door, the children had caught a glimpse of how other kids were spending their pandemic days. In lush, spacious yards they spied boys and girls enjoying trampolines, swing sets, Slip 'N Slides. Kara hated when this happened. Her kids' ardent, unselfconscious pointing and staring felt like a commentary on her own inability to provide such things. Fortunately there were no children or play structures where the Willy's order was going. Kara turned onto Kirkwood Road and stopped in front of an attractive courtyard-style apartment complex. She was grateful for the contactless drop-off method that had become the default during the pandemic: if she was quick enough, she could leave the tardy delivery on the stoop without having a confrontation. After she set the food down, however, the front door opened and a young woman's masked face appeared. "Thank you so much!" she hollered. "You're welcome, hope it's good," Kara replied with a wave. Later, she saw that the woman had left her a generous tip. Kara suspected that she had spotted the car full of kids.

As the day went on and the orders began thinning out, Kara considered calling it quits. There were certain hot spots in the northern suburbs, such as Smyrna or Sandy Springs, where she could be assured of a greater quantity of orders and nicer tips, but the mechanic who had changed her oil had warned her to go easy on the car. The prospect of breaking down far from the HomeTowne Studios where she and the kids were living was not appealing. "What do you think?" Kara asked Grace. "Should we head back to the room?"

Grace lit up whenever her mom sought her advice. Earlier that week, Kara had gotten an email from Grace's fourth-grade teacher, who'd expressed concern that Grace had not been logging on to remote class sessions. He referenced a meeting he'd had with Kara before the pandemic, during which he had shared the results of an achievement test that had been administered to Grace. Kara still seethed at the memory. She recalled the word *challenged* being used to describe Grace, and how badly it had stung when she skimmed the document that he'd handed her. "According to overall comprehensive evaluation results, Grace demonstrated no academic strengths. . . . Grace exhibits deficits with reading, writing, and math skills." *Who the fuck do you think you are?* Kara had thought. In the meeting, however, as in her response to the recent email, she'd held it together, promising to help her daughter get on track.

But for now, Grace had a bigger job: ensuring that her younger brothers stayed in line and, above all, encouraging Kara to keep going, to not give up. "Naw, c'mon," she said. "Let's do a couple more."

BEFORE LONG, a dozen children between the ages of four and thirteen were showing up at Celeste's door each day. Some arrived around noon and stayed for two or three hours; some were with her from early in the morning until dark. Most were Micah's friends and had already been coming around for the past few weeks, but a few were the children of parents Celeste hardly knew.

The "daycare" itself consisted of Celeste sitting in a blue camping chair near her door and keeping an eye on the kids riding bikes or running through the parking lot, while Jalen supervised the ones playing videogames or watching movies inside. When Celeste grew fatigued and needed to lie down, she and Jalen would switch. For the majority of kids, virtual schooling was a moot point: since the hotel lacked stable

Wi-Fi, students had to either use a smartphone to get online or—as Celeste had done for Jalen and Micah—purchase a mobile hotspot device. But the reality was that, for many at Efficiency, grades and class assignments had taken a back seat to more pressing concerns.

Perhaps the most important benefit that Celeste provided, during this time of mounting hunger, was food: breakfast, lunch, and, when needed, dinner for the children in her care. Sometimes Nyah, who was now pregnant and had moved in with her boyfriend Mike several doors down, would assist with the cooking. Celeste was afraid for her daughter—she still thought Mike was bad news—but she'd been careful not to alienate the seventeen-year-old by voicing her misgivings too forcefully. When Nyah helped out, Celeste would slip her a portion of the money they'd made. Her "give whatever you can" policy usually brought in $25 or $30 a day.

By the end of April, a handful of people at the hotel had managed to start working again. Most hadn't. Pretty much everybody, though, was behind on rent. On the last Tuesday of the month, Lisa finally made it known that she'd had enough. After weeks of threatening residents individually, Lisa typed up a brief letter.

> Thank you for choosing to stay here with us at
> Efficiency Lodge. While we have been making every
> effort to work with all our guests, we are sure our guest
> understands that Efficiency Lodge has overhead that
> has to be paid as well.
>   As of today you are _____ days late on your rent.
>   At this time we ask that you come into the office no
> later than Wed 4/29 to make a payment in full or meet
> with Lisa to set up a payment arrangement.

Lisa ended by promising to evict anyone who failed to pay their rent in full. She then printed off a stack of letters and slid one under the door of anyone who had been delinquent. The notices went out in the morning, and gradually, as residents read them, they started gathering on the walkways outside their rooms. Celeste, holding her own letter, joined her neighbors. People were mad—and they were nervous. Greg, the out-of-work housepainter, turned to Celeste.

"What do we do?" he asked.

"Don't worry, love," she said. "There's no way they could just put all of us out."

LATER THAT SAME WEEK, while the kids busied themselves with an art kit their dad had bought them, Natalia sat Shantel's Chromebook on her lap and typed in the web address for Georgia's social services portal. She had just checked the balance on their bank account and saw that it was dangerously close to zero. Their hotel rent was crushing them: at $550 a week, or $2,200 a month, living at Extended Stay America cost them $750 more than they had been paying at The Whitney, and $1,250 more than their monthly rent at Victoria Heights. The only reason they had been able to remain at this extended-stay was the supplementary unemployment payments Natalia was receiving; combined with the money Maurice was bringing in, they were effectively breaking even. But she had been informed by HR that if she wished to keep her job at State Farm, she would need to begin taking calls again—it was up to her to figure out how to work remotely. Ironically, going back to work would mean a $300 reduction in her weekly income, since her enhanced unemployment benefits would be cut off. Her income would be returning to what it had been prior to Covid.

Something had to give. If they were already barely getting by, how could they possibly stay afloat on even less? Maurice thought he should start delivering food again for Uber Eats; Natalia said she'd most certainly lose her shit if she was left alone with the kids all day and night. She pointed out that after their rent and car payment, their largest expense was groceries. Going on food stamps, she said, would free up several hundred dollars a month. Yet Maurice objected to the idea. Food stamps were his childhood. It wasn't how things were supposed to be here in Atlanta; this was where they'd made a fresh start. "You're being irrational," Natalia said. He knew she was right. "Fine," he said. "We can sign up."

On the social services website, Natalia filled out a SNAP preapplication screener, which asked whether anyone in her household had a disability, what the family's total monthly income was, and how much they paid in rent. She then moved on to the application itself, and was stopped short by one of the very first questions.

"Are you homeless?" the application asked.

Its matter-of-fact directness startled Natalia, and she put the computer aside. She'd been asked that question only once before, during a phone conversation with Breanna, the co-worker who'd helped her the day of the panic attack. Although Maurice and Natalia still hadn't told their family in D.C. what had happened to them—they'd kept it hidden not just from their children but from everyone else as well—Natalia had chosen to confide in her friend, who was shocked at what had taken place. "So . . . y'all are homeless now?" Breanna asked. Natalia hesitated before responding. "We try to be impeccable with our words," she said, "and that's a title we really don't want to put on ourselves."

But maybe it was time, Natalia thought, to quit pretending. Returning to the application, she clicked "Yes."

PART THREE

Possibility

15

LaQuana Alexander eased her ailing beige sedan past Efficiency's busted security gate, waving at a cluster of young men hanging out nearby. They stared blankly back at her. It was a Saturday morning in early May, and LaQuana—or LA Pink, as she was known—had set aside the next several hours to give away food and clothing at the hotel. Efficiency's residents were accustomed to such activities: a few area churches had begun making sporadic visits to the extended-stays lining Candler Road, dropping off nonperishables and sack lunches for the kids. But the residents had never met anybody like LA Pink. Her car was so weighted down with plastic bags full of clothes and shoes and other accessories that its rear tires were barely visible from behind. Strangers often assumed that she was living out of the sagging vehicle, and now, as she parked near the rental office, it was easy to mistake her for someone in search of a room.

"Hey hey! How's everyone feeling today?" she greeted the people eyeing her, relishing their surprise at her tone of playful familiarity. She introduced herself, and there was a moment of awkwardness verging on hostility as they sized her up: a youthful-looking Black woman in her midforties, covered in tattoos from neck to ankles and sporting a neon pink mohawk, pink yoga pants, black Crocs, a large, overstuffed fanny pack, and a black T-shirt with the words THE COMMUNITY BOUTIQUE WITH LA PINK: EMPOWERING DIGNITY THROUGH FASHION emblazoned in hot pink across the front of it. On the back of the shirt it read PINK DIAMONDS ALWAYS SHINING. In lieu of a protective mask, she wore a handmade face shield bedecked with pink and purple sequins. A repurposed school bus driven by her friend, stacked top to bottom with cardboard boxes of groceries, pulled into the space beside hers. "Doin' fine," one of the men cautiously replied.

This was Pink's first foray into the world of Atlanta's extended-stay hotels. Born in Lamesa, Texas, and raised in Denver, she'd relocated to Atlanta in her early thirties. She quickly launched her own business, a custom jewelry line called Creative Creations. But the venture failed to take off, and when a toxic roommate situation resulted in the loss of her apartment, she ended up with little money and nowhere to live. Things got so dire that, for a brief period, she resorted to sleeping in an abandoned building. "That was a divine blessing, to have to go through that," she would later say.

It was during this time of instability that she started befriending the men and women she was meeting on the streets. Characteristically, her attention zeroed in on the donated clothes many of them were wearing. The items they'd received at local charities and clothing closets, she discovered, were essentially garbage, "nasty, raggedy" castoffs that only deepened their humiliation. The assumption seemed to be that unhoused people didn't care about their appearance and needed to be grateful for what others gave them. Pink's own conviction was that how you dressed reflected not just who you were but who you might become. Giving someone rags—or, alternatively, stylish, high-quality apparel—could be a self-fulfilling prophecy. And so, shortly after she managed to secure an apartment for herself, she set about soliciting new and lightly used clothing from retail stores, acquaintances in the fashion industry, and parishioners at wealthy churches, storing the garments in the warehouse of a West Side food bank. Soon she was spending her weekends at Woodruff Park or the tent encampments around Gateway Center, and the Community Boutique was born.

Pink's extreme empathy, preternatural energy, and unwavering belief that even the most hopeless circumstances were redeemable gradually earned her a reputation as somebody who could be counted on to be there no matter what. She was the person who would come through—with dinner, with tampons, with bail money or simply a prayer and a hug—when no one else would. "I'll meet you where you're at," she liked to say, "but I've gotta take you where I'm going."

She refused to be labeled: social worker, activist, humanitarian, evangelist, therapist—Pink was all and none of these things. She enjoyed defying expectations. A passionate, Spirit-filled follower of Christ (*"not* a 'Christian'"), she'd stopped attending church and loudly proclaimed her disdain for holidays like Christmas ("a pagan invention"); a fierce advocate for social and racial justice, she mostly avoided protests—although she had taken part in a handful of demonstrations against police violence over the years. In her work, she was unfazed by the volatile, sometimes aggressive behavior of those she served. Her adult son in Denver had long battled drug addiction, and Pink herself had spent time in jail and been involved with gangs when she was younger, so she was no stranger to such struggles. And though her charisma and dedication attracted a broad array of collaborators and donors, whose financial support she now relied on, her desire for autonomy remained steadfast. So strong was her commitment to independence that when a given agency or nonprofit inevitably offered to bring her on as a paid staff member, she always turned them down. Friends cautioned Pink against overextending herself, concerned that her tenacity and lack of boundaries, her radical availability, would prove unsustainable. But she said this was the job she had been called to do.

Within minutes of arriving at Efficiency, Pink was enlisting a motley group of residents to assist her. She coaxed a retired mechanic named Davis into putting down his tall boy in order to help Nikki, her friend with the bus, set up card tables for displaying sneakers and dress shoes. A girl in cutoff pants and with tightly cornrowed hair, who at first had been standoffish toward Pink, was soon going around collecting people's clothing sizes; the girl's next-door neighbor, a very sociable, very muscular Samoan woman who called herself Tony Montana, after the protagonist of *Scarface,* was trying, unsuccessfully, to get everyone to form a line.

Already, Pink had casually disrupted the hotel's tacit social order.

One of the guys she'd put to work was Turbo, whose real name, though hardly anyone knew it, was Christopher. A developmentally disabled, illiterate twenty-four-year-old, Turbo had been hanging around the extended-stay since his release from prison, sleeping wherever he could: in the trash-strewn breezeway, on an upstairs landing, sometimes in an abandoned room. People frequently made fun of him for his body odor and unkempt hair. Now Pink had him knocking on doors, asking who needed food and running back to the bus to grab boxes for older residents unable to get one themselves.

Meanwhile, a gaggle of small kids were enthusiastically taking orders from Pink, who was telling them to sweep up cigarette butts, retrieve belts and purses out of bags—anything to make them feel included. Pink was especially taken with Mason and his five siblings, the youngest of whom, infant Kayla, kept trying to eat Pink's radiant mohawk. Glancing up at the children's hotel room window, she saw an outward-facing poster that read WITH MOM ALL THINGS ARE POSSIBLE. Pink looked at the children's mother, Christina, and said, "Oooh, I *love* that!" Christina flashed a rare smile.

Eventually Celeste, who had been resting all morning, came outside to see what was happening. Although she thanked Pink for being there, she seemed to bristle at the arrival of another strong personality. Hanging back, she coolly offered to lend a hand if Pink needed help.

It wasn't long before the parking lot had been transformed into something between a block party and a fashion show. Women disappeared into their rooms to try on shirts and blouses and fancy platform shoes, emerging with a twirl to whistles and catcalls. One guy opened the doors of his Charger to allow its bass-heavy sound system to reverberate across the property. Another man in a tank top and sagging shorts was giving ten-dollar haircuts, a cigarette in one hand and a pair of clippers in the other. When LeAnn, the assistant manager, poked her head out of the office, Pink invited her to join them. "We don't discriminate!" she exclaimed. Fifteen minutes later, LeAnn left with new jeans and shoes. Even Celeste was getting in on the action, joking that any pants bigger than an "extra-extra-extra small" would be too baggy for her increasingly gaunt frame.

Pink was in her element. She hated the notion of "charity," so it was important that the day bear no resemblance to a charity event. This was accomplished, in large part, through the sheer force of her presence. She had a way of putting people instantly at ease, of creating a "we're in this together" sense of solidarity, while at the same time refusing, as she often put it, to "cosign people's bullshit"—refusing, in other words, to validate the stories they'd told themselves, to grant them the pity or victimhood they sometimes sought. "We're kings and queens," she would say, "the sons and daughters of the Most High."

It was this orientation that determined not just the quality of the clothes she provided but the sort of food she gave away. Pink had seen plenty of food pantries distributing expired or even moldy products, and she made a point of offering only items that she herself would want to eat. Those she worked with became not her "clients" but her friends, for better or worse. In the absence of nearby family or romantic relationships—she hadn't dated anyone in twenty-six years, since her son was born—the vast network of people she served and partnered with made up the whole of her social world. It was not unusual for her to invite someone (never a man) to stay at her apartment in Douglasville, and she freely gave people her phone number, encouraging them to call at any hour. For those inured to the condescending, even indifferent demeanor of caseworkers, Pink's openness and generosity often created an immediate bond. Nothing felt more enlivening to her than these moments of connection—and there were a number of such moments that day at Efficiency.

And yet, as the afternoon went on, something troubled Pink. In late February, she had been sorting through clothes at Fountain of Hope, the food bank that had come to function as a home base for her boutique, when a mother and her young daughter showed up to get a free bag of groceries. Pink spotted them in line and walked over to say hello.

"How you doin'," the woman said, shaking Pink's outstretched hand.

"I'm beyond excellent. My name's LA Pink."

"I'm Michelle. This is Skye."

Pink had never heard of Efficiency Lodge, and she was taken aback by Michelle's description of the hotel: the awful living conditions, the constant threat of being locked out. When Michelle mentioned the school buses that arrived each morning to pick up the many children who lived there, Pink shook her head in disbelief. "That's insane," she said. It hadn't occurred to her that the run-down, featureless extended-stays she'd been driving by every day were filled with families. These were people, according to Michelle, who had jobs, often more than one, but still lacked housing—a kind of homelessness previously unknown to Pink. She and Michelle exchanged numbers, and Pink promised to visit them at the hotel as soon as possible.

Then the pandemic hit, and Pink's work suddenly took on a new urgency. For months, she had been preparing to open a version of the Community Boutique at Frederick Douglass High School; the plan, which she'd come up with in collaboration with the school's social worker, was to offer low-income students a relaxed, stigma-free environment to "shop" for clothes during lunch and after school. (Pink had insisted on installing speakers in the boutique, convinced that streaming rap and R&B would make the students feel more at ease.) When Covid erupted and the school shut down, she swiftly pivoted to emergency food distribution, coordinating with Atlanta Public Schools to get seven-day meal kits to needy households in the district and going door to door in Bankhead and Grove Park, delivering food boxes to seniors on fixed incomes.

Throughout this time, she kept in regular contact with Michelle. Over a series of long, intimate phone conversations, Michelle told Pink about aspects of her life—early childhood traumas, her history of abuse at the hands of her ex-husband—that she rarely divulged. There was an affinity, a closeness between the two of them, and they began calling each other "Sis." But in the weeks after the SoulShine job fell through, Pink could tell that Michelle was sinking into "something dark," as Pink described it. Michelle told her that she'd at last dropped out of her online social work program, and on the phone Pink could hear her snapping angrily at Skye and DJ with greater frequency. Her occasionally slurred speech made Pink wonder if she was high or drunk, but Michelle claimed it was merely a lack of sleep, that she was beside herself with fatigue.

Finally, about a week before Pink's first visit to Efficiency, she called Michelle and got a message that her number was no longer in service. Pink considered driving to the hotel to check on her, but being a one-woman crisis response team meant that there was always something more urgent requiring her attention. She told herself that she'd catch up with Michelle at Efficiency the following weekend. But so far there had been no sign of her.

Earlier in the day, Pink had asked a group of residents, including Christina and Celeste, if they happened to know Michelle. Nobody did. Celeste told Pink that if anyone had information about her friend, it would be Travis, the hotel's maintenance guy. Celeste called him over—Travis, too, was in the process of picking out a new wardrobe—and he quickly recognized Pink's description of Michelle. On a recent weeknight, he told her, police had showed up at the hotel after an ugly fight in room 137. Travis hadn't interacted with the room's occupants, he said, but the next day he was mad as hell at the damage they'd inflicted. Their bathroom door had been knocked off its hinges, and a hole had been punched through the wall.

"But what happened to the family?" Pink asked.

"Lisa put them out."

THAT EVENING, Pink drove around the area looking for Michelle. She stopped at gas stations and fast-food places, hoping that Michelle and her kids had managed to get into a different hotel. In her line of work, people's phones, nearly all of them prepaid or on pay-as-you-go plans, were constantly being disconnected. To lose phone communication was, in many cases, to lose the person. Pink dealt with this abrupt separation by entrusting their fate to God, reminding herself of the hubris of presuming that it was *her* unique support or intervention that could decide anybody's future. "God's got 'em" was among her oft-repeated axioms. But this situation felt different, not least because a child was involved. She continued searching, to no avail.

A couple of days later, Pink received a message on Facebook. It was from Michelle. She and Skye had been sleeping outside, the message said, and they were scared and hungry. They were in the parking lot of Gulf American Inns, an extended-stay down the road from Efficiency.

When Pink got there it was almost dark. It had been more than two months since she'd seen Michelle, and as Michelle and Skye approached her car, each of them wearing a backpack, Pink was stunned at Michelle's appearance. Her hair and clothes were noticeably unwashed, and she seemed to have lost at least fifteen or twenty pounds. Her eyes were drained of all vitality.

Michelle crumbled in Pink's embrace. "It's okay," said Pink. "You're okay." Although she hardly ever cried, Pink almost broke down, too, at the sight of tiny Skye standing subdued at her mother's side. Michelle said that her daughter had been having nightmares lately. "Let's get you some dinner," Pink said.

Experts often talk as if there are discrete types of homeless Americans. It is widely assumed, for instance, that a family dealing with "episodic" homelessness has stumbled into their predicament for economic reasons (job loss, an eviction), whereas "unsheltered" or "chronically homeless" individuals are believed to be in that position because of mental health issues, a disability, or substance use. Yet Pink had witnessed, again and again, how such things could become a *by-product* of homelessness rather than causing it. Michelle's experience demonstrated how rapidly one variant of homelessness could morph into another—in other words, how porous all those ostensibly firm distinctions could be. The "hidden homeless" could very quickly find themselves on the street; today's worker, given enough adversity, might lose their job and spiral into addiction or mental illness. Pink had to remind herself that only recently the woman walking toward her had been in school and renting her own apartment. Homelessness, seen in this light, was never a fixed state or a static condition. It was a point along a spectrum: in a motel today, on a couch tomorrow, possibly in a tent a year from now.

Between bites of a chicken sandwich outside Popeyes, Michelle recounted the events of the last several days. Shortly after her phone was cut off, she told Pink, her EBT card had stopped working as well. She thought maybe she'd been reported for selling her food stamps, which could cause her to permanently lose the benefit or even face arrest. Broke and unable to feed her kids, she withdrew further into herself. "I didn't want to talk to nobody, see nobody. I just wanted to disappear," she said.

Her last hope of paying her growing rent balance at the hotel and maybe having a bit of money in reserve was the stimulus check that, according to the IRS's Get My Payment website, seemed not to have been mailed yet; when she'd entered her Social Security number, it said "Payment Status Not Available." Pink had heard the same thing from several people at Efficiency. While those with direct deposit, such as Pink, had received their stimulus payment weeks earlier, roughly seven million "unbanked" households—and up to ten million more who hadn't used direct deposit to receive their most recent tax refund—were forced to wait for a paper check to show up at their last known address. There were media reports that it could take another month or longer for the first stimulus checks to reach this largely low-income, overwhelmingly Black and Hispanic segment of the population.

Michelle said that she and DJ had been at each other's throats since the pandemic started. Confined to their room, the two of them had been bickering nonstop. She told Pink that DJ was a good kid but had an awful temper, and that he'd kept forgetting that *she* was the parent, that they weren't equals. "He thinks he can criticize me, disrespect me all he wants," she said. Their arguments had grown worse and worse, until one night, according to Michelle, DJ "went berserk." The cops arrived, and Lisa, seeing the damage to their room, ordered them off the property by the next morning.

It was clear that Michelle didn't want to dwell on the details of what happened after they left Efficiency. She said that DJ had gone to stay with Regina, Michelle's disabled elderly aunt, whom Danielle was also now living with. "She told him Skye and I couldn't come," Michelle said bitterly. She spent the day asking for money at the Chevron station beside Gulf American, but she didn't collect enough to pay for a night at the hotel. So she and Skye found a secluded corner of the hotel parking lot and remained there until the sun came up. At some point, a man staying at the hotel told her that she and Skye could sleep in his car, and this was where they spent a couple of restless nights, with Michelle wondering whether the man could be trusted. When he checked out of his room, she and Skye were back outside. Then a woman allowed Michelle to use her phone, but a call to 211, the United Way helpline, yielded nothing. "They said there were no shelter beds in DeKalb, Fulton, *or* Gwinnett, and that the only thing they could suggest was that I move in with relatives or ask a church to let us sleep in their building."

That was what it took for Michelle to finally send the Facebook message to Pink.

As she listened to Michelle, Pink registered the elements of her story that didn't add up. Why would DJ explode unprovoked? Why didn't Michelle borrow a phone and reach out to Pink much sooner? Why would her aunt allow DJ and Danielle to come stay with her but not Skye and Michelle? Only later, when Pink spoke to DJ, did a fuller picture emerge. He said his mom's drinking had been getting worse in recent weeks, and that on the night the police were called, she had been completely drunk. When he'd made a comment about her throwing money away on beer—"And I admit," he said, "I used some harsh language"—Michelle began cursing and screaming at him. He'd tried to keep his cool, he said, but then she'd told him that he was just like his father, the man who had kicked and punched Michelle while DJ, a young boy, looked on helplessly. "I lost it," DJ said.

Pink decided to put her questions aside, at least for now. Her first priority was finding a safe place for Michelle and Skye to go. She had no idea where that would be; if necessary, she'd take them to her own apartment. Pink's dream was to someday have a big house where people in these sorts of situations could stay as long as they needed. But in the meantime, she would have to improvise.

She told Michelle and Skye not to worry. They weren't alone anymore.

16

When the pandemic struck, Britt turned her back porch at Gladstone into a hair salon. A self-taught stylist, she had been doing hair for several years, though rarely for pay. In a family full of girls and women, hairdressing was a useful talent, and Britt had discovered that she had a knack for it. People had long encouraged her to capitalize on this gift: to go to cosmetology school or, at the very least, to showcase her abilities on a dedicated Instagram page. Britt had always brushed them off. But after she lost her job in Grady Hospital's food services department during a round of Covid-related layoffs, finding new ways to earn money became a necessity. She put the word out among her relatives and friends and neighbors that she was available to handle any of their styling needs, for a fraction of what they would be charged at other places. It didn't hurt that all those other places were now closed. Since her $550 a month rent was so affordable, she figured that she could take care of it with just a few four- or five-hour appointments each week. And she was right: by May, she was doing enough box braids and twists and soft locs to cover not only the rent but her other expenses too.

Everyone was complaining about being stuck at home, but Britt actually enjoyed these days in the apartment. Life had become more predictable; things felt manageable, contained, in the best sense of the word—like at QLS, but without the constant hustle and, later, the many houseguests. She shuddered to imagine trying to weather the pandemic without a place of her own. Not only was she using the apartment to generate income—she was immensely proud of this modest venture—but with the world seeming to come unglued, her home had become a refuge. "I'm safe, *we're* safe," she would sometimes tell herself after reading the news, and she believed it. Another couple hundred square feet in the apartment would have been nice. And a dishwasher. And maybe a TV she could watch in bed. And a second bedroom, so her children wouldn't have to sleep in the living room. Yet one major unforeseen perk of her garden-style unit was the big expanse of grass lying just beyond her front door. Desiree and Kyrie could play with the neighbor kids to their heart's content, and invariably, no matter the time of day, there would be adults outside keeping an eye on them.

Gladstone was like that: a place where people usually looked out for each other. Pretty much everybody knew everybody else's business. When a nonprofit showed up to distribute groceries, neighbors could point them to the unit where the elderly stroke survivor lived alone; they could tell you whose lights had been disconnected, or whose cousin had overdosed, or whose grandmother had passed away. If there was an emergency, there was always someone you could call. It was no paradise: there were break-ins and instances of domestic violence, and on one occasion Cindy, the leasing manager, had to lock herself in the office when a man threatened her with a knife. But in an age of impersonal apartment towers, Gladstone was something of an anomaly. Partly this was because a large contingent of those who had once lived at East Lake Meadows and Bowen Homes now resided at the complex, thanks to Yateshia. Britt was surprised, upon moving in, at the number of men and women she recognized from years earlier. On a Sunday morning before the pandemic, she and the kids had walked across the street to visit Church of Atlanta Lighthouse, the congregation she had attended growing up. The church was full of Gladstone tenants.

Most of Britt's neighbors were in a position similar to hers: without Gladstone, they might not have had a place to live. Just a couple of years earlier, in 2018, an article had appeared in *The Guardian* about the loss of low-income housing in the city: "Nowhere for People to Go: Who

Will Survive the Gentrification of Atlanta?" Nearly all of Gladstone residents were classified as "extremely low-income," defined by HUD as earning less than 30 percent of the area median income, or AMI, which in Atlanta for a family of three was about $27,000 a year. The many seniors at the complex subsisting on Social Security or disability payments had incomes that fell far below this threshold. Those earning wages at or slightly above the federal minimum wage had it even worse: working full-time at minimum wage amounted to a gross income of $15,080. Gladstone offered these tenants a degree of stability that was growing rare in Atlanta, at least for people like them. It had become known as a place where your rent wouldn't drastically increase from one year to the next—and where, unless you did something stupid, like throw parties that got the cops called out or use your unit to engage in illegal activities, you could be relatively assured of your lease being renewed. You wouldn't be living in luxury, far from it. But you would have a home with a rent you could afford.

How did a place like Gladstone still exist in Atlanta? Part of the answer had to do with its reputation as a "tax credit" complex. In 1996, the property's owner, Grant Park Homes, had been awarded a Low-Income Housing Tax Credit (LIHTC) to renovate the forty-seven-year-old buildings. Subsidizing the acquisition, construction, and rehabilitation of apartments for lower-income families and individuals, LIHTC (often pronounced "lie-tech") was the nation's largest program for the production of affordable housing. Much like Section 8 vouchers—the other federal program intended to support low-income tenants—LIHTC was born of a political and ideological opposition to public housing. Instead of fixing the chronic underinvestment in public housing that had led projects to deteriorate, the federal government tried to encourage the private sector to step in. The culmination of these efforts, LIHTC was a last-minute addition to President Reagan's Tax Reform Act of 1986, famous for slashing the tax rate on the wealthy. No longer would the government act as a direct party in the construction and maintenance of low-income apartments. As a public-private partnership, LIHTC introduced a model whereby the federal government was now only *indirectly* involved. The program quickly took off. It gained bipartisan approval, and before long LIHTC was helping to finance the overwhelming majority of affordable housing in the United States.

From the beginning, housing advocates have pointed to various flaws in the LIHTC model, but the biggest is that the affordability is temporary. Federal law stipulates that a LIHTC property maintain its rent restrictions for a period of thirty years, at which point its owner can do whatever they wish with the property: they can sell it, redevelop it, or convert it to market-rate rents. In 2018, a study by the National Low Income Housing Coalition sounded the alarm on this issue. Affordable housing in America, already in perilously short supply, was a ticking time bomb: roughly 25 percent of all current LIHTC units were set to reach the thirty-year mark between 2020 and 2029. Atlanta's forecast was particularly grim. A monthly rent of $600 is the maximum amount considered affordable for households bringing in $24,000 a year, and in Atlanta, the number of such units was dropping significantly; since 2012, the city's low-income housing stock had declined by about 5 percent each year, a trend that was expected to accelerate over the next decade. The properties most at risk of converting to market-rate housing were those either owned by for-profit entities (as opposed to non-profit or "mission-driven" owners) or located in high-desirability areas.

Gladstone was both. It's what made the complex so unique: here were apartments that were truly affordable for the city's seniors and low-wage workers and people with disabilities, in a neighborhood whose property values were continuing to soar. To be sure, it was unlikely to last forever. A BeltLine report had noted that Gladstone was the largest remaining low-income housing development within close proximity to the trail. The report recommended "interventions" to preserve the complex's below-market rents, since keeping existing properties affordable, as difficult as that could be, was far more economical—and politically viable—than attempting to build new low-income housing.

But for the time being, Gladstone's residents could stay where they were. According to the BeltLine report, the complex's LIHTC status wasn't set to expire until 2025. In Atlanta, knowing your housing would be secure for another half decade was no small thing.

■

TOWARD THE END OF MAY, Britt was fixing lunch when she noticed that her mom had been trying to call her. Then came the text. Cass and Aaliyah, oil and water, had just had a big falling-out. This was no surprise: Aaliyah's apartment had become a pressure cooker. Cass's hours at Twelve Hotel had been steadily reduced because of the pandemic, and then, a few weeks earlier, she was finally laid off. Aaliyah's boyfriend had also lost his job. With Britt's brother Devin in the mix as well, life at the apartment had turned into a bad reality TV show. There was incessant bickering about the most trivial matters—whose fault it was that the toilet paper hadn't been replaced, whose turn it was to take out the trash. Four strong-willed, stubborn, exceedingly bored adults were confined to a one-bedroom unit. Now there had been a blowup, and Cass needed somewhere to go. Could she stay with Britt for a little while?

Britt groaned when she read the message. She had been here before, and she had reason to worry. Her mom wasn't easy to live with. Most of Cass's immediate family could tolerate her short temper and foul moods only in small doses, even though they sympathized with the painful turn her life had taken years earlier.

Born in 1976, Cass and her sisters spent the first few years of their lives shuttling between their mother, Theresa, who by the time Cass was seven had fallen prey to the city's burgeoning crack epidemic, and their grandmother. It was while staying at East Lake Meadows with Granny that Cass and Yateshia had become close friends. Yateshia, too, had been sent to stay with her grandmother; she, too, had a mom struggling with addiction. But unlike Cass, Yateshia's family was big and sprawling. Lois Mae Evans, Yateshia's grandmother, had nine children, and as many as eighteen people had been living in her five-bedroom unit at one point. The first time Yateshia invited Cass over, she quietly explained why her grandma had become so withdrawn. The year before, Lois's son, Alfred, who was thirteen, had gone missing. He was later discovered strangled to death in a vacant lot. He was the first victim in what would come to be known as the Atlanta Child Murders, which saw a total of twenty-nine children and youth, all of them Black and from the city's poorest neighborhoods, kidnapped and killed between 1979 and 1981. Long after his body was identified, Lois would sit for several hours a day beside her living room window, looking expectantly toward the sidewalk, saying her boy would be arriving home soon.

Throughout her childhood and teenage years at the housing project, Cass tried to keep her head down, mostly avoiding the ubiquitous drugs and gangs. But the world of East Lake Meadows, while familiar, was also stifling, and when, in the summer of 1992, an opportunity arose to leave Atlanta, she jumped at it. She had just graduated from high school, and Theresa was preparing to relocate to Cleveland with her boyfriend, who had family in Ohio. Cass decided to join them. She enrolled in Job Corps and, before long, met Alonzo Wilkinson, a fellow student. Four months later she was pregnant. She was eighteen, the same age Theresa had been when she'd had Cass. In the weeks after Britt was born, Cass considered moving with Alonzo to his hometown of Milwaukee, but in the end she opted to return to her "safe haven," as she referred to it: Granny's apartment at East Lake Meadows. "I can't say I was 'disappointed' to be on my own with Britt," Cass recalled, "because I never really expected a man to look out for us. It was, like, a foreign concept to me."

Her relationship with Eric Evans, Lois's youngest son, would help remedy that. Although he was Yateshia's uncle, he was just a couple of years older than her, and Cass had long had a crush on him. To her surprise, the feeling was mutual. More surprisingly, he treated Britt as if she was his biological daughter, not only showering her with affection but paying for her diapers and clothes and baby food. In 1996, with conditions at East Lake Meadows fast deteriorating, the couple had their first child and were determined to make a home together. Cass, Eric, Britt, and Devin, along with Yateshia and a host of others from East Lake Meadows, were eventually approved for a transfer to Bowen Homes, a housing project off Bankhead Highway.

Eric worked for the city doing road construction while Cass found a clerical job at the police department. She made it a point to tell people that although some of her female co-workers had been hired on as part of a welfare reform program, which compelled recipients of public assistance to enter the labor force, she had landed the job before them. "Nobody ever had to force me to work," she would say, joking that the only time she *hadn't* worked was in the days immediately following giving birth to her kids. These kids now included another son and daughter, Aaliyah and Josiah. Cass and Eric took pride in being able to offer them the sort of upbringing they had never known themselves. Evidence of their children's success accumulated on the living room wall, in the form of medals and trophies and honor roll certificates.

When Britt was thirteen, Cass discovered that Eric had been cheating on her. It wasn't so much the infidelity that angered her as his disrespect. She accused him of not even trying to hide the affair. Eric began looking for his own place; it would be better for everyone, he told the kids, if he and their mom lived apart. Cass was devastated. To make matters worse, she was informed by her boss that the city was making staffing cuts across a number of departments and that she would soon be out of a job. Between the layoff and the sudden loss of Eric's income, she missed one month's rent, then another and another. Yateshia offered to lend her money, but Cass refused, insisting that she had the situation under control. The family lost their apartment before the year was out—just a few months before Bowen Homes, slated for demolition, announced that a number of residents (including Yateshia) would be receiving Section 8 vouchers to move elsewhere.

Cass and the children started bouncing around from place to place, dependent on—and gradually exhausting—the generosity of friends and relatives with apartments. At the time, moving in with Granny at The Villages of East Lake was not an option; in contrast to the leniency that had prevailed at East Lake Meadows, those managing the mixed-income development that replaced it had made it clear that "off-lease" interlopers would not be tolerated. Many nights were spent at seedy motels on Fulton Industrial Boulevard. Again and again the kids were forced to switch schools—Britt would attend four different schools over the same number of years—and the family rarely knew where they'd be living from one week to the next.

Since splitting up, Eric had been pleading with Cass to allow the kids to come stay with him and his girlfriend. At last, after two years, Cass relented. But Britt, she said, would remain with her. It was a decision she would come to bitterly regret. The two of them went to stay with Trisha and her boyfriend. Several months later, when Trisha broke up with him and he moved out, Britt finally told her mom what had happened to her: he had been sexually abusing her for months. She was fifteen years old. When Cass found out, she was beside herself, screaming and promising to kill him. She and Britt moved to a motel.

Those who had known Cass from an early age were mystified by her inability to find her footing. She continued to work, taking whatever minimum-wage, often physically demanding job she could get. But she rarely kept a job for more than a few months. She seemed listless, adrift. To the recurring, usually impatient question "So what's your plan?" she would become defensive, attributing her inertia to an array of vague, undiagnosed health problems. Sometimes, however, she acknowledged a harder reality: that something inside of her had died when Eric left.

Yet she still took an active role in her children's lives and educations. She was a vigorous presence at PTA meetings ("I was always speaking up, making a fuss," she recalled), and somehow, despite the family's tumultuous circumstances, she ensured that the kids stayed on top of their schoolwork. Cass also encouraged them to take part in extracurricular activities like sports and ROTC, shuttling them to an endless stream of practices and events in the barely drivable car her father had given to her before he passed away. Later, when Josiah was a star quarterback at Mays High School, Cass had T-shirts made with a portrait of him posing in his jersey. She wore the shirt to every game, both home and away.

At Britt's high school graduation, a small crowd of relatives gathered in the bleachers to cheer her on. But nobody cheered louder than Cass when Britt's name rang out over the PA. Not only had Britt managed to graduate, but she'd been admitted to Alabama A&M, a historically Black university in Huntsville. Her tuition would be paid by the I Have a Dream Foundation, whose mentorship program was designed to "empower children in under-resourced communities" to "have an opportunity to earn a college degree and fully capitalize on their talents, aspirations, and dreams of fulfilling careers and productive global citizenship." Britt had been part of the program since the second grade. During the drive to Huntsville, Granny and Cass told Britt what a big deal it was that she'd gotten into college. Cass's sister, Kimi, who went to Valdosta State, was the only other family member who had achieved this milestone. Britt planned on majoring in early childhood education.

No sooner had Britt settled into her dorm room, though, than she grew horribly nauseous. Before she knew it, she was staring at two bold pink lines on a home pregnancy test. For years, the women in Britt's life had been cautioning her against unprotected sex; now, just a couple of months after losing her virginity to Javon, the football player she had started dating as a junior, she was struggling to fathom what it would mean to have a baby. By fall break of her first semester, she had taken a Greyhound back to Atlanta, yearning to be near family, to give them the news in person. Cass's reaction was surprising. "You worked so hard to make it to college," she told Britt. "Please don't throw this away." She gently urged Britt to consider an abortion. Britt was so hurt by the suggestion that she refused to speak to Cass for several weeks.

Britt never returned to Alabama. When she gave birth to Desiree in the spring of 2013, she was living temporarily with Javon's mom and older sister. Javon was in Mississippi, playing football at Hinds Community College. Not long after the delivery, Britt realized that one of the things she'd left behind in her dorm room was her graduation gift from Granny, a beautiful hand-stitched quilt. Britt felt terrible for having forgotten it. But, holding Desiree, she tried to focus her thoughts on what she had gained, not on what she had lost.

That summer, Cass proposed that she and Britt get a place together. She had found an apartment that seemed promising, located in a complex close to the Steak n' Shake where she'd just started working. Britt would stay home with the baby, she said, and would be responsible for keeping the fridge stocked (using her food stamps) and covering their utility bills (using the money Javon was still sending her). Cass would pay the rent. There was only one issue: the lease needed to be in Britt's name, because she had a clean rental history. Cass's application had been denied.

After nine months in the apartment, Cass switched jobs. An administrative delay caused her to start the new position later than expected, and the long gap between paychecks led her to fall behind on rent. When Cass finally got paid, it was too little too late. The eviction that ensued felt just as shocking and shameful as her first eviction from Bowen Homes. Except this time, the black mark was on her daughter's record. It was Britt's credit that would be ruined by the eviction.

Over the next five years, because of her poor credit, Britt was turned down for every apartment she applied for. Then came the voucher. After leaving QLS and losing the voucher, she had again become convinced that no landlord would ever rent to her. Gladstone had given her one more chance.

"SURE," BRITT SAID in response to Cass's request to come stay with her at Gladstone. "That's fine." She couldn't bring herself to say no to her mother. "I mean, I love my mama to death," Britt told her friend Yasmine. "But it's getting to the point where I wanna be like, 'Please, just let me have my own space.'"

Their eviction in 2015 had marked a turning point in their relationship. Cass had always told Britt, "Baby, you can't bring everyone to the top with you," but Britt had begun to wonder if this included her mother. As she put it to Yasmine, "I feel like I need to say, 'Mama, you can't go with me, you've gotta work out your own shit.'" Cass assumed her presence in the apartment would be a relief to Britt, since she'd be able to help with Desiree and Kyrie; Britt had mentioned wanting to start driving for Instacart to bring in extra money—Cass could watch the kids while she was gone. Britt didn't see it that way. But she held her tongue.

Late that night, Cass rode the bus to Gladstone, arriving at Britt's apartment with a backpack and suitcase. Britt had cleared Desiree and Kyrie's things out of the living room to make space for her mom's air mattress. After greeting Cass with a hug and showing her around, Britt said good night and went into her bedroom, where the kids were already fast asleep.

On the first day of June, Kara and her kids left their downtown hotel and walked to a nearby parking garage. It was eight-thirty on a Monday morning, and Peachtree Street was all but deserted. Evidence of the previous night's turmoil was everywhere. Little pieces of glass flecked the sidewalk. Next door to the hotel, Wilbourn Sisters Designs had replaced its busted-out windows with sheets of plywood. WE ARE BLACK OWNED. WE ARE HURT! PLEASE STOP, was spray-painted across the wood. A digital billboard read: CITY OF ATLANTA CURFEW CONTINUES. 9PM TO SUNRISE.

Across the country, in more than 140 cities large and small, the streets had exploded in recent days. The demonstrations following the gruesome murder of George Floyd at the hands of Minneapolis police were stunning in their breadth and scale and ferocity. People were protesting not only decades of racist and unrestrained police violence but the degradations and disparities that, for many Black Americans, had come to define everyday life. Minneapolis's Third Precinct police station went up in flames, luxury stores in New York and Chicago and LA were pillaged and vandalized, and in Fayetteville, North Carolina, Floyd's place of birth, crowds set fire to the historic Market House, where enslaved people had been bought and sold. State leaders deployed some seventeen thousand National Guard troops to subdue the uprising; within days, more than ten thousand people had been arrested nationwide. Atlanta witnessed one of the earliest eruptions of protest. At an emergency news conference, Mayor Keisha Lance Bottoms accused rioters of "disgracing" Atlanta. "This city don't deserve this," said rapper and city luminary T.I., who spoke alongside the mayor. "This is Wakanda. It is sacred, it must be protected."

Kara had watched and rewatched the bystander video of Floyd's killing, of that cop kneeling on his neck for nearly nine minutes. What got her were his words, his voice—"I can't breathe," and then "Mama! Mama . . . I'm through!"—even though his mother had been dead for two years. And the lies that followed: the department's claim that Floyd had resisted arrest, that he'd died after a "medical incident." Kara felt this brutality and deceit in a personal, visceral way, and she'd sympathized with the impulse to burn the whole country down. But the nightly protests were becoming an annoyance. And then, three days earlier, Vice President Mike Pence had been in Atlanta to attend the memorial service of Christian evangelist Ravi Zacharias, leading to the closure of numerous roads and two major interstates—and causing Kara to deliver several DoorDash orders egregiously late. Over the weekend, she'd worked fewer hours in order to get back to their room before dark. She wanted justice. She also needed to feed her kids.

In the parking garage, Kara loaded her groggy, hungry children into the Toyota. Settling behind the wheel, Kara was careful to remove their room key card from her jeans pocket, so as to avoid bending it. She worried that even the slightest infraction—eliciting a noise complaint from a neighboring room, having to request a new key card—could cause her to lose her current hotel room. About two weeks earlier, her car had broken down and its radiator needed to be replaced. This unanticipated expense led Kara to miss a week's rent, and she and the kids were forced to leave their room at HomeTowne Studios. They spent that night in the car, returning to the same QuikTrip they'd parked at the summer before. In the morning, while the kids ate breakfast outside a Burger King, Kara aimlessly scrolled her Facebook feed. One post caught her eye. It had been shared more than four thousand times.

"Are you facing a housing emergency due to Covid-19?" the post read. "If your landlord or mortgage holder is threatening your housing, we urge you to call us immediately. Now is not a time to feel ashamed of your struggle, it is a time to come together to protect human life during this unprecedented crisis." It went on to say that members of Housing Justice League were fielding calls: ready to answer questions, help identify assistance, and connect tenants with legal resources. At the end of the post was a phone number.

Like many residents, Kara had never heard of this Atlanta-based organization prior to stumbling upon the post. Housing Justice League was still relatively young—it had been founded in 2014—but the group's roots went back to the foreclosure crisis of the preceding decade. Predominantly Black neighborhoods in Fulton, DeKalb, and Clayton counties had been targeted by predatory subprime lenders, and so it was these neighborhoods that saw staggering foreclosure rates when residents were unable to repay their risky, high-cost mortgages. Witnessing a growing number of neighbors being forcibly removed from their homes ("The banks got bailed out, but our families are getting kicked out," went a slogan at the time), a group of Atlanta activists, many of them involved with a local offshoot of the Occupy movement, began organizing to prevent such seizures from taking place: protests were staged outside courthouses, foreclosed properties, apartment complexes, and the banks responsible for the ongoing disaster.

Occupy Our Homes Atlanta, as the activists called themselves, eventually became Housing Justice League (HJL). Reflected in this name change was a significant shift in orientation. With the recession quickly giving way, in Atlanta, to rampant gentrification, the group broadened its focus. They helped form tenant associations at more than a dozen low-income complexes, distributed eviction defense manuals, campaigned for stronger renter protections, and, as the group's membership base expanded, called attention to the myriad ways in which the "new Atlanta" was fueling an epidemic of housing precarity. With Research Action Cooperative, Housing Justice League published a galvanizing report titled "Beltlining: Gentrification, Broken Promises, and Hope on Atlanta's Southside" in 2017. The terrain of struggle had shifted. The organization's members and those they stood with were no longer dealing with the fallout of an economic downturn. They were fighting the effects of their city's renaissance.

In March, during the early weeks of the lockdown, it became apparent that Covid was only heightening the inequality and insecurity that had already been plaguing Atlanta. For HJL's members, mobilizing in support of the city's most vulnerable renters had never seemed so necessary, but collective organizing amid a rapidly spreading virus proved challenging. How to shelter in place while fighting on behalf of tenants at immediate risk of losing such shelter?

It was in response to this dilemma that the emergency hotline was born. By the time Kara came across HJL's Facebook post, roughly a hundred volunteers, some of them seasoned organizers and others with no prior experience with housing activism, were fielding a flood of calls nine hours a day, seven days a week. As the nation's unemployment numbers continued to soar and the patchy state-level protections that had kept people in their homes were on the verge of expiring, renters were on a precipice. This was true across the country, but in Georgia— one of just seven states that had never imposed even a partial moratorium on evictions—the outlook was especially bad. (A letter signed by more than 135 service organizations, religious groups, and elected officials urging Governor Brian Kemp to impose a statewide eviction pause was effectively ignored.) Although local courts were closed, Georgia landlords were able to electronically file dispossessory affidavits undeterred, creating a giant backlog of evictions that would be carried out once the courts reopened.

And then there were the landlords who did not wish to wait for the courts to open. Day after day, tenants from across the city called the hotline with reports of illegal lockouts, open intimidation, and attempts to coerce rent payment by cutting off utilities. These were renters who had lost their jobs, who were caring for children or loved ones, who were immunocompromised and afraid of venturing out; people whose stimulus checks had come and gone, whose rent had been paid down using credit cards and title loans and who still faced the threat of homelessness. Hotline volunteers, a number of whom were themselves precariously housed, saw the call center as a form of mutual aid, but instead of money or food what they were sharing was knowledge and sympathy and, crucially, solidarity.

When Kara called the hotline, she shared the story of what she and her kids had gone through and explained that, a year earlier, before their first stint in the car, she had reached out to several shelters. None had helped: they either hadn't called her back or she didn't qualify for assistance or they couldn't accommodate a family of five. But the hotline volunteer mentioned one nonprofit she hadn't heard of, a place called Nicholas House. A couple of hours later, Kara was on the phone with Carla Wells, a case manager with the agency.

Courteous and professional, she asked Kara a series of questions and then, to Kara's amazement—it was the point in the conversation when she expected to hear a noncommittal "We'll contact you if something opens up"—the case manager said she could get Kara into a hotel room that afternoon. "You mean . . ." Kara paused. "Y'all can help with the cost?"

"Actually," said Carla, "you won't have to spend any money at all. We should be able to cover you for at least a couple of weeks." Because of the pandemic, she explained, the federal government had temporarily loosened the rules surrounding housing assistance, allowing agencies like hers to move quickly and flexibly, getting support to families who desperately needed it.

Kara was barely listening. She felt lightheaded with relief. Later, when she and the kids arrived at the address Carla had given her, a Residence Inn by Marriott, they found themselves in the plush, marble-walled foyer of a "beautifully converted historic boutique property," as the hotel's online description put it. Muzak wafted through the otherwise silent lobby. "Don't you be touching anything," Kara told the children as the five of them approached the front desk.

Her admonition was unnecessary. The kids, taking in this strange environment, remained frozen at Kara's side. A smiling man with a neatly trimmed beard checked them in. He didn't mention this to Kara, but the hotel's nineteen floors of rooms—which normally were filled with tourists and conference attendees and business travelers—had been almost entirely empty since March. Indeed, the only hotels that had continued to thrive during the pandemic were dingy extended-stays such as the one Kara had just been evicted from. This Marriott, by contrast, had been running at close to zero occupancy, and its general manager had jumped at the chance to partner with Nicholas House when approached with the idea of placing families there. It was a win-win, the general manager had said.

After receiving her room key, Kara promised herself that she wouldn't squander this blessing. *Nope, not this time,* she thought. Their room was by far the nicest they'd ever stayed in.

Still, Kara was unable to let her guard down, refusing to cut back on her grueling delivery schedule. She encountered other families staying at the hotel, and her instinctive sense that there weren't enough re-sources to go around made her feel that she had to fight to maintain an edge. Now, on this first day of June, she was going to find out what was in store for her and the kids. She had an appointment with Carla Wells, who had told Kara that she had something exciting to share with her. Kara wondered if it was a job opportunity. Or maybe an apartment?

The meeting with her case manager was scheduled to begin at noon, so Kara decided to squeeze in a few hours of work. If she was lucky, she could make $40 or $50.

CARLA LOWERED HERSELF into a cushioned chair and arranged her things on the table in front of her: a thin stack of blue folders, a water bottle, her iPhone, a ballpoint pen, her eyeglasses case. She had arrived at the hotel's barren conference room ten minutes early, giving her a chance to steady herself and collect her thoughts ahead of an afternoon packed with client meetings. The events of the past week—Floyd's kill-ing, the mass demonstrations, the inordinately violent police response to this uprising—were weighing heavily on her. Over the course of her twenty-plus-year career, Carla had become known as a sort of gadfly, a thorn in the side of the social services establishment, because she called attention to the political and economic forces shaping the lives of those she worked with, pointing to the profoundly racialized character of the insecurity afflicting them. For her, the fact that eight out of ten people experiencing homelessness in Atlanta were Black was inseparable from what protesters had been railing against. "It's *all* connected," she'd said with some frustration during a recent staff meeting. "Can't y'all see that?"

Born in Chicago in 1975, Carla considered herself a product of that city's progressive Black churches, where the gospel was synonymous with social justice and faith took a decidedly public form. It was at Grant Memorial AME that she was "first encouraged to think outside the box, to challenge the dominant narratives," and it was there, amid the relative comfort of a middle-class upbringing, that she was persistently reminded of how poverty and "hypersegregation" continued to afflict large swaths of the city's population. Her family had deep roots in Chicago: her mother and grandparents had grown up in the Ida B. Wells housing project, her maternal grandmother had worked as a housecleaner for wealthy white families in Evanston, and several generations of other relatives had resided in the Englewood neighborhood. Between her church's organizing efforts and her parents' own activist commitments, Carla developed a keen political sensibility from an early age, deciding in high school that the only careers worth pursuing were the ones that would enable her to give back to her community.

She eventually received a master's degree in child, family, and community services from the University of Illinois-Springfield, then cut her teeth first with the Salvation Army and later with an organization called Youth Guidance, where she was dispatched to "inner-city, high-risk schools" on the West Side. Carla would come to refer to her time at Youth Guidance as her "real education": a period when, under the tutelage of colleagues with extensive knowledge of urban history and sociology, she started to perceive the interlocking systems and policies that were choking the life prospects of low-income students. After getting married—"Of course we met at church," joked her husband, Kyle— giving birth to two daughters, and resettling in Atlanta, Carla was hired at Nicholas House. She had now been with the organization for eight years, immersed in the difficult, often vexing work of homeless services.

When Kara gently knocked on the conference room door at twelve sharp, Carla stood to welcome her with a handshake. "Come in and grab a seat," she said. "It's great to finally put a face to the name."

"Yes, ma'am," Kara replied stiffly. Turning to her children, she said, "You not gonna say hello?"

"Hello," her three older kids said in unison. Kara remained in the doorway, unsure where to sit; more than two dozen chairs had been arranged around a grid of eight long tables. Carla motioned to a row of chairs across from her, under an abstract art print resembling a desert horizon, and since another family was scheduled to meet with her at twelve-thirty, she got straight to the point.

"So, Ms. Thompson . . ." she began. Whether addressing a client directly or speaking about them with a colleague, Carla never called a client by their first name. In part this was intended as a sign of respect for men and women who, in encounters with welfare agencies or government bureaucracies, were often made to feel small. Carla had known any number of direct service providers whose default assumption was that people like Kara were attempting to game the system or were to blame for their predicaments, or both, and that they deserved to be treated accordingly—a view that Carla most definitely did not share. But her decorum was also meant to set boundaries. She rarely divulged anything about her personal life, opted for emails over text messages, and generally maintained an air of sympathetic but in no way chummy professionalism. Many of her clients would have been surprised to read, in one of her online bios, that among her favorite activities was watching *Carnival Eats* with her daughters Nia and Naomi and then, as she put it, creating "their own version of whatever sugary, gooey, messy concoction seen on the show."

"So, Ms. Thompson," Carla said. "I've been discussing your situation with my executive director, and there's a Nicholas House program that could be a very good fit for you. I think you would be an excellent candidate. If it's okay with you, I'd like to recommend you for the program."

She paused, and when Kara again simply responded, "Yes, ma'am," distracted by her kids on the floor with their coloring books, Carla went on to describe the program.

Homeless to Homes, or H2H, as it was known, was a "rapid rehousing" program that offered rental subsidies for families exiting homelessness. Participants leased an apartment in their own name and, as with a Section 8 voucher, paid only 30 percent of their income toward rent; Nicholas House, via funds from both federal and state sources, covered the rest. The idea was that, by working with a case manager to gradually increase their income, households would be able to renew their lease and pay the entirety of their rent by the end of the year-long period. Unlike homelessness interventions involving intensive, long-term supports—typically referred to as "permanent supportive housing"—rapid rehousing was intended to get people out of shelters or off the street as quickly as possible through the provision of more minimal, time-limited assistance.

H2H fell outside her purview, Carla continued, so Kara would be assigned a different Nicholas House case manager upon her acceptance to the program. The only thing Kara needed to do in the meantime was go to Gateway to obtain a homeless verification letter, which Carla characterized as a mere formality. Along with other factors, including income level and employment status, Kara's eligibility for rapid rehousing hinged on her being certified as "literally homeless." Most families languishing in hotels and motels were denied this designation, but because Nicholas House was paying for Kara's room, the Marriott could technically be considered a "shelter," and Kara and her kids could, for the purposes of the assistance program, be defined as "homeless." The arbitrariness and harm of this semantic gatekeeping, which deprived countless families of crucial aid, were not lost on Carla. But when speaking with clients, she tended to keep these criticisms to herself.

"Does all that make sense?" Carla asked.

"It does," Kara said.

"All right, great." Carla jotted down some notes and closed the folder in front of her. Then she looked up at Kara, seeming to remember something she'd meant to say earlier. "Before we conclude here," she told Kara, "I just want to commend you for really going above and beyond. I don't know that I've ever seen someone work as hard as you. It's honestly quite remarkable."

"Thanks," said Kara. "I'm just trying to put us back on solid ground."

"I get that," said Carla. "And H2H really does have the potential to help you achieve that."

Kara's eyes lit up at this last statement, as if finally grasping the significance of the program: how much money she'd be able to save each month, and how a lessening of her rent burden could improve her family's overall quality of life. "Yeah," she said, almost to herself. "You're right."

For Carla, such hopeful moments were never fully satisfying. She had grown disillusioned in recent years. It wasn't just the knowledge that programs like H2H were reaching only a tiny fraction of those in need. It was that even the most successful outcomes—and Carla was convinced that if anybody could benefit from H2H, it was Kara—were failing to address the underlying reasons why so many families lacked stable housing in the first place. To her mind, the "homeless industrial complex"—by which Carla meant the government agencies, nonprofits, businesses, and philanthropic groups that made up Atlanta's Continuum of Care—was always trying to persuade itself, and the public, that it was tackling the crisis when it hadn't even begun to address its true nature and magnitude. The idealism that had once animated her work in social services had, after she'd sat through countless webinars and conference plenaries and unveilings of strategic plans, been eroded by a creeping suspicion: that both the local and national response to homelessness was being hobbled by a kind of willful myopia. Instead of an honest assessment of why scores of people were continuing to become unhoused—poverty wages, out-of-control rents, greed, racism, gentrification—there was bloodless technocratic talk of "leveraging resources" and "program deliverables." Instead of tenants' rights workshops and political advocacy, there were mandatory parenting classes.

"Not everything that can be faced can be changed," James Baldwin, Carla's favorite writer, observed in a 1962 essay. "But nothing can be changed until it is faced." For Carla, that summed it up. Even if genuine solutions remained out of reach, even if they were deemed too radical or unrealistic, Carla felt it was necessary to at least reckon with the actual causes of the problem. And chief among those causes, she felt, was a fundamentally unjust, profit-maximizing rental market—the "housing Hunger Games," as she referred to it. She and Kyle and their two daughters had experienced its effects firsthand a couple of years earlier, when they were priced out of their rental home in Grant Park, located down the street from Nicholas House, and had to move to a neighborhood near the airport. The couple had worried about eventually being forced out of Atlanta altogether; in soon-to-be-revitalized neighborhoods around the city, they'd seen chartered buses filled with investors, getting tips on how best to take advantage of these "opportunity zones."

Someday, Carla thought, America would awaken to the immorality of allowing one of the most basic human necessities to be auctioned off to the highest bidder. "In this country," she said, "it's simply a fact of life that if you're a renter, especially a poor renter, you're always going to be at the mercy of a landlord who may or may not have an interest in keeping you housed. As soon as it becomes more lucrative for them to sell the property, or to raise the rent, or to get wealthier tenants in—if the market allows that, they're going to follow the market."

Financial support was important. But Carla had grown convinced that what her clients really needed was not assistance per se. It was power. "Most people I work with, they don't just feel hopeless. They feel powerless. Because they're constantly subjected to forces beyond their control—even beyond their understanding."

As the meeting drew to a close, Carla stood to walk Kara and the kids to the door. "You're going to make it through this," she said, shaking Kara's hand.

There were days when Carla wondered why she stayed. It certainly wasn't the pay. And as for giving back to the community, her initial impetus for pursuing a career in social work, it seemed that for every family she was able to help, another four or five were turned away; for every family she was able to assist in finding housing, another few lost their homes. No, what prevented her from leaving was something else: a hope that her outspoken presence—"until they throw me out," she'd joked to Kyle—would help dismantle some of the self-serving myths and simplistic narratives surrounding homelessness. She would keep on saying what she had to say, even if nobody wanted to hear it.

DELIGHTED SQUEALS ECHOED through the playground at Bessie Branham Park. The children couldn't believe their luck: they had the whole place to themselves. The first and only time Kara had brought them here, before the pandemic, the popular playground had been overrun with kids from a local after-school program, so there were lines for the climbing wall, the tire swing, the zipline, the seesaw. But now Nathaniel could ride back and forth on the zipline to his heart's content; the four of them could have their own private fortress atop the steep yellow climbing structure. Though a laminated sign indicated that the playground was still closed because of Covid, Kara ignored it—after all, Georgia businesses such as movie theaters and bowling alleys had re-opened nearly two months earlier. And since Kara couldn't afford those places, this was the next-best option for an impromptu birthday party.

"No way is my little girl nine years old," Kara had said to Grace that morning, holding an unwrapped present behind her back.

Grace's birthday wish, she'd made clear over the preceding days, was to get her hair braided. Deeply self-conscious about her appearance, she found her hair a particular source of embarrassment; she hated how patchy it was, and how eczema sometimes left her scalp pink and itchy. "Why you bald?" a boy at school had once mockingly asked her. Kara wanted to give Grace this gift—one of the few nice things Kara could say of her own mother was "she always made sure my hair was done"—but she'd decided that, given the cost (at least $200, excluding treatment and hair prep), it would have to wait. Instead, Kara had surreptitiously bought Grace a discounted floral dress at Walmart, and when she gave it to Grace with a hug, telling her to put it on before they left for the day, Grace tried to hide her disappointment.

But a few minutes later, in the hotel lobby, she brightened when two front desk clerks greeted her with "Happy birthday!" as the family stepped out of the elevator. "Wow, what a gorgeous birthday girl," one of the clerks, a slim blond woman, said. "I love your dress." Grace beamed. The clerks presented her with a gift bag packed with blue tissue paper, underneath which were snacks culled from the rack of candy and toiletries and potato chips beside the check-in area. Grace was grinning from cheek to cheek. Jermaine, however, burst into tears at the unfairness of the situation. "Oh no! Don't cry," said the other clerk. "How about if everyone picks out candy?" Jermaine, Joshua, and Nathaniel each chose the peanut butter M&Ms.

At the park, Kara watched her kids from a shaded picnic table some forty feet away. Ever since Grace had eagerly asked, in the car, whether her dad had sent a birthday message, Kara had been quietly seething, resentful of the callous neglect exhibited not only by Darius but by her own parents and relatives, none of whom had texted or called. *Fuck all y'all,* she'd thought. Now, though, Kara was willing herself to relax, letting the stillness, the sound of birdsong, soothe her nerves. After being with the kids for so many weeks, hour upon hour, it felt odd to view them from a distance. Affection welled up in her. On YouTube, she'd begun following a channel called *Proud Mommy of Eight,* which chronicled the daily activities—doctor visits and pool outings, spaghetti dinners and homework sessions—of a single parent and her brood in Fort Myers, Florida. While standing in line at the grocery store or sitting in a parking lot between DoorDash orders, Kara drew inspiration from the woman's example. Her videos made no effort to hide the hardships of raising eight kids on her own, but neither did she seem crushed by the responsibility. "Blessed and highly favored" was how the woman described herself. Observing Nathaniel's glee on the zipline, Kara imagined the scene as an entry in her own video diary. This, she thought, was what motherhood was supposed to be like—not the joyless grind that it had become. This was how children should be spending their Friday afternoons.

"Who's ready for pizza?" she shouted. The children raced to the picnic table, where Kara had laid out four napkins, four cups of fruit punch, and four plastic plates with a slice of Ultimate Pepperoni on each of them. Except for Joshua, who was hopelessly picky, the kids quickly reached for a second slice. Only Grace was allowed a third. After the pizza was polished off, Kara handed out cupcakes she'd picked up at Publix. Everyone laughed when Joshua's mouth and hands and even, somehow, the side of his head became smeared in blue and green frosting.

A moment later, Nathaniel accidentally spilled his juice on the table, soaking his mom's phone. The laughter abruptly stopped.

"Goddammit!" Kara exclaimed, lunging at the phone. And then, louder: "What is *wrong* with you, boy?" Had a stranger been walking by, they might have been alarmed at Kara's outburst and the enraged look on her face. Her reaction, however, stemmed from a single, over- whelming fear: without her phone, she couldn't work. Driving for DoorDash required a smartphone with internet access, so a broken phone meant instantly losing her sole source of income. But the phone turned out to be fine.

"Go on," she told the kids, who were now subdued. "Go play some more. We'll be leaving in a little bit."

Grace stayed behind, wiping at a grease spot on her new dress. In the distance, Jermaine was cautiously joining Nathaniel on the seesaw. Kara seemed far away, lost in her own thoughts. After she announced to the boys that they had two more minutes, her phone dinged. Kara read the email. "This right here is divine," she told Grace. She read the email again, this time out loud. Twelve days had passed since her meet- ing with Carla, and five since obtaining a homeless verification letter from Gateway—as Carla had predicted, she'd had no trouble getting it. Now Carla was writing to say that Kara had been approved for Home- less to Homes. Congratulating Kara and wishing her family well, Carla mentioned that Kara would be receiving further information from her new Nicholas House case manager within a few days. "Isn't this the best birthday present?" Kara said with a giggle. Grace nodded.

Michelle took a languid drag on her Marlboro Red. She was perched on a bench outside the Salvation Army shelter where she and Skye were living, watching her daughter play with a princess doll in one of the patio's neglected planters. Having exhausted the time-killing strategies—folding laundry, browsing the internet in the shelter's computer lab, finishing the chores she had been assigned—that Michelle had come to rely on to keep herself busy during their six weeks at the shelter, she was now in the middle of that dull, sluggish part of the morning where the hours dragged on and on. A few minutes earlier, she had heard drumming off in the distance and wondered if it was coming from the Juneteenth event Pink had helped organize. Michelle had declined Pink's invitation to attend, saying she just wanted peace and quiet. And besides, the shelter had implemented a Covid protocol intended to limit the number of people coming and going from the facility. You had to remain on the premises all day, or you had to leave in the morning and come back at night. Michelle wasn't about to risk missing a free dinner.

The shelter sat between Luckie and Marietta Streets, only a short walk from Atlanta's most popular tourist attractions, the Georgia Aquarium and the World of Coca-Cola. Spread over two sprawling floors, the cream stucco building contained separate accommodations for men, women, and families, in addition to dorms specifically for homeless veterans, men who had recently been released from jail or prison, and those enrolled in Harbor Light, a drug treatment program. There were also five common areas, a small playground, several class-rooms, a food pantry, and a cafeteria that doubled as a chapel on Sunday mornings. With its 320 beds, the shelter was among the city's largest. On most nights, every bed was occupied.

At first, Michelle had found the place intimidating. It was exactly what she'd imagined an urban homeless shelter would look like. But the lady at the intake desk had been warm and welcoming, and when she and Skye were shown their room, Michelle was overcome with re-lief. It was spartan but tidy, with white cinderblock walls, a wooden dresser, two beds, and a window. Best of all, it was private, and free—or at least it was for Michelle. Since one of Pink's contacts in the mayor's office had managed to get her into the shelter, the city had agreed to cover the $10 daily fee. Only women with children, Michelle discov-ered, were given their own rooms. Everyone else was spending $70 a week to stay in a crowded dormitory filled with bunk beds and metal lockers, where physical fights (and, by many accounts, bedbugs) were common and sleep was hard to come by.

She and Skye quickly adapted to their new environment. Michelle took to heart a dictum drilled into residents from the moment they set foot on the property: that if you followed the rules and attended all the classes and showed initiative, you could eventually leave the shelter in a better state than when you'd arrived. You might, in other words, never have to resort to staying at such a place again. And in fact, as Michelle "worked the program," a ubiquitous phrase carried over from the realm of addiction treatment, she was surprised to find that all the benefits and services she'd been trying to access over the preceding year and a half suddenly materialized. The caseworker she had been as-signed made a phone call, and soon Michelle's CAPS application, stuck for so long in its online purgatory, was approved. The caseworker also helped get her food stamps reinstated—they'd been cut off since April, and Michelle hadn't been able to figure out why—and Michelle at last received her stimulus payment. Most significantly, she was re-ferred to an outside organization, Project Community Connections,

Inc. (PCCI), for housing assistance. "Knock on wood," her PCCI case-worker had told her, "but I think there's a real chance you could be in an apartment by the end of July." Michelle thought of her fruitless visits to the Division of Family and Children Services office and her note-book full of phone numbers that had yielded nothing but busy signals and unanswered voice messages.

Skye was adored by the shelter staff. They gave her donated toys to play with, and in the cafeteria she was always offered extra dessert. "You people are spoiling this girl," Michelle would say with mock dis-approval. She loved seeing Skye doted on. It was only when Michelle thought of DJ and Danielle that a wave of sadness swept over her. The stress of living at Efficiency had messed her up, she had told them during a recent phone call, glossing over the drinking that had caused her and DJ to part ways in such an ugly manner. Her aunt Regina, afraid of contracting Covid, insisted that DJ and Danielle not visit their mother and sister at the shelter. Michelle had sent Regina a few hundred dollars to go toward food and utilities, but this did little to soften her aunt's resolve. And so, for the time being, Michelle's com-munication with DJ and Danielle was limited to the rare call from Regina's landline.

When Michelle caught herself complaining about the food or the tedium or the many rules and restrictions at the shelter, she tried to remember where she'd come from and focus on where she hoped to go. On the Tuesday before Juneteenth, Pink had been delighted to hear about the opportunities opening up for her friend. Michelle told her that with Skye starting daycare the following week, she was scheduled to begin working as a door monitor on the men's side of the shelter— an unpaid job but one that, according to her caseworker, could be a stepping-stone to a full-time staff position with the shelter. There was even talk of Michelle returning to school to become a social worker. Her own apartment, a stable job, her family back together: this was Michelle's north star. She could put up with pretty much anything in the meantime.

Michelle stamped out her cigarette. "Let's get out of this heat," she told Skye.

THE JUNETEENTH CELEBRATION was about to begin, and the plaza outside the King Center was almost filled to capacity. The atmosphere was electric. While a college drum line unleashed a tight, staccato rhythm near the entrance on Auburn Avenue, people kept streaming in, greeting one another and taking in the scene.

Pink was in the middle of it all: one minute making sure the banners were almost finished or giving out T-shirts designed specifically for the occasion, and the next standing for an interview with a local news outlet. She had grown up in Texas, where Juneteenth originated—it marked the date in 1865 when enslaved men and women in the state belatedly learned of their liberation—so she'd been celebrating the holiday for as long as she could remember. After moving to Atlanta, she had linked up with a group that organized an annual festival. But whereas in the past these Juneteenth events were sparsely attended, the mounting demonstrations across the nation had given this year's Emancipation Day a new urgency. The celebration would double as a protest march. "WE READY!!! WE READY!!! WE READY!!! FOR YALL," Pink had posted on social media that morning. The day before, she'd swung by Efficiency to hand out flyers. Celeste wanted to be there but hadn't been feeling well. Christina said there was no way she was going to trek to the event with six kids. And Travis, the maintenance guy, was scheduled to work.

The only resident who would be attending was Geraldine, a woman in her late fifties. Soft-spoken and introverted, Geraldine lived at the hotel with her disabled adult son and two teenage grandchildren. They had been at Efficiency for seventeen months. Their last home had been a shabby, rodent-infested three-bedroom in South DeKalb whose kitchen and living room windows were cracked and whose lone bathtub wouldn't drain. Geraldine had pleaded with her landlord to address these problems, and when, after several months, he refused, she'd called code enforcement, hoping this would spur him to action. But her plan had backfired. The house was condemned, and her landlord opted to sell his property instead of making the required repairs. Now, crammed into a room on the second floor of Efficiency, the four of them rarely ventured out. Justin, her thirty-one-year-old son with severe autism, watched TV all day, and her grandson and granddaughter left only to visit their mom, who was living at a rooming house, trying to save enough money for an apartment. Geraldine stayed in unless she was going to church or a doctor's appointment.

Geraldine had met Pink during one of her Community Boutique events at the hotel, gratefully accepting a food box from the younger woman. Though their personalities couldn't have been more different, Geraldine felt drawn to Pink, and when she saw the flyer for the Juneteenth march she knew immediately that she would go. She'd never considered herself political, let alone identified as an activist. But just a week earlier, an Atlanta police officer had shot and killed Rayshard Brooks outside the Wendy's on University. The city's police chief had resigned and the white cop had been charged with murder, but still Geraldine couldn't watch the footage of Brooks's final moments without crying. What if that had been her Justin, failing to "comply" with an officer's command? Brooks had been married for eight years and had three daughters and a stepson. How many more fathers and mothers, sons and daughters would be killed on camera before summer's end? Geraldine felt so impotent, so disconnected sitting there in her room.

Zyniah, her granddaughter, had been feeling the same way. Some of her classmates had been taking part in the downtown protests with older friends or siblings, and as Zyniah scrolled through their photos and videos on social media, she wished she could join them. "If you want," she'd said to Geraldine after her grandma mentioned the Juneteenth celebration, "maybe I can go with you?"

Geraldine no longer owned a car, so she and Zyniah took an Uber to the King Center. Their driver, an older Black man, said he'd been tempted to attend the march but couldn't afford to take the day off. Addressing Zyniah, he said that if things were ever going to get better it would be because her generation had chosen to take a stand. "Yes, sir," the thirteen-year-old replied.

Geraldine and Zyniah were kindred spirits: both quiet, observant, and easily overstimulated. As they got out of the Uber and made their way through the packed plaza, they found themselves questioning their decision to come. Over the drum line's pounding beat, a woman somewhere was speaking angrily into a megaphone. "We had a mayor named Kasim and now we have a mayor named Keisha, and tell me—where has that gotten us? Are our people any better off today?"

Finally they spotted Pink's mohawk and made their way over to her. Only then did they start to feel more at ease. Pink was thrilled that they'd made it. "Look at you!" she said to Zyniah after Geraldine introduced them. Zyniah had carefully planned her outfit for the day: black high tops, army camouflage-style tights, a black headband and Covid mask embossed with LOVE in silver sequins. Pink was clearly impressed, insisting that one of her friends take a picture of her, Geraldine, and Zyniah. To their right was a reflecting pool containing the crypt of Dr. and Mrs. King, with the famous words from the "I Have a Dream" speech: "We will not be satisfied until justice rolls down like water and righteousness like a mighty stream."

When the march finally began, Pink was at the very front of a thick column of people spanning nearly four blocks. Along with a dozen others, she held a segment of an enormous red, black, and green Juneteenth banner depicting two hands breaking free of their chains. "What do we want? Justice!" she chanted. There were still another two and a half miles to walk, and already the sizzling midday heat and humidity were causing sweat to pour down her face. Pink had gotten little sleep over the past three weeks. Her anger at the recent episodes of police violence overrode her usual aversion to demonstrations, and her days had been packed with rallies and planning meetings for the Juneteenth march, all on top of her usual frenetic schedule. So it was all adrenaline at this point. "When do we want it? Now!"

"You good?" Geraldine asked Zyniah between chants. Zyniah said she was fine, but she seemed tense. She'd never experienced anything like this. Soon a passing car honked its horn for several extended seconds. "Grandma, is something happening?" she asked anxiously. "Are they mad at us?" She'd heard of drivers plowing into demonstrators during protests.

"No, that means they agree with us," Geraldine said. "Don't worry."

At the intersection of Auburn Avenue and Jesse Hill Jr. Drive, the march came to a brief halt. Towering overhead was a six-story mural of Georgia congressman and civil rights icon John Lewis, who would succumb to cancer only a few weeks later. "As a nation and as a people, we're going to get there," Lewis had said earlier that month, when the protests started. "We're going to survive, and there will be no turning back. There may be some setbacks, there may be people who will stand in our way, but we will not go back. We've come too far, and we're not going to give up now."

"Don't shoot! Don't shoot!" the marchers chanted in the direction of a group of APD officers watching impassively from the sidewalk. Mixed in among the Juneteenth flags and banners were signs reading I CAN'T BREATHE or SILENCE = VIOLENCE or IF ALL LIVES MATTER THEN WHY AREN'T YOU MAD? One guy was wearing a sign that read ATLANTA: A CITY TOO BUSY TO HATE BUT NOT A CITY TOO BUSY TO KILL. After a young man, a student at Morehouse, gave a rousing extemporaneous speech about lynchings and poverty and the carceral state and reparations, the marchers continued toward Centennial Olympic Park, their final destination. "You guys hangin' in there?" Pink hollered over her shoulder. "This is incredible!" Zyniah yelled back.

Another line of cars honked their horns. This time Zyniah and Geraldine raised their fists and cheered.

IN THE KITCHENETTE of their hotel room, Maurice was preparing four tuna sandwiches, two for him and one each for Anthony and Shantel. Matthew was slung over one of his broad shoulders like a sack of potatoes. When Maurice was growing up, his mom usually fed him and his siblings the same thing seven or eight or ten days in a row: beans or bologna or, most often, the dreaded Spam—whatever bulk item at the store happened to be cheapest. Even years later, the mere thought of Spam made Maurice feel sick. A can of tuna fish, on the other hand, was a rare treat, and once he was an adult, to his own children's chagrin, tuna sandwiches became a go-to meal whenever he was in charge of lunch or dinner. "Come and get it," he told Anthony and Shantel, who were locked in a fierce wrestling match on the Xbox their godfather Aaron had bought for them before he'd died. "In a minute," Shantel mumbled, pounding away at her brother.

Maurice poked his head into the bedroom where Natalia was working. Holding his plate, he pointed to the sandwiches and mouthed, "Do you want one?" Natalia, on the phone with a customer, shook her head, indicating that she'd be finished soon.

At the end of April, when State Farm threatened to fire her if she didn't start working remotely, she and Maurice decided that they'd need to upgrade their room at Extended Stay America; until the kids returned to in-person school, there was simply no way she'd be able to field calls for six to eight hours at a time without a separate bedroom. Though moving to a larger room meant that their already-staggering weekly rent would be even higher, they discovered—almost five months after arriving at the hotel—that they were eligible for a small discount through Natalia's job, effectively keeping their rent at the rate they'd been paying.

The discount was a nice surprise, and the modicum of privacy made possible by the separating door was definitely welcome. And yet the whole thing made them uneasy. They were still living paycheck to paycheck, still spending nearly twice as much on this dreary room as they'd spent on their old apartment while getting a quarter of the space. And they knew that the more comfortable they got, the more normal the whole awful, unaffordable arrangement would begin to feel. They had met neighbors who seemed to have settled into life at the hotel, resigned to their circumstances, and Maurice and Natalia feared becoming similarly "desensitized," as they put it. "This is *not* a home," Maurice said, "and I'm scared we'll start to think it is." No matter how long they stayed at the hotel, they were determined to remember that this was not how it was supposed to be.

"Phew, all done," Natalia announced a couple of minutes later. She always felt slightly off-kilter after staring at her computer screen and talking into a headset for several uninterrupted hours. A nap with Matthew was sounding good to her. But it was Juneteenth, a day she had been raised to regard as practically sacred, and it seemed wrong not to mark it in some way. Natalia had just turned thirty-six, and she'd told her family that instead of a present or a special take-out dinner what she really wanted for her birthday was for the five of them to attend a protest rally together. She'd seen on Instagram that a family-oriented event would be taking place in Sandy Springs—a perfect chance, she thought, to finally get out, to stop observing passively from their hotel room in a suburban strip mall as a once-in-a-generation movement unfolded around them. Shantel, however, was afraid to go, citing the police response to the protests: the tear gas and beatings and rubber bullets that her parents had been discussing. And Maurice, the most cautious in the family where Covid was concerned, was nervous about the health risks. He also wasn't feeling well. For weeks, an abscess in one of his back teeth had been causing him tremendous pain. It wasn't constant, but when the pain flared up, as it had just now, while he was eating his sandwich, it could be unbearable. Lacking dental insurance, which they'd opted out of to save money, he'd avoided going to the dentist. He had been downing Tylenol and ibuprofen instead.

So they'd decided to stay put. Then, that morning, a tentative plan with her sister in D.C. to do a Zoom call with all the cousins—they were hoping to read and discuss a children's book about Juneteenth that her sister had found—had fallen apart after Natalia realized she was scheduled to work. The day was unraveling.

Natalia asked her family to join her around the coffee table. Maurice, plainly in distress, said he had to lie down. "Babe, I'm so sorry," Natalia said, telling him to yell if he needed her. Then, turning to Shantel and Anthony, she said, "I wanna play something for you." She did a quick search on her phone and propped it up on the table. As a montage of civil rights images started appearing on the screen, the hymn "Lift Every Voice and Sing" began streaming out of her phone's tinny speakers.

Penned by lawyer and educator James Weldon Johnson in 1900, the song had long been considered the "Black national anthem"—it was officially adopted as such by the NAACP in 1920—and Natalia described to her kids how she'd been made to memorize its first verse in a youth group when she was Shantel's age. The hymn's marching tempo and soaring lyrics ("Sing a song full of the faith that the dark past has taught us / Sing a song full of the hope that the present has brought us") never failed to move her.

But now its invocation of "the harmonies of Liberty" and "the rising sun of our new day begun" caused her thoughts to drift to a conversation she'd recently had with Maurice. In a rare act of spontaneity, Natalia had enrolled, not long after going back to work, in a remote associate degree program at Georgia State, paid for by State Farm. She was taking two classes, college algebra and U.S. history, and as part of the latter course she had been learning about the post–Civil War era.

One night, with the kids asleep, she and Maurice were up late; he was watching sports with the volume turned low and she was completing the assigned reading from her textbook, *The American Promise*. "What I was reading blew my mind," she later said. The book detailed the wreckage of Reconstruction, the successful attempt by southern elites to resubjugate the Black population. She learned that the promise of labor rights and land ownership, of "forty acres and a mule," had been swiftly rescinded by President Lincoln's successor, Andrew Johnson, setting the stage for an entire legal, political, and economic order designed to consolidate white wealth and power through the coerced toil—what her textbook referred to as the "compulsory free labor"—of Black bodies. She learned that states had enacted strict "Black Codes" penalizing Black people if they tried to work in occupations other than farming or domestic servitude; she read about laws aimed at preventing Black people from migrating in search of safety and economic opportunity. Sharecropping and debt peonage, vagrancy laws and the "neoslavery" of convict leasing: it was all meant to force the formerly enslaved into a vast system of exploitation and, in many cases, because of the Thirteenth Amendment's slavery loophole for those convicted of crimes, involuntary and unpaid labor.

Natalia shared these revelations with Maurice. Though he, too, was unfamiliar with much of this history, he seemed unsurprised by what he heard. "I mean, it makes sense, right?" he later said. "If there was actual freedom, who would they get to work those fields for practically nothing? How would they build up their profits? It's simple: they free you with no money, no education—nothing. And then you realize that if you can't own your own property, you have to pay someone else for a place to live. Then they've got you." He said there were always going to be people who had to stay poor in order to make others rich.

The following day, Natalia devoured a magazine article by the acclaimed writer Ta-Nehisi Coates, which showed how the spirit of Jim Crow had extended even to northern cities. She felt as if she was reading the story of her family's own predicament: an account of housing insecurity that began with four million formerly enslaved people deprived of land and forced into an economy of low wages, rent, and debt—and continuing with the devastating effects of urban renewal, redlining, restrictive covenants, and, more recently, subprime lending. A long history of discrimination and dispossession. A question stuck with her: *Emancipated into what, exactly?*

When the song ended, Shantel and Anthony were itching to get back to their Xbox. Natalia wanted to discuss the song's meaning with them. She wanted to discuss the significance of Juneteenth, and all the things she had been learning about, and how it related to what was still happening in America. But she let it go. She needed to finish a math assignment by midnight.

AT EFFICIENCY, the mood was festive. Everyone seemed to be outside. Since Lisa, the manager, was away visiting relatives in north Georgia, a number of her prohibitions—including her much-reviled rule against grilling—were being openly flouted. At least three separate barbecues were underway, and a child's birthday celebration, complete with water balloons, goody bags, and, most remarkably, a bouncy castle, was in full swing in the parking lot. An ice cream truck had just pulled up beside the party.

Near a stairwell on the rear side of the hotel, Celeste and her neighbor Valencia were sipping tequila out of plastic cups. They said hello to Geraldine and Zyniah, who had just returned from downtown, as they walked upstairs to their room. "You enjoy yourselves," Geraldine said with a shy smile.

Relaxed and a little tipsy, reclined in their camping chairs, Celeste and Valencia joked and traded stories on the walkway, occasionally raising their voices to be heard over the thumping music or the roar of dirt bikes. Hours passed. Every so often Valencia, who was dressed in cut-off jean shorts, a baseball cap, and sandals, reached into her tank top and took out a pack of cigarettes. Various neighbors stopped and chatted with them. Celeste fixed herself a plate of chicken and rice; Valencia briefly left to intervene in an argument between her two daughters. Even though it was now dark, Micah and his friends were still hopping away in the bouncy castle, savoring every last minute before it needed to be deflated. Younger teens flirted, while older teens like Mike, Nyah's boyfriend, milled about stone-faced, selling weed and other stuff, on the verge of getting into bigger things but still more or less broke, still dependent on family.

At one point—it could have been seven o'clock, given the still-boisterous scene, but it was actually closer to ten—two guys rushed down the stairs next to where Celeste and Valencia were seated. One was clutching an Uzi-style weapon; the other held what looked like a submachine gun. They were older, in their twenties, and their drug game was more established: nicer clothes, nicer TVs and furniture in their rooms, and making enough money to buy expensive weapons. "These fools," Celeste muttered after they hurried by.

Micah, sweaty and out of breath, came to get a box of juice. Celeste called after the seven-year-old as he disappeared into their room, "Hey, where'd you get that cotton candy?" Celeste's neighbor James, an Iraq war veteran who had kicked a heroin habit years earlier and now worked at the VA hospital, came over to say that he and Shay, his fiancée, were heading out to grab food. He asked if Celeste and Valencia wanted anything. "Naw, we good," Valencia replied. She and Celeste continued their conversation.

About fifteen minutes later, a volley of automatic gunfire—*tat. tat-tat-tat-tat-tat*—rang out.

Celeste and Valencia instinctively ducked. "Young man, *stay inside!*" Celeste yelled at Micah, who had poked his head out the door. She dialed Jalen's phone. He had been riding his bike around the property.

"Where are you? No, where *are* you? Get back here now." Valencia ran to check on her daughters.

The hotel was dead silent. Upstairs in her room, awakened by the shots, Geraldine was in tears, crouched beside her bed, next to her son and grandkids. "Oh, they were just shootin' off their guns," her next-door neighbor would later tell her. Nobody had been hit.

Out on Candler Road, James and Shay were driving back to the hotel with their food. They were waiting at a red light, behind a couple of other cars, when a different kind of explosion filled the air. Fireworks lit up the sky. The elaborate spectacle appeared to be coming from Decatur Square, an area full of bars and restaurants where, the previous night, a Confederate monument had been taken down by court order. The thirty-foot obelisk stood mere steps from the DeKalb County courthouse. It was there, in 1960, shortly after county officials allowed a Ku Klux Klan parade through its corridors, that Martin Luther King Jr. was sentenced, jailed, and led off in chains to endure four months of hard labor on a false traffic charge. Although the Georgia General Assembly had recently updated state law to make it harder for local jurisdictions to remove Confederate monuments, the monument had finally been declared a public nuisance because it kept getting vandalized. At close to midnight, a crowd of hundreds had cheered as a crane plucked it from its pedestal. One attendee told a reporter, "I can think of no more fitting start to Juneteenth."

Now the day was ending with this unexpected display overhead. Even after the light turned green, not a single car moved. There were no impatient honks or attempts to bypass the stopped vehicles. Instead, for one minute and then another, everyone stayed put, their eyes lifted to the sky, captivated. Soon it would be over: the fireworks would fade, and James and his fiancée would be back at Efficiency, where the gun-shots had abruptly forced people back into their rooms. Yet for these fleeting moments there was a shared calm. Candler Road was awash in color.

PART FOUR

Rupture

K ara was in her car, scanning a list of apartment complexes. Her new Nicholas House case manager had kept her word and promptly emailed the acceptance materials for Homeless to Homes (H2H). At-tached to the message were three separate documents: a letter for pro-spective leasing agents verifying Kara's participation in the program; a detailed overview of the program's guidelines; and the piece of paper Kara now held in her hand, which contained the names, addresses, and phone numbers of twenty rental properties in the Atlanta area. Kara had asked the front desk clerk at Residence Inn to print these docu-ments for her, and the woman happily obliged.

Kara had been discouraged when she'd first read the letter outlining the terms of H2H and learned that she would be responsible for paying all the application fees. She remembered from her last experience hunting for an apartment how quickly these fees could add up—and how much money she had wasted applying for units that she probably had no chance of getting anyway. The second disappointment was that, in order to receive assistance, she would be required to rent a three-bedroom unit—the number of bedrooms was determined by family size—priced at $1,000 or less per month. At the time, the average rent for a three-bedroom in Atlanta was close to double that amount. What really wor-ried her, though, was the letter's mention of a deadline. "Your admission [to H2H] is based," it stated, "on your ability to locate suitable housing

within the allotted time period." Otherwise, it continued, "your tentative admission to the Nicholas House Inc. Homeless to Homes program
will be cancelled." The letter was dated June 10. She had until July 3 to
find an apartment. *That's three weeks,* she thought in disbelief.

Yet she remained optimistic. It was her first day without the kids in
over four months—their daycare had at last reopened—and she felt
much lighter. The list of apartment complexes Nicholas House had sent
seemed promising. Kara guessed these were properties that had some
kind of relationship with the organization—had partnered with them
in some way. During her recent visit to Gateway Center, she'd heard
talk of such arrangements between agencies and landlords. If that was
the case, Kara concluded, then it was simply a matter of deciding which
apartments on the list were the best fit for her family.

Parked outside a drugstore after dropping the children off, Kara
grabbed a pen and began crossing out the complexes she knew were
dilapidated or located in high-crime parts of the city. She was surprised
to find some of these properties on the list, considering their reputation.
On the Nicholas House website—as in the literature of nearly every
homeless-service organization—the emphasis was on helping people
secure "safe and stable housing." What good was an affordable unit that
had backed-up sewage, or whose roof was caving in, or where you were
afraid to step foot outside? Kara didn't even want to consider Deerfield
Gardens. Or Sunny Cascade. And certainly not The Hills at Greenbriar, which everyone knew was a war zone. (According to an *Atlanta
Journal-Constitution* investigation, the police had answered more than
4,100 calls from this Campbellton Road property in the past three years,
one-third of them involving shootings, armed robberies, rapes, and reports of shots fired.) She then put little asterisks next to the addresses
that were more appealing. A couple were located only a short distance
from the children's daycare; others she had driven by while out delivering for DoorDash. These were the properties she would be contacting
first. She said a prayer and started dialing.

"Hello," came a robotic voice after seven rings. "Thank you for calling Heritage Reserve apartment homes: quality living at an affordable
price. Our staff is busy helping other customers—"

Kara pressed zero. The line began ringing again.

"Heritage Reserve, Rochelle speaking."

"Hi, Rochelle, how you doin'. This is Kara Thompson."

"Hey, how are you."

"I'm pretty well. I was calling to see if y'all have any three-bedrooms available before, um . . . between now and July the third."

The agent said she did have a three-bedroom unit, but that moving in by the first week of July would be difficult. The middle of the month was more feasible. "No problem," Kara responded cheerfully. "But let me ask you a question." She explained that Nicholas House would be paying 70 percent of her rent—"and I *do* have a job, I do work," she hastened to add, preempting what she figured Rochelle was thinking. Would that be an issue? she asked.

"No, I think that should be okay," said Rochelle. She was familiar with Nicholas House, she said, but she needed to check with her manager before giving Kara an answer. "If she approves it, we can definitely move forward with you. Can I get your phone number and email?"

Kara thanked the woman and hung up. She was off to a good start.

But her luck didn't last. Out of seventeen calls, she was able to speak to only five leasing agents. The last one told her, as two others had, that his property didn't accept "assisted tenants." Why, then, Kara wondered, had these complexes had been included on the list? Clearly it was outdated.

In fact, only a few years earlier, there had been an entire binder in the Nicholas House office full of landlords willing to work with the agency. But in Atlanta's red-hot rental market, that binder's worth of properties had been whittled down to a single page—and even those were turning out to be dead ends. Carla Wells and other Nicholas House case managers had been pushing for the agency to hire a dedicated "housing navigator," someone to help clients like Kara in their apartment search. But the funding for such a position had not yet materialized.

The days that followed brought more of the same. The handful of leasing agents who bothered responding to Kara's voice messages told her that they had no available three-bedrooms, were "no longer working with programs," or both. Like Section 8 vouchers, most landlords were reluctant to take on families supported by Homeless to Homes and similar programs, either out of prejudice or because of the administrative burden, since additional paperwork was required for these tenants. At most of these places, the rent was too high anyway. One agent, from Harmony Plaza on Myrtle Drive, was "almost positive" he had a three-bedroom that would be available soon, and he strongly suggested that Kara submit an application—which would entail paying a nonrefundable $60 application fee *and* a $150 administrative fee—in order to "reserve" the unit. When she went online to look at the apartments, she saw that three-bedroom units were renting for between $1,200 and $1,300 a month. She cursed the agent, glad she hadn't taken his advice and applied.

Heritage Reserve, the first place she'd reached out to, called her back to say that sadly all their apartments set aside for subsidized tenants were currently leased. But of course she was welcome to apply for a regular unit.

"Does that mean I wouldn't be able to use the support from Nicholas House?" she asked.

"Yes, that's right," the agent replied.

As her options dwindled, Kara's initial optimism gave way to anxiety. And then, on June 16, that anxiety gave way to panic. Nicholas House emailed her to explain that their funding for hotel assistance had run out. After June 30, the agency would no longer be able to cover her family's room at Residence Inn. "Please begin to plan and prepare to pay for your accommodations afterwards," the email read.

Kara broadened her search beyond the list Nicholas House had given her. She scoured apartment listings for any mention of Section 8, thinking that landlords who accepted those vouchers might be willing to take other forms of assistance as well. She also found herself calling The Hills at Greenbriar and other complexes she had crossed out early on. But even at these places of last resort, there was no sure thing. Her need for a three-bedroom, along with the rent cap and inflexibly narrow time frame, was severely limiting her prospects. The logistics of the search only compounded her stress. As it became obvious that calling and emailing properties was insufficient, she began to spend her days driving around the city. This required not just time—time she should have been spending delivering food—but a great deal of gas. So even though she hadn't yet paid for a single rental application, the search was costing her. And she could only look for apartments while the kids were at daycare. She didn't want them to get their hopes up.

With the deadline looming, she grew obsessed. She called rental offices multiple times a day, leaving messages she knew wouldn't be returned. She was barely working, hardly sleeping or eating. She could no longer be polite when speaking to unhelpful leasing agents or property managers. Now she hung up on them or started walking away when they told her something she didn't want to hear. The thought of losing the H2H assistance was bad enough. But the possibility of being back in the car with the kids during the hottest months of the year—she had only saved enough money to pay for two, maybe three weeks at an inexpensive hotel—was even more dreadful. All she needed was one yes, just one place that checked all the boxes.

And then she found it: a three-bedroom house in Marietta, a large suburb situated about twenty miles north of downtown. She'd spotted the ad on Craigslist. When she dialed the number, a representative from Invitation Homes, the company that owned and managed the rental, immediately answered.

Yes, the man said after looking up the listing, they would consider accepting the subsidy from Nicholas House.

Yes, he said, the house was currently vacant and could be ready for move-in by early July.

Yes, he said, the price listed in the ad was correct. It was $950 a month.

"When would you like to see it in person?" he asked.

THE NEXT MORNING, Kara got the children up earlier than usual in order to be in Marietta by nine. It was Saturday, and their daycare was closed on weekends, so she was forced to break her own rule and bring the kids with her to see the house. It was either that or wait until Monday to tour the property—and she didn't want to let this one slip away. "We've been receiving a lot of inquiries," the leasing agent had told her. He said he understood her desire to see the rental as soon as possible.

Kara had been awake all night. Again and again she had reached for her phone in the dark, checking the Craigslist ad and zooming in on every photo, scrutinizing the walls and floors and appliances for any flaws that might account for the rental's low price. She recalled that her old duplex, the one whose hot water heater had stopped working, had also looked inviting in the pictures posted online. But aside from appearing a bit dated—the home seemed like it could use new carpet and wallpaper—the Marietta house looked ideal. The place was lovely, and by the time the sun rose, Kara had furnished and decorated it in her mind's eye.

"Mama, you all right?" Nathaniel asked from the back seat as they headed north on I-75. Kara seemed to ignore the question. The cumulative stress of the past several days was catching up with her. She hadn't eaten since the afternoon before, when she had picked at a salad, and she now felt weak, completely sapped of energy. She was driving fast, doing seventy-five in a sixty-five, and a couple of times, noticing that she was drifting into the next lane, she had roughly jerked the car back into her own lane. "I'm just tired," she eventually responded.

She was about a mile from her exit when her phone rang. "Hi, Ms. Thompson, it's Norman from Invitation Homes." He said he was sorry for the last-minute call, but there had been a change of plans. The home she was scheduled to tour had just been rented. But the good news, he told her, was that another, nicer house, even more spacious than the first but in the same neighborhood, had become available. The only catch was the rent: it was $1,100. But he assured Kara that this extra cost was well worth it.

"If you're interested—"

"Yes, yes, absolutely," Kara said while exiting the interstate.

"Excellent. I'll send you the address." He told her she could drive straight there.

Kara's heart was racing after hanging up. She was disappointed but not surprised to learn that the first house had been rented out. Norman had predicted it would go quickly. Soon a text message came in, and she pulled over to the side of the road to read it. Along with an address on Dover Crossing Drive, he had sent Kara a lockbox code—because of Covid they were only offering self-guided showings—and a link to the new listing. The house was indeed huge: 2,900 square feet, with three bedrooms and two-and-a-half baths. It was $100 more per month than what Nicholas House had agreed to pay, but you'd have to be crazy, Kara thought, to walk away from a place like this because of $100. She felt confident she could persuade Nicholas House to allow her to pay the difference.

For Kara, driving toward the house down Shallowford Road was like entering a parallel universe, one she had longed to inhabit. She had never been in this part of Cobb County. They passed Lassiter High School, and she remembered seeing, during her predawn sleuthing, that it had received 10 out of 10 on the GreatSchools rating, just slightly above the scores of the nearby elementary and middle schools. Now Kara had to suppress an urge to say to her kids, "There's the school you might be going to someday!" The immaculately clean streets and sidewalks, the trees, the quiet: she loved it all. They were only three minutes away from the address, according to the GPS, when Grace pointed and exclaimed, "Look, it's a sign!" On the corner was a Smoothie King, her mom's favorite.

When they arrived at the house, Kara pulled into its driveway and told the children to wait in the car. Situated in a modest but well-manicured subdivision, the home had a two-car garage, a covered entrance, and a freshly mowed front lawn. Norman called her as she was punching in the code. She put him on speakerphone.

"Did it open?" he asked.

"Yes, it opened."

"Are you in?"

"Yeah, I'm going in." And then, a moment later: "Oh *God*." She said it softly, in awe.

"It's nice," the agent said. "Didn't I tell you it was nice?"

But Kara was no longer listening. She was walking through the empty living room—taking in the plush carpeting, the fireplace, the abundance of natural light, the cathedral ceiling—and experiencing pure joy. Glancing across at the expansive kitchen, she put her hand over her mouth and gasped. Moving from room to room, she kept smiling, shaking her head in amazement, until she came to the master bedroom and began to laugh. It was overwhelming. In the en suite bathroom, she stood gazing at the soaking tub. "Oh my God," she whispered again.

Norman, still on speakerphone, had been talking the whole time, telling her to be sure to check out the vanity sinks, the breakfast bar, the fenced-in yard. He had a strong, unplaceable accent—vaguely Australian or South African—and Kara, distracted, had to ask him to repeat himself. After several minutes of this, Norman recommended that she apply for the rental right there and then. His company utilized a new technology, he said, that allowed them to evaluate applications within a half hour or less. She simply needed to complete an electronic form, which he was about to send her, and submit a $70 fee. He told her he would call her back as soon as it was processed. Kara sat in a hallway and filled out the application on her phone: her Social Security number and date of birth, her rental history and annual income and employment history.

She had just paid the $70 via Zelle, as instructed, when Grace appeared at the front door and asked if she and the boys could come inside. Kara went to the car to fetch them, and her reluctance to get the kids' hopes up suddenly crumbled. She knew she shouldn't be saying such things—"Go look at the bedrooms!" "See that big backyard?"— but she couldn't help herself. The children, taking a cue from their mom's exuberance, began exploring the house with glee, opening doors and cabinets, giggling, rolling around on the living room carpet.

By the time Norman called to congratulate Kara on having been approved, Grace and Nathaniel had decided which room would be theirs, determining that the other, smaller one would go to Jermaine and Joshua. "So if you like it," the agent was saying, "look around, take your time and if you like it—"

"I like it," Kara cut him off. "I like it. I want it. Take it off the market."

Norman chuckled, and she did, too, as if they had reached a new level of familiarity. She no longer cared if she sounded desperate. As he went on to talk about lease terms and potential move-in dates, Kara wandered into the kitchen, stopping in front of the refrigerator. A small green and white magnet was stuck to it. "This home is owned and managed by Invitation Homes," the magnet read. "Please be aware of fraud. Lease and payments for this home must be made in contract with Invitation Homes. If anyone is trying to convince you otherwise, it is a scam." Under "Signs of a Scam," it included "Bad grammar," "No background checks," and "Eager requests for cash or wire payments." Kara stared at the magnet, her expression unchanged. Then she kept pacing around the kitchen, continuing the conversation without missing a beat.

At one point, Norman told her to go outside and remove the Invitation Homes For Rent sign. "So that people will stop inquiring about the property," he explained. Kara, thrilled to hear this, did a happy walk-jog to the front door, like a game show contestant going to collect her prize. But there was no For Rent sign on the lawn. "Oh, that's strange," said Norman. "I guess we haven't put one up yet."

The only thing left to discuss, he said, was the security deposit of $1,100. Would she be paying it herself?

He made no attempt to hide his disappointment when Kara responded that Nicholas House would be taking care of the security deposit. "That's a shame," he told her. "I was hoping we could get this wrapped up today." He said he had worked with many such organizations before, and that if she paid the deposit herself she would definitely be reimbursed. He was growing impatient. He suggested that Kara simply wire the money from her bank account.

"Well, I'd need to see some paperwork first," she said, pushing back. "I'm not gonna send off a bunch of money without getting a lease."

"Yes, of course, of course," he said, his tone becoming gentle and accommodating again. "I only wanted to be sure you could make the payment before I get the documents together."

"Is it possible to meet you? Because it would be very helpful to meet you in person," Kara said. "I'm a single parent of four. I'm really trying to do the right thing."

"I understand," Norman said reassuringly. He said he would be glad to meet her on Monday. But by then, he added, the house might be rented to someone else. "I can't hold it for you without a deposit," he told her.

Kara thought about the $1,100. If she paid it and Nicholas House refused to reimburse her, it would wipe out her savings—money she had been holding onto not only for gas and food and application fees but for the hotel room she and the kids would need in just over a week. In that moment, however, the only thing worse than losing all the money would be losing this house to another family.

As she was about to tell Norman that she would wire the deposit, Grace yelled from the other room. "Mommy, Jermaine pooped!" Kara had been spellbound, almost in a daze, and this jolted her back to reality.

"I'm sorry," she told the agent. "I'll have to call you right back." Kara realized that she was out of Pull-Ups; they'd have to run to the store to buy more. She got the children in the car, texted Norman to explain the situation, and, pulling out of the driveway, looked back at the house.

She thought of the magnet.

Minutes later, in line at Walgreens, a PDF document arrived in her inbox. It was a lease. Her breath caught at the line in the first paragraph that read, "Kara Thompson shall be referred to as 'RESIDENT.'" The move-in date was listed as July 1.

Her phone rang. "I emailed you the lease," Norman said. "I hope that makes you feel better?"

He just needed the deposit, he told her—then he could cancel the showings scheduled for later that afternoon. Kara was now in the parking lot, standing beside her Toyota. How could this be a scam, she reasoned, if she had been given the correct code to the lockbox? That's what she kept returning to. This had to be real. *But what if it wasn't,* she thought. What if there was no way in hell she and the kids would be moving into that beautiful house, living in that safe, quiet neighborhood? She thought again of the magnet, and the fact that there had been no mention of Invitation Homes in the lease; the landlord was listed as "Norman Thomas," and the document stipulated that rent and deposit payments were to be made by wire transfer to a Bank of America account in the name of a "Miki Gress." She thought of the rent amount. No way was a home like that renting for $1,100.

And yet Kara didn't want to let it go. She couldn't bring herself to accept that anything good was probably too good to be true.

Pink lingered in the home decor aisle at Family Dollar. Michelle had moved into her own apartment the night before, and although Pink had a hectic day ahead of her, she couldn't resist surprising Michelle with some housewarming gifts. In her shopping cart she had already placed a bulky comforter, a scented candle, and a bouquet of red and yellow polyester flowers. Now she was trying to choose between two framed inspirational quotes. The first was a verse from Isaiah: "Those who trust in the Lord will find new strength." The other read, in folksy cursive, "Home Is the Story of Who We Are and a Collection of All the Things We Love." Unable to pick just one, she grabbed them both.

Michelle was waiting for Pink on the little balcony outside her first-floor unit. When she saw her friend, she hopped over the railing and ran to her.

"Look at this place!" Pink exclaimed as they embraced.

"Can I show you around real quick?" Michelle asked. Pink had told her on the phone that she had a car full of food boxes to deliver and could only stay a few minutes.

"Girl, I want the complete tour."

Situated in a wooded complex off Memorial Drive not far from Stone Mountain, the two-bed, two-bath unit was roomy and spotless. "That man hooked us *up*," Michelle said of her caseworker. Not only had he found her the apartment, convincing the property management company to rent to Michelle despite her lack of employment over the previous nine months, but he had also gotten her an appointment with a local furniture bank—a charity that collected used furniture and redistributed it to families in need. Because of the pandemic, their earliest available appointment was a month away, so she and the kids would be sleeping on blankets and eating meals on the floor until then. But it was worth the wait: the nonprofit would be furnishing each room of the apartment *and* delivering these items free of charge. This helped alleviate Michelle's concern about the fact that her rent alone would be swallowing up 80 percent of her take-home pay from the Salvation Army, where she'd begun working full-time. PCCI, the agency assisting her with housing, had taken care of her security deposit and first month's rent, but going forward she would be responsible for the $1,100 a month rent herself.

After guiding Pink through the kitchen and living room, which was barren except for a few cardboard boxes and, on top of the fireplace mantel, a painting of a bluebird that a co-worker's daughter had made for them, Michelle knocked on one of the bedroom doors before opening it. DJ and Danielle were on the carpet with their Chromebooks, and Skye was rolling around between them.

"Guys, Ms. Pink's here," Michelle said. Skye let out a yelp and rushed to Pink, who scooped her up into her tattooed arms.

"Hey, sweetie," Pink said. "You lookin' mighty fine." Skye was sporting a black Levi's T-shirt and Michelle's white sunglasses, which covered most of her face.

Pink asked the older kids if they liked the apartment. "We *love* it," replied Danielle. "It's so nice," DJ echoed. Michelle said there were no words for how good it felt to be reunited with her children. The three of them had never gone so long without seeing one another. "It's like we're whole again," said Michelle.

Standing there, Pink realized she had never seen Michelle so relaxed, so unencumbered. To Michelle, the events of the previous year— Jacob's lies and *Divorce Court* and the eviction; the panhandling and their stay in the storage room; the shouting matches and depression and nights with Skye in the parking lot—felt like a terrible dream that she had finally woken from.

"Hold up," Pink said. "I've got some stuff to give you." She went to fetch a box of food and the bag from Family Dollar.

Before leaving, she asked the kids to join her and Michelle in the living room. Holding hands, she led the five of them in a prayer of thanksgiving and protection, beseeching the Holy Spirit to make their new home a "sanctuary of comfort and peace and rest."

BACK IN HER CAR, Pink was glad to have started the day on a celebratory note. Her next stop was Efficiency, where things were getting bleaker and bleaker. Her last visit to the hotel, about two weeks earlier, had been prompted by a hysterical call from Geraldine, whose room had just flooded. At the time, Pink was in the middle of a Community Boutique event on the other side of Atlanta, but when she arrived she heard the whole outrageous story. While her grandson was in the shower, Geraldine told her, he was startled by what sounded like a pipe bursting somewhere in the ceiling. Geraldine had been at her new food services job at Georgia Regional Hospital, and when she finally made it back to her room, alerted by a barrage of panicked text messages, the brownish water seeping from above was well over her ankles. Her son and grandkids had salvaged what they could, but the damage was extensive: virtually everything they owned, including a box containing birth certificates and Social Security cards, was soaked through.

The worst part, Geraldine told Pink, was Lisa's reaction. When Geraldine knocked on the manager's door, a ponytailed guy came out and said it was Lisa's day off. He was wearing a shirt that read DON'T FOLLOW ME, accompanied by a skull and crossbones, beneath which was written, CUZ I'M ABOUT TO GET INTO SOME SHIT. Geraldine told him what had happened. "It's not my problem!" Lisa bellowed from the couch. Only once the police and firefighters showed up did she stumble to the door. She had one other room available, she said impatiently, clearly annoyed, and Geraldine was more than welcome to it.

This room, Geraldine discovered, was in fact a "bando"—short for abandoned—inside the squalid breezeway where addicts loitered. One of the room's windows was missing, and since there was a pair of bed frames but no mattresses, Zyniah and her brother had to haul two sopping mattresses from their old room down a flight of stairs. Later, Pink bought them sheets and blankets and tried to help them make their new room more habitable. As she was leaving, she glanced back and saw, through the opening where glass should have been, Geraldine and her granddaughter sliding a dresser behind their door, creating a barricade. She had been unable to shake the image.

Now as she drove through the front gate, she braced herself. "Here we go," she muttered. Her window was rolled down, and the stench hit her right away: the smell of sun-broiled garbage, emanating from the trash bags piled up in the parking lot and along the walkways. A few of these bags had torn or been left untied, scattering spaghetti noodles and banana peels and soiled diapers on the ground. Christina was sitting on a metal folding chair in front of her room, holding a cigarette whose long, curving ash appeared ready to fall on her lap at any moment. She acknowledged Pink with the smallest of nods and thanked her for the box deposited on the ground beside her chair. Then she continued staring off into space.

Pink had spent time in the most neglected parts of the city. But Efficiency struck her as uniquely awful. A kind of seething despair had come to pervade the place. From Travis's wife, Eboni, Pink learned that Travis had been fired by Lisa in retaliation for threatening to report her drug use and erratic behavior to the higher-ups in Mableton, where Efficiency's corporate office was located. The hotel had not yet hired another maintenance person—this explained the trash and the fact that an increasing number of air-conditioning units were broken and remained unfixed—and Eboni and Travis and their two kids were suddenly at risk of being forced out of their room. With the exception of Geraldine, who at last had been approved for an apartment down the road, almost everyone Pink encountered was in similar straits. A recent spate of violence at the hotel seemed to heighten the despair. In the parking lot, a longtime and beloved resident named Slim had been intentionally run over by a car after some dispute; he was taken to Grady, where he soon died. That same week, Christina's next-door neighbor, a young pregnant woman, had been kicked and punched by her boyfriend, causing her to miscarry.

Now, only a few days after firing Travis, Lisa herself was gone, apparently for good. Some claimed she had run off with an enormous sum of stolen cash. Others said she'd merely been transferred to the Efficiency in Douglasville. But the theory that had gained the most traction, the one that seemed most plausible, was that Lisa had been let go for allowing too many people to fall behind on their rent. Until the pandemic struck, she had never hesitated to lock people out. Yet the sheer number of residents out of work and late on rent payments had made this task difficult. Although Lisa had been promising since April to evict anyone whose rent balance went unpaid, she had never actually followed through on these threats.

The person who replaced Lisa in the rental office, a humorless woman from the East Point location named Camille, refused to utter a word about her predecessor. But she'd made it abundantly clear that if anyone owed money, they would be thrown out. It was as simple as that. Whether and how she would be able to enforce this was an open question.

As Pink was dropping off her last box of food, Celeste pulled up in a U-Haul. "I'm done with this shithole," she said by way of greeting. Pink asked her where she was headed. "To my friend Ricky's place," Celeste said, and then quickly added, "but please don't tell Nyah if you see her." Nyah despised Ricky. Celeste said that the social worker at Micah's school knew a property manager who was willing to rent to her; they would be staying with Ricky for a week or two until an apartment became available. And she had landed a new job at Talk of the Town, a local soul food restaurant. Best of all: she had been informed that her cancer was in remission.

"So things are finally looking up," she said. Nyah, who was due to give birth in a month, had gotten a job as well, at the Taco Bell on Candler Road. She hoped that she'd become eligible for employment benefits prior to the baby's arrival and ultimately save enough money to get an apartment with Mike.

"All right, well, you be safe," Pink said. "Don't be a stranger."

"Thanks. I'm sure we'll see you around."

Pink drove off while Celeste surveyed her cluttered room, estimating how long it would take to pack everything. What she hadn't told Pink was that she'd been feeling weak all day, like she might pass out— an effect of her final chemo treatment. Nor had she told Pink that, after renting the U-Haul and a storage unit, she had just $18 to her name.

She heard shouting in the parking lot and closed her door. "At least we're getting out of here," she said. After twenty months at the hotel, she'd begun to wonder if they would ever leave.

IN THE END, Kara decided not to wire the deposit. Her resolve was strengthened by the discovery of a Zillow listing identical to the one Norman had sent her. It had the same photos and floor plan and address as the Craigslist ad, the same wording about "making long-lasting memories" and spending "cozy nights in" and "relaxing after a long day." There was just one difference between the two ads: on Zillow, the home was listed for $2,125 a month. When Kara confronted Norman with this discrepancy of more than $1,000, he calmly explained it away, claiming the Zillow price had been a mistake. But Kara was unconvinced. She realized now that she was being scammed. She told the man that he wouldn't be getting another penny from her. Later, she tried calling him back to say that she would be reporting him to the police. But his number had been disconnected.

The episode left her shaken. How had she nearly fallen for such a thing? Her explanation to the kids was that the house hadn't "worked out," and when Grace kept asking questions, sensing there was more to the story, Kara angrily told her to let it go.

A few days later, still reeling, Kara was checking out at Walmart when the cashier struck up a conversation with her. The older woman mentioned her fear of Covid—the virus's death toll in the United States had recently surpassed 125,000—and then asked Kara how she was holding up during this challenging period. "I'm managing," Kara said.

The cashier looked at her. Something in Kara's body language made her pause. She said she was about to go on break and told Kara to meet her at the store entrance, next to Subway, in five minutes. The woman told her to hold out her hand and said, "I just feel that I'm supposed to give this to you." When Kara opened her hand, there was a fifty-dollar bill.

That afternoon, less than two weeks before her deadline to secure an apartment, Kara received a call from Chelsea Gardens, one of the complexes on the list Nicholas House had given her; she had left several detailed messages with the leasing office but hadn't gotten a response. The manager now told her that a three-bedroom had opened up and could be ready for move-in within a week. Since Nicholas House would be paying the bulk of her rent, the manager said, they were willing to overlook the eviction Kara had alluded to in her message. But they still needed her to go through the application process in order to verify her lack of criminal history.

"No problem," Kara said. "How much is the fee?"

"Fifty dollars," the manager replied.

Kara applied immediately. She had visited the College Park complex only once, at the beginning of her search, and had been less than dazzled by what she saw. The leasing office was closed, so she had been unable to look at the apartments themselves, but there was a mound of discarded furniture outside one of the buildings, never a promising sign. And security appeared nonexistent. On the mental scorecard she had started keeping, Kara had given the place a C, a good enough grade to merit following up. But after submitting her application, she made the mistake of skimming reviews of the complex, and she suspected a C had been overly generous. "I've lived here since October and it's been hell," wrote one man. "Mold in my bathroom. . . . Constant water leaks. Wiring out the wall which they promised to take care of and NOTHING." Another tenant wrote: "Sewage water has been leaking into my apartment from the apartment next door. These people don't care about anything or anybody. . . . I have small kids that I have to lock in their room so they don't go into the water."

If the deadline to find a place hadn't been bearing down on her, Kara would have expanded her search to other parts of Georgia, maybe to Macon or Fayetteville. But she was almost out of time, and this was the closest she had come—the closest she had come with a *real* landlord, she thought bitterly—to hearing a yes. When the complex called again to say her application had been approved and that the three-bedroom was still available, Kara said she'd take it. "We got accepted!" she told the kids after hanging up.

She was given a move-in date of July 1. Nicholas House authorized the rent amount of $1,075 a month, not including utilities, on the condition that Kara pay the extra $75 herself.

"So we're good to go?" she asked Ms. Gilbert, her case manager.

"Yes, we're all set."

Actually, Ms. Gilbert corrected herself, there was one additional thing. The Homeless to Homes program was funded in part by the City of Atlanta, and the city required that an environmental review be conducted on any city-subsidized house or apartment. The purpose of the review was to ensure that the property in question did not "negatively impact the surrounding environment." Ms. Gilbert said it could take up to ten days for the city to complete the review, but she expected it to be finished sooner. Worst-case scenario, she said, was that Kara's move-in date would be pushed back to July 5. "At the latest," she assured Kara.

With an apartment finally lined up, Kara turned her attention to other pressing matters. Ms. Gilbert had recommended switching the kids to a school and daycare closer to her new home, and since finding childcare could be almost as daunting as finding a place to live, Kara began making phone calls right away. The nearest daycare center to Chelsea Gardens that accepted CAPS was Step of Faith Christian Academy in Union City, about a fifteen-minute drive from the complex. The kids could start right away, the director told Kara. This was a small miracle. Next Kara had to figure out where she and the children would stay after leaving the Residence Inn on June 30. Her frustration at having to check out of the hotel was tempered by the knowledge that she would need accommodations for only a couple of days—five or six tops. Because she would be paying by the night, not the week, she settled on Garden Inn, a motel near Step of Faith whose nightly rate— $78 after tax—was the cheapest around.

Three days later, after a long, stressful afternoon of DoorDash deliveries, Kara packed up their belongings at Residence Inn, drove to get the kids, and opened the door to their new room at Garden Inn. The contrast with the hotel they had just left couldn't have been starker. The dark room reeked of cigarettes and sweat, the bedspread was filthy, and there was hair all over the sheets and pillowcases. "Don't worry," she told her kids. "We'll be out of here soon."

A week later, however, they were still there. Every morning Kara emailed her case manager to see if the environmental review had been completed, and every afternoon she had received the same reply: not yet, not yet, not yet—but hopefully tomorrow. As the city's ten-day processing period came and went, Ms. Gilbert said she would contact the Department of Grants and Community Development, the city agency that handled the reviews, to complain about the delay. "I will contact you as soon as I get a response," she wrote, "but I plan to email them daily until the form is completed and returned."

At week two, Kara received a message from DoorDash.

> Hi,
>
> This email is to notify you that your DoorDash Dasher account has been deactivated due to multiple incidents of extreme lateness. This is a violation of our DoorDash Independent Contractor Agreement. After our review and in the interest of maintaining safety of all users, we have deactivated your DoorDash Dasher account.

Kara was dumbfounded. She had been given no advance warning. A quick Google search revealed that by "extreme lateness" DoorDash meant any order dropped off eleven minutes or beyond the anticipated delivery time. Kara thought about the five months she had spent racing around Atlanta and running breathless to people's doorsteps and forcing her kids to pee in bottles. She fired off a desperate reply:

please this is my only income right now please forgive me
its not me I have multiple orders and I have to wait for
the next order to get prepared and if they say wait thats
what I have to do

She hit send. "You have reached an email that is not in use," came
the automated response.

Kara began applying for other jobs, but she knew that even if one
came through, it could be two or three weeks before she received her
first paycheck. (She thought about trying to drive for a different delivery app, such as Grubhub or Uber Eats, but she assumed that losing
her job with DoorDash would preclude her from working for a com-
petitor.) Their room at Garden Inn was bleeding her dry. In order to
continue paying the nightly rate—it still seemed foolish to pay by the
week—she had skipped her car payment, and now, on top of everything else, she was worried about her Toyota getting repossessed. And
because their room contained only a minifridge, no microwave or
stovetop or oven, she and the kids had been eating most of their meals
out, creating an extra financial burden. "I feel like I'm losing it," Kara
confided to one of the workers at Step of Faith. "It's like I keep going in
a circle, and I'm getting dizzy, and I can't find a way out."

She called the leasing office at Chelsea Gardens and pleaded with
the woman who answered the phone. Couldn't she simply pay a pro-
rated amount to get the keys to her unit, she asked, and then Nicholas
House could send the remainder of the funds once the environmental
review was finished? "I don't care if there's no furniture in there," she
said. "I just want the keys so I can lie down on the carpet and go to
sleep." The woman explained that they couldn't hand over the keys
until the lease was signed, and that the lease couldn't be signed until
they had the security deposit and first month's rent. "I'm sorry but you'll
have to wait," she told Kara.

The morning after paying for their twenty-third night at Garden
Inn, which brought the total amount she'd spent on their room to
$1,794, Kara was driving the kids to daycare and almost hit a young
man and woman crossing a street near the motel. When the woman

made a motion to the effect of "Watch where you're going," Kara slowed to a stop, rolled down her window, and began screaming at the couple. She had been doing this sort of thing lately: honking furiously if the car in front of her hesitated when the light changed, aggressively tailgating other drivers until they switched lanes.

She seemed ready to snap at the slightest provocation. She had also been yelling at the children more and more. When they cried, as they inevitably did, it made her angrier, leading her to shout even louder. One morning, she drove to Nicholas House, convinced the organization wasn't putting enough pressure on the city. Ms. Gilbert was away from the office when Kara arrived, but she emailed Kara later that day. "I understand your frustration," she wrote. "But please understand that Nicholas House has done everything possible to get your family housed. Yelling, cursing, and being disrespectful will not get the form completed any quicker."

ON THE EVENING OF Wednesday, July 29, thirty-five days after the environmental review was first submitted and twenty-eight days past her original move-in date, Kara received the call she had been waiting for. The necessary forms had all come back, Ms. Gilbert told her. She could move into her apartment.

"Oh my God, thank you," Kara said. "Thank you so much. Thank you, thank you, thank you." She was laughing and crying at the same time. The kids were watching TV on the bed, and they began jumping up and down when their mom shared the news. Later, Kara went into the bathroom and took out her notebook. At the top of a fresh page, she wrote FUTURE in big bold letters and started outlining what she wanted her life and the kids' lives to look like in a year, in two years, in five years.

The next morning, Kara put on her nicest dress, the pink one she saved for special occasions. The plan was for her to drop off the kids at daycare, swing by Nicholas House at ten o'clock to pick up the checks, and then drive to the complex to sign her lease. Around nine, Ms. Gilbert called to ask if they could make it ten-thirty instead; she had to run a quick errand. Kara said that worked for her. Twenty minutes later, while cleaning their room in preparation for checking out, Ms. Gilbert called her again. "Don't tell me you need to make it eleven," Kara answered playfully.

Ms. Gilbert told Kara she had just heard from a leasing agent at Chelsea Gardens, who was calling in response to her brief email informing them that Kara would be arriving soon with the rent and deposit payment. Ms. Gilbert had been in contact with the complex over the preceding weeks, explaining the situation with the city and apologizing for the delay. They had said it was fine. But there must have been a mix-up, she told Kara, because now they were saying her unit had been rented to someone else. Apparently they had grown impatient waiting for the review to be completed.

"I know this is disappointing," Ms. Gilbert said. She assured Kara that she would write to the management company to find out what had happened, and to request that her family be prioritized for another unit.

Kara was too stunned to speak. After hanging up, she sat on the edge of the bed, staring at her phone. Then she grabbed her purse and car keys. "These motherfuckers," she said. "These evil, evil motherfuckers. Hell no. That is *my* apartment. That is *my apartment.*" She repeated these words again and again, becoming more irate by the minute. Her impulse was to drive straight to the complex with the kids, but when they were almost there she turned the car around and drove them to Step of Faith. She could feel herself about to crack, and she still had enough self-composure to make sure the children didn't see her in such a state.

She dropped them off and, heading in the direction of Chelsea Gardens, suddenly had the feeling she was being scammed again. The people in the leasing office *knew* how badly she needed this apartment. The female agent she'd spoken to had heard the desperation in her voice. She could now imagine the woman mocking Kara with her colleagues, mimicking Kara's begging tone. She could see them deliberately sabotaging her future. And as for Ms. Gilbert, and probably Carla as well, they, too, had been playing games all along. For all she knew, the environmental review had been completed and returned weeks earlier. Out of resentment or jealousy or just plain cruelty, Ms. Gilbert didn't want to see her get ahead. Like Kara's parents, she wanted to hold Kara down, to keep her in her place. In a flash, it became clear to her: these people *wanted* her to explode. They wanted her to crash her car at that very instant. They wanted to show that she was the kind of mother who gets arrested and whose kids wind up in the foster system. They wanted to prove that she belonged in the psych ward where she used to work.

"Don't let that happen," she told herself. "Don't let them win."

There were two leasing agents in the office, both men, and they were both sitting with prospective tenants when Kara came through the door. Like many such complexes in Atlanta, the refined interior of the office—gray hardwood floors, expensive-looking leather chairs, framed art prints—was incongruous with the rest of the property. Kara marched to the nearest desk and, without waiting for the agent to acknowledge her, demanded the keys to her apartment. "Give 'em to me," she said. Then, raising her voice: "That's *my* apartment! You don't *do that* to a family. You not gonna do that to my children!" The agent, whose name was Andre, immediately figured out who she was; he was the one who had emailed Ms. Gilbert earlier. He told her to calm down and wait for him to finish with his other client. His response set Kara off. "You don't *do* that to a family!" she bellowed, pointing her finger at him. "You don't fucking do that!"

Andre was about to call the police when his co-worker, Ian, a slim, light-skinned man wearing an Oxford shirt and round tortoiseshell glasses, approached Kara and, placing a hand on her shoulder, said quietly, "May I sit with you for a moment?" She allowed herself to be guided to his desk while the prospective tenant he had been talking to moved to a sofa. Ian pulled his chair around in front of Kara's so that their knees were almost touching. He asked Kara about her children. How old were they? Did she have any photos of them? He had a young daughter himself, he said, speaking softly. Parenting could be so challenging, he said; there's so much responsibility, and often so little support. Kara dabbed her eyes with a wad of tissues Ian had handed her.

He told her this was actually his last day with the property management company. It had been a summer job while he finished grad school at Clark Atlanta. He and his wife were preparing to start their own business, a home daycare. He asked Kara other questions about her life. He never came out directly and said it, but what he seemed to be telling her was: *I see how hard you've been trying to provide for your kids. I see how tired you are. I can only imagine what you've been dealing with.*

Kara sat in the leasing office for more than two hours. When Ian and Andre's boss eventually showed up, Ian went to talk with her privately. Several minutes later, they rejoined Kara and said they had another unit to offer her. It was a two-bedroom, not a three, but if Kara wanted it she could move in at once. The three of them were huddled around Ian's desk, and Kara called Ms. Gilbert on speakerphone, to ask if Nicholas House would approve the smaller apartment. Yes, Ms. Gilbert said, the agency would allow that. Everyone looked relieved. Ian pumped his hands in the air in celebration.

There was just one problem, Ms. Gilbert continued. In order to receive the twelve months of assistance through Homeless to Homes, this new unit would have to pass an environmental review as well. The city, she said, required that each individual apartment unit undergo a separate assessment. So Kara would be forced to wait—again—for the review to be completed. Or, Ms. Gilbert said, Kara could move in right away, in which case she would be ineligible for the Homeless to Homes twelve-month subsidy. The agency would have to switch her over to a different Nicholas House program, one that covered only the deposit and first month's rent.

Determined not to let the apartment slip through her fingers again while waiting for the environmental review, Kara made up her mind: she would forgo the year of assistance. She would figure out a way to make it work. Two jobs, three jobs, ninety hours a week—whatever it took.

21

The rickety luggage cart was rolling away, but Celeste managed to run and grab it just in time. Struggling to catch her breath, she apologized to the woman whose minivan the cart had nearly collided with. "My *son*"—she looked pointedly at Jalen—"was supposed to be holding it instead of messing with his phone." "My bad," Jalen mumbled, looking remorseful. He went to fetch a pillow and soccer ball that had fallen near Celeste's Durango.

When they finished loading the cart with every item it could conceivably hold, they carefully wheeled it through the parking lot and into the hotel lobby. This was their third time unpacking the Durango in as many weeks. After leaving Efficiency, Celeste had taken Micah and Jalen to her friend Ricky's apartment in Decatur, as planned. Celeste and Ricky had dated briefly a couple of years earlier, but they had never clicked romantically; for Celeste, ambition was among the most attractive qualities a man could possess, and Ricky manifestly lacked it. But an easy camaraderie had developed. Although he technically lived alone, Ricky always had people crashing with him, and one of his two bedrooms was already occupied by a cousin and his girlfriend. If they didn't mind sleeping on the floor, he had told Celeste, she and the boys could stay as long as they wanted.

This arrangement lasted four days. One morning, after Ricky left for work and while the boys were still asleep, Celeste was in the bathroom when the door opened behind her. It was Ricky's cousin, who accused Celeste of flirting with him since her arrival. He then attempted to force himself on her. "I was able to get out before it went too far," she later said, "but it scared the shit out of me." She woke the boys and told them to collect their stuff. She wanted to tell Jalen what had happened but was worried that he would confront the man, so she kept it to herself. That night, they stayed in the SUV with the windows cracked, trying to sleep despite the heat.

In the morning, they drove to Talk of the Town, the restaurant where Celeste was now working. Before heading inside, she made an effort to clean herself up, putting on a fresh T-shirt over a pair of yoga pants and brushing her teeth with a bottle of water. The boys were less than thrilled to be spending the entirety of their mom's shift at a table beside the cash register, but they stopped their pouting when Val, the restaurant's middle-aged owner, brought them a big tray of breakfast.

As the day went on, Val asked Celeste if something was bothering her. She seemed distant, not her usual chatty self. Without telling her about the incident with Ricky's cousin, Celeste said the apartment she'd hoped to get into had fallen through: her old eviction debt was still an impediment, and even the $13 an hour she was making at the restaurant wasn't enough to meet the complex's requirement of earning three times the monthly rent. She and the boys had nowhere to go. Val took a pen from her apron pocket, scribbled something on the back of a receipt, and handed it to Celeste. "That's my address," she said.

Celeste was not the first Talk of the Town employee to benefit from Val's hospitality. Over the years, Val and her husband, Nate, had offered shelter to a near-constant stream of families in the finished basement of their ranch-style home in Lithonia. As the person who signed their paychecks, Val saw up close how hard her servers and cooks and dishwashers worked to make ends meet—and she knew that in Atlanta, where the bulk of those paychecks were being devoured by soaring rents, having a job was no longer enough to prevent someone from becoming homeless. It wasn't only employees who lived with her and Nate for varying lengths of time: relatives and fellow church parishioners regularly stayed at their house as well.

When Celeste was at work, Micah and Jalen, who had resumed virtual school in early August, remained at Val's house, ostensibly to log on to their classes but more often to while away the hours watching movies and playing video games. Celeste tried to give Val and Nate money for utilities, but they wouldn't accept it. They wanted to help Celeste build up her savings.

This plan was derailed, however, when Val pulled Celeste aside a few weeks later. She said her daughter, who also lived at the house and worked at Talk of the Town, was accusing Micah of exposing himself to her four-year-old. The daughter was incensed, and although Val, upon further investigation, believed that nothing inappropriate had occurred—it seemed that her granddaughter had accidentally walked in on Micah while he was using the toilet—she nevertheless thought it best that Celeste go somewhere else. "Just to keep the peace," she said.

Fearful of losing her job if she pushed back, Celeste went to gather their things. On her phone, she looked for the cheapest available hotel rooms in the metro area. For reasons more psychological than financial, she was determined to avoid extended-stays, Efficiency most of all; the idea of going back there was too demoralizing to contemplate. She sorted the search results by "price, low to high," and the Howard Johnson in College Park—the same one they had gone to after her house burned down two years earlier—was near the top. She paid for six nights in advance. *So much for the eviction debt,* she thought.

After successfully guiding the luggage cart through the lobby and up the elevator, Jalen and Celeste entered their fifth-floor room and found Nyah and Micah staring out the window, transfixed. The Howard Johnson sat adjacent to the airport, and from their room they had an unobstructed view of one of its five busy runways. They were watching the planes take off and land.

Nyah's gentler side always seemed to come out around her baby brother, but that afternoon she was feeling particularly tender. The past two weeks had been harrowing for her. In early August, at thirty-five weeks pregnant, she was finishing a shift at Taco Bell when she was hit with the most severe bout of nausea she had ever experienced. Her vision was blurred, and she had difficulty breathing. She dialed Celeste, who, trying to sound calm, told her to hang up and call 911. An ambulance rushed Nyah to Emory Decatur Hospital, where she underwent a battery of tests, including a CT scan. Her high blood pressure and other symptoms pointed to preeclampsia, a potentially life-threatening pregnancy complication, and it was decided that she would be kept overnight. Nyah was scared to death. She looked up *preeclampsia* on her phone and read that it was a leading cause of maternal mortality.

Because of the hospital's pandemic-related ban on visitors, Celeste was unable to see her daughter. But she stayed on the phone with her for long stretches of time. Nyah's tears, her vulnerability, reminded Celeste that for all her toughness and independence, the eighteen-year-old was still very much a child. "I'm here, sweetheart, I'm here," Celeste said soothingly. After forty-eight hours, Nyah was discharged with a plan to induce labor at thirty-seven weeks, provided her blood pressure remained under control. The day was now at hand: Celeste would be dropping her off at the maternity center at five the next morning.

"Micah, get over here and help us unload," Celeste commanded, hoisting a suitcase. Nyah stood up to lend a hand, but Celeste waved her off. "Please, rest," she told her. "The doctor said you're not supposed to exert yourself."

A moment later, Nyah's phone rang. It was Mike, checking to see how she was feeling and confirming that he would be meeting her at the hospital in the morning. She was permitted just one visitor in the delivery room, and Mike, to her great relief, had been adamant about attending the birth. He had, in Celeste's words, begun to "step up" over the previous month, even prior to Nyah's medical emergency. Not only was he showing newfound concern for Nyah's health and well-being and starting to voice excitement about becoming a father, but he had also found a job. Earlier that summer, Celeste had spent hundreds of dollars on a crib and stroller and other baby items for the couple while Mike passed his days hustling and smoking weed with friends. Finally, Celeste could no longer contain her frustration. She let him have it. He still had a clean slate—no criminal record, no real debts. Did he really want to be that guy who gets locked up and never sees his kid again? The guy who has to ask his girlfriend's mom for money whenever his drug dealing hits a slump? Mike had insulted her and stormed away, but her lecture hit its mark, because he was soon applying for jobs. Since late July, he had been making $11 an hour packing batteries at a Duracell warehouse; some days he would work overtime, pulling twelve-hour shifts. When he was first hired and needed steel-toed boots, Celeste purchased them herself. She saw the boots not only as a gift to Mike but as a way of looking out for her daughter and grandchild.

Once the cart was emptied and their belongings had been arranged in semi-tidy heaps around the hotel room, Celeste announced that it was time to eat. They were going to Annie Laura's Kitchen, an Atlanta institution and one of Nyah's favorite restaurants. They arrived at the drive-thru-only establishment a little after six o'clock—sufficiently early, Celeste had hoped, to beat the dinner crowd, but the line of cars waiting to place and pick up orders already wrapped around the building three times. As they inched along toward the order window, Nyah peppered her mom with questions about what to expect during the labor and delivery process. The phrase "high-risk pregnancy," repeated by the doctors and nurses who had attended to Nyah, hovered unnervingly over their conversation. But Celeste reassured her. Tonight, she had assigned herself one task: to empower Nyah, to convince her that she was strong and capable and that everything would go smoothly. "You think so?" Nyah replied doubtfully when Celeste told her what a wonderful mother she would be. "You know I wouldn't bullshit you," Celeste said.

They exchanged a grin at the sound of Jalen rapping quietly in the back seat, next to Micah, who was trying to find his way out of a maze in a children's activity book. Jalen wore headphones and was typing lyrics to go with a new beat he had come across online. It was this project that had kept him on his phone all day. His mom and sister were able to catch a snippet of his newest song. *I know it's hard with your back against the wall / when you ain't got the strength but you still conquering defeat / the outsiders call it weak but they don't see why you don't speak / It's shit going on at home but you don't say that / kick it in your room but trouble always find the way back.*

It took almost an hour for the family to get their food. Celeste parked in an adjacent lot and the four of them started digging into their catfish and greens and mac 'n' cheese. While they ate, they swapped stories and laughed at memories of outings and shared meals from the years before Efficiency—before their house burned down, before the cancer diagnosis. Then suddenly, out of nowhere, thick sheets of rain began pummeling their vehicle. It grew so loud that it was impossible for them to hear one another; through the windows, everything was obscured. Celeste looked over at Nyah, then glanced in the rearview mirror at her sons, munching contentedly at their dinner. She felt nothing but gratitude. *These are my babies,* she thought. After a few minutes, the rain finally stopped. It was one of those surreal summer storms so common in Georgia: clear and radiant one moment, a monsoon-level deluge the next, and life resuming just as quickly.

FOR MAURICE AND NATALIA, the start of the new school year marked a bitter milestone. They had never imagined, back in January when they were scrambling to secure temporary accommodations, that they would still be without a home eight months later. And there was no end in sight. Natalia had lost count of the number of rental applications she'd filled out, not only for apartments in Sandy Springs and Dunwoody but farther afield, in suburbs they had never heard of. She had lost count of the number of times they had been rejected, the money they had thrown away on application fees, and the comments she had left on housing forums to the effect of "Anyone know of a private landlord willing to take a family with an eviction?" Eight interminable months of this, with nothing whatsoever to show for it.

A recent trip to D.C., the family's first since attending Aaron's memorial service in early 2019, had been occasioned by another death: Natalia's cousin Gary had overdosed on heroin. In the days leading up to the funeral, Maurice and Natalia considered canceling the trip. There was the issue of cost. Even though they would be gone for three nights, they would still be required to pay the weekly rent for their room. The only alternative, which was less appealing, was to pack up their room, check out of the extended-stay, and, depending on availability, check back in upon returning. This was in addition to the cost of gas and the motel room they would need in D.C. But there was also the emotional burden of returning home. For Maurice and Natalia, it was easier to deal with the present moment, however dismal, than to be reminded of the future they had failed to build for themselves.

They ended up driving to D.C. at the last minute, and the visit was even more taxing than they had anticipated. Among relatives on both sides of the family, they were perceived as the couple who had made it out. They were the ones who had laid down new roots, the ones who, with their solid marriage and stable jobs at well-known companies, with their date nights and family dance parties and amusement park excursions, all of it displayed in Natalia's social media posts, had found a city where they could thrive. That story was no longer true, but a mixture of pride and shame kept the couple from admitting it. Even their siblings and closest friends in D.C. were unaware of their current circumstances. On the long drive, they asked Shantel and Anthony, who themselves still hadn't been told the real reason they had left their apartment at The Whitney, not to say anything about living at Extended Stay America. "People love to gossip," Maurice explained. But it turned out that most of their relatives were preoccupied with their own troubles. The disappearance of affordable housing across the D.C. region had only accelerated in the years since Natalia and Maurice had left. "It seemed like everybody," Natalia said later, "was either struggling to maintain or had already moved elsewhere. The D.C. we had grown up with was basically gone."

Back in Atlanta, the family returned to what Maurice had begun calling their "expensive prison." He and Natalia had recently calculated the total amount of money they had spent on their weekly rent at the hotel. This proved to be a painful exercise: since January, they had spent upward of $17,000. "Holy *shit,*" Maurice said, incredulous. "These people are making a killing."

He wasn't wrong. In 2020, as Covid led thousands of midrange and upscale hotels to close their doors, Extended Stay America kept each of its 652 locations in forty-four states and D.C. open. As with other "economy" or "budget" chains geared toward families like Maurice and Natalia's, the occupancy rate at Extended Stay America remained close to 80 percent throughout the pandemic, with numerous properties at full capacity. Extended Stay America would record $96 million in profits on revenues of $1 billion in 2020. Observing the phenomenal success of the extended-stay model, institutional investors had started flocking to this asset class. Soon Blackstone, the private-equity behemoth, would partner with Starwood Capital Group to buy Extended Stay America for $6 billion, followed by the purchase of a portfolio of more than a hundred WoodSpring Suites properties—another budget extended-stay chain—for $1.5 billion.

One industry publication described this flood of capital into the extended-stay market, which in the past had been considered a marginal, even disreputable backwater within the wider industry, as a "gold rush." "To be sort of flip," said Jan Freitag, the senior vice president at STR, a hospitality analytics firm, "when in doubt: extended-stay." Today, of the 5.6 million hotel rooms in the United States, more than half a million are now classified as extended-stay—more than double the number that existed in the early 2000s. And that number is slated to multiply in the coming years. New construction of extended-stay hotels is growing at four times the rate of traditional ones; regional chains like Efficiency Lodge and Intown Suites are now competing with global conglomerates like Choice Hotels. Choice has been especially ambitious, projecting 10 to 15 percent growth in their budget extended-stay brands over the next decade. They take pride in their "proprietary data platform [that assists] developers in identifying the best sites for extended-stay hotels."

But there is little mystery as to where these hotels are situated: places where working people are most likely to be deprived of housing. What kept these hotels and motels full during the pandemic was not a sudden upsurge in business travel. It was the fact that the people residing in them had no other options. The flood of investment money can be seen as an attempt to capitalize on—and indeed exacerbate—this state of affairs. Efficiency Lodge once acknowledged in an annual SEC filing that housing-insecure families and individuals were a target demographic for its properties. More recently, Greg Juceam, the chief executive of Extended Stay America, confessed that rapidly rising rents across the country had been a "tailwind" for his company.

In a 2018 survey of extended-stay guests in Gwinnett County, one of eleven counties in Atlanta, 84 percent of respondents indicated that the hotel or motel was their "primary place of residence"; 69 percent reported having one or more full-time jobs. Each day, Gwinnett County school buses made ninety-one stops at these hotels. A more recent analysis by the Southern Poverty Law Center estimates that between thirty thousand and forty-seven thousand people are now living in metro Atlanta's budget extended-stay hotels, charged rates that are often double what an apartment down the street would cost. "It's a reinforcing cycle," argues Michelle Dempsky, a Legal Aid attorney who litigates on behalf of extended-stay residents. "If you're in emergency need, you're paying a premium for necessity, which puts you in more financial distress, which makes you less able to secure housing, which means you're stuck there." Maurice's description of their room as an expensive prison was entirely accurate: the success and future growth of this industry relied on a captive customer base.

Natalia and Maurice were at their wits' end. Their low credit score and the stain on their rental history had become a seemingly insurmountable obstacle. Among the perverse realities of the extended-stay trap, they had discovered, was that paying your hotel rent consistently for months or even years did nothing to repair your credit or rental record. You couldn't ask the hotel manager to write you a reference letter. When applying for an apartment, all that mattered was where you lived *before* you ended up in the hotel. In fact, it wasn't just the exorbitant rates—and subsequent inability to save—that prevented people from being able to leave extended-stays. As with Section 8, landlords were widely known to discriminate against applicants coming from extended-stays because of the stigma attached to such places. Natalia stopped listing Extended Stay America under "current residence," but that created a several-month gap between their last apartment and the present. So she went back to including it—and still they got rejected. There had to be some other way.

For Maurice, that other way was to clear their debt to Liberty Rent. Liberty had told Maurice and Natalia they would consider working with them again only if the money they owed the company—$2,900, for the two months' rent Liberty had paid The Whitney following their eviction—was paid off. Maurice believed that taking care of the debt offered the surest route to getting out of the hotel. If nothing else, doing so would likely raise their credit score. And while the eviction, publicly accessible in online court records, would continue to show up in tenant screening reports, a document from Liberty showing they were debt-free might at least increase the likelihood of being approved some-where. And if not—if they *still* couldn't get approved—then maybe paying the $2,900 would earn them another chance to use Liberty as a cosigner.

Maurice's openness to working with them again was itself a sign of his desperation. It was Natalia who, after losing their condo at Victoria Heights, had pushed the idea of using Liberty, even though it meant spending far more than they could afford—and it was Maurice who had vigorously opposed the plan, and who had attributed their subsequent eviction to having taken on this greater rent burden. But even a luxury apartment, he now pointed out, would cost less than what they were spending at the hotel. He knew that clearing the debt would exhaust the small savings they had accumulated, largely from their pandemic stimulus checks. But he felt they had no other choice.

"You do realize we're out of options?" he said, exasperated at Natalia's objections. "You get that, don't you?"

For her part, Natalia thought paying the debt now would be a grave mistake. She felt they should continue to save. She was convinced that if they could set aside another couple thousand dollars, they could then offer to pay a landlord two or three months up front. Surely *someone* would be willing to rent to them when presented with a large sum of cash? Emptying their checking account while they remained at the hotel just seemed too risky. What if their car broke down and needed repairs? Maurice was still tormented by his tooth pain—what if he required expensive oral surgery? What if one of them lost their job? Their tiny financial cushion would be gone—and then, the ultimate fear, they could be forced to vacate their room. If they were going to deplete their savings, Natalia at least wanted assurance that they would have a place to live. She had already looked into the possibility of receiving emergency rental assistance in the event that they were unable to pay their weekly rent; the CARES Act had provided funding for eviction prevention programs. But hotel residents, she learned, were explicitly barred from receiving such aid. They would be on their own.

"Tell me," she said to Maurice, equally agitated. "Where exactly would we go if this plan of yours didn't work? You want us to wind up in a tent?"

As for Liberty Rent, Natalia had come to see it as a racket: forcing tenants to pay yet another fee to get into an apartment they couldn't afford, and then, if they fell behind, leaving them to fend for themselves. She had even begun to suspect that using Liberty had made them more, not less, susceptible to losing their apartment. The "Liberty Guarantee," as the company had dubbed it, ensured that the landlords they contracted with got paid regardless of whether a tenant remained in their unit. If an eviction took place, Liberty promised to continue paying the tenant's rent for a maximum of six months or until the unit was rerented, whichever came first—hence the $2,900 charge passed on to Natalia and Maurice, from the last month they were late and the one additional month it had taken the complex to find new tenants. With Liberty, Natalia saw in hindsight, there was no reason for The Whitney not to push her family out. From the landlord's perspective, if Natalia and Maurice and their kids stayed, they *might* get paid. If the family was evicted, on the other hand, The Whitney was guaranteed their rent money.

Now that they were unable to agree about the best way forward, the couple's morning meetings in the car became heated. Hurtful words were spoken; old resentments resurfaced. A harshness uncharacteristic of their relationship caused discussions to end abruptly, with slammed doors.

By mid-August, they were still at an impasse, and Maurice was fed up. He started making payments to Liberty behind Natalia's back.

■

THREE DAYS AFTER the birth of her grandson, Celeste returned to
Gateway Center. It had been more than a year and a half since her first
visit, when she had walked away empty-handed, and this time she arrived with a different strategy. The night before, in the lobby at Howard Johnson, she had met another guest, a young mother with a toddler,
whose room at the hotel was being covered for an entire month by a
local nonprofit. They had also enrolled the woman in a program that
would take care of her move-in costs once she found an apartment.
"You gotta be tellin' these people what they want to hear," the woman
said of her own recent assessment at Gateway, which had referred her
to the organization. For months, she had been bouncing between motel
rooms and relatives' couches, always a hair's breadth from finding herself on the street. But that's not what she told the Gateway caseworker
who had interviewed her. Aware of the bizarre logic governing who
was considered "homeless" and thus qualified for assistance, the woman
had said that she and her child were sleeping in an abandoned house. It
had worked: she received the support she needed. Celeste began craft-
ing a similar story.

Like her last trip to Gateway, Celeste got there before the sun came
up. She was the ninth person in line. Soon another woman joined the
queue directly behind her. Her name was Samantha. She had bright red
hair, a silver hoop in her nose, and the palest skin Celeste had ever seen;
she had been staying in an encampment for the past six weeks. She
looked no older than eighteen or nineteen. Before long, the two of them
were deep in conversation. At one point, the younger woman went to
search for a bathroom, and when she came back fifteen minutes later
there were three more people ahead of her in line, separating her from
Celeste. But they picked up right where they'd left off. An hour later,
they were hugging; Celeste promised to lift her up in prayer. Eventually, around eight-thirty, a security guard allowed the first ten people to
enter the building—the number had been reduced that day because of
a staffing shortage. Because of her trip to the bathroom, Samantha was
now thirteenth in line. As Celeste proceeded up the stairs and through

the metal detector, she turned and saw Samantha sitting on the curb, her head in her hands.

The waiting area had been rearranged to accommodate social distancing, and Celeste, double-masked as usual, selected a seat between the two people who appeared least likely to be sick. A peculiar hush blanketed the space, like a library, and when someone spoke to a neighbor or took a call they generally kept their voice low. Even the infant girl in a stroller near Celeste seemed to be observing this unstated rule.

Ignoring her hunger pangs—the only thing she'd had all morning was a bag of Ruffles and a pineapple-orange Faygo—Celeste closed her eyes, lulled by the quiet. A text from Nyah caused her to smile drowsily. It was a video of Caleb—in the baby tub Celeste had bought for him. The birth had gone smoothly: once Nyah was induced, it had taken about twenty hours for her to go into labor, which ultimately ended in a Cesarean section. Throughout the process, Mike had been mercifully quick to respond to Celeste's requests for updates, and when they finally FaceTimed with her, after the delivery, Celeste marveled at the tiny body filling her phone's cracked screen. Now, with Nyah continuing to recover, she and Mike were back at Efficiency with their baby. Nyah's father, Robert, had flown in from Florida, and Nyah sent Celeste a picture of him holding Caleb. They rarely saw each other in person, but Robert and Nyah talked frequently—whenever he called, "DAD" appeared on her phone with heart emojis next to it—and he was the only man whom Nyah had ever told she loved. Although Celeste had her own issues with Robert, who had long ago remarried, she was grateful that he had shown up.

After six hours at Gateway, Celeste was still waiting for her name to be called. By her count, a mere four people had been seen in the time she had been in the building. Weak and in need of food, she was considering complaining when a woman her age with bleached hair, a plastic face shield, and a clipboard marched into the waiting area and announced: "Anyone who has income and a negative Covid test, come with me if you want housing." Then she walked out the front entrance. It was unclear if the woman was with Gateway or some other agency, but nearly everyone waiting, including Celeste, stood and followed her.

On the sidewalk, the woman had set up a large canopy tent, the kind you might find at a farmers' market. She was seated on a folding chair, already filling out paperwork for the first person in line. She never introduced herself to the group as a whole, but after several minutes of listening in on her conversations with others, Celeste gleaned that her name was Joya. She was some sort of outreach worker with an organization Celeste had never heard of. She had a gruff, no-nonsense manner, and it was only when Joya snapped at a man standing in line that Celeste understood what kind of housing was on offer. "A *rooming* house?" the man had said. "Ain't you got some apartments?"

"If you want an apartment, go look for one," Joya retorted. The man stalked away.

Celeste was furious. No way would she have left her place inside the building if she'd had this information. She'd heard horror stories about Atlanta's rooming houses—and besides, every rooming house she knew about allowed only single adults, not families with children. But it was almost her turn to talk to Joya, so she maintained her composure and continued waiting. Since Celeste was polite, all "yes, ma'am, no, ma'am," Joya was friendlier with her. The rooming house for women, she said, was on the West Side, near Joseph E. Boone Boulevard. She had one room available. Rent was $580 a month. If Celeste felt comfortable with the arrangement, Joya said, her boys could stay in the house as well. The three of them could live in that one room.

Celeste thanked her and said she would have to think about it. They traded numbers. "Next," Joya said to a young man standing behind Celeste.

At work that evening, Celeste received a call from Joya. She said she needed a decision right away; there were other women interested in renting the room. Celeste was still reluctant. She hadn't gotten away from Efficiency only to wind up in a situation that was likely worse. The lower rent was no comfort. *Half the price,* she thought, *and probably half as nice.* She was scheduled to check out of the Howard Johnson in the morning, though, and after paying her car note and insurance and putting $9 of gas in her Durango, she didn't have enough money for even one night at a cheaper hotel—which was why she had gone to Gateway. She told Joya she would take the room, sight unseen.

22

Nyah was in bed with Caleb, sweating. For weeks, the window AC unit in her room at Efficiency had been functioning only as a fan. Though September had arrived and summer was finally giving way to fall, temperatures remained stuck in the high eighties. Mike had left for work about forty-five minutes earlier, at one o'clock; Nyah had just finished nursing their nearly two-week-old son and was tenderly rocking him to sleep. After the initial swirl of activity following Caleb's birth, after the countless pictures and videos and the visit from her dad and all the emotional peaks and valleys, she and her baby had ventured out of their room only a couple of times. Instead, they had settled into a cycle of feeding and napping, feeding and napping—and sweating.

As Caleb was drifting off, Nyah heard a commotion in the parking lot. She typically ignored such disturbances, but whatever this was sounded like it was coming from directly outside her door. Placing Caleb in his bassinet, she carefully lifted herself out of bed—her stomach was still sore from the C-section—and went to the window to investigate. "What the hell?" she whispered. She saw a group of men armed with handguns and assault rifles. She felt a stab of fear, and her pulse quickened. Sporting bulletproof vests, combat-style pants and boots, and other tactical gear, they looked like members of a SWAT team or police task force, but there was nothing on their clothing identifying them as law enforcement. They continued past her room. Before they disappeared around a corner, heading toward the front of the property, she heard a woman yelling obscenities and one of the armed men ordering her to keep moving.

At her apartment in Douglasville, Pink's phone was blowing up. The first frantic call came from Travis. He and Eboni and their two boys had been in their room when someone started banging fiercely on their door. "Open up!" a man's voice boomed. As Travis turned the lock and opened the door a crack, it was pushed open by five guards brandishing semiautomatic weapons. Travis and his wife and kids were being evicted for failing to pay their rent, said one of the guards, and they needed to vacate their room immediately. Carter, who was three, burst into tears at the sight of a gun trained on his dad.

Travis tried explaining that there had been a mistake—that until recently he'd been employed as the hotel's maintenance technician, that they still owed him money for work he'd done. A guard said he would have to take that up with management later. "We need you out *right now*," the guard repeated. The only possessions they could take with them, he told Travis, were things they could grab quickly and carry with their hands. Everything else would have to stay. Eboni and Travis looked around their room. They had been at the hotel for more than a year and had amassed a large quantity of toys and kid clothes and play equipment. Eboni reached for a diaper bag and her carrier for her six-month-old. Travis found a backpack and hastily stuffed it full of clothes and toiletries. As they exited their room under the watchful eyes of the guards, another man, whom Travis hadn't spotted, stepped behind the family and started changing their lock with a power drill. Leading them off the property, a guard informed the couple that if they reentered the premises, they would be arrested for criminal trespass.

"Where are you now?" Pink asked. She saw that she had missed several calls during the ten minutes she and Travis had been talking.

He said a few residents who had been evicted, including his family, had gathered across the street, on a strip of grass; others were at the gas station next door. Travis had no idea how many armed guards had descended on the hotel, but he thought at least six families had been forced out. In reality, the number was double that.

Pink said she would be there as soon as she could. Meanwhile, Eboni was on the phone with Housing Justice League, whose emergency hotline number had been making the rounds at Efficiency. After hearing her story, the volunteer who took the call sent out an urgent appeal on the organization's Slack. Families at a "long-term hotel in Decatur" were being evicted en masse, she wrote, and HJL members were needed there at once. She requested legal support as well. A Legal Aid attorney who was involved with tenant rights' advocacy replied that he wasn't able to go but would be available to offer guidance via telephone. Within minutes, Eboni received a call back from the hotline volunteer who said that people from the organization were on their way.

By the time Pink arrived, the scene was tense. A small crowd had assembled at the grassy area; maybe a hundred feet separated them from the hotel's front gate. It resembled a standoff. After carrying out the evictions, a team of guards had positioned themselves at the broken, permanently open gate, essentially barricading the premises, preventing anyone from entering. The hotel was eerily silent, devoid of its usual bustle; the only people visible on the property were the guards, rifles slung over their shoulders. Many residents who hadn't been evicted were afraid to come out of their rooms, including Nyah.

Pink parked in a nearby lot and walked over to join the group. Half a dozen HJL members had already shown up and were conferring with the families. "Y'all, this is unreal," Pink said. "We can't let them get away with this." She was outraged to see all the babies and toddlers among the group, and all the men and women with whom she had formed relationships over the past five months. There was Valencia and her daughters, and there was LaToya, who had recently lost her job at the airport, holding her infant son. There was Ms. Sharon, who a year earlier had suffered a stroke a mere ten days after burying her adult son and had been working as a housekeeper when everything shut down; there was Stephanie, a medical receptionist still recovering from surgery to remove a benign tumor, standing with her three boys. The decision to forcibly remove these particular families and not others seemed weirdly arbitrary. Pink knew for a fact that Christina, for instance, hadn't paid her rent in months, and none of the dealers who had stayed at the hotel rent-free under Lisa had been evicted either. Valencia, by contrast, was only a couple of weeks behind.

"Whoa," said Quinn, one of the HJL members. "Check this out." ProPublica, a nonprofit investigative outlet, had created a searchable online database of every American company given a low-interest loan as part of the federal Paycheck Protection Program. On April 9, Efficiency Lodge Inc. had been the recipient of a loan in the amount of $329,200. (The loan was later forgiven in its entirety.)

People were growing more and more enraged. It wasn't just the surprise mass evictions at gunpoint, terrifying as those were. It was that the guards had barred the evicted families from retrieving their belongings. Like many extended-stays operating under states' "innkeepers' lien" laws, the hotel had a practice of holding hostage a resident's personal property—medical devices, essential documents, even pets—until their balance was cleared. Absent such payment, any possessions in their room could eventually be sold or otherwise disposed of.

"Fuck it," someone declared. "I'm 'bout to get our shit." He crossed the street, dodging traffic, and a moment later could be heard loudly demanding to be let through the gate. A cluster of guards converged in front of him, hands on weapons. The man was gesturing, pleading. Then he turned around and walked back, shaking his head.

REFUSING TO LEAVE without their belongings and with nowhere else to go, the families remained on the strip of grass, waiting and fuming. The stalemate dragged on for almost two hours until Pink spotted a beige SUV approaching the hotel, trailed by a police cruiser.

"Oh, good, it's the commissioner!" Pink exclaimed, trotting to meet the vehicle. Over the years, because of her deep involvement in the community, Pink had come to know a number of elected officials. Some were brazenly opportunistic, seeking to lend credibility to their personal brands—and broaden their voter base—through association with her. But she considered DeKalb County commissioner Larry Johnson to be the real deal: a political leader who was actually committed to improving the lives of those in his district. Raised on the South Side of Chicago and with a background in public health, the commissioner struck Pink as more attuned than most politicians to issues of poverty and inequality, and he had participated in a handful of Community Boutique events over the years. True to the tagline she had given him ("One call, that's all"), Johnson was indignant when Pink alerted him to what was unfolding at Efficiency.

At the front gate, the guards stepped aside to allow the SUV and police car to pass. Pink followed the cars on foot, practically daring the armed men to stop her. After greeting Johnson, she accompanied him to the rental office, where Johnson insisted on talking to whoever was in charge. Pink stood at the door, using her phone to film the encounter.

Emboldened by Johnson's presence and the sight of Pink entering the hotel parking lot, the group across the street quickly migrated there as well. The same guards who earlier had pointed AR-15s at them, threatening to have them arrested if they reappeared, now stood quietly as the families walked toward the rental office. Lieutenant Adam Quigley, the DeKalb County police officer who had arrived with Johnson, seemed intent on de-escalating the situation. A hulking figure with a cleanly shaved head, he was polite and courteous, if flustered by the torrent of grievances coming at him all at once from the displaced residents. "Hold on, hold on," he said, lifting his hands. "Please, one at a time." Travis, the de facto spokesperson for the group, gave a concise account of the day's events. "A bunch of us been living here not for weeks but *years*," he said, "and they just put us out like we trash, like we criminals." He held his son in his arms. "They won't even let me get the bouncer for my six-month-old."

Quigley seemed disgusted by what he was hearing. He said he could understand why they were so angry. "But you all keep using the word 'illegal,'" he said. "What do you mean by that?"

It was at this point that Natalie McLaughlin, a lead organizer with HJL and coauthor of the organization's *Eviction Defense Manual*, stepped forward. She pointed out that, since the families had been residing at the hotel for such a lengthy period of time—a few people even had Efficiency's address on their driver's licenses—their relationship to the extended-stay was no longer that of "innkeeper" and "guest" but "landlord" and "tenant." Under Georgia law, she explained, establishments like Efficiency were obligated to pay hotel-motel taxes only for the first ninety days of someone's occupancy; after that period, the property owner ceased to be an innkeeper—and the occupant ceased to be a guest. He or she was now a tenant. As such, an occupant was entitled to the same rights as any other tenant facing eviction: the owner needed to go through the judicial process of obtaining a writ of possession, and the occupant had a right to fight their eviction in court. In attempting to bypass due process, Natalie argued, the hotel had perpetrated, through the use of private security guards, what were known as "self-help" evictions. And evictions of this kind were highly unlawful. "You can't just point a gun in someone's face," she said, "because you've decided it's more convenient than getting a court judgment."

She offered to call a Legal Aid attorney, and soon the lawyer was on the line with Quigley, confirming Natalie's assessment. If Quigley was persuaded by their argument, however, he didn't show it. Handing the phone back to Natalie, he told the residents to hang tight. He went to confer with the guards and then he walked to his car to make some additional calls.

While all this was playing out in the parking lot, Commissioner Johnson was in the rental office addressing Camille, the manager who had replaced Lisa, through a sheet of bulletproof glass. "Is the owner here?" he asked. "I want to discuss what's going on." She said the owner wasn't on the property. When he asked her to call her superiors at the hotel chain's corporate office, she demurred. "They close at five," she said, "so they're not going to answer anyway." Johnson wasn't satisfied. "Yeah, but they have cellphones, right? And I've got a cellphone." It went on like this for a while. At every turn, Camille rebuffed his demands—not defiantly but indifferently, as if the whole exchange was boring her. Even talk of revoking the hotel's license did nothing to elicit her cooperation. To Johnson's question of where the families were supposed to go, Camille said it was simple. They needed to get jobs and pay their rent—end of story. Her terse answers offered a preview of what would become the hotel's stock response over the coming weeks. Efficiency, it was claimed, was no different than any other hotel. If a guest withheld payment, they had to leave. It was as straightforward as that. A Hilton or Holiday Inn didn't need a writ of possession from a judge to remove a nonpaying guest. Why should Efficiency?

Yet Efficiency's management had, on multiple occasions, acknowledged the legal reality they were now pretending to misunderstand. "Those guests who have been with us for over ninety days," Lisa had explained in the typed notices back in April, after many residents had lost their jobs, "may no longer be 'guest[s],' you may be 'tenants at will.' This means we may have to go through the courts to evict you for non-payment. Efficiency Lodge is trying to avoid this because per your rental agreement YOU will be the one responsible for all COURT COSTS."

It was unclear why the hotel had shifted tactics between April and September, but the closure of DeKalb County's eviction court, resulting in the accumulation of an enormous backlog of dispossessory filings, was no doubt a factor. When going through the courts served the hotel's immediate interests—using the threat of legal costs to further pressure residents into scraping together their rent—Efficiency was willing to recognize the unique status of the people staying there. But once it became expedient to circumvent the judicial process, to simply force these families out through extralegal means and replace them with new residents, acknowledging their status was a liability. By purporting to be "just a regular hotel," Efficiency could justify the lockouts.

Efficiency's position, if not its methods, aligned with that of most extended-stays throughout the country. Their business model, after all, was premised on a straightforward proposition: that it was possible to reap the financial benefits of a traditional landlord-tenant relationship while avoiding its costs, legal and otherwise.

With Camille unwilling to budge on the evictions, Johnson rejoined the others outside. Before long, Lt. Quigley came back to the group, asking everyone to gather around. He said he had an update. "First," he began, "I want to be very clear about my position. I cannot take sides." Typically, he said, his department wouldn't get involved with an eviction, which was a civil matter. But this seemed to be, as he put it, "a different kind of scenario." He said he had notified his chain of command, who had decided to reach out to the Marshal's Office, the agency responsible for carrying out evictions—and that they, in turn, had turned the decision over to a judge. That judge—Judge Nora Polk of the DeKalb County Magistrate Court—had determined that his department did not have the authority to stop Efficiency. "Don't be mad at me," he said defensively as grumbles of "Huh?" and "This is bullshit" spread among the residents.

"What about the ban on evictions?" someone asked. They were referring to the national moratorium announced only eight days earlier by the CDC. With an astonishing twelve to seventeen million American households reportedly at risk of losing their homes for nonpayment of rent, the federal government had been under growing pressure to avert an "eviction tsunami." The CDC moratorium did not cancel people's rent or keep it from accruing; tenants would still be responsible for paying any rent arrears once the moratorium expired. But it was a way for the federal government to delay catastrophe.

That the moratorium was issued by the nation's public health agency was significant. For months, housing activists and health officials had been arguing that during a lethal pandemic, being deprived of shelter could quite literally be a death sentence. This was not hyperbolic: a study published in the *American Journal of Epidemiology* would soon find that lifting local bans on evictions prior to September had resulted in an additional 10,700 Covid-related fatalities.

And yet, buried in the fine print of the CDC moratorium, as the HJL members had already discovered, was a striking proviso. Those residing in hotels and motels were not protected by the moratorium; as with emergency rental assistance, they were unambiguously excluded from the relief it promised. Judge Polk had apparently said as much. "Yeah, I was told that doesn't apply to this situation," Quigley said to the group.

He was able to offer the families only one piece of good news. In negotiating with the guards, who had then consulted with Camille, he had convinced the hotel to allow the evicted residents to retrieve their belongings—not right away, the guards had said, but the following day, in two shifts, one room at a time, escorted by security. That was the most that he, as an officer of the law, could do for them. He seemed unsatisfied with this outcome. "I want to tell you that I empathize with what you all are going through," he said. "And I appreciate everyone staying calm and professional. Because I can't say that if I was in your shoes, right now, I can't say I'd be this . . ." He trailed off. "I've gotta be careful, but you get what I'm saying."

The sun was beginning to set, and any lingering hope that the families might be given a reprieve was now lost. The focus turned to where all these families would go. The guards were getting antsy; they wanted everyone off the property. Johnson stepped aside to make a few calls, and when he was finished he had found a solution, albeit a temporary one. New Life, a large church and community center in the neighborhood, had received funds from United Way and DeKalb County to support its homeless prevention services. After hearing about the evictions, the church's pastor had agreed to use some of this money to pay for a block of rooms at a Budgetel down the road. It would just be for a couple of nights, but it was better than nothing. Johnson asked Pink if she could help with the logistics—organizing transportation, lining up food, and taking care of any other needs that might arise. "Absolutely," Pink said. Natalie and the others from Housing Justice League were arranging to give people rides, swapping phone numbers with the families. "This isn't over," said Graham, one of the HJL members. "We've gotta fight this," said Travis. Several residents nodded in agreement.

As Pink was preparing to leave, a guard beckoned her over. The hotel, he said, was in the process of planning another round of lockouts. They hadn't settled on a date, but it would happen soon, likely within a week. "I thought you might want to tell your friends," he said.

The next morning, it was revealed that a list of rooms had already been drawn up. Warning notices were slipped under residents' doors. One of them went to Mike and Nyah.

| 23 |

At first, Britt thought her mom was joking. It was an afternoon in late August, and she had just dropped off an Instacart order when Cass, who was home with the kids, left a message telling Britt to call her back right away. A letter had arrived saying their apartment building was going to be torn down.

"Mama, stop playin'," Britt said when Cass picked up.

"No, this is for real. Let me read it to you."

"'Dear Resident,'" Cass began.

> We regret to tell you that, by the end of this month, you
> will receive official notification that your lease will not
> be renewed and all apartments must be vacated by
> October 31, 2020. After that date the Gladstone Apartment
> community will cease operation. All apartments must be
> vacated and the buildings will be demolished. The closing
> of Gladstone Apartments is a painful decision for the
> ownership, but unfortunately there is no reasonable—

Britt cut in before Cass could finish. "I'm sorry," she said. "I can't even deal with this right now." She said she would be home in a little while. After hanging up, she thought of Desiree and Kyrie. Britt wondered if Cass had told them.

The answer was clear as soon as she saw her children's faces. Desiree appeared to be taking it especially hard, and once again, like so many other times during the past four years, Britt knew she would have no explanation—or at least no good one. The fact that everybody at Gladstone, not just her family, was about to be forced out was little consolation to Britt. Rationally, she was aware that she had in no way brought this upon herself. Yet she couldn't help but feel that there was something intrinsically wrong with her, some personal defect beyond bad luck that caused these sorts of things to happen.

As Britt changed out of her work clothes, Cass was outside with their neighbors, congregating the way people might after a flood or fire. Through an open window, Britt heard the fear in their voices. "Where are we supposed to go?" was already a refrain. So was the phrase *déjà vu*. East Lake Meadows, Bowen Homes, Englewood Manor, Bankhead Courts, Herndon Homes: the complex was filled with tenants who had experienced this before, whose lives had been upended by a "painful decision" made in an office somewhere and communicated to them in a letter uncannily similar to the one they had just received. Britt's next-door neighbor Bobby, a construction worker who had known Cass since they were teenagers at East Lake Meadows, said it was the same old story. He had been at Gladstone ten years, he said, but it didn't matter. The message remained the same. "It's always 'Fuck you, it's not our problem, go figure it out yourself.'"

Bobby scoffed at the letter's mention of relocation assistance. In order to "help make your move-out and transition to another home easier," as the letter had put it, management was offering money to residents willing to leave their apartments early. If a tenant moved and handed in their keys within thirty days, they would be given a payment of $2,500; if they left within sixty days, before the end of October, they would get $1,500. This, of course, created an incentive to leave even if they hadn't yet lined up another apartment.

And not all residents were eligible for these payments, only those "in good standing," meaning their rent had been paid up through the month they chose to vacate. The complex's most vulnerable tenants—those who had lost jobs during the pandemic and had fallen behind on rent as a result—would be getting nothing toward application fees and a security deposit, making it that much less likely that they'd be able to rent a new place. Cass would later learn that at least two of the neighbors gathered with her outside Britt's apartment were among this group. They all agreed that the relocation funds were intended to shield the complex from criticism, or to keep residents from complaining, or both. "These people don't give away money to be *nice,*" Bobby said. His guess was that the combined payments made up "maybe half a percent" of whatever the bulldozed property would be worth.

It went like this over the following weeks: tenants panicking and commiserating and trying to ease one another's fears; their anxiety growing day by day; residents weighing their need for the relocation funds against the difficulty of securing a place to live. Neighbors reported back on the waiting list at this complex, the application fees at that one. Two complexes in the nearby Thomasville Heights neighborhood, Park Vista Apartments and Forest Cove, kept coming up in conversations, but Park Vista had no available units and Forest Cove, arguably the most dilapidated and dangerous property in all of Atlanta, was widely regarded as beyond the pale—in fact, the entire complex would eventually be condemned.

Attempts to get information from Gladstone's rental office—about what would be happening to the property, and why it was necessary to remove everybody now, in the middle of a public health emergency, while businesses remained closed and schools were still remote—went nowhere. Cindy, the longtime leasing manager, was no longer in the office. In her place were white people nobody had seen before. If you asked them what was going on, they pleaded ignorance, saying they knew only as much as the residents themselves did; any talk of the property being sold and redeveloped, it was claimed, was merely rumor. If you pressed, they handed you a slip of paper with the phone number of an apartment "representative," a former *Atlanta Journal-Constitution* editorial board member and self-described expert in "crisis communications" recently hired by Gladstone's management. There was also an increased security presence. Cass said they were probably worried the residents would riot. For Britt's part, when she wasn't out driving for

Instacart, she mostly kept to herself. The situation was too depressing. She had no plan. She hadn't even begun to formulate one.

Yateshia, Cass's childhood friend from East Lake Meadows whose daughters and mother and brother and aunt and uncle all rented apartments at Gladstone, started stopping by the complex on her way home from work. With the end of September fast approaching, Yateshia had been calling news organizations and local politicians, hoping to thwart the impending demolition—or at least buy her friends and relatives a little more time. The idea that hundreds of people would manage to find an apartment within thirty to sixty days while a pandemic continued to rage was, to her, absurd. She was most worried about residents with disabilities. Both her elderly mother and oldest daughter, Rosa, who had a developmental disability and had lived at Gladstone for more than five years, were dependent on SSI. Rosa received $783 a month; her mother got slightly more than that. In Atlanta, the average rent for a basic one-bedroom unit was now equivalent to 174 percent of the maximum SSI payment of $943. Nationally, the situation was just as bad: there was not a single city or county in America where someone with a disability who received SSI could afford an apartment without other forms of assistance.

"For most of the people here," said Cass, "this is it—this is the end of the line. They call it a 'second-chance' complex, but really, it's a last-chance complex."

ON AUGUST 31, just days after Britt and Cass and their neighbors were told they would have to vacate their units, a man named Kevin Norton submitted a permit application to the City of Atlanta's planning department. As vice president of land acquisition and development at one of North America's leading privately held residential builders, Norton was no stranger to the permitting process. His employer, the Ontario-based developer Empire Communities, had come to be a major player in cities like Austin and Charlotte, and since entering the Atlanta market with a $225-million growth-capital boost from the Carlyle

Group, one of the largest "mega-funds" in the world, the company had rapidly established its presence in the metro area. The developer showed a particular interest in deals along the BeltLine. Projects were in the works in Blandtown, Boulevard Heights, and at the old Stein Steel factory in Reynoldstown. Now, unbeknownst to Gladstone's tenants, Norton was disclosing what would become of the thirty-four-acre property at 1335 Boulevard once the apartment buildings were torn down. It promised to be one of Empire's most ambitious undertakings yet.

The plans filed by Norton called for the construction of 782 high-end rental units, 398 townhomes and condos, and twenty thousand square feet of retail and restaurant space. Positioned alongside Boulevard Crossing Park, which would connect the new development to the BeltLine's Southside Trail, the mixed-use project would also include several interior parks and "amenity features." Preliminary site plans and artist renderings were attached to the application. They showed no trace of the Gladstone property in its current form. Not even the streets intersecting the complex would retain their names. Burroughs and Roberts, Gault and Park (the street Britt lived on) were provisionally labeled "Street A" and "Street B" and so forth, later to be rechristened "Warmbreeze Road" and "Cozy Court" and "Zodiac Drive."

Missing from Norton's proposal was any mention of the affordability restrictions that, under the rules of the Low-Income Housing Tax Credit program, were supposed to be tied to the property. If Gladstone's land use covenant was meant to provide residents with stable, affordable housing until at least 2025, when it was set to expire, how could Empire possibly move forward with its market-rate project? How could all these people be summarily displaced?

The answer lay in an obscure but fateful loophole in the federal housing credit program. In 1989, when lawmakers expanded LIHTC's affordability requirement from fifteen to thirty years, there was concern that this longer period of rent restrictions might deter investors from putting up capital for new developments. So a provision was added to Section 42 of the IRS code enabling owners to exit the program prematurely—as early as year fourteen of their thirty-year commitment. According to the provision, an owner could request a "qualified contract" from their state's housing finance agency; the agency then had one year to find a buyer willing to keep the property affordable. It was a virtually impossible task. The IRS code specified the price that a prospective purchaser had to pay in a qualified contract scenario, and in most cases that price was far higher than its market value. If no buyer was found, the property was released from the program. It could be sold or converted to market-rate units, at which point all affordability requirements would be removed.

For two decades, this loophole drew little notice. A 2012 HUD study revealed that very few property owners were aware that such an opt-out strategy even existed. But gradually, as rental markets heated up and more and more properties approached the fourteen-year mark, word of the qualified contract provision began to circulate among LIHTC investors and owners. Soon analysts were detecting an alarming trend: as property owners availed themselves of the loophole, the country's affordable housing stock began to plummet. Unlike public housing, the LIHTC model of privately owned, government-subsidized rental housing came with an expiration date. But qualified contracts were cutting *in half* the amount of time an apartment complex remained affordable to low-income tenants. Nationwide, by 2023, more than one hundred thousand affordable units would be lost prematurely via the qualified contract process. Most were located in gentrifying neighborhoods, where the financial benefits of redeveloping and converting to market rate were greatest—in other words, at properties exactly like Gladstone.

For Gladstone's owner, the decision to exit LIHTC early through a qualified contract must have been a no-brainer. Although his identity was a mystery to residents at the complex, his name was Nathan Metzger III, a prominent figure in Atlanta real estate. In 1995, when Metzger purchased the property, the BeltLine hadn't yet been conceived, and Chosewood Park was considered little more than a poverty-afflicted place of "distress and blight," as a city report put it, suffering from the effects of chronic disinvestment. It was an area that, from the perspective of real estate capital, was good only for some tax credits. Eighteen years later, when, according to documents released by the

state through an open records request, Gladstone's affordability requirements were removed, Chosewood Park still appeared very much
the same; no major redevelopment projects were yet underway. But
now, with the BeltLine's Southside Trail slated to run through the
neighborhood, land values in the area were soaring. It would have been
easy for Metzger, who had been busy buying up other properties along
the BeltLine, to look at the transformation occurring in areas like Old
Fourth Ward and determine that exiting the LIHTC program would
be enormously lucrative. This proved correct. Metzger had bought the
property for $3.7 million. He sold it to Empire, the Canadian developer,
for $33.25 million.

While Gladstone's tenants were calling news outlets and knocking
on City Council members' doors in a desperate bid to keep their homes,
Empire's plans for its new development sailed through the approval
process. Norton presented Empire's proposal to the BeltLine Design
Review Committee, a city-appointed advisory group tasked with guiding development around the BeltLine corridor. When Norton met with
the committee on September 16, there were no questions about the
property's current tenants. There was no discussion of LIHTC or qualified contracts or the fact that the complex that Empire wished to de-
molish had long been subsidized by taxpayers—a startling omission,
considering the BeltLine itself had published a report arguing for interventions that would enable "the preservation of existing deed restricted
affordable housing developments," with priority given to "at risk" units
that would be expiring soon, were under for-profit ownership, and
were located inside the BeltLine Tax Allocation District. Gladstone was
cited in the 2015 report as the largest complex fitting all three criteria.

The committee members seemed not to have read this report. They
were mainly concerned about specific design choices: too many parking
spots, porches that weren't high enough. They did, however, note the
developer's refusal to go beyond the minimum number of lower-rent
units required by law. Under the city's inclusionary zoning ordinance,
passed in 2017 under intense public pressure, any new apartment buildings near the BeltLine had to set aside 15 percent of units for people
making 80 percent of the area medium income. In Empire's proposal,

that amounted to 72 (out of 482) apartments renting at $1,240 a month for a one-bedroom and $1,490 for a two-bedroom—or nearly triple what Britt and her neighbors had been paying each month. Notwithstanding these reservations, the committee signed off on the project, as did the Atlanta Regional Commission, which was responsible for reviewing permits for large-scale residential buildings.

And in truth, there was nothing nefarious going on: no illegal maneuvering, no bribes or shady backroom deals. There was nothing that would elicit protests or petitions. It was all perfectly typical of the new Atlanta. It "generally align[ed]," as the Atlanta Regional Commission's review put it, with the "policies and principles" guiding development in the city. What was unfolding at Gladstone had happened elsewhere too many times to count, if anyone even cared to.

Most projects of this magnitude also went through a community review process, in the form of a presentation to the relevant Neighborhood Planning Unit, or NPU. Established in 1974 by Atlanta's first Black mayor, Maynard Jackson, the NPU system had come to function as the city's "official avenue for residents to express concerns and provide input in developing plans to address the needs of each neighborhood." But because the Empire development did not involve a rezoning application—the land was already zoned MRC-3 for "high density commercial and residential uses"—the project never came to the attention of NPU-Y, which included Chosewood Park. During NPU-Y's September virtual meeting, there were updates from the local police and fire departments; there was debate about a proposed ordinance to limit the spread of short-term rentals, and there was an announcement that the NPU's book club would be reading *The Color of Law,* a history of housing segregation in America. But there was no discussion about the fate of 1335 Boulevard.

In Atlanta, as in other cities, ambitious projects like Empire's often sparked debate within affected communities; various "stakeholders" were then invited to discuss and provide feedback on development plans, whose basic outlines they often had little chance of influencing. But in this case, there was no organized opposition. The Chosewood Park Neighborhood Association (CPNA), composed almost entirely of homeowners, made no complaints, formally or informally, regarding the removal of Gladstone's residents from their homes. This was largely because they didn't see these low-income renters—many of whom had been living in the neighborhood for more than a decade—as part of the community.

Paul McMurray, the association's vice president at the time, recalled that most of his neighbor's qualms about Empire's redevelopment plan concerned the threat to the area's old-growth tree canopy. Later, on the CPNA private Facebook page, one member complained about the clearing of the former Gladstone site. The towering trees, he wrote, were "possibly the best thing those apartments had going for them." Another member, lamenting the "displacement" of local wildlife, posted a photo of a deer wandering the neighborhood.

SINCE RECEIVING THE LETTER from Gladstone's management, Britt had felt paralyzed, unable to do or even think about anything pertaining to the move. Her inertia was born less of fear than a sense of futility: a feeling that no matter how hard she worked or how punctually she paid her rent and other bills, she would never be able to escape this cycle. She would never be able to look her kids in the eye and assure them that in a year's time they'd be going to the same school or sleeping in the same bedroom or playing with the same friends next door.

But one morning toward the end of September, some of her old optimism returned. She felt compelled to go out and tour an apartment complex she'd had her eyes on for months. The Skylark was a sparkling new property located at 1099 Boulevard, just a short walk from Gladstone. Like most of the construction happening in Chosewood Park, the project's owner, Pollack Shores Real Estate Group, had been drawn to the neighborhood in part because it was "directly in the path of redevelopment already taking shape in Atlanta," as the company's CEO had put it, and in part because of its status as an Opportunity Zone. Created by the Trump administration and passed into law with the Tax Cuts and Jobs Act of 2017, the program was intended to spur private development in "economically distressed communities," allowing investors to defer or avoid taxes on their capital gains if they bought and transformed properties in such areas. A number of these communities were already experiencing rapid income growth—in New York, thoroughly gentrified neighborhoods like Williamsburg, Greenpoint, and Dumbo had been classified as Opportunity Zones—but for Pollack Shores and Empire and other developers, the tax breaks served to sweeten the pot. Along with Red's Beer Garden, a gourmet hot dog and craft beer establishment that had recently opened across from Gladstone, The Skylark signaled what was in store for this stretch of Boulevard. Its fresh, contemporary white-and-glass façade was Gladstone's aesthetic opposite.

Britt considered walking to the complex—fall had arrived, and it was a beautiful crisp morning—but she worried it might look strange, as if she had wandered in off the street. And so, wearing a bright orange sweatshirt and black spandex pants, a style she liked to think of as "sporty chic," she grabbed her car keys and announced to her mom that she was heading out to run errands.

The rental office resembled a hotel lobby, but it was prettier and more inviting than any hotel lobby Britt had ever been in. It was exactly how she had visualized it: all vibrant reds and greens and soft woods and big leafy plants. A masked leasing agent was helping someone else, but the affable young woman gave Britt a brochure and told her she could look around. Trying hard to project a casual self-assurance, as though this were just one of several upscale apartment buildings she would be visiting that day, Britt took a cursory stroll outside and then returned to the office. She sat down on a stylish sofa and began reading the brochure. Under "In-Home Features," she saw that each unit included a "chef-inspired kitchen" and "your choice of color scheme," in addition to stainless steel appliances, a walk-in closet, and a washer and dryer. *A washer and dryer!* No more driving to the laundromat. Then there were the amenities: the fitness center, the pool pavilion. "Step outside your apartment," she read, "and into our community to enjoy the pool deck, social clubroom, or take a trip down the BeltLine." The complex even featured a handful of "artists in residence," whose works were displayed throughout the premises. It was easy for Britt to picture herself living there. The place didn't seem stuffy; it seemed fun, kid-friendly. "The Skylark," Britt read, "offers exceptional features so that you can live the way you were meant to."

And yet, even as she imagined a future there, Britt knew that it was a fantasy. When the agent was finished with the other person, she asked Britt if she wanted to see a model unit. During her previous apartment searches, at places on the QLS/Gladstone end of the spectrum, Britt had grown accustomed to leasing agents asking, "You got any evictions?" or "What's your credit score?" before offering to show a unit. There was none of that crassness here. The complex looked amazing, Britt told the woman. And then, with all the nonchalance she could muster, she asked how much the apartments were renting for. A one-bed, one-bath unit started at $1,355 a month, the agent said. Driving there, Britt had entertained a vague notion of spreading the relocation money from Gladstone across twelve months, allowing her to pay a higher rent. But $1,355 was inconceivable. And they probably wouldn't allow a parent with two kids to rent a one-bedroom. Other doubts came flooding in. Who was she kidding? She would never be approved at a place like this. Britt checked her phone and coolly told the agent that she would have to come back another time, that she had to be somewhere else. She hoped her embarrassment wasn't obvious.

A week later, on the last day of September, Britt picked up the items remaining in her apartment. Most of the kids' things had been taken to their father's place; though Zack and his fiancée had two toddlers of their own, he'd said that Desiree and Kyrie could stay with him while Britt figured out where the three of them would go next. It looked like she and the children would be able to crash at her friend Janeka's apartment, in South Fulton. When Britt had first broached the subject, Janeka seemed hesitant—she had a boyfriend and a puppy, and Britt and the kids would have to sleep on the living room floor—but Britt offered to give her a chunk of the relocation funds, adding, reluctantly, that she would try to convince Zack to keep the children a bit longer. Janeka said that was fine. Britt had almost resorted to reminding her friend of the eight days she had slept on Britt's couch at QLS. She was glad it hadn't come to that.

Using a cardboard box as a carrier, Britt went back and forth between her apartment and the dumpster, discarding anything that wouldn't fit in her sedan. Through repetition, she had grown inured to this dreary ritual. In the seven years since Desiree had been born, she figured that they had relocated at least ten times.

Earlier, Britt had gotten a text from Cass, who was out looking for jobs. She had yet to find a place to stay. Granny had told her no; Theresa, her mom, lived in a subsidized senior high-rise with strict rules prohibiting "off-lease" guests. Aaliyah had just given birth to a baby girl, and she and her boyfriend had made it clear that they had no extra space. Cass refused to ask one of her sisters to take her in. With her kids or grandmother, she could feel that she was helping by being there, but her sisters, to Cass's mind, only judged her, treating her like a freeloader. Cass planned on asking Granny again, hopefully catching her in a better mood. Until then, Britt had agreed to let her sleep in her empty apartment; the people in the office had told Britt that if it was only for a few days, she could still receive her relocation payment. "Don't worry about me," Cass had said when Britt expressed concern. "All I need is my air mattress and my George Foreman grill."

The text from Cass had a link to an 11 Alive story about Gladstone. Britt pressed play on the brief news clip. She was surprised to see Yateshia. "A lot of people is still in square one," Yateshia said. There was a reference to the development that would be replacing the complex: Empire's plans had finally been revealed in the *Atlanta Business Chronicle*. The clip ended with the reporter musing about what would happen if residents couldn't secure new housing by the deadline to leave. "A representative for the property manager," she told viewers, "said no residents will be left homeless. Residents we've spoken to hope that promise will be kept."

Britt filled the box and made one last trip to the dumpster. Two U-Hauls were on the street, and several people's cars were as packed as hers. Bobby had moved out the day before, as had the family of seven across the way; a crew of workers had already boarded up their units with plywood. According to Cass, most residents were taking their relocation money and checking into hotels. That's what Yateshia's

daughters were doing. Yateshia's elderly mother was going to a rooming house.

The only things still in her apartment, when Britt returned to lock
up, were Cass's belongings in a corner and the LIVE LAUGH LOVE plaque
on the living room wall. On the rear porch was Kyrie's Paw Patrol
scooter. Britt had bought it for him for Christmas a few years back; she
remembered the euphoric look on his face as he unwrapped it. He had
since outgrown the scooter, and it wouldn't fit in her car, but she didn't
have the heart to throw it out. She pictured it buried in rubble when the
bulldozers came.

PART FIVE

The New American Homeless

24

One by one they arrived at Flat Shoals Park. They carpooled from Budgetel, and they shared Uber rides from Efficiency. Some came from work; one man came from the junkyard where he'd just been hired; one family drove up in the van they had been sleeping in. Some had been locked out during the first round of evictions at gunpoint; others during the second. Still others continued to languish at Efficiency, no less bitter than the people who had been forced out.

They came to vent, to let loose their anger. They came to rail against the latest in a long series of outrages: two days earlier, Tasha, a thirty-nine-year-old mother of three, had been found dead in her room, a few doors down from Camille's office. On the morning of her death, she and her children had been scheduled to be evicted—it would have been the third round of lockouts—and she had told a neighbor that she had been unable to sleep or eat and had been experiencing piercing headaches. The paramedics thought she'd died of a brain aneurysm, perhaps a heart attack. But those arriving at Flat Shoals Park had little doubt about the true cause of death.

The meeting was being facilitated by Housing Justice League. Members of the organization had stopped by a grocery store to buy party-size bags of Doritos and chocolate chip muffins, brownies and orange Fanta, and as the current and former Efficiency residents ambled into the park's pavilion, they piled food onto Styrofoam plates while talking quietly with one another. The mood was somber. "That place is death, death, death," Valencia said of the hotel, while others talked about the fear and uncertainty they were living with. New Life, the church paying for the rooms at Budgetel, had received funding to cover another ten days for the people marooned there, but that time was quickly coming to an end. And this aid was offered only to families who had been evicted in the initial lockouts. Those evicted the following week were on their own.

HJL had maintained close communication with both groups, in addition to those still hanging on at Efficiency, and there was a growing sense that the harm inflicted by the hotel couldn't go unchallenged—that something needed to be done. During a recent discussion among members of HJL's eviction defense team, it was unanimously agreed that supporting the families and drawing attention to their plight was a matter of utmost urgency. Extended-stay residents, it was pointed out, were arguably the most vulnerable renters in the country. Unprotected by the federal eviction moratorium, ineligible for assistance, and denied even the meager rights afforded to other renters, these "guests" (as the hotels insisted on referring to them) had been exposed to all manner of intimidation and abuse, with no legal recourse. Tenants across the country were under threat, on an unprecedented scale. But there was, at that moment, one thing more perilous than being a tenant: not being considered a tenant at all.

By the time the meeting started, more than thirty adults were present—the children had bolted for the adjoining playground. Pink was there, and so was Celeste. When Nyah had told her about the lockout notice, the result of a debt that had accumulated before Mike began working, Celeste sprang into action. Horrified at the thought of her daughter and grandson suffering the same fate as the other evicted residents, she took out a high-interest payday loan and, later, used her stimulus check to pay off the remaining balance. It pained Celeste to give Efficiency even one additional cent. In her mind, it was no longer just a shitty hotel; it was the embodiment of all the people and institutions that had mistreated or taken advantage of her. It was anyone who had told her, tacitly or overtly: *You'll do this because you have no other option.* Who had said: *You'll put up with this because you can't go any-where else.* In retrospect, she saw the cruelty with which the evictions had been carried out as merely an extension of the hotel's usual treatment of its residents.

Celeste wasn't sure what to expect from this gathering today. She'd never seen herself as the activist type. But for the past two weeks, since Nyah had called to tell her what was happening outside her door, she had been incensed, and the prospect of forcing some accountability was enough to get her to leave work early.

"How's it been at that place you at?" asked Valencia after hugging Celeste. She was referring to the rooming house. "You don't want to know," said Celeste.

Travis suggested that everyone introduce themselves. He went first, enumerating the awful things he had witnessed as the hotel's maintenance person. This was as much a confession as a complaint: he felt that he could have spoken up more assertively on behalf of his neighbors. He was especially anguished by Tasha's death. Her room had been infested with mold, he said, and she had been facing eviction because she had refused to pay rent until the problem was addressed. "It's fucked up how they treated her," he said, referring to Lisa and Camille.

His remarks set the tone for the rest of the introductions. Pink was among the few attendees who simply said her name and sat back down. She seemed less interested in talking than listening, shaking her head in anger as one person after another detailed not only what they had endured at the hotel but the circumstances that had led them there. In their accounts of vindictive landlords and unrenewed leases, tanked credit scores and ruined rental histories, a picture emerged of the housing caste system that allowed extended-stays like Efficiency to flourish.

The members of Housing Justice League were the last to speak. Natalie, the HJL leader who had pleaded the residents' case on the day they were evicted, began by providing a brief overview of the organization's background and mission. A marathon-running twenty-six-year-old with curly brown hair, Natalie was HJL's soft-spoken dynamo. After graduating from college in Pennsylvania, she had moved to Atlanta in 2017 for a yearlong fellowship with Quaker Voluntary Service

(QVS). Although she had been engaged in activism since high school, she had little experience with housing policy, so her placement with HJL (which received financial support from QVS, through the latter's Atlanta Economic Justice Program) was something of a crash course. The more she learned about the power asymmetry between landlords and tenants, and about the displace-and-replace tactics afflicting the city's poorest renters, the more she came to regard housing—who is deprived of it, who is getting rich off it—as an urgent moral and political issue. She was now one of two full-time paid organizers at HJL.

"There's no excuse for what you all have been dealing with," Natalie told the group. "It's complete exploitation." She said the simple act of coming together was a show of strength. Those responsible for their pain wanted nothing more than to keep them isolated, since as individuals they could be made to feel ashamed and defenseless. "But as a *collective* we're powerful," she said. Which was why gatherings like this were so crucial: building relationships was a vital part of any organizing effort. The energy in the pavilion was palpable. Among the residents, who were spurring Natalie on with interjections of "That's right" and "Amen," there was an eagerness for what she and the other HJL members were bringing: a radical, empowering new perspective on their predicament. Natalie pointed out that, in terms of organizing, they were in uncharted waters; there was no clear blueprint or precedent for the fight ahead. She was aware of no prior campaign, in Georgia or elsewhere, that involved extended-stay residents uniting in solidarity. But that was also what made it so significant.

"We would love to join you in this struggle," said Natalie.

"Hell, yeah," a woman named Frederica said loudly. She had been evicted the week before. "If we go down, we go down swinging."

Quinn, a recent addition to HJL's eviction defense team, stood to address the group. In preparation for the meeting, he had been doing research on Efficiency and had made a striking discovery: for years, the hotel chain had been co-owned by the prominent attorney and former Georgia governor Roy Barnes. Although Barnes, whose financial disclosures when he ran for office showed a net worth of $16.6 million, had sold his shares in the company, he continued to represent the hotel in legal matters. His brother, Ray Barnes, remained Efficiency's owner and chief executive. "You all were getting put out of your rooms," said Quinn, "and the Barnes brothers were counting their money." The people behind the evictions, the people who had kept the hotel in squalor and had brought in the armed guards, were no longer nameless, faceless entities. The residents had a target for their ire.

Quinn read a quote from Ray Barnes in an old *Atlanta Business Chronicle* article. "You'll always have undesirables," Barnes had said of his hotel chain. "The question is how quick can you get rid of them."

For a moment, these words lingered in the air. Then Pink spoke up. "All right," she said with a clap of her hands. "When's the protest?"

A PLAN BEGAN TO CRYSTALLIZE. At the end of the meeting, a WhatsApp group was formed, and by midnight nearly everyone who had been at Flat Shoals Park had joined it, along with several current residents who had not attended the meeting for fear that it could further jeopardize their ability to stay at Efficiency. Apart from future in-person gatherings, the WhatsApp group was meant to serve as a means of real-time communication, connecting people scattered throughout Atlanta and allowing them to brainstorm ideas, strategize, and alert one another to emergency situations.

Someone proposed sharing photos and videos of the conditions at the extended-stay, which could be used to draw media attention, and soon there was a torrent of images depicting hideous mold infestations; broken fridges, stoves, and showerheads; busted doors; and ceilings close to caving in. "They got us living like this," wrote Veronica, who stayed in room 117 with her girlfriend. "Don't want to fix nothing but want to take money from us. . . . This is not right." Her message was preceded by the news that four neighboring rooms had just flooded, with videos attached showing water seeping out of light fixtures and covering bedroom floors. Camille was refusing to refund the affected residents' rent or switch them to other rooms. They could leave or "deal with it," she had told them. Such reports were met with exhortations to stay strong, to channel rage into action. "Team work makes the dream work," wrote Pink beside a flexed biceps emoji. "We all we got," wrote LaToya.

During their second meeting at the park, it was agreed that a major protest outside Efficiency would be timed to coincide with the next series of lockouts. There were indications that these evictions would be taking place in the next ten days or so, but the exact date was still unknown. Graham, one of the HJL members, brought poster boards to the meeting, and for about an hour the group sketched out a broader plan, dividing it into three phases: (1) "Outreach/Research," (2) "Launch Campaign," and (3) "Escalation!" Under these phases were listed a set of corresponding tasks, and teams of two or three people volunteered to take each of them on. Then, over the next week, they got to work.

One team of current residents slid flyers under people's doors, encouraging them to call the HJL hotline if they were threatened with a lockout. Another team drafted an online petition, as well as the sample script for an upcoming "phone zap" to Efficiency's corporate office. Travis borrowed a video camera and started interviewing evicted residents about their experience. Quinn and an evicted resident named Rashana continued to dig up information about the hotel's earnings and ownership; Stephanie, Vernando, and Marissa launched a campaign website and sent emails to the Georgia NAACP and Stacey Abrams. Pink met with a group of nine residents and their children to make protest signs, while Eboni and Natalie drafted a demand letter that would be sent to Efficiency's corporate office and the media, along with a press release. The letter called for an end to lockouts during the pandemic and the cancellation of late fees. It also insisted that Efficiency fix the plumbing to prevent flooding; clean up the piles of trash; remove mold infestations; allow former residents to retrieve their mail; and compensate families who were wrongfully evicted. Everybody, it seemed, was doing something, whether printing flyers and coordinating transportation or recruiting additional residents to join the group.

In the midst of all this activity, the group drew inspiration from tenant mobilizations occurring across the country. In city after city, renters were banding together, asserting their right to safe, affordable housing and organizing against displacement, landlord profiteering, and intolerable living conditions. Animated by the conviction that meaningful change would come only through collectively imagining and then demanding it, tenants had begun reclaiming control over their own fates.

A vibrant new tenants' rights movement had been taking shape long before Covid, but tenant unions were now sprouting up everywhere—not just in Massachusetts and New York but in Kentucky and West Virginia, Texas and Arizona. People's Action, a national grassroots organizing network, had launched a Homes Guarantee campaign calling for the creation of a tenants' bill of rights. In California, unhoused Black and Latino families had started occupying vacant properties, part of a coordinated effort to call attention to the immorality of allowing houses to sit empty while rates of homelessness skyrocketed. The pandemic poured fuel on the fire of this tenant activism. In the span of a month, the LA Tenants Union saw its membership double from four thousand to eight thousand. "Rent strike now!" became a rallying cry from the Bronx to Alexandria, Virginia, where newly unemployed tenants at the Southern Towers apartment complex organized an almost four-hundred-unit strong rent strike. Members of KC Tenants, in Kansas City, blockaded the county courthouse, successfully shutting down most of its eviction docket. Seventeen members of the Philadelphia Tenants Union were arrested for attempting to do the same.

On September 30, lockout notices were distributed to at least ten families at Efficiency. They were given one week, until Wednesday, October 7, to pay their rent balances in full. Otherwise they would be immediately forced to leave. Somebody shared one of the notices on WhatsApp. The group was ready: when the hotel's guards started putting families out, a throng of protesters would be waiting for them.

"Good morning everyone," Travis wrote to the group on the seventh of October. "Justice for all and all for justice, let's go team."

"See y'all soon," wrote Stephanie, "and just to let everyone know, I'm so extremely proud of y'all for standing up to fight for what's right!"

Both she and Travis had woken up early to send press releases to local reporters and news outlets. According to the notices, the lockouts would be happening at noon, so the plan was for the group to meet at

11:00 a.m., on the strip of grass where they had congregated after the first evictions. But at 10:15 a.m., messages from current residents began streaming in. "They are locking ppl out," wrote Veronica. "Small children and newborn babies." Several members of the group responded that they were rushing to get there right away.

An hour later, a crowd had assembled across the street from the hotel. Using a megaphone, Stephanie was leading them in a chant. "Fight, fight, fight! Housing is a human right!" The night before, Natalie had put out a call to the HJL listserv, and the organization's members had turned out in force. In less than three days, more than four hundred people had signed the residents' online petition and demand letter. Now many of those people were standing alongside families who had been evicted, some of them that morning. Pink held a neon pink sign that read No Justice, No Rent. A young boy's sign read Remove the Armed Guards! No More Guns Pointed at Children. Off to the side, Celeste was being interviewed on camera by a reporter from CBS 46. "Nobody *wants* to be living at a place like this," she said. "They stay here because they have no other options."

A number of protest signs singled out Roy Barnes, the ex-governor and Efficiency's former co-owner. The Atlanta Legal Aid Society had just filed a lawsuit against the hotel chain, arguing that removing residents outside the judicial process was illegal. Roy Barnes would be defending the hotel in court. Yet he had long cultivated a very different public persona. Two weeks earlier, Barnes, along with Georgia's current governor, Brian Kemp, had presided over the groundbreaking ceremony for a new faith-based homeless shelter. An *Atlanta Journal-Constitution* article about the event had been shared among the Efficiency residents. Helping the homeless, Barnes said at the ceremony, had always been in his family's DNA. "We have an obligation as a community," the paper quoted him as saying, "for those that have fallen on bad times to take care of them."

The protest lasted well into the afternoon. But it did nothing to stop the lockouts. Families continued to be forced out throughout the day. A few of them crossed the road and joined their friends; others simply drove off in their cars, in search of a new place to live. The guards seemed unfazed by the presence of the protesters; Camille was said to have been joking about the gathering. Nonetheless, a news crew had shown up, as had three other reporters and a representative from the NAACP, so the day was deemed a success. The situation at the extended-stay was finally receiving the attention it deserved. Eventually the story would be picked up by the national press. "For Many Hotel Dwellers, Eviction Ban Provides No Relief," went an Associated Press headline. A headline in *The New York Times* read: "Falling Behind on Weekly Rent and Afraid of Being Evicted."

That evening, after the protesters left, word went out that the guards had retaliated against newly evicted residents who had participated in the protest by not allowing them to retrieve their belongings. On Whats-App, the consensus was clear. They needed to keep turning up the heat. The "escalation" phase was about to begin.

THE GROUP WAS STILL riding high at their next meeting four days later. Attendance was a bit sparser than at previous meetings, but the smaller turnout allowed for a more focused discussion. There was a strong desire to build on the momentum of the protest and resulting news coverage. They started plotting their next move: an even-larger demonstration in front of Roy Barnes's mansion in Marietta. That it was his brother, not him, who currently owned the hotel seemed inconsequential. After all, his law firm was representing Efficiency in the lawsuit filed by the Atlanta Legal Aid Society, and he was vigorously justifying the hotel's conduct in news interviews, insisting that the evictions were completely lawful. And he had profited handsomely from his past involvement with the extended-stay, selling his stock shares for nearly $1.5 million—a paltry sum by Wall Street standards, but almost unfathomable to people who had been forced out of their rooms because they were unable to pay off an $800 or $900 rental debt.

During the meeting, ideas for the protest came pouring in. They would enlarge the photos taken at the hotel and glue them to poster boards; there would be a long row of pictures lining Whitlock Avenue, the affluent street Barnes lived on, depicting mold and rodent feces. They would bring shoes and clothing ruined by floodwater and mold stains and pile them in Barnes's driveway. They would create flyers to pass out to Barnes's neighbors. They would invite other activist groups in Atlanta, ones who had helped plan the protests against police violence, to join them. Pink would draw on her political connections; they would get city council members—maybe even a state senator or two—to take part. There would be an aggressive media blitz in the lead-up to the protest, with the Legal Aid lawsuit against Efficiency adding legitimacy to their cause. They would time it to take place on the Saturday before Thanksgiving.

The discussion, however, quickly moved beyond this particular event. What if they dreamed bigger? asked Natalie. Bigger than a protest, bigger than publicly shaming those responsible for the misery at Efficiency? She was a firm believer in the efficacy of protest, seeing it as an important weapon in the group's arsenal. But there were no shortcuts, she said, to rectifying the power imbalance between landlords and renters, to dismantling a system that sanctified ownership rights and property at the expense of human lives. Building tenant power was a tedious, demanding, necessarily communal process. "What might that look like in our case?" she asked.

They could go door to door at the other Efficiency locations, one person said, finding out whether the conditions there were equally bad, whether people were being evicted without due process. There could be a tenant association that any Efficiency resident would be able to join. Even at a single location, a majority of residents collectively withholding the rent until their demands were met could force action. Then, later, they could go door to door at the other extended-stays on and near Candler Road. A2B, Gulf American, United Inn—the families living there were no less exploited, no less vulnerable to sudden lockouts. They, too, needed support.

When the meeting ended, a sense of possibility, of being part of something momentous, pervaded the group. A precise road map for long-term organizing hadn't yet emerged, but nearly everyone felt energized for the work ahead.

AND THEN, as the weeks went by, this momentum slowly but steadily waned. La Toya's car was totaled in an accident. Valencia's phone was disconnected and she became unreachable. Celeste's living situation was deteriorating, and she, too, disappeared. Travis got a new job that made it difficult to attend daytime events. Stephanie, one of the group's most active members, tested positive for Covid and was admitted to Grady for a week. At the fourth meeting, even fewer people showed up. Afterward, on WhatsApp, it took days to find a time for a follow-up meeting that worked for more than a handful of people—and even then it was canceled at the last minute because of a severe thunderstorm.

Logistical factors such as lack of transportation and unpredictable work schedules contributed to diminishing participation. But there was another, more unyielding element: the majority of the group's members were struggling to take care of their most basic material needs. This had been the case since the very first meeting, but now it was crushing them. Tenant organizing required a reservoir of time and energy, and this was exactly what most in the group lacked. They had been given two jobs, essentially: providing for their families and fighting for change. Doing both was beginning to seem impossible.

When the church stopped paying for the rooms at Budgetel, a few people from the initial round of lockouts moved elsewhere. Most stayed on, however, paying their own way at a rate considerably higher than what they had been charged at Efficiency. Some people had been working since June or July, but for those who were unemployed, finding a job, *any* job, became a critical task, as did securing childcare and keeping their kids fed. Then there were the other evicted families, the ones trying to scrape by in their own ways: Two weeks at this temp job, one week at another. A week at the women's shelter while the children were with an aunt. A couple of days in the van, a couple at a hotel. And, for the determined few still holding out hope for an apartment, despite the odds: applications, applications, applications.

At a gathering on November 7, tensions that had been roiling under the surface finally spilled out into the open. While waiting for the meeting to begin, Ms. Sharon overheard Vernando complaining about having to sleep in his car. "At least you've *got* a car," she snapped. Someone suggested that she go to Atlanta Mission, which supposedly had open beds, and Ms. Sharon said that she had already been turned away there, and the conversation devolved into a you-don't-know-what-the-hell-you're-talking-about squabble. Everyone seemed a little raw, sleep deprived. Aside from a brief chuckle at a headline about Trump's loss to Biden ("Queens Man Evicted"), there was no talk of that week's presidential election. People were dealing with more pressing matters.

Twenty minutes after the meeting was supposed to start, there were just thirteen people present. Quinn proposed coming up with an agenda for the meeting, in addition to continuing to plan the protest at Barnes's house. But Pink, already agitated, went in a different direction. "Let me ask you a question," she said. "What's the point of all this"—she gestured at the poster boards—"if these families don't have a place to live?"

For several weeks, Pink had been working nonstop to find jobs and accommodations for those who had been evicted or were soon to be locked out. And she had been doing it largely on her own: calling landlords and driving to hotels and apartment complexes, acting as an intermediary between the residents and various caseworkers, helping parents obtain birth certificates and Social Security cards, and on and on. In the process, she had begun to express frustration at the lack of a more coordinated effort to address these immediate needs. She recognized the value of activism, but she had grown weary of planning a demonstration while families were unable to get so much as a bed at a homeless shelter. In her mind, these pursuits—political organizing, on the one hand, and providing direct assistance on the other—were always in tension, but in recent days, partly because of sheer exhaustion, they had hardened into an impossible binary. The HJL members didn't see the matter in such stark terms. They thought it was feasible to do both: to figure out ways to meet one another's needs *and* to push back against the policies and systems that had created those needs. Yet the time for nuanced discussion had clearly passed. After Natalie ventured a diplomatic response to Pink's question, it was obvious that not only Pink but others had disengaged. When Pink was excited about something, her enthusiasm was infectious. The opposite was also true.

From the outset, the group's driving force had been its fervent, righteous anger—at Lisa and Camille, Ray and Roy Barnes. With every passing week, this anger had dispersed. The group's members were now angry at Gateway and all the other organizations that had declined to help; at the food pantries that had run out of groceries after hours-long waits; at teachers who were threatening to report them for their children's chronic absences; at bosses who refused to give them more weekly hours. They even became angry at one another: at Pink for showing favoritism toward particular families (Pink's retort was that *some people* wanted everything to be done for them); at those who were perceived as selfish or attention-seeking; at HJL for not doing more to mobilize and distribute resources. With so many people to blame, Efficiency Lodge itself was fading into the background. For some of the group's members, it had been two months since they had lived there. The extended-stay had become one terrible place among many. A couple of despairing families would even end up returning to the hotel, lured back by the relatively low rates.

As the meeting dragged on, several former residents made it known that the main reason they had shown up was to talk to Pink, to find out if she had any news for them about housing aid. A week later, when Graham asked on WhatsApp whether anyone was interested in gathering to finish the preparations for their upcoming protest, nobody replied.

In the days after Britt moved out, Gladstone became unrecognizable. Its unnatural quiet was disturbed only by the sound of hammering. At the end of the month, when the mass exodus of residents had begun in earnest, sawhorses stacked with plywood had appeared on the lawn outside the rental office. As each unit was vacated, a crew of three men arrived, sometimes within minutes, to start boarding it up: first its windows and then, last, with a finality that recalled the sealing of a tomb, its olive-green front door. Security guards patrolled the property, warding off potential squatters. The stacks of plywood grew smaller and smaller. Soon there were just enough sheets remaining for the handful of still-occupied apartments.

It was unclear what would happen to the people living in those units if they failed to leave by the demolition date. Their forcible removal seemed imminent. One tenant, a sixty-seven-year-old woman, had lived alone at Gladstone for twelve years. Someone from the rental office had tried persuading her to go to an extended-stay, but she refused; she would hand over her keys, she said, only when she had another apartment to move into. Yet her income, a total of $1,100 a month in Social Security, had so far precluded that. Born and raised in Atlanta, she was facing homelessness for the first time in her life. Others were in a similar position. An undocumented woman with three kids; a mom and her teenage daughter; another disabled senior who, when her next-door neighbor said goodbye, kept repeating, "I got nowhere to go, I got nowhere to go": these were among the tenants who had yet to relinquish their homes.

Cass was still there as well, though she had been using Britt's apartment solely as a place to sleep. In its present state, she found the complex unbearably bleak, and she stayed away as much as she could. She'd started working with ("not *for*," she emphasized) her sister Kimi, who had a housecleaning business called Miracle Maids. Most of Kimi's clients were Airbnb hosts. Covid had put a dent in the short-term rental industry, but things were gradually picking up again. In preparation for arriving guests, the sisters were hired to deep-clean houses and condominiums that had been unoccupied for weeks, in some cases even months. To Cass, the whole concept was outlandish. It seemed incredible that you could own not just one house but two or three; that such extra houses, according to Trisha, could generate six-figure incomes; and that all this was happening at a time when people like her were barely able to keep a roof over their head. *The rich get richer,* she thought, quoting a rap lyric, *and the poor get fucked over and out.* As she vacuumed and dusted and scrubbed bathtubs and kitchen tile, Cass decided that if she ever won the lottery and was able to buy a house, she wouldn't need anything fancy, just enough space for her kids and grandkids to spend the night, maybe a playroom for the little ones—and a Jacuzzi for her aching bones.

In the evening, Cass rode the bus back to Gladstone, getting off at the stop almost directly in front of Red's, the new beer garden. The warm glow of bistro lights, together with the muffled din of laughter and conversation, stood in sharp contrast to the gloom enveloping the newly deserted apartment buildings.

With the gas turned off in Britt's old unit, Cass could neither use the stovetop nor take a hot shower, so she was limited to making grilled cheeses on her Foreman and bundling up in blankets to fight the chill. Before falling asleep, to take her mind off her woes, she sat on her air mattress reading ESPN articles about her son Josiah, the one in Florida on a football scholarship. When she had last spoken to him on the phone, she had lied and said everything was fine, that she had already found another place. She didn't want him to worry.

DJ DREADED RETURNING HOME.

Michelle had sent him to buy groceries with her EBT card, and now he parked himself at a table outside the store in order to prolong the trip. He wished he'd brought his notebook. Aside from Danielle, he had no friends or relatives to confide in, and writing poetry had become a primary means of letting out the sadness and resentment that had been building up in him. He never showed his poems to anybody. They were too dark, too despairing, and, he feared, not very good. Yet writing was becoming a compulsion, much as drawing had long been for him. Sitting at the table, his head buried beneath a hoodie, he considered trying to find a pen and napkin, but he stayed put, watching the passersby and wondering how things at home had so thoroughly unraveled.

After they'd moved into their apartment, it had felt like old times, at least initially. He and Michelle, Danielle, and Skye were a family again, no longer forced to live apart or burdened by the incessant effort to pay for food and their hotel room—or, going back a bit further, by the seething tension between Michelle and Jacob. During those first few days in their new place, despite seeming bone tired, Michelle was outwardly affectionate in a way she hadn't been since their eviction from Eastwyck. But her job at the Salvation Army was already taking a toll. Her shifts ran from midnight to 8:00 a.m., five days a week. If she'd had a car, she could have driven to the downtown shelter from Stone Mountain in about thirty minutes. Without one, she had to rely on MARTA, which required three bus transfers and meant a commute of nearly two hours. Afraid to walk alone, she had DJ accompany her to the bus stop at ten o'clock each evening. Then, since their school district had not yet returned to in-person instruction, he and Danielle would be responsible for Skye until Michelle arrived home around ten the next morning.

After months of spending virtually every moment of every day with her mom, Skye often melted down when Michelle headed for the door, crying, "I want Mommy! I want Mommy!" while Danielle held her. Some nights, it took hours to get her to sleep.

The work itself, Michelle had told her kids, was easy. She simply sat at a desk near the shelter's emergency entrance—the part of the facility for single men and women, no families—and made sure nobody came or went in the middle of the night. Periodically she would do a walk-through of the dormitories, checking to see if there were any issues; when an incident occurred, say an argument or a mental health episode, she would call security or, if it was particularly bad, 911. And that was the extent of the job. She liked her supervisor, who was still encouraging Michelle to pursue a degree in social work, and although her $11-an-hour pay was only barely enough to cover rent and utilities, her impression was that the Salvation Army was the kind of organization where she could eventually have a career, with a salary and benefits.

Yet her grinding commute and schedule, which sometimes involved being called in at the last minute on one of her days off, proved more taxing than she expected—not just physically but emotionally too. Being back at a place, five nights a week, that represented one of the lowest points in her adult life, that signified, to her, failure and desperation, had a corrosive effect. DJ and Danielle bore the brunt of it. At home, Michelle was increasingly irritable and distracted, never fully present. "Like she's here but not here" was how Danielle put it to DJ.

The teens left the apartment only to go grocery shopping, or, in Danielle's case, to occasionally meet up with a friend. Their grades had suffered the previous year, and they had both expected to regain their footing now that they were settled in their own place. But DJ, especially, continued to struggle. Skye's erratic sleep patterns made it impossible to get a full night's rest, and he had difficulty staying awake during online sessions. More than once he realized his classmates had been mocking him as he dozed. It wasn't long before he was behind in each of his classes—even literature, his favorite. Not only was he late in completing assignments, but sometimes he was unaware that work had been assigned.

DJ hoped his teachers would email Michelle to alert her to his poor performance. He thought about bringing it up himself, but he didn't want her to feel guilty. He also didn't want to make her feel bad for failing to follow through on her earlier promise to enroll Skye in a daycare program, which at least would have allowed DJ and Danielle to focus on school while Michelle napped between shifts, instead of chasing their sister around. But no teachers contacted Michelle. His French teacher didn't even respond to DJ's own email regarding a quiz he had forgotten to turn in. He figured his teachers were probably as overwhelmed as everyone else.

Finally, Michelle announced one morning that she would no longer be working at the Salvation Army. She said she was going to find a different job, a regular nine-to-five near the apartment, and that she would try to line up childcare for Skye. A neighbor had told her that a nearby plasma center paid $12 an hour, and Michelle said she was planning on applying there. DJ—always analytical, always on the lookout for signs of trouble—couldn't understand why she would seek employment at such a place. Surely a plasma center would be just as triggering as the shelter had been.

But it was a moot point. The plasma center, Michelle learned, wasn't hiring. That week, she dropped off applications at a discount clothing store and a couple of restaurants, but mostly she stayed in bed, saying she wasn't feeling well. Soon the first empty beer can appeared in the kitchen trash: a single twenty-four-ounce Bud Ice. When additional cans started showing up, DJ and Danielle voiced concern. Michelle told them not to worry. Days passed, and then one evening around dinnertime she arrived home with a man she had begun seeing. DJ and Danielle were stunned. They had no idea she had met someone. His name was Nick: a wiry, light-skinned man wearing a baseball hat backward. He seemed full of himself, and he looked to be half her age; in fact, he was twenty-six, seventeen years younger than Michelle. "What's going on," he said, nodding at DJ and Danielle.

DJ detested Nick from the moment he met him. For Danielle, it took a little longer. Her distrust of this man—who was now showing up each night, disappearing into the bedroom with her mom while barely acknowledging her and DJ's existence—gradually turned into loathing as she saw the effect he was having on Michelle. When Nick was at the apartment, he and Michelle stayed in her room, the pungent smell of weed wafting through the unit. Michelle was at pains to let her kids know that it was Nick who smoked, not her, as if expecting DJ and Danielle to be impressed by her moral fortitude. Yet she was equally keen to emphasize how much Nick cared about her, pointing out, a couple of weeks into their relationship, that he had paid their light bill for the month. "I can't force you to like him," she said. "But I *do* ask that you be cordial and show him just a tiny bit of respect."

DJ and Danielle couldn't fathom how their mom could be attracted to someone like Nick, much less spellbound by him. They found her hunger for his presence, her willingness to so fully surrender herself to him, at once embarrassing and scary. "It's like you're choosing some random guy over your own kids," Danielle said with disgust. Michelle turned and walked away.

The breaking point for Danielle came early on in their relationship, in mid-October. Nick had spent the night, and he and Michelle were still in bed when Skye entered their room to ask for breakfast. From the living room, Danielle heard Nick brusquely tell Michelle, "Have your daughter take her." A moment later, Skye was in the hallway. The three-year-old tried to open the door her mom had just shut behind her, but it wouldn't budge; lacking a lock, Michelle and Nick had used a piece of heavy furniture to keep it closed. The blowup that ensued later that day, once Nick left, was ugly. Afterward, sobbing, Danielle hastily packed a bag and told DJ she was moving back in with Regina, their great-aunt. Then she took off.

With Danielle gone and Michelle spending more and more time either at Nick's place or sequestered with him in her room, DJ was left to take care of Skye on his own. He felt like a single parent. He gave his sister baths and prepared her meals and allowed her to sleep beside him on his twin mattress. He had yet to have even one conversation with Nick. When he talked to his aunt Regina on the phone and she asked him what he knew about his mom's boyfriend, he replied, "I know his name, and I know he lays around all day. That's pretty much it."

He assumed Nick had stopped contributing financially, because a letter appeared stating that October's rent hadn't been paid, and he spotted a text on Michelle's phone warning that their electricity could be cut off. DJ waited until they could be alone before raising the issue with Michelle. Her response was unusually combative. It became clear that she was drunk—*tipsy* was the word she insisted on—and she told him to fuck off. When he suggested Nick was partly to blame for their deteriorating state—"You put your trust in these dudes, and they don't do shit for us in the end"—she exploded. "I'm grown, *you're not!*" she yelled in his face. "You're just a child. You don't get to tell me how to live my life." As for the drinking, she attributed it to what she'd been through the year before. "*You* weren't there with me when I was holding that fucking sign. *You* weren't there with me and Skye when we were sleeping outside." DJ felt the sting of her accusation: that he could have been doing something, *should* have been doing something, to get them out of that situation. On the one hand, she wanted DJ to mind his place, to remember that he wasn't "grown." On the other hand, she was burdening him with the responsibilities of an adult and blaming him for not behaving more like one.

I'm going crazy, DJ thought as he now sat in front of the grocery store. The only reason he eventually stood up and began the long walk back to the apartment—the only reason he hadn't already run away, or worse—was Skye. Recently he had finished school for the day to find his baby sister in Danielle's old room; she had pulled a heavy lamp off the dresser and was playing with the cord. He could hear Michelle and Nick watching a movie, oblivious. Tormented by the thought of Skye hurting herself or starting a fire, he headed home sooner than he wanted.

The next several days were hellish. One screaming match blurred into another, culminating in a brutal fight after Michelle appeared at DJ's door to tell him Nick would soon be moving in with them. "Did you hear that? Do you hear me?" she said, obviously intoxicated, until DJ erupted in rage. "You're the same as your dad!" she taunted him. "What? You gonna beat me like he did?"

DJ threw a glass at the wall. It was the same vicious dynamic each

time: the more Michelle told him he was like his father, the more incensed he became, proving her point. He hated his temper; he hated the
look of fear in Skye's eyes when he cursed and yelled. Afterward, alone,
he wondered if his mom was right about him.

On November 2, the day before Nick was set to bring his things
over, DJ was awakened by Michelle gently tapping him and saying his
name. She apologized for how she had been treating him, and she
promised to find a job and cut back on drinking. She then told him to
get dressed: Pink was coming to pick him up. "Ms. Pink? Why am I
going with her?" he asked. He hadn't seen her since the day she'd
dropped off the housewarming gifts.

As Pink had dealt with the aftermath of the Efficiency lockouts,
she had assumed that no news from Michelle was good news—that
she was merely busy with work. But she missed her friend and was
eager to see her, so that morning Pink had texted Michelle to ask if
she wanted to help sort clothes for an upcoming Community Boutique event. Michelle replied immediately. She was busy, but maybe DJ
could join her? Ordinarily DJ would have chafed at the thought of his
mom making plans without checking with him first, but he was grateful for Michelle's conciliatory words, and he welcomed any excuse to
get away from the apartment. As if anticipating his hesitation to leave
Skye behind, Michelle added that she had talked to Mercedes, her old
co-worker at A2B, who had offered to take Skye for a week or two.
Mercedes and her wife had two children of their own, and DJ knew
Skye would be happy with them. "I think we could all use some space
right now," Michelle said.

DJ hadn't spent much time around Pink, and at first he was quiet
and reserved. But she quickly put him at ease. As they folded and sorted
clothes at Fountain of Hope, the food bank where Pink stored the donated apparel she received, DJ began to open up about the circumstances at home. He spoke rapidly and then haltingly, struggling to be
precise. Pink was shocked and saddened by what she heard. She was
also struck by the fact that although DJ was plainly hurting, he never
denigrated his mother. His loyalty to Michelle, his desire to present her
in the best possible light, emphasizing how hard she had always worked

to take care of her kids and how much she loved the three of them, was deeply moving to Pink. "Now I know why your mom is always bragging on you," she said. He smiled under his Covid mask.

Later, when Pink dropped him off, she walked DJ to the front door. But the apartment was dark and empty. Pink hugged DJ and told him to call her if he needed anything.

His call came sooner than she expected. Less than an hour after leaving him, Pink answered the phone and heard Michelle shouting in the background. "I can't do this no more," DJ said to Pink. It sounded like he was fighting back tears. And then again, this time to Michelle: "I can't do this no more!"

"Shut your bitch ass up!" Michelle yelled back.

Pink's first instinct was to tell DJ to put his mom on the phone and to ask Michelle what the hell was wrong with her. But Pink's father had been an alcoholic, and she knew that trying to reason with someone in Michelle's state was futile. Instead, she told DJ she was coming to get him. "You're going to stay with me for a little while. Does that sound okay?"

"Yes," DJ replied, his voice filled with relief. "That sounds really good."

BRITT WAS TRYING, and failing, to keep her cool. She and the kids were racing to catch a flight, but Kyrie wouldn't stop pestering her to buy him a soda. "I told you, they'll have drinks on the plane," she snapped while navigating her rolling carry-on around the oncoming travelers. "If you ask me again, you won't get anything at all."

In the past, Britt had never felt nervous about flying, but today, for some reason, her anxiety was off the charts. If they weren't already cutting it close—if their MARTA train hadn't been delayed, and if it hadn't taken so long to get through security—she would have been tempted to calm her nerves with a quick rum and Coke. This was her first time at the airport since leaving her job at Low Country. She was relieved to be flying out of a different concourse, lest she run into any of her old co-workers. It had been hard enough exiting their train at the exact spot where she'd read the email from Atlanta Housing Authority about her voucher. She remembered how hopeful she'd felt that night almost two years ago, how excited she'd been to tell her friends at work what awaited her. "Let's go, let's go," she urged the kids, pushing them to walk faster.

The three of them were headed to Milwaukee, where Britt's father, Alonzo, lived. He had been released from prison two weeks earlier, after spending a decade behind bars on drug charges. During this incarceration, Britt and Alonzo stayed connected by exchanging long, intimate letters, and she had known that he would soon be getting out. Even so, it was a shock to hear his voice when he called her from a welcome-home dinner organized by relatives. He said he wished she was there with them. The terms of his parole prohibited out-of-state travel, but he asked if there was any way she could come to Wisconsin. "I've gotta meet my grandbabies!" he exclaimed.

Britt was touched by his eagerness to see her and the kids. Growing up, she had traveled to visit her dad every other summer, and she wanted Desiree and Kyrie to bond with her dad and his side of the family just as she had as a child. Yet the cost of such a trip seemed prohibitive. It would require using what was left of the relocation funds she had received from Gladstone. She was still debating whether or not to go when she got word that her grandmother—Alonzo's mom—had unexpectedly passed away; she and her son had been reunited for only a couple of days. Her memorial service was going to take place the following weekend. Britt bought their tickets that evening.

Once they were seated on the plane, Britt started to feel better. "I am *so* ready for a break," she had told a friend the day before. Cass had been calling Britt incessantly over the past three weeks about her problems with Granny, who had eventually relented and let Cass move in. There had been signs of trouble from the beginning. When Britt drove her mother to the apartment and helped carry her things upstairs, Granny insisted that they put the bags in her bathtub and close the curtain. Alluding to an impending "inspection," she said she was scared of being kicked out if management discovered she had a long-term guest. Cass explained—too impatiently, in Britt's opinion—that no such inspection would be taking place, that she was confusing her current apartment with her old public-housing unit. But this only agitated Granny further. Her Alzheimer's, it became clear to Cass over the next few days, was growing worse. Yet she remained as headstrong as ever, determined to continue living life the way she always had: independently. Cass felt ill-equipped to deal with Granny's worsening symptoms. She took it personally when Granny berated or insulted her, often shouting right back—and yelling at Britt or whoever else tried to defend Granny. Britt saw the arrangement as a powder keg. She gave it one more week.

Her own situation at Janeka's place was only slightly less tenuous. In the month she and the kids had been there, her friend had asked probably half a dozen times how much longer they would need to stay with her. Britt wondered what it would be like to make a fresh start in Wisconsin. She had never seriously considered leaving Atlanta. But maybe her time in the city had come to an end. Maybe the "relocation assistance" would end up going toward its intended purpose after all.

In Milwaukee, Britt ordered an Uber to take her and the children to her half sister Ashley's apartment. Of her four half siblings on her dad's side, she had always been closest with Ashley. They were just a couple of years apart in age, and Britt had fond memories of the last summer they'd spent together, when she was sixteen. Britt attributed their many shared tastes and interests to the fact that they were both Geminis. Although their communication over the years had been infrequent, confined mostly to text messages and comments on each other's social media posts, Ashley seemed thrilled to hear that Britt was coming into town. If Desiree and Kyrie didn't mind sleeping on the floor in her son's room, she said, Britt could have the living room couch. Britt told her that sounded perfect; she caught herself before adding that it would probably feel like a luxury resort compared to where she was currently staying. In the Uber, she thought about all the nights they had stayed awake talking and eating junk food as teenagers, and she imagined picking up with Ashley right where they'd left off.

But after she arrived at the apartment, it quickly became apparent that Ashley's life was no more charmed than Britt's. She seemed worn out from the two part-time jobs she was working, and she apologized for the mess. Their conversations were stilted. Even during an excursion to an indoor water park for her son's birthday, Ashley was frazzled, distracted. She said she hated Milwaukee. She hoped to move somewhere cheaper, with better jobs. *At least Des and Kyrie are having a good time,* Britt thought.

A bigger letdown was the reunion with her father. Britt and the kids had arrived on Wednesday, and it wasn't until late Friday night that he finally came by to see them. "I could tell when we hugged that he sincerely missed me," she said later, "but I also sensed right away that the whole 'father-daughter back together' thing wasn't gonna be happening."

In his letters to Britt from prison, Alonzo had seemed eager to know everything about her. There was none of that interest now. Britt tried to put herself in his shoes—to empathize with how painful it must have been to be locked up for all those years and then, so shortly after returning home, to lose his mother. Still, their time together left her cold. After making small talk for several minutes, he at last gestured to Desiree and Kyrie, who were passed out on the couch. Britt thought it best to let them sleep, but Alonzo asked her to wake them up. Disoriented and bleary-eyed, they were less than enthusiastic to be meeting the middle-aged man towering over them. Desiree said something rude about wanting to be left alone (with her "attitude and sassiness," Britt once observed, "my daughter is me all over again"), and Alonzo told her to mind her manners. His tone, Britt thought, was harsh and inappropriate, and she suppressed an urge to tell him so. "Say sorry to your granddad," she admonished Desiree instead.

The next day, following the memorial service, a throng of relatives and friends gathered at a house belonging to one of Alonzo's cousins. Britt grabbed a plate of food and sat alone, looking at her phone. Earlier, at the funeral home, she had felt awkward and out of place. Ashley and her siblings were mourning the loss of someone Britt hadn't seen or talked to in more than ten years; their shared remembrances and inside jokes only underscored Britt's outsider status. The whole trip,

Britt told herself, was a mistake. She thought of all the other ways she could have spent the relocation money.

Her dad walked by, en route to the dining room. "You all right?" he asked. She smiled and gave him a thumbs-up. She felt like sobbing. He had hardly spoken to her—he had barely even looked at her—since the night before, at Ashley's apartment. "We were closer when we were separated," she said later, "than when we were sitting in the same room together." Their return flight to Georgia that evening couldn't come quick enough.

Before ordering an Uber to the airport, she got a text from Aaliyah: their mom was no longer at Granny's. In the middle of the night, Granny had barged into the room where Cass was sleeping. "What are you doing here?" she'd yelled. "Who let you in?" The outburst had so unnerved Cass that she immediately packed her things. Reluctantly, despite the presence of their newborn, Aaliyah and her boyfriend had agreed to let Cass move back in with them. "I don't want to see Mama out on the street," she wrote to Britt.

On the plane, when the landing announcement came over the PA system, Desiree and Kyrie cheered. They couldn't wait to get home—even though that meant an air mattress on someone else's floor. Through the darkness outside their window, the lights of the city gradually came into view. Britt let out a sigh. She and Atlanta were stuck with each other.

CLUTCHING A BAG FULL OF men's shirts with one hand, Pink reached into her fanny pack with the other and tossed her car keys to DJ. He opened her trunk and carefully pulled out a stack of prepared meals: aluminum foil-covered trays of chicken parmesan with a side of vegetables. They were at the Budgetel on Candler Road, delivering food and clothing to the families evicted from Efficiency who were still there. Driving to the hotel, DJ was struck by how much of his life had revolved around this particular stretch of road. He pointed to A2B (newly renamed Economy Hotel) and the stop where he and Danielle would catch the bus to school; he pointed to the Eastwyck apartments and the Days Inn where Jacob took them after they lost their apartment. "I bet you never imagined you'd be coming back to Candler Road to do *this,*" Pink said as they began unloading.

It had been a week since Pink had brought DJ to stay with her, and DJ had fast become, in Pink's words, her "right-hand man." Over the weekend, he joined her at Fountain of Hope for a big Community Boutique event: taking people's sizes, replenishing the supply of clothes, disassembling the metal wardrobes at the end of the day. During the week, he attended school from Pink's kitchen table. And then, after school, the two of them got to work. They went door to door distributing food to seniors in Bankhead and Grove Park; they dropped in on the many families Pink assisted, and they gave men and women rides to job interviews or check-cashing stores, praying with them before parting ways. DJ adored Pink, and the feeling was mutual. Within a couple of days of being together, DJ was affectionately referring to her as "Auntie."

After completing their deliveries one afternoon, Pink asked about the notebook she had seen him writing in. Was it something for school? she asked.

He told her he had started writing poetry, and when she asked if he'd feel comfortable sharing a poem or two, he surprised himself and obliged. "*What?* That was dope," Pink said when he finished reading. An idea occurred to her. She made a phone call, and ten minutes later she was pulling into the parking lot of Paradise Missionary Baptist Church. The church's pastor had allowed a friend of hers to build a recording studio in an unused office upstairs, and it had become a space where young people in the community could hang out. DJ and Pink spent the next several hours in the studio with her friend and a group of other teenagers. Pink beamed with pride as DJ—at first tentatively, and then with growing confidence—recited his poetry and freestyled over beats he had helped create.

Back at her apartment that night, the two of them stayed up until sunrise, lost in conversation. DJ talked and talked and talked. He talked about his real dad, about how much he both resented and missed him;

he talked about Michelle's anger and pain, and his worry that he was the cause of it. He said he wished he could go back to the days before they left Eastwyck, when Jacob would take him to play basketball and he and Danielle would spend Sundays at South DeKalb Mall—when his mom had seemed so hopeful, so full of life. He was confused by how quickly it had all fallen apart. He said he had begun to think there was something wrong with him, something deeply messed up.

Pink listened, and after DJ had unburdened himself, she said, "All right, now I'm gonna say my piece." She told him he had done nothing at all to cause his family's hardship. She said he was not his father. She said that someday he might have children of his own and that, if so, he would be an amazing dad. But in the meantime, she said, they were going to get his grades up. They were going to make sure he graduated from high school. They were going to find ways for him to cultivate his artistic gifts.

"You've been carrying so much," she said.

Now, at Budgetel, she watched DJ pass out trays of food. At one point, he hoisted a toddler and tried to get the little boy to laugh by making silly faces. Earlier, Pink had called Michelle to see whether DJ could stay with her a little longer, telling her that he was coming alive serving others. "I'm not surprised one bit," Michelle said. "That kid has a lot to give the world."

In the parking lot, Pink asked someone to take a picture of her and DJ. He stood stiffly beside her, looking tough, but Pink was having none of it. "You'd better get over here," she said, pulling him close.

Before leaving Efficiency, Celeste had thought it was impossible to hate a place more. But the rooming house proved her wrong. Situated on a dead-end street in a particularly distressed corner of Dixie Hills, on the West Side, the redbrick bungalow was one of those Atlanta homes that had been bought and sold, flipped and foreclosed upon and abandoned so many times that neighbors were often unsure who was living in the house at any given moment. It was built in 1965, and its current owner was an entity called Ackland Realty, LLC. The actual person or persons behind this name remained a mystery to the home's occupants.

Celeste's first reaction to the house when she pulled into the driveway was to pray she had the wrong address. But then she spotted Joya, the caseworker she'd met at Gateway, and she reminded herself that the rent was cheap. As Celeste approached the front porch where Joya was waiting, she nearly stepped on a sharp object lying on the unmowed lawn; it was a nail file with a thick wad of duct tape at the bottom, forming a handle. "That's always a good sign," she said to Joya, showing her the shank. Joya squinted and shook her head. "Let me take you around."

The house was in disrepair. Entire chunks were missing from the hardwood floor, making it risky to walk barefoot or in the dark, and its once-white walls were covered in grime. Dust bunnies the size of rodents hovered in corners—and real rodents appeared to be a problem as well, given the many traps visible throughout the property. In the kitchen, a pastel-colored bedsheet had been nailed over the windows, casting a pinkish glow over the grease- and sauce-stained appliances and cheap plastic bins used for food storage in lieu of cabinets. The room Celeste, Jalen, and Micah would be sharing was in the basement, adjacent to the washer and dryer. It was dank and musty and poorly insulated, the kind of room that was freezing when you wanted it to be warm and sweltering when you wanted it cool. Celeste entered the room but jumped back at the sight of a huge wasp, "one of them African killer wasps," in her words, perched on the doorknob. She noticed that the screens on the open windows were torn. "I'd make sure those windows stay closed," Joya called from the foot of the stairs.

Yet the house itself turned out to be the least of Celeste's concerns. Walking through the upstairs hallway that first day, she peeked inside one of the bedrooms and saw a woman dozing on a rubber air mattress with no sheets, pillows, or blankets on it. Celeste recognized her from Gateway. Or rather, she recognized the soiled denim bag resting beside her mattress, which had HOT MESS printed across it.

"Hey there," Celeste said as the woman, whose name was Paris, opened her eyes. "Where's your little guy?" At Gateway, Paris had been accompanied by a boy who looked to be about three or four, clutching a Thomas the Tank Engine toy. "They took him from me," Paris said. She then launched into a tirade against the Division of Family and Children Services. Later, Celeste learned that Paris and her son had been sleeping under the Cheshire Bridge Road overpass. She had three other children, each of them now in foster care. She also had a long history of drug use and mental illness, which, as Celeste would discover, manifested in bouts of volcanic rage.

The woman in the next room over was much older and suffered from dementia and schizophrenia. Joya told Celeste that the woman couldn't cook for herself, and she asked Celeste to make extra food whenever possible. "I should have turned around and run out the door right then and there," Celeste said. Instead, she and the boys moved their things in, as did four additional women in quick succession. (Although Celeste had been told there was just one room available, this

seemed not to be the case.) Celeste was the only tenant who didn't receive a SSDI check every month, whether because of mental health issues or a developmental disability, or both.

Like extended-stay hotels, rooming houses were proliferating across
the country, filling the vacuum created by the steady loss of affordable
housing. And, again like extended-stays, their quality and living conditions varied greatly, from the higher-end to the barely habitable.
What Atlanta's rooming houses had in common was their questionable
legality—these were often homes in neighborhoods zoned for single-
family residences that had been converted into multiple individual
units. They were also extremely profitable. It was not unusual for landlords to double or even triple their rental income simply by subdividing
an existing home. The house Celeste and her boys were residing in, for
instance, might have fetched $1,500 a month as a normal rental, but as
a rooming house it generated $4,200 a month from its seven tenants.

Proponents of this model, which caters almost exclusively to single
adults, portray it as a win-win for property owners and renters: a
supply-side solution to the housing crisis that circumvents the expensive
and time-consuming process of constructing new apartments. Yet such
depictions often belie a darker, more precarious reality. Rooming houses
are notorious for attracting slumlords, who, in the absence of legal over-
sight and (as with Celeste and her housemates) formal leases, can evict
tenants at a moment's notice, typically outside the judicial process. Not
surprisingly, it was the poorest, most desperate tenants—as opposed to
the upper-middle-class professionals drawn to "co-living" start-ups like
WeLive and Common—who were especially vulnerable. And it was
this population that most rooming houses explicitly targeted.

Celeste endured four months on Tremont Drive before she started
to crack. "Hell House" is what she called it. Joya had appointed
Celeste the house manager ("The competition wasn't exactly stiff,"
Celeste quipped), an uncompensated role she took on entirely for selfish
reasons: if there was going to be a semblance of order in the house, it
would depend on her ensuring that everyone took their meds and ti-
died the common areas and helped take out the trash. Celeste wrote up
a list of weekly chores and, for a little while, succeeded in getting her

housemates to complete them; she did most of the cooking but insisted they do the dishes; she reminded them to bathe and attend to their personal hygiene—all while parenting her kids and continuing to work part-time at Talk of the Town and searching for other housing options.

But it was only a matter of time before the bottom fell out. "I'm gonna beat this bitch to death!" she cried to a friend one evening after a fight with Paris, which ended with the other woman nearly slamming the hallway door on Micah's hand. "I can't stay here! Y'all testing *my* sanity!" she erupted on another occasion, after the housemate with dementia fell down the stairs early one morning, waking everyone up with her screaming. Whenever Celeste complained to Joya—"These women need professional care," she said, "and I can't keep exposing my children to this"—Joya would alternately promise to make things better and remind Celeste that nobody was forcing her to live there. She was free to leave anytime.

The mounting chaos at the rooming house coincided with Celeste's worsening physical state. This was the main reason she and the boys stayed put, spending more and more time confined to their basement room—which, with their two twin mattresses and narrow futon taking up every inch of floor space, was effectively one giant bed. Although her cancer was in remission, she was suffering from an inability to absorb nutrients (an aftereffect of the treatment). She grew emaciated, her bones starting to protrude. Soon she was down to eighty-five pounds. Her doctors said she needed to have a feeding tube surgically placed without delay. She was hospitalized for three days following the surgery; her niece got the boys and took them to her apartment.

Before she was discharged, she was informed by a nurse that Medicaid would cover only a stationary feeding tube pump. A portable pump—essential for continuing to work at the restaurant—was deemed not "medically necessary" and would cost her a copay of $450. "But I can't afford that right now," Celeste told the nurse. She had used her last stimulus check to pay off Mike and Nyah's debt at Efficiency, to catch up on her car note, and, since her health had prevented her from working as much as usual, to make up the difference on that month's rent. And so, from her hospital bed, she scrambled to put together a

GoFundMe. "If I cannot continue working," she wrote, "my boys and I will be evicted from the rooming house where we are temporarily staying. Please consider helping us during this extremely difficult time." She then posted it to her social media pages. It was shared and reshared, and by the next day, incredibly, she had raised enough to pay for the portable pump.

Frail and listless, she returned to the rooming house and discovered that, in her brief absence, the conditions there had further deteriorated. There was hardly any food, or at least nothing edible—it usually fell to Celeste to pool everyone's EBT funds and drive to the store for groceries—and the house had sunk into a state of alarming disarray: maggots on unwashed plates, trash piling up, mouse droppings everywhere.

At first, Celeste felt a kind of maternal guilt at how badly things had gotten, as if her housemates' welfare was her responsibility. Then she felt angry for feeling guilty. "I didn't sign up for this," she told Joya, who Celeste was convinced was receiving some sort of kickback for this arrangement. "You think I did?" Joya shot back. She had once told Celeste that in addition to her "work with the homeless"—Celeste put the phrase in air quotes when relating the conversation—she also had a job at Macy's and temped as a paralegal. She'd made it clear that the house's "drama," which seemed to encompass everything from maintenance issues to psychotic episodes, was not a priority for her.

FINALLY, ON A WINTER MORNING almost six months after they'd arrived at the rooming house, Celeste pulled herself out of bed and said to her sons, "We're moving to Florida." During the past week, she had been in touch with Micah's grandmother, an internist who ran her own medical practice in Tampa. Celeste had swallowed her pride and reached out to her—itself a sign that she was out of options. Ever since Celeste and Micah's father, who was now in prison, had separated, Celeste had hated asking his mother for anything, knowing such requests would just confirm the older woman's dim assessment of her.

When Celeste told her about the rooming house, her response was predictable—something to the effect of *How could you put my grand-baby through that?* But she agreed to help Celeste in finding a job and a place to stay in Tampa.

For Celeste, going back to Florida, where she had spent much of her early life, was hardly a homecoming. Florida signified defeat. Florida was a childhood wrecked by the foster system. It was heartache and abuse, frustration and futility. Celeste had never hesitated to tell people about her dream of opening a restaurant. But she rarely divulged the whole story: that she and her younger brother, Leonard, had long planned on embarking on Passion Foods together; that Atlanta was the city where they would realize this ambition; that just weeks before they were set to move, he was shot and killed. After Leonard's burial, she had resolved to stick with their plan and before long was setting down roots in Atlanta without him. Returning to Florida was an acknowl-edgment that the restaurant, and so much else, had failed to come to fruition.

After telling Micah and Jalen of her decision, Celeste was anxious to get away from the rooming house as quickly as possible. A few days later, she and the boys were ready to hit the road. They drove to Micah's and Jalen's respective schools to drop off their Chromebooks and mo-bile hot spots. Celeste had already contacted the school administrators to let them know she was having to withdraw her second- and tenth-grader from the district. Then they headed to their closet-sized storage unit to finish packing the Durango.

The storage facility was situated directly beside Efficiency. Through a gap in the wall between the two properties, you could look down at the hotel from the facility's long driveway. As Micah sat in the front seat of the car eating his breakfast—a slice of Domino's from earlier in the week—she and Jalen went and stood at this gap, peering at their old room.

Jalen remarked on how desolate the place appeared. Aside from the armed guards, not a single person was outside. The day before, they had met up with Nyah and Caleb at Big Bear, a local grocery store. Celeste paid for everything; she wanted to get her daughter stocked up on food and diapers, one last time. At the store, Nyah was sullen and with-drawn. She was hurt that her mom and brothers were leaving her be-hind. Celeste had invited her to come with them, but Nyah refused to separate Caleb from his dad. "I get that. You need to do what's best for your child," Celeste said. Nyah told Celeste about a letter from the DeKalb Health Department that had been distributed to the hotel's residents. It informed them of two confirmed cases of tuberculosis at Efficiency. "Oh God," Celeste said. "Please stay in y'all's room, okay?" Her warning was unnecessary. Except for going to work at Taco Bell, when Mike would stay with Caleb, Nyah hardly ever left the room.

Bundled up against the cold, with her skeletal frame hidden beneath two bulky sweatshirts and a pair of flannel pajama pants, Celeste sorted through the storage items as Jalen carried their things to the trunk. At one point, Celeste came across a painting that Slim, the man from Ef-ficiency who had been run over and killed the previous summer, had made for them in exchange for dinner from Celeste's makeshift eatery. It was a picture of a Native American chief. "Sweetie, check this out," Celeste called to Jalen. They'd both forgotten about the painting, and it brought them back to their earliest days at the hotel.

"Can we put it in our house in Florida?" Jalen asked. The question was aspirational. They still didn't know where they would be living.

"Of course," Celeste replied. It took just a few more minutes to fin-ish loading the car. Celeste typed "Tampa" into her GPS, and they began the six-and-a-half-hour drive to whatever awaited them.

| 27 |

When Natalia found out that Maurice had secretly begun paying down their debt to Liberty Rent, she was only half-heartedly upset. Maybe he was right, she thought. As much as she wanted to hold on to the money they had set aside from their stimulus checks, perhaps clearing the debt was in fact the surest route to securing their own place. Who was she to say what would ultimately allow them to escape the hotel? Her experience with Atlanta's housing market, her tenacity in applying and in some cases reapplying to apartment complexes in the area—offering cash up front, exuding competence in friendly, person-alized voice messages, attaching notes explaining their eviction and low credit score, all in vain—had left her convinced that there was little rhyme or reason to getting approved. The whole thing had come to feel inscrutable, as if their lives were in the hands of a capricious god.

It seemed fitting, then, that what finally got them into an apartment was not strategy but serendipity. Natalia spotted a new post on the "In Need of Housing in GA" Facebook group, clicked the attached link, filled out an application, paid the nonrefundable fees, and several days later received a call saying they had been approved for a three-bedroom unit—albeit with the requirement that they pay a "risk management fee" because of their poor credit, effectively doubling the amount of their security deposit. Afraid of losing it if they delayed, they agreed to take the unit, located in Sandy Springs, without seeing it in person.

That night, the family celebrated with hot wings and, for dessert, an ice cream cake. But when they finally drove to the complex, they saw it had the dated, somewhat dingy appearance of other large complexes in this part of suburban Atlanta that had been built in the 1970s and '80s. Despite Maurice's insistence that Natalia and Shantel stay in the car, they peeked through the window of their unit. "*Okay,*" Natalia said, forgetting to sound excited for her daughter's sake. "Okay. I guess this is . . ." She didn't finish the sentence, but she was going to say, "I guess this is what $1,500 a month will get you." "It's so big!" Shantel said hopefully.

The family's departure from Extended Stay America was unceremonious. They had no fondness for the place, even though Matthew had taken his first steps and celebrated his first birthday there. So few were their possessions in the room that, were it not for Natalia's work computers, they could have transported everything in one load. When they returned to the hotel to grab two remaining suitcases and Matthew's stroller, Maurice said, "I'm not going to miss pulling into this parking lot." Natalia made a joke about coming back to the hotel on date nights: she and Maurice could sit outside their old room and relive their private sessions in the car. Nobody laughed. It was that kind of morning: oddly mirthless, given how desperate they'd been for this day to arrive. As Maurice loaded their things, Natalia locked their room for the last time.

"Y'all taking off?" Natalia turned and saw Drea, a woman in her early thirties who lived at the hotel with her kindergarten-age daughter. She and Natalia had gotten to know each other in recent months. Before the pandemic, Drea had been a driver for Uber and Lyft, and when her daughter's school closed she got by on unemployment insurance, expanded under the CARES Act to cover gig workers like her. But those payments had ended in late July. Lacking childcare and unable to find remote work, she had now fallen behind on rent and was facing an impending lockout. Now there was some awkwardness as both women realized that Natalia had been about to leave without saying goodbye.

"Maybe once you get settled," Drea said, "you can swing by here for lunch."

"Yeah, of course," Natalia replied. But she had no interest in ever stepping foot on the property again.

Shantel appeared and said she was ready to go. She had become friendly with a girl upstairs, but when she knocked on the girl's door to give her Natalia's phone number, nobody answered. Relationships were ephemeral at these places.

"Well, I'll see you soon," Natalia told Drea. She and Shantel walked to the car where Maurice, Anthony, and Matthew were waiting for them.

That afternoon, Maurice drove to the Public Storage off Roswell Road to pick up some of the items from their storage unit, now that they finally had a place to put them. When Maurice arrived at the unit's roll-up door, however, the key Natalia had given him failed to open the padlock on it. "You sure there's not another key somewhere?" he asked her on the phone, staring at the disk-shaped lock. Natalia said that was all she could find—they must have lost the original one. Maurice hung up and drove to the nearest hardware store, where, for $45, he purchased the one pair of bolt cutters they had in stock. Back at the storage unit, he tried over and over with all his might to break the lock, but it wouldn't budge. A small band of sweat began to expand at the collar of his pale blue polo shirt. He drove to Home Depot, where he spent $70 on what he was told was a better pair of bolt cutters. Standing in line, he added up the amount of money the storage unit had cost them: $80 a month for nine months, and now $115 to get it open—a grand total of $835.

Luckily, the more expensive bolt cutters did the trick. But when the gate finally rolled up, Maurice was hit with the overpowering smell of mildew. On the day of their eviction from The Whitney, the movers had laid out blankets and bedspreads on the curb and then dumped the family's belongings onto them, tying up the corners when they were finished. Their furniture sat beside these bundles. By the time Maurice arrived with a truck he had borrowed, there had been a heavy rain, and the furniture was drenched. Some of these pieces Maurice threw away; others he hauled to the storage unit, expecting them to dry off and hoping that whatever was inside the blankets had stayed dry. The whole day had been a harried blur. Now, going through their stuff, Maurice wished he had taken the time to air everything out. Their things were moldering, "gross," as he put it to Natalia, and in the end he was able to salvage only two TVs, a stack of framed family photos, and one of Matthew's plastic playsets. "Looks like we're starting with a clean slate," Natalia said.

Over the next few months, Natalia and Shantel began frequenting yard sales and flea markets, buying a side table one day, an old bookshelf on another. Then they would paint and, in some cases, repair these items. "Our mother-daughter DIY project," Natalia posted to Instagram. For his tenth birthday, Anthony's room underwent what Natalia referred to as a "Pac-Man room makeover." She and Maurice spent hours decorating Anthony's bedroom walls to resemble his favorite videogame, using special tape that wouldn't leave any damage. But it wasn't until they received their second round of stimulus checks in December that they were able to properly furnish the apartment, making it feel a bit less shabby.

On New Year's Eve, exactly seven years to the day after they arrived in Atlanta, Maurice prepared steaks on a propane grill he'd found on clearance at Walmart. His friend Stephen was visiting from Baltimore, in town for a baseball tournament. After dinner, while the kids watched a movie and ate popcorn in the living room, Maurice and Stephen drank beers on the small concrete patio outside their unit. Natalia declined their entreaties to join them. She'd decided to turn in early. "You guys enjoy yourselves," she said. She gave Maurice a kiss on his forehead and wished him a happy new year. Neighbors were shooting off firecrackers in the parking lot.

"If this year didn't destroy us," she said to Maurice before sliding the glass door shut, "then nothing will."

A MONTH LATER, in early February, Natalia was pacing back and forth in the living room as Maurice's reassuring voice came over the speakerphone. In less than an hour, her first intake session—tellingly, she kept referring to it as an interview—with the nonprofit Neighbor-hood Assistance Corporation of America, or NACA, was scheduled to begin on Zoom. She was a nervous wreck. She had barely slept the night before, convinced she would do or say something during the "in-terview" to ruin her and Maurice's chances of owning their own home. "Ugh," Natalia groaned. "Why didn't I wait until we could both be on the call?" Maurice was at work. "You'll do great," he said. "Just be hon-est and be yourself." He added that his birthday was only three months away. Who knows, he said jokingly, maybe they would have a house by then. "Babe, for real," Natalia said, "how wild would that be?"

When they had first moved to Atlanta from D.C., becoming home-owners had been their goal. Maurice compared it to a long, winding hike whose summit could not be seen but would eventually—hopefully—be reached, as long as they stuck to the trail. Setting aside a bit of money from their annual tax refunds, slowly trying to repair their credit: this was their trail. The abrupt loss of their rental home had thrown them off it. At the hotel, they'd seemed doomed to remain part of the nation's renter class—that is, if they could manage to pull them-selves out of homelessness and rent a place at all. But Natalia's sister had recently told her about NACA, and suddenly their dream of owning a home was revived.

Founded in 1988, NACA's mission, as Natalia read on the organiza-tion's website, was to make affordable homeownership a reality for working families, overwhelmingly people of color, who had been sys-tematically denied this opportunity. Natalia and Maurice were ac-quainted with the grim statistics: that the homeownership rate for white Americans was nearly 75 percent, while for Black Americans it was 44 percent; that the country's owner-renter divide was a key driver of its racial wealth gap, with the net worth of the median white house-hold exceeding that of the median Black household by a factor of ten. NACA's home purchase program was intended to fix this injustice. Eli-gible families received a below-market interest rate on their mortgage and weren't required to make a down payment or cover closing costs. Scanning the FAQs, one item in particular jumped out at Natalia. "NACA's home buying process is not based on credit score. . . . Even those with poor credit are encouraged to work with NACA, as they will receive comprehensive financial counseling and be put on a path to homeownership."

One night after dinner, Maurice and Natalia sat in front of her work computer and the two of them went through NACA's online handbook together. Natalia wanted to be sure that she wasn't allowing her enthusiasm to cloud her judgment. And indeed, they both laughed when they came to the part where the organization addressed directly how scamlike the whole proposition sounded—especially since, as the website put it, "there is more fraud and abuse in the mortgage industry than any other industry." Maurice opened the calculator on his phone, and he found once again—he had done this many times before—that their housing costs as homeowners, including mortgage payments, insurance, and property taxes, would likely be less than the cost of continuing to rent. And of course the accumulation of equity would enable them to begin building wealth for the future. An added benefit: with a fixed-rate loan (all of NACA's mortgages were fixed-rate for either fifteen or thirty years), they wouldn't be subjected to the volatility of rising rents. Nor would their ability to stay housed be contingent on the whims of a landlord, whose power to terminate a lease or refuse to renew it had proved so fateful in their own lives.

"Let's do it," Maurice said. That weekend, they attended a free four-hour virtual Homebuyer Workshop and paid $25 to become NACA members. They were then able to schedule an intake appointment with a NACA counselor.

"Hello. Hello?"

"Yes, sorry. I'm here," said Natalia. The man on the other end introduced himself as Marcus, and he explained that the purpose of this session was to determine Natalia and Maurice's qualifications for the homebuying program and to develop an "action plan." His formal, businesslike manner threw her off.

"Yes, sir," Natalia replied after he finished his preamble. She became more flustered when Matthew, whom she had set up with Nickelodeon and a snack, climbed her chair and began lunging at keys on her keyboard. "Oh, I'm so sorry," Natalia stammered, trying to keep Matthew from ending the call. But Marcus loosened up at the sight of the toddler. "Hey! I see your big hand waving," he said to Matthew.

"I'm so sorry," Natalia repeated.

"No worries," said Marcus. "That's what kids do." Natalia thanked him and relaxed—until the questions started.

Marcus dug into her and Maurice's entire financial history, from student loan debt and credit cards to their eviction and the amount of money they spent each month eating out. For Natalia, it was like surgery without anesthesia. Finally, Marcus turned to the one topic Natalia was looking forward to discussing.

"Okay, so . . . When would you want to buy a home?" He gave her three possible answers. She picked the last one. "Now," she said, her voice regaining strength. "And where is buying a home in your life priorities?" Again she went with the last choice. "Top," she said. There was a long pause, and then Marcus said that based on their income, an affordable mortgage would be $1,085 a month. "That would put you at, let me see here . . . $203,009 in terms of buying power."

"That sounds great!" Natalia exclaimed. She resisted the urge to reach for her phone and begin looking up listings.

"And you would need," Marcus continued, "a minimum of $4,777 at closing."

This caught Natalia off guard. Was he talking about a down payment? What happened to the "no down payment" thing? She wanted to seek clarification but was afraid of asking a dumb question. Later, rereading the handbook, she would discover that what he was referring to was not a down payment but the "minimum required funds" needed for an earnest money deposit, the cost of a home inspection, prepayment for property insurance and taxes, and other miscellaneous expenses.

"You mentioned earlier that you and Maurice have about $800 in savings. Based on your current savings, how long do you think it would take to come up with your minimum required funds of $4,777?"

"Umm . . ." Natalia had no idea how to answer this. She felt deflated. It wasn't Marcus's fault; he was gracious and polite. It was her and Maurice's fault. Their naivete, their childish optimism, their talk of owning a house by Maurice's birthday: it made her want to crawl into a hole. She tried to keep her composure. "Umm, probably a year?"

"Okay, I'll make a note of that. So that would put us at February of next year for a follow-up." The call concluded shortly after.

THE FOLLOWING SUNDAY, Natalia woke up with a strong desire to be outside. "Come on, no more screens," she announced to Shantel and Anthony. "That goes for you too," she told Maurice, who had settled in front of the TV to watch pro wrestling. As they grudgingly got dressed, Natalia threw together a picnic lunch. The kids had made a last-ditch appeal for Sky Zone, an indoor trampoline park, but Natalia and Maurice, who were not yet vaccinated, were still leery of enclosed public spaces. Natalia assured Anthony and Shantel that a little fresh air wouldn't hurt them.

An hour later, at the riverfront not far from their apartment, Natalia and Maurice sat on a blanket facing the water. Anthony and Matthew were playing on the sandy bank; Shantel was sitting on a nearby boulder, listening to music on her headphones. The morning was gray and overcast—slightly warmer than it had been in recent days but still cold enough to necessitate jackets and beanies. During the spring and summer months this area of the Chattahoochee tended to be crowded. But today there were only a handful of other people.

Natalia was finding it difficult to shake the NACA interview. For her, the takeaways seemed clear: there were firm limits on what they could achieve, and no matter how hard they worked they would be handing over the bulk of their income to a landlord for the foreseeable future. Their security was tenuous. And it was likely to stay that way.

Maurice was less discouraged about their prospects. To him, saving $4,000 over the next year while paying down their debts would be a challenge, but it wasn't out of the question. Sure, their hope of getting approved by NACA in their current financial state had been unrealistic. Yet they weren't fated to remain renters. If need be, he told Natalia, he would take on a second job to bring in extra money, just as he had when they were at The Whitney. And Natalia was in the process of embarking on her own side gig. A few months earlier, eager for a diversion, she had begun making bath and body products: candles and hand lotions, soaps and children's bath bombs. She had given these items to friends and relatives for Christmas, and the response had been enthusiastic. Now she was considering launching a pop-up shop at an upcoming vendor expo. Maurice told her he would do anything he could to help facilitate this.

"It might take a little while to get there," he said, reclining on the blanket. "But we'll get there."

Matthew was ready for a nap, and before long he was asleep on his dad's belly. Natalia sat beside them, hugging her knees to her chest and looking out at the river. She told Maurice this was the sort of thing she had pictured them doing when they decided to move to Georgia, and Maurice replied drowsily, "Yeah, me too."

28

Michelle stumbled through the darkness of the apartment, searching for her phone. Like the day before, and the day before that,
she had awoken with a ferocious hangover. Her head throbbed vio-
lently; she felt parched, as though every last drop of moisture had been
wrung from her body. She was alone, with a hazy recollection of Nick
having told her earlier in the morning that he was going out. Or maybe
it was already the afternoon. The only indication that it was day, not
night, was the thin bar of sunlight underneath a curtain. Michelle went
from room to room looking for the phone, until all of a sudden she
stopped, remembering what had happened to it. During a recent fight
with Nick, she had thrown it at him, just barely missing his head, and
had watched it smash to pieces against the wall behind him.

The apartment reeked of cigarette smoke, and it was frigid too.
Since the electricity had been disconnected, the sole source of heat was
the gas stove, which stayed on for hours on end. Michelle's bedroom,
with its tangle of sheets and blankets and unwashed clothes and food
wrappers littering the floor, was the one room in the apartment that
appeared lived in. The rest of the unit had a vacant feel. There were a
few traces of more recent activity: cigarettes stubbed out in the fireplace and in upside-down coffee lids, empty beer cans on the counter.
But when Michelle looked around, most of what she saw seemed like

artifacts from another life. The blue painting her Salvation Army co-worker's daughter had made for her. An old Mother's Day card from DJ ("For You, Mom, With Loving Thoughts"). The framed Bible verse and inspirational quote from Pink. And, finally, an E-Z Build Gingerbread House Kit that Michelle had purchased in a moment of sobriety, hoping that the kids might return for the holidays and that they could re-create the fun they'd had building a similar house two years earlier. It was now a month past Christmas. The kit sat unopened on the mantel.

Michelle's estrangement from her children had deepened in the nearly three months they'd been away. The kids were now together at their aunt Regina's house. On the morning of Thanksgiving, Michelle had texted Pink that she wanted DJ home with her that evening. He was excited to share a meal with his mom—and later, he was too hurt and ashamed to tell Pink that, after an argument, Michelle ended up leaving him alone in the apartment, choosing to go out with Nick instead. DJ stayed with Michelle for a few more days, afraid of imposing on Pink, of continuing to be the burden that he felt himself to be. Then Skye joined Danielle at Regina's, and soon DJ did as well. "It's because my work schedule's about to get crazy," Michelle told Mercedes, referring to an overnight job she hadn't even applied for. "It's better for them to be with Regina." When her stimulus payment arrived, she impulsively Cash-Apped the bulk of it to her aunt, provoking Nick's ire.

When Michelle was drinking, she told herself that Danielle and DJ were simply jealous of Nick, that they couldn't accept that she needed companionship beyond the kind they could provide. For years and years, she had been single-mindedly preoccupied with ensuring their well-being. She was so *tired*. Why couldn't they let her have this one thing? When she wasn't intoxicated, she knew that such rationalizations were bullshit. She saw herself the way Pink and her kids and Regina and everyone else saw her: a woman bent on self-sabotage. She despised what she saw, so she drank to see differently.

Instead of her phone, Michelle located her backpack. She reached into it and removed a tall can of Bud Ice, her first of the day.

■

As winter turned to spring, DJ's and Danielle's communication with their mom became more infrequent. And when they did talk to Michelle, they had to sift meaning from inebriated, often disjointed monologues. They were able to gather that, after working at KFC for a month, she and Nick had found a job with some sort of traveling fair or carnival, until during their last stop—in Albany, Georgia—Nick had had an altercation with their supervisor and gotten them both fired. The injustice of this firing, and the convoluted account of how they'd managed to make it back to Atlanta without a car of their own, took up an entire perplexing conversation. DJ and Danielle also gleaned that she had lost the apartment: that she had attempted to pay down her rental balance by handing over a whole paycheck but that the leasing office would accept only the full past-due amount; that she and Nick had used her March stimulus check—or what remained of it after again sending money to Regina—to rent a room at Haven Hotel in Stone Mountain. But much of what she said, from one phone call to the next, was contradictory and easily disproved. It was hard for the teenagers to know what, if anything, they could believe.

By April, her calls were growing frantic. They were now almost exclusively to Danielle, usually in the middle of the night, and they had a breathless, frenzied quality. To Danielle, picking up on Michelle's cues, it was obvious that Nick was physically abusive, and—although Michelle never came out and said it, always defending Nick or explaining away his actions—it seemed clear that her mom was scared of him. As Michelle described it, Nick's fury was most severe when he felt slighted or belittled by her, or when he supposedly caught her flirting with some stranger. In one breath, she would gush about how much he cared for her, the various gifts he had given her and so forth, and in the next she would detail his threatening and controlling behavior. A couple of times, she mentioned needing to get away from him, but Danielle's pleas for Michelle to leave Nick for good were barely acknowledged, much less heeded.

After a late-night call during which Michelle declared that she no longer had anything to live for, Danielle and DJ were wrecked, unable to sleep for days or to concentrate on their schoolwork. Regina, observing the toll all this was taking on her great-niece and -nephew, reminded them that praying for their mom, asking angels to surround her, was the most they could do for her. A quiet, diminutive woman whose lifelong disability had made her accustomed to depending on God, Regina encouraged DJ and Danielle to do the same. More practically, she suggested that they turn off their phones when they went to bed.

One morning in early May, Michelle showed up unannounced at Regina's house in Decatur. Over the preceding days, she had grown fixated on Skye, telling Danielle that she wanted her baby back with her. "She's my child, I want my child," she cried, as if Danielle weren't her child too. She talked as though Skye had been stolen from her. When Danielle responded that Skye was better off at Regina's with her and DJ, Michelle exploded. "*I'm* her mother! *I'm* her mother! Don't you dare tell me where she's better off!"

She pounded on Regina's front door, demanding to be let in. There was no car in sight; she appeared to have arrived on foot. Regina had already set the deadbolt when she asked Michelle what she was doing there. "I'm here to get my daughter. Now open the door!" she yelled.

Regina was grateful that DJ and Danielle were at school and that Skye was in the den with Regina's church friend, who tried to help with Skye during the week. Through the window, Regina was stunned at Michelle's appearance. Michelle had told Danielle that she had lost so much weight she was no longer allowed to donate plasma. But it wasn't just her gaunt figure that shocked Regina. Michelle looked as if she was staying on the street—and in fact she had been, though she hadn't told anyone. Spending the night at bus stops, sleeping on the floors of MARTA stations: this was now her life.

Michelle refused to leave without Skye, and Regina refused to open the door. She told Michelle that it wasn't good for her daughter to see her in this condition, that Skye would be frightened. "This isn't you," the older woman said. "I don't know what's happened. You're not in your right mind." When Michelle resumed banging on the door, Regina declared loudly that she was calling the police. "There, I called them," she said a couple of minutes later. The look of betrayal and disbelief on Michelle's face stung Regina. She and Michelle had long bumped heads, going back to when her sister, Michelle's mom, was still alive. There was a history of unresolved hurts. Regina knew she could have been better to her niece, but she really did love her. "All right then," Michelle said. Regina watched as she walked down the driveway and then out of sight.

Five weeks later, toward the end of June, an unknown number appeared on Danielle's phone. It was Michelle, calling from the DeKalb County Jail. From what she told Danielle, Nick had started beating her, and she had fought back, cutting him with a shard of glass. The cops arrived, and both she and Nick were arrested. She was being charged with simple battery, criminal trespass, disorderly conduct, and carrying a weapon without a license, all misdemeanors. The weapon charge was for the gun in her backpack, which belonged to Nick. To protect him, she had told the police it was hers.

Michelle begged Danielle to bail her out, and Danielle, in turn, begged her great-aunt to put up the $265 needed to secure her release. Regina didn't have that kind of money. After paying her bills each month, she had scarcely anything left over from her Social Security check. But she was able to scrape it together. Her friends advised her to give Michelle an ultimatum: she would bail her out if Michelle promised to leave Nick and go to rehab. Yet Regina was familiar enough with these matters to know that you couldn't force somebody to change. Michelle would seek help for her addiction—to alcohol and to Nick—only when she was ready to do so.

After six nights in jail, Michelle was released on June 28. Then she vanished.

THE MORNING WAS already hot and muggy, even though the sun had only just risen. In another five or six hours, Rockmor Plaza shopping center, a strip mall off Memorial Drive near the DeKalb County

Jail, would be teeming with activity. Saturday was the busiest day of the week for many of its shops and restaurants: Wing Master, KJ Nails Spa, Cricket Wireless, Professional Barber & Beauty Salon, the St. Vincent de Paul thrift store. But right now their doors were locked, and the shopping center was silent. There was just one establishment, First Coin Laundry, open twenty-four hours a day, seven days a week, whose bright fluorescent lights were always on. It was here, on a hard plastic chair, that Michelle had spent the night, occasionally lulled to sleep by the rhythmic whirr of a nearby washing machine. It was late August, two months since she had been arrested.

A large cut ran from her left eye down to her cheek, and her face was badly swollen. The day before, Nick had accused her of trading sex for cash, and the more she denied it, the more enraged he became. But that wasn't when he'd punched her. That happened later: after she'd managed to get away, after he'd eventually located her in a corner of the Five Points MARTA station and convinced her to return to his hotel room, after he'd begun accusing her again. Now everything she owned was back in that room, including her phone and wallet, which was why she had been unable to drink or even smoke a cigarette, despite her body's longing for both. She had no money, not a single penny. Yet for the first time, her determination to leave Nick—as when she had fled her ex-husband nearly a decade earlier—outweighed all else.

She had run panting and bleeding from his room. She knew that this was it. He had taunted her, telling her she had better run, that if he caught up with her, he was going to kill her. She wasn't sure he was capable of such a thing, but she didn't want to find out. (It turned out he *was* capable: less than a year later, he would plead guilty to the murder of another girlfriend, a twenty-four-year-old woman.)

Michelle had sensed this day was coming, and during the past week, aided by a woman she had worked with at the Salvation Army, she had started reaching out to domestic violence shelters. The only place with an available bed happened to be the farthest away; it was in a rural part of the state, in a town she had never heard of. They also offered treatment for substance use disorders. When she'd called them, it was simply to ascertain her options should she need somewhere to go in an emergency. It had been difficult to fathom leaving Nick for good.

But the spell had finally lifted. She was ready: ready to get her life back, ready to figure out what exactly had broken in her when she'd watched the eviction squad pile her furniture on the grass at Eastwyck, or when she'd asked strangers for money using Skye to elicit sympathy, or when she'd languished at Efficiency waiting for her daycare subsidy to be approved. Or maybe the break had occurred much earlier—with her ex-husband's betrayal or her own mother's struggle with addiction— and everything over the last two years had merely reopened these wounds. Soon, immersed in a community of women who were them- selves engaged in the agonizing but vital work of wrestling with such questions, one truth—a truth that would lead her to other truths— would come shining through: that while she may have been done with her pain, her pain wasn't yet done with her.

At the laundromat, Michelle closed her eyes, and when she opened them a couple of hours had passed. The assistant manager, a Middle Eastern woman in her late twenties, was standing over her, asking if she needed anything. Michelle had spent the night there before, and the woman had always shown her kindness. That morning, she had brought Michelle some snacks and a bottle of water and had allowed her to use her phone. "Actually," Michelle said, "do you mind if I make one last call?" The woman told her to take as long as she needed.

A moment later, Danielle's face appeared on the screen. She and Skye had just woken up, and the three-year-old immediately leaped into the camera's frame at the sound of her mom's voice.

"Mommy!" she squealed.

"Hey, pumpkin," Michelle said. "Oh, I've missed you guys so much." She told them they would be together before long. "But there's some- thing I have to talk to you about," she said. She asked Danielle to get DJ, who was still asleep.

When he joined them, DJ looked startled to see his mother, frail and battered, for the first time in months. He seemed guarded at first, muttering hello. But as Michelle began to speak, there was a flash of recognition. The mom they knew, the mom they had started to doubt they would ever see again, had clawed her way back to the surface. They could hear it in her voice, so clear, so confident.

Michelle explained that she was going away for a while. She would be safe, she told them, and she promised to give them all the details later. "I've gotta get myself straightened out," she said. Then she started to weep. DJ and Danielle began crying too. She asked them to forgive her for everything she had done, for everything she had put them through. "I'm so sorry. I'm so very, very sorry," she said again and again.

29

Britt was a heavy sleeper, and it took a good minute of Janeka yell-whispering her name before she stirred.

"What? What'd you say?"

"I *said*," Janeka hissed, "that someone's tryin' to take your car."

It was 2:30 a.m. on the last Friday in January. Janeka and her boyfriend had been in bed, having just finished watching a movie on his phone, when they heard the *beep, beep, beep* of a tow truck backing up. "Whoa, that's Britt's car," the boyfriend said, peering through the blinds.

In the half-light of Janeka's living room, Britt fumbled for her flip-flops and then bolted downstairs to the parking lot, into the freezing cold. The truck was already pulling away with her car. She had to run to catch up with it.

"They never sent me any sort of notice!" Britt yelled at the driver as he rolled down his window. "I think there's been a mistake." Some states required creditors to send a "right to cure" notice before repossessing a vehicle. Georgia was not one of them. "Can I at least grab my things?" Britt pleaded.

The man told her to be quick. He didn't want trouble from her, he said. As he lowered the car using his truck's hydraulic system, Britt stood shivering, rubbing her bare arms for warmth. Along with the flip-flops, she was wearing only the shorts and tank top she had been sleeping in. *How the hell did it come to this?* she thought, hoping none of Janeka's neighbors were watching.

When the driver motioned for her to proceed, Britt popped open her trunk and removed a security guard uniform, a large flashlight, and a baton, hiding the latter within the uniform so as not to alarm the driver. For the past couple of months, she had been dating a man, Derick, whose three part-time jobs included guarding a local shopping center. The night before, she and Derick had gone out for dinner, and he had left his uniform in the trunk when Britt dropped him off at the apartment he shared with his brother. She was relieved that the tow truck hadn't taken off before she could retrieve these items. She had no intention of telling Derick the truth about her car. She would tell him it was in the shop. In the name of maintaining "emotional boundaries," as she put it, she hadn't let herself be vulnerable in this way with him. She hadn't yet told him about her housing situation or allowed him to meet her kids. She couldn't even bring herself to refer to him as her boyfriend. He was her "male friend"—a term her mom and sister found amusing. After closing the trunk, taking care not to drop the flashlight, she grabbed Kyrie's Batman figure from the back seat. Without another word to the repo guy, she turned and hurried back inside.

The kids were still asleep on the air mattress she shared with them. Britt crawled under the covers but remained wide awake for the next three and a half hours, her mind racing, cursing her own carelessness. In the morning, she took Desiree and Kyrie to school in an Uber. Then back at Janeka's apartment she gathered herself and dialed the number of Exeter Finance.

The irony was that Britt hated driving. If she'd had her way, she never would have bought a car to begin with. But in Atlanta, driving was a necessary evil—and a car an inescapable expense. At the Hyundai dealership a year earlier, Britt had told the salesman helping her that she was looking for something cheap but functional—a car for school drop-offs and work commutes, not for turning heads. When the man asked her price range, Britt told him that she had $3,000 left over from her tax refund, and she was hoping not to spend much more than that. She mentioned her low credit score, but he said that wouldn't be a problem. In the end, she wound up with a used 2017 Sonata. She was given a contract to sign, and she saw that after factoring in her $3,000 down payment and then adding taxes and a $798 dealer fee and the $1,850 "car care" plan the salesman convinced her to purchase, there was a remaining balance of $12,834.48. This was the amount that would be financed—at an annual rate of 26.84 percent. If and when her car was eventually paid off, the total spent, at that APR, would be $23,698.80. But Britt didn't do these calculations. She had no idea that she was being charged almost four times the interest paid by used-car borrowers with strong credit. She was just happy to no longer have to stand at bus stops when she was late for work.

Six days after the purchase, a welcome letter arrived from Exeter Finance, the Irving, Texas–based lender to whom, for the following five years, she would be making monthly payments of $395. Founded in 2006, Exeter had established itself as one of the nation's major subprime auto lenders, specializing in loans to consumers with low FICO credit scores. When Britt bought her Sonata, Exeter's portfolio valuation stood at $7 billion. In 2019, the Massachusetts attorney general sued the company, alleging that its practices "put car buyers in economic danger" by originating loans that Exeter knew they could never repay. The following year, Santander, another subprime lender, reached a $550 million settlement to resolve similar abusive lending allegations made by attorneys general from more than two dozen states. Meanwhile, as of 2023, an astounding 30 percent or more of subprime auto loans typically defaulted, a percentage approaching the highest default rate for subprime mortgages near the peak of the foreclosure epidemic.

Britt had been careful not to miss a car payment. But in December, on the heels of her disappointing trip to Wisconsin, she'd made a decision that she would soon regret. She "went overboard" on Christmas gifts for Desiree and Kyrie. "It was a way of saying to them, 'We are okay. Life is normal. We are not in a crisis right now, just because we don't have our own place.'" After buying the gifts, she'd made only a partial payment on her car note. Then, in early January, in an attempt to mitigate the growing tension between her and Janeka, she'd decided not only to pay the light bill—which, in addition to buying groceries, she had been doing since they moved in—but Janeka's rent as well. This coincided with her seasonal job at Amazon coming to an end. She'd get caught up on her car note the following month, she told herself. But by then her Hyundai would be gone.

Now, on the phone with Exeter, Britt was informed that her car would be sold at auction within two weeks unless it was "redeemed" beforehand. Usually redeeming a repossessed vehicle meant paying off the full remaining amount of the loan all at once. But Britt got lucky. She apologized profusely, explaining to the customer service agent that she had lost her apartment and more recently her job. She promised to never miss another payment. The Exeter agent said he would need to talk to his manager. Three days later, Britt was told that because of the ongoing pandemic, Exeter was willing to make an exception: they would allow her to redeem her car if she simply paid her past due balance and late fees plus the expenses incurred by the repossession: towing and storage costs, and so on. "I think I can handle that," Britt said, knowing she would need to borrow money from one of her aunts or cousins. She was given an address in Greenville, Georgia, located more than an hour's drive away.

Her friend Yasmine agreed to take her to pick up the car. On the way, she thought about the New Year's resolution she'd made four weeks earlier. Since leaving Gladstone in late September, afraid of the rejection she'd believed was inevitable, she hadn't applied for a single apartment. But then her horoscope said that a "fear of stepping out" was preventing her from moving forward, and she resolved to start applying again. She was planning on setting aside money for this purpose. *So much for that,* she now thought. Not that it mattered: with the repossession showing up on her credit report, it was now even less likely that any rental applications would be approved.

WHEN THE CHILDREN'S spring break rolled around, Britt was anxious to get them out of the city—or rather, out of Janeka's place. The situation there had reached a breaking point. At first, Britt had been able to tell herself that her presence in the apartment was helping her friend. Janeka had long struggled with depression, and there were moments—always with Desiree and Kyrie gone—when she seemed to appreciate Britt being there. But six months of living together had been disastrous for their friendship. They had once been close enough to refer to each other as sisters. "My sister's gonna be staying with me," Janeka had told people back in October. Now they couldn't stand to be in the same room.

For Janeka, the resentment stemmed from "a few weeks" turning into half a year. It stemmed from having to share her one-bedroom unit with a six- and an eight-year-old, and all the whining and bickering and daily annoyances this involved. It stemmed from the loss not only of her living room but of any real privacy; it seemed insane to her that she and her boyfriend had to go to his place in order to be intimate, conscious that Britt or the kids might knock on her bedroom door at any time to use the en suite bathroom.

For Britt, the resentment stemmed from being made to feel that she was a problem. Early on, she had to force herself to stop apologizing to Janeka; she was sick of constantly saying sorry. "You think we *want* to be here?" she had an urge to scream. And there was Janeka's new puppy. One evening Britt and the kids entered the apartment to discover a large hole chewed out of their air mattress. For several nights, until Britt could buy another mattress, they had to sleep on the fake wood floor (the living room was uncarpeted), with only a couple of blankets offering the barest cushion. Worse, the dog was not yet potty trained, and they had to be careful not to step in the puddles of urine that began appearing.

While scrubbing the kitchen and living room, Britt imagined confronting Janeka. "You act like my children are *such a headache,* but it's not my kids that's pissin' and shittin' on the floor. This place is *nasty.* And if you're with a dude who don't mind laying in an apartment like this, then you know what? *He's* nasty too."

In mid-March, Janeka had texted Britt to say that she was breaking her lease and would be moving out during the summer. (Britt had looked into renting an apartment in the same complex but was told she wouldn't be approved.) Janeka's boyfriend's mom, Britt later learned through a mutual friend, was a real estate agent and had secured a rental house for the couple. "Must be nice," Britt said. She had a deadline now for finding a new place for them to live. But she still had three or four months to line something up, and it was with this knowledge that she decided to take Desiree and Kyrie to Florida over spring break to visit her brother.

The seven hours in the car, once they left the city, were therapeutic for Britt. She was able to clear her head, get perspective. A season of growth, of necessary transitions: that's how she decided to approach the months ahead. She had a new job—after a short-lived stint at a Dollar General warehouse, where her shifts consisted of sorting items in a walk-in freezer for hours on end, she had recently been hired on at the Chick-fil-A across from Centennial Olympic Park—and she had a newfound clarity about the sorts of relationships, romantic and otherwise, she would allow into her life. No more guys like Derick, so content with their mediocrity, still obsessed with videogames in their twenties. No more fair-weather friends like Janeka. She was going to spend the next five days giving her kids their first experience at the beach while drinking strawberry daiquiris and hanging with her baby brother, and then she was going to return to Atlanta with a new attitude.

She received a voicemail message from Janeka on the drive back to Georgia. Britt listened to it, and then she listened to it again, trying to make sense of it. Between this recording and a subsequent, no less confusing exchange of texts, Britt was able to glean two things: Janeka had abruptly moved out of her apartment, and a number of Britt's possessions—the things that Janeka couldn't squeeze into her car, that she intended to grab later but hadn't—were still in the unit. Britt drove straight to the complex. But when she tried opening the front door, her key no longer worked; the lock had been changed. The next morning, she learned that a maintenance crew had disposed of everything that had been left behind in the apartment, including a shoebox containing her and the kids' Social Security cards and birth certificates and immunization records. Janeka had taken the new air mattress and a duffel bag full of clothes and toys, but Britt was too angry to make a plan to get them from her. None of it added up: Janeka's sudden decision to move out, her lack of communication. Britt couldn't imagine that Janeka would deliberately screw her over like this, but there was no other explanation. In the end, Britt chalked it up to Janeka's "issues" and accepted that their friendship was over.

Where can we go? Where can we go? The question played on a loop in Britt's brain. How many times had she asked it over the last seven years?

She and the kids ended up at her friend Yasmine's studio apartment. Britt had sworn that it would only be for a few days, perhaps a week. Yasmine's own car repairs had caused her to miss a rent payment, and she was afraid of giving her landlord another reason to put her and her daughter out. "I'm not tryin' to fuck up yet another relationship by overstaying my welcome," Britt said. The other option was Aaliyah's place, but whenever Britt talked to her sister on the phone, she sounded more and more overwhelmed. In February, her fiancé had been laid off from his job, and with her new five-month-old baby, Aaliyah delayed her return to work. *I was back at work three weeks after my son was born,* Britt thought but didn't say. So the couple was scrambling to make ends meet. They were also fighting constantly, a result, Aaliyah had confided in Britt, of the stress of having not only her mom but her youngest brother, Devin, crashing in their living room. "It's too much," she'd said.

Britt knew there was no way she and the kids could move in as well. She would sooner go to a hotel. Or sleep in her car—maybe *that* was the reason the universe had caused Exeter to take pity on her, because someone knew she would eventually need the vehicle for another purpose. As for Desiree and Kyrie's dad, Javon, his wife had recently given birth to their third child, and even if Kyrie hadn't cried and fussed each time Britt needed the kids to go to their father's apartment ("He's a mama's boy," Javon had said derisively in front of Kyrie), Britt was well aware that they were in no position to accommodate two additional children. Yasmine suggested asking one of her aunts to take the kids for a little while. But Britt's memory of what she'd been through as an adolescent—her aunt's boyfriend molesting her—was never far from her mind. She was determined to keep the kids with her.

Since she was a young girl, Britt had always had faith in herself and her abilities. She had believed the adults at the Young Entrepreneur convention and her mentors in the I Have A Dream program who had told her she was destined for great things. Now she wasn't so sure. She felt a kind of cognitive dissonance, a sense that she had landed in the wrong life—as if she just wasn't *made* for circumstances such as these. What could seem like apathy or resignation was in fact a state of perplexity and disorientation. At Yasmine's, she looked in the mirror and said, "How is this happening to you? How are you twenty-six with two kids and you don't have anywhere to live?" It was startling to realize that the person staring back at her was not the person she had imagined herself to be. It was not a woman who was fun-loving and confident and ambitious. It was not a woman with the career she'd hoped for. It was a woman with no "career" at all: a woman scraping by and taking whatever part-time position or fast-food job she could get. It was a woman who had become a burden, who burned through relationships. It was a woman who looked tired and worn out. Like she had given up.

Despite her housing woes over the years, Britt had resisted seeking help from agencies that aided homeless families. "It's not a 'too proud to beg' thing," she had said. "I just don't like using the H-word. I'm not saying I'm better than anyone, but that's not me. That's not me and my kids." She associated the word with the "bag ladies and winos" that children in her neighborhood used to make fun of. But now she found herself calling agencies, leaving messages along the lines of "Hi, I'm calling to see about getting housing assistance for my children and me," followed by a phone number and a weary "Thanks, I look forward to hearing from you."

Three days later, a caseworker called her back. She told Britt that in order to be eligible for the kind of support she was looking for, she would first need to go to Gateway and try to get a referral to a shelter: having to stay with a friend, she said, didn't qualify her. It wasn't only families in extended-stays who were locked out of assistance. Families doubled-up with others were similarly excluded—even though men, women, and children in these arrangements made up the overwhelming majority of homeless families in the United States.

On the phone, Britt hid her disappointment, thanking the woman and promising to do as she instructed. But she knew she would never take Desiree and Kyrie to a shelter. She would not allow that to become their reality.

OVER THE NEXT FIVE MONTHS, Britt and the kids bounced around between cheap hotels and a dizzying assortment of living rooms belonging to friends and old acquaintances, relatives and friends of relatives, even her manager at work. The more time dragged on, the longer they went without a home of their own, the more Britt tried to assuage her guilt by surprising her children with unexpected presents—a new bike, a set of walkie-talkies they'd been asking for—and by getting as involved as possible in their extracurricular activities. She supplied snacks for Kyrie's football team. She drove Desiree three hours to a cheerleading competition in Augusta.

She had given up on being approved for an apartment. At the last complex where she'd applied, she decided to tell the leasing agent about her low credit score and the eviction and repossession prior to forking over application and administrative fees. The agent encouraged Britt to go for it, even showing her the newly renovated two-bedroom unit she was promising to "reserve" for her and the kids. Not only was Britt not approved for this apartment; she never even heard back after submitting her application.

The sole bright spot was her job at Chick-fil-A, where she had been promoted to shift captain and had become part of a team that was occasionally sent to other cities to help open new locations. Although she wasn't paid extra for these trips to Los Angeles and Houston, New Orleans and Phoenix, her food and airfare and lodgings were covered—relieving her of the need to find a place to stay that week—and she was able to see the country, which she found thrilling.

Cass's support was indispensable. Britt felt comfortable leaving town only if the children were with her mom, who was still at Aaliyah's apartment. Cass welcomed the opportunity to watch her grandkids. It gave her something to do, a way to feel useful. Since moving in with Aaliyah, she had been offered a handful of jobs: a cashier position at Goodwill, a janitorial job back at the airport. But she declined each of them at the last minute. In part, this was because her stimulus checks and tax refund had given her a bit of a cushion, even after contributing to Aaliyah's rent and utility payments. But the main reason, she told a friend, was that she had arrived at the point in her life where she was simply tired of working "underpaid bullshit jobs," as she put it. "More than half of my life is over," she said. "Is this really how I want to spend the rest of my days, cleaning toilets at Hartsfield-Jackson?" Now that she was no longer struggling to put food on the table for her family, she was resolved that the final chapter of her life would involve doing something she found fulfilling. At the top of her list was enrolling in culinary arts school to start her own catering business.

And yet, to her kids' frustration, she had taken few tangible steps in this direction. When she wasn't babysitting her grandchildren or keeping the apartment meticulously clean, she was watching standup comedy or weepy melodramas on her old laptop. Sometimes she took the bus over to Greenbriar Mall, which was usually empty. On one rainy afternoon, she went to a bookstore in the mall and, drawn to the title, purchased *Just as I Am,* a memoir by Cicely Tyson, who had recently passed away. She spent the rest of the day reading it in the food court, riveted.

But there was one thing Cass was doing to break out of her rut. She was trying to get her driver's license reinstated fourteen years after it had been suspended. She had lost it when she was unable to pay some overdue traffic fines; there just hadn't been a moment during those years, she said, when she could spare the $229. But she had finally gone to the courthouse to pay the fine, and then she took a bus to the DMV to obtain a handbook. She had been studying for the driving test ever since. She told everyone that by her next birthday she would have her license. Her plan was to rent a car and travel cross-country to Las Vegas, all by herself.

After returning from one of her work trips, Britt drove to Aaliyah's apartment to get the kids and ended up spending the night. In the morning, while the others were still asleep, she floated an idea to her sister that had been germinating for weeks. With her poor credit, Britt had come to the conclusion that she would never again be able to rent an apartment in her own name. But what if Aaliyah, who had a relatively high credit score, filled out a rental application on Britt's behalf, as though she herself would be living in the unit?

Even as Britt asked her sister to do this, she felt a stab of guilt. She remembered back to when she was nineteen, after she had just given birth to Desiree, and Cass had convinced Britt to rent an apartment for the three of them in *her* name. The ensuing eviction had done irreparable damage to Britt's credit, and so much more. Now Aaliyah had her own infant daughter, and with her current lease set to expire in a couple of months she was nervous about doing anything to mess up her prospects. She knew that what Britt was proposing was risky, that if anything went wrong she could easily find herself in the same predicament as her older sister.

But in the end she agreed to go along with it. A week later, Britt took her to pick up a money order in the amount of the application fee, and then they drove to a nearby apartment complex where, according to the agent Aaliyah had spoken to on the phone, there was a one-bedroom unit coming available soon. Britt waited in the car with Layla, Aaliyah's daughter, while Aaliyah went inside the rental office to drop off the application. When she returned to the car, she stared at Britt without saying anything. "It'll be fine," Britt assured her.

Not long after that, on one of her days off from Chick-fil-A, Britt's aunt texted her to see if she could help with a last-minute Miracle Maids appointment near Grant Park. Always on the lookout for ways to bring in extra money, Britt had told her to let her know if she ever needed a hand. She and her aunt spent about two hours cleaning the Airbnb. When they finished the job, since Desiree and Kyrie were at school and there was nowhere she had to be, Britt took the slightly longer way back to Aaliyah's, where the three of them had continued to stay for the time being. She drove down Boulevard, passing the Skylark apartments on her right, and then she slowly turned into the parking lot in front of Red's Beer Garden.

The day was as clear and crisp as the morning she'd moved out of Gladstone almost a year earlier. It was hard to believe it had been that long. What she'd assumed would be a temporary setback, maybe even a blessing in disguise, had become a seemingly intractable condition. She had last been in the neighborhood in March, when the old buildings at Gladstone were still boarded up, the property sealed off by a chain-link fence around the perimeter. Now those buildings had been razed. The site had been cleared of the former complex and most of its trees and grass and shrubbery as well. As if the whole thing had been blotted out of existence.

A signboard near the road announced what was in store for the property: COMING SOON—EMPIRE ZEPHYR. On the website of the developer, Empire Communities, the project's "community amenities" page noted that Chosewood Park "finds itself in a transformative time in its history." This was not an exaggeration. Investment capital had continued to pour into the area. Five major residential projects were in the works nearby, and the BeltLine's still-unfinished Southside Trail, which was spurring much of the growth, had just received a $16 million federal grant to help speed up its completion. The *Atlanta Business Chronicle* used the word *explosion* to characterize this surge of development dollars into Chosewood Park and the surrounding communities. The demographic shift underway was equally dramatic. "The influx of younger people and higher-income residents is attracting more interest from businesses, something the area has long needed," Jacob Mills, the president of Chosewood Park Neighborhood Association, told the *Chronicle*.

On the Empire website, a description of the project could be found underneath a digital rendering. There was a mix of condos and farmhouse-style townhomes "starting from the low $400s."

> Located just south of Grant Park and across from the future BeltLine Park, Empire Zephyr is a 34-acre community that will flourish into a destination for exploration,

creativity, and harmony on the southside. Here, residents will get a taste of Atlanta's southern flair, forge new connections, reach new personal milestones, and dive deep into the spirited nature that Zephyr has to offer. It's time to carve out your place in the city against a backdrop of lush greenery, budding culture, energy, and soul.

Britt had no desire to linger in the neighborhood, and after gazing for a minute at the construction site where she and her children had once lived, she got in her car and left. There was a time when she would have felt excited about what her city was becoming. No longer.

"I was just like, 'Wow, this will be really nice when it's done,'" she said later. "'But me and my kids? There's no place for us here.'"

The first few weeks in her apartment at Chelsea Gardens brought a shift in Kara's outlook. After more than a year of homelessness, she had finally allowed herself to "breathe," as she put it, relieved at last of the anxiety of not knowing, from one night to the next, where she and her children would be sleeping. The kids, ecstatic to have their own bedroom, seemed to relish the change in their mom's demeanor, which conveyed a simple message: *It's okay to be excited. This time it's for real.*

It had been an impossible choice: go back to Garden Inn, wait for another environmental review to be completed, and, if there was another delay, risk having to start the entire housing search over again; or give up the Homeless to Homes support but have a place to live. Confronted with two terrible alternatives, Kara had gone with the option that seemed slightly less bad.

On the living room wall beside her kitchen, she hung a decorative sign that she had come across at a discount store. It succinctly captured how she was feeling. TODAY IS A NEW DAY, it read. A new day, a new apartment—and also a new job, or at least a return to an old one. Kara began working again as a home health aide, and since the kids' daycare remained opened until eight o'clock, she was able to stay with her elderly clients for up to twelve hours at a time.

A schedule this demanding was far from ideal, for Kara or the children. After picking them up in Union City and driving home to College Park, Kara had to feed them, bathe them, and get them ready for bed, and it was often 10:30 p.m. or 11:00 p.m. before they fell asleep. Earlier in the pandemic, when all the daycares were closed, Kara had yearned for even a few minutes of alone time. Now things were reverting back to how they had been immediately preceding and following Joshua's birth: working as much as possible and seeing her kids hardly at all. Kara wished she could find some sort of balance between these extremes. But keeping the apartment would require making sacrifices. "Ain't nothin' too tough for me," Kara told herself.

But gradually, like storm clouds gathering, her perspective darkened. Bills came due. There was her car insurance and car note, which she had fallen dangerously behind on after spending nearly $2,000 during their prolonged stay at Garden Inn. There was her cellphone and gas and light bill, and there were new expenses, such as the $44 a week she had agreed to pay a local rent-to-own store for furniture. She had opted for the bare minimum, in both price and quality, where furnishings were concerned: a bed for herself, a bed for Nathaniel and Grace to share, a cheaply constructed bunk bed for Jermaine and Joshua; a modest sofa; a dresser. Rent-to-own stores were infamously predatory, typically saddling customers with the equivalent of a 60 to 80 percent interest rate. But these stores appealed to (and aggressively targeted) financially strapped people who wanted or needed a particular item right away—and who, lacking a credit card, might never be able to save or spare the cash necessary to purchase it elsewhere. And so, like other things in their life, they ended up paying much more for much less. Soon the transmission went out on Kara's Avalon, and she had to empty her checking account to get it repaired. She was scared to revisit her budget. All these expenses, and that was before factoring in her single greatest burden: rent.

Everything she had been imagining for herself and the kids, everything she had recently mapped out under FUTURE in her notebook, had been predicated on the assistance she was supposed to have received through Nicholas House's Homeless to Homes program. It was this full year of support that was going to enable her to accumulate a bit of savings—that was going to alleviate the pressure of working so many hours, allowing her to focus more attention on the kids and their needs, and making her a more patient, tender, affectionate mother. Now she had lost that support.

Maybe she'd made the wrong choice. Maybe she'd blown her one real chance at stability. Or perhaps, if she'd chosen to wait for another environmental review to be completed, she and the kids would still be at that disgusting hotel. All she knew was that the relief she'd felt after moving into the apartment had now evaporated. A familiar feeling had returned with a vengeance: a sense of treading water, of trying not to drown. The stress of finding a home had been replaced by a fear of losing it, as if she were living on borrowed time. "Why does this have to be so fucking hard?" she wondered. She didn't do drugs, she didn't get wasted, she didn't squander her money on frivolous things. And yet, no matter how hard she worked, it was never enough.

Her thoughts kept circling back to that awful phone call from Ms. Gilbert, her Nicholas House case manager—when she'd told Kara that her apartment had been given away to someone else. Her mind went over every detail, every word. Lying awake at night, she obsessed over the call, unable to let it go. And the more she dwelt on it, the angrier she became. *She was just pretending to feel sorry for me,* Kara told herself. *People like that, they don't want to see a woman like me succeed.* Losing the apartment was not the result of an unfortunate sequence of events. Ms. Gilbert and the apartment management had seen her desperation. They had conspired to sabotage her long-term assistance, Kara decided. They had intentionally set her up for failure.

In the morning, she sent an aggrieved, threatening message to Ms. Gilbert's email address. She accused the case manager of lying to her, and she promised to file a lawsuit against her and Nicholas House and the City of Atlanta for what they had done to her family. And it wasn't just Ms. Gilbert and Nicholas House who were out to get her. It was also the director at the kids' daycare: she had been trying to knock her down, as Kara put it, when Nathaniel was sent home with a runny nose and told he couldn't return without a doctor's note. Kara also suspected her ailing client. The woman was coughing on Kara, trying to make her sick, trying to prevent her from being able to work and pay her rent.

Later, Kara would rebuke herself for indulging such thoughts. She didn't know where they were coming from. "I feel like a piece of shit," she wrote. "I don't feel like a woman. I don't feel like Kara. I feel stupid. I feel like I am letting my kids down again. All I want is a nice place for my kids with peace."

There were moments of reprieve, small pockets of grace amid the fatigue and financial strain. The mechanic who repaired her car's transmission worked overtime in order to get it back to her the next day; Kara thanked him profusely and wrote a glowing Yelp review. On her thirty-first birthday, she signed the kids out of school early and took them to This Is It! Southern Kitchen & Bar-B-Q on Panola Road, and then drove them to the park, where they enjoyed a glorious fall afternoon together. Kara couldn't stop hugging and kissing them. Around the same time, she checked her food stamp balance and saw that she had received more than $1,000 over the usual amount. Whether this was deliberate or an error, she was grateful for it. She went to the store and bought as much frozen meat and veggies as her freezer would hold. Afterward, she was constantly on the lookout for ways to pay this blessing forward to others. On three separate occasions, she pulled her car over to the side of the road to help women holding signs asking for food or money; two of them had young children with them. Kara prayed with the women, took them out to eat, bought them toiletries. "I've been where you are," she would tell them. "Don't give up."

Early each morning, while the kids slept, she had started writing a chronicle of her life on the lined pages of her notebook. *Things I Had to Endure,* she titled it. "Hey guys, thanks for choosing to read my book," she wrote in the preface. "Lord, thank you for giving me the encouragement to share my life story with the nation." But she eventually abandoned the project. The adversity and distress she had begun describing weren't just in her past. They were her present.

Toward the end of October, Kara found a second job with a company called SAS Retail Services. She had barely slept in recent days, apprehensive about her ability to make the following month's rent. The work, mercifully, required little mental exertion—she simply drove from one Atlanta grocery store to another, restocking their magazine sections—but it was physically taxing, with penalties for failing to go fast enough. At Kroger one morning, she had just finished up and was about to hurry to the next store when she decided to grab a bag of chips and iced tea for a quick snack. While standing in line to check out, she began to sob uncontrollably. She was heaving and shaking. Other customers huddled around her, asking if she needed anything. Kara could only shake her head. She put the chips and iced tea down and ran to her car.

"HELLO MS. THOMPSON," the email read. It was sent midday on March 8.

> Chelsea Gardens is currently in the process of having our buildings cross inspected by a certified electrician to find out what is truly causing the high electric bills. We are not sure that it is an error on our end but that it may be on the city. I will keep you posted on our findings. In the meantime, please note it would be best to pay your balance owed to avoid shut-off.
>
> Warmest regards,
> Octavia James, Senior Manager
> Meridian Management Group
> Chelsea Gardens Apartments

When Kara read the email, she almost had to laugh. The past four months had been a surreal nightmare, and this email—*it would be best to pay your balance owed to avoid shut-off*—told her that it was far from over. Before all this began, she had already been teetering on the brink. How had she not completely snapped?

It had started with her November light bill. Since moving into her apartment in August, Kara's electric bills had been higher than expected, in the $150 to $200 range. But in November, she opened her mail and was floored to discover, next to "current charges," that she owed $387.61 for the previous month's usage. She assumed this was a mistake. But when she called College Park Power, her electricity provider owned by the city of College Park, she was told that the amount was accurate; it was based on a direct meter reading, said the woman on the phone. Kara kept her cool. She explained that she had been a renter for more than a decade, and that she couldn't remember having ever received such an expensive light bill. Her current place, she said, was a two-bedroom unit measuring just over a thousand square feet. She asked the woman if it didn't seem strange to her that an apartment so small would generate an electric bill this high. "It's not impossible," the woman said flatly. Kara had no choice but to pay.

She became vigilant about avoiding excessive electricity use. Although temperatures outside were dropping, Kara set the apartment's thermostat in the high sixties when she and the kids were home; when they were gone, she set it much lower. She plugged in appliances and other devices, including her phone charger, only when she was using them. She made sure everything was switched off before going to bed. And yet, when her December bill arrived from College Park Power, it was even higher than the last one. For a period of thirty days, she had been charged $673.51.

Kara marched her paper bills to the leasing office, demanding an explanation, an investigation—any insight at all into what was going on. No, she said, she hadn't been using a space heater; she didn't even own one. No, she hadn't been running her heat 24/7, and no, she wasn't leaving her TV on through the night. They told her to talk to College Park Power. It was likely their fault. The meter was probably broken. At CPP, they asked her the exact same questions—"What's your thermostat set at? Are you unplugging your devices?"—even though she had already told them how careful she'd been to reduce her electricity consumption. Kara suspected that even if she *had* been blasting her heat all day and night, it still wouldn't produce a nearly $700 bill for a two-bedroom apartment. The woman helping her, the same person she had spoken to on the phone after Kara received her first bill, offered to send someone to check the meter, but once they confirmed that there had not, in fact, been a misreading—which they quickly did—she said Kara would be responsible for the charges. She should talk to her apartment management, the woman said. It could be faulty wiring; it could be any number of issues. "We have a lot of older apartments in College Park," she explained, "and a lot of times the complexes don't want to spend the money to address these problems. So they try to use the power company as a scapegoat."

Around and around and back and forth it went like this over the following days: calling and emailing the leasing office, begging them to have an electrician inspect her building; calling and emailing CPP, asking them to conduct further inspections. The complex kept blaming the power company. The power company kept blaming the complex. What they all agreed on was that Kara needed to find the money to pay her balance. She spoke to her neighbors and learned that several of them had also received these kinds of bills in the past. One neighbor told Kara that she had tried challenging the bills but had gotten nowhere. "You just have to suck it up and pay," she said.

After the bleakest holiday season of Kara's life, most of it spent working as many overtime hours as she could get, her electricity was finally cut off in mid-January. Her latest bill had been $608.27, and even skipping her car payment hadn't freed her up to pay the minimum amount to avoid disconnection. The shut-off approached with a grim inevitability. Kara went into her "shell," as she put it, cutting off all contact with the few people she was still in touch with; the fact that her phone had also been disconnected meant that this withdrawal was less a choice than a concession. It was too cold to stay in the apartment, so she and the kids slept in her car with the heat running, just a stone's throw from the unit whose rent she had paid that month.

When her next paycheck rolled around, she was able to get the power restored. By then, a few hundred dollars' worth of meat in her freezer—the food she had purchased with her extra EBT funds—had thawed and spoiled. She emptied the contents of her freezer and refrigerator into a big garbage bag and carried it to the dumpster.

January to February, February to March, March to April: each month brought a new ordeal, another crisis as the mounting electricity bills spun a web of interconnected misfortunes. She was awarded a "financial hardship" grant from the power company, but this merely lowered her balance until the next bill. She applied for emergency rental and utility assistance from Fulton County, but two months later she still hadn't heard from them. CPP put her on a payment plan of $175 a week, but she couldn't keep up and eventually her power was cut again. In March, when Octavia in the leasing office emailed to say that an electrician would be coming out to "cross inspect" the building, Kara had been hearing the same thing from everyone else in the office for the past eight or nine weeks.

Kara wasn't sure how much more she could take. Knowing she wasn't responsible for these outrageous bills, and yet continuing to receive them, was like being subjected to a sadistic experiment. Compounding all this, she had yet to receive a single stimulus payment. Her last address on file with the IRS had been the extended-stay where she and the kids were living before the pandemic struck, and she had been trying and trying to get new checks sent out, so far unsuccessfully. January was the last month she had paid her rent in full; likewise her car note and car insurance. Keeping her lights on had become her main priority. She took a screenshot of her "pending" status on the IRS's Get My Payment page, and swore to everyone—the apartment manager, her auto creditor, a co-worker she'd borrowed from—that they would receive their money just as soon as her checks arrived.

On May 24, Kara drove to the offices of College Park Power for what she guessed was the seventh or eighth time—she had lost track of the exact number. She was no longer trying to contest her bills. She was simply hoping to convince them to lower the minimum payment required to avoid another disconnection. In lieu of the $400-plus they were saying she would have to pay by the following day, she had come to ask them to accept $200. The woman behind the counter was someone Kara had seen before but never talked to. When Kara explained her situation and mentioned the name of her complex, the woman sighed. "Unfortunately, I hate to say it, but that's one of the worst apartments you could live at." She said she had encountered "many, many customers" from Chelsea Gardens whose bills were as high as hers. This was not news to Kara; others from CPP had been telling her the same thing.

When Kara asked why the power company would continue to send these bills, month after month, to customers they knew were not actually responsible for the electricity usage they were being charged for, the woman's answer was also familiar: because that's what the meters were reading. It wasn't CPP's job to figure out *why* the meters were putting out these numbers; if the meters were working properly, the customer was charged. The woman was sympathetic, though: she accepted the $200, but she warned Kara that her new bill would be hitting her account soon. Kara asked the woman what she would do if she were in her shoes. "Honestly," she said, "I'd find another place to live."

Two days later, Kara was running an errand for her home health client when the kids' daycare called. She had recently switched them back to KinderCare, the location just down the road from Chelsea Gardens. On the phone was Kimberly, the daycare chain's regional director. She said Kara needed to pick up Jermaine immediately: the three-year-old had scratched another child and then pushed over a shelf of books. The center was suspending him for two days.

Kara knew what she would have wanted the director to say next. "Ms. Thompson," Kimberly would have continued, "we're going to figure out a solution together. You've told us what you're going through. We understand that you have to be at work in the morning, and that you can't go to work if you've got nobody else to watch your kids. We know you're doing this on your own, that you don't have any kind of support. We can't be having this rough behavior, but we're going to see what we can do for you. It's going to be all right, okay?"

But Kimberly said nothing of the sort. She said their decision was final. Kara began to cry, saying, "Please don't do this to me, please don't do this to me." When Kimberly refused to budge, Kara began unloading on her, insulting her, telling her to go to hell.

By the end of the call, all four of Kara's children had been kicked out of the daycare.

LACKING CHILDCARE, Kara was forced to quit her job as a home health aide. It was a wonder that she had been able to hold on to it for so long. The ordeal with the electricity—the shut-offs, the nights in her car, the endless trips back and forth between the power company and the leasing office—had long ago caused her to lose her other part-time position with SAS Retail.

The day after the fateful phone call from KinderCare, Kara had started searching online for jobs that would allow the kids to stay home with her: school was out for the summer, and it would likely be weeks or even months before four spots opened up at another daycare. A remote call center position would have been ideal, but the few she came across required prior experience in customer service or bilingual proficiency, or were obvious scams intended to prey on desperate people like her. She considered returning to food delivery but assumed that since her DoorDash account had been deactivated, she was ineligible to drive for the company's competitors. Her next payment to CPP would be coming due in just over a week, and then there would be a seven-day grace period before her electricity was disconnected. She was determined not to let that happen.

An overnight job seemed to be her only option. She quickly found one with a security firm she had worked for in the past. Kara knew it was risky: she hoped the kids would remain asleep while she was gone, but the job was in Buckhead, and if there was an emergency it would take her twenty-five minutes to drive back to the apartment.

Kara thought about asking one of her neighbors to be on call during her shift. But her capacity for trust, justified or not, had drastically diminished over the last year. In December, a brush with the Division of Family and Children Services had left her shaken. A nurse at College Park Elementary had contacted the agency after noticing a small cut on Nathaniel's head. Nathaniel had told the nurse that his baby brother had accidentally hit him with their mom's keys while she was in the shower, but the nurse reported it anyway. That evening, a DFCS investigator showed up at the family's apartment. It was a scene Kara had dreaded for as long as she had been a parent. After speaking with the children individually, however, the man established that Nathaniel had been telling the truth, and that was the end of it. Before he left, Kara asked him if DFCS could help with her light bills and rent. He said the agency didn't have the resources to offer such assistance.

The episode was enough to keep Kara from telling her neighbors that she would be away overnight. She was worried somebody might report her. She told the kids not to mention it to anyone.

KARA PREPARED A special dinner of blackened fish and french fries for the kids, and then she gave her three boys a bubble bath, allowing them to linger in the tub as long as they wanted, to splash and play with their bath toys. Grace, whose tenth birthday was fast approaching, got her own bath when they were finished. Later, Kara cuddled with the children in their room. They watched part of a Disney movie. Kara assured the kids that everything would be fine. She would be home by the time they woke up, she said.

In recent weeks, during fleeting moments of calm, she had been thinking about something that Carla Wells, her first case manager at Nicholas House, had said on the phone after Kara sent the threatening emails to Ms. Gilbert. Carla had told Kara that she wasn't crazy. Her anger, her mistrust of others: it made sense. She had experienced a great deal of injustice. She had taught herself how to survive. But coping with it on her own, "it's taking a toll on you," Carla said.

She had strongly encouraged Kara to see a therapist, and although Kara responded defensively—*I don't need that, and I don't need you* was the essence of her reply—she had begun to realize that Carla was probably right. Lately she'd felt an urge to talk about the things she'd been through, the things she carried with her. "I have a damaged heart," she wrote at one point.

She hated it, she absolutely despised it, when people looked at her like she was unhinged and told her she "needed help." Such statements, as she heard them, seemed to discount her genuine needs: her need for a functioning water heater; her need not to be scammed and exploited; her need to keep her lights on, to keep her food from spoiling. Her need not to be homeless or to be shoved back into homelessness. That's what she "needed."

But she had become open to the idea that another kind of help, the kind Carla had alluded to, might be beneficial as well—might help her to feel less isolated, less dejected, less prone to rage. Yet when she had finally worked up the courage to call Georgia's Medicaid office and ask which counselors in her area accepted her insurance, she was told that her insurance did not cover therapy, or any other mental health services, or even primary care. Kara's children had healthcare coverage through the state's PeachCare for Kids program, but Kara's own Medicaid coverage, unbeknownst to her, was active only while she was pregnant. Along with some 274,000 other adults in Georgia, Kara had fallen into Medicaid's "coverage gap": poor people whose annual income exceeded their state's eligibility threshold. (In Georgia, a parent with four children had to earn less than $9,000 annually to qualify.) If Georgia had been among the states to expand Medicaid coverage under the Affordable Care Act, she would have received the help she was seeking. But in Georgia, she was now eligible only for subsidized "family planning services": contraception, sterilization, STD treatment, and the like. Kara put the idea of therapy out of her head.

It was getting late. Tucking her children in, Kara handed Grace the inexpensive phone she had recently purchased for her. She told her to keep it beside her at all times.

"Listen to your sister," she told the boys. "She's in charge."

Kara switched on the nightlight and sat down on the carpet next to their beds. The kids drifted off to a recording of Kara singing. She had made the recording back in September, the night before her birthday, and she had listened to it intermittently since then. The kids loved it. The improvised words and melody were Kara's own. Like her book, the recording began with Kara addressing an imagined audience. "I just want to let y'all know how good my God is, because he's brought me through *a lot*." She sang about her trials and tribulations, and about the people who had told her she was "broke" and "hopeless." She sang about her God, who had another plan for her life. Her voice, mighty and plaintive, filled the room.

When the recording stopped, Kara realized that she herself had started to fall asleep. She needed to be at work soon. She shook herself awake and went into the kitchen. She removed the knobs from the stove and took all the sharp knives out of their drawer, hiding them in a cabinet above the refrigerator. Then she locked the front door behind her and walked to her car.

| EPILOGUE |

Throughout my reporting for this book, one image in particular stayed with me. It was a Monday night in January 2020, and I had signed on to participate in the annual census of Atlanta's homeless population. Mandated by HUD, this "Point-in-Time" count aims to provide a comprehensive snapshot of homelessness in America. About thirty teams of five or six volunteers each would be canvassing every block within city limits. Our task was to tally and survey each unsheltered person we encountered: those staying in parks, on the street, under bridges, and in other areas not meant for habitation.

I was assigned to a team that included a graduate student in social work, a middle-aged woman employed by the state of Georgia, and a retired couple whose church had put out a call for volunteers. Our leader was a seasoned street outreach specialist from a local nonprofit. At nine o'clock, the six of us climbed into a van that would be driving us around the city. Earlier, in a meeting hall on Peachtree Street where everyone had convened before heading out, the CEO of Partners for HOME (the lead agency for Atlanta's Continuum of Care and the organization responsible for coordinating the yearly census) had delivered a galvanizing speech. Her words infused the gathering with the energy of a pep rally. The data we were setting out to collect, she said, would play a crucial role in the city's fight to "eradicate homelessness," building on the progress already underway. In recent years, citing the results of the

Point-in-Time count, headlines had touted a considerable decline in Atlanta's homeless population. The work we were doing that night, we were told, would help reduce the numbers further.

Over the next four hours, wearing winter jackets under orange reflective vests, our team methodically covered the highlighted portion of the map we'd been given. Some teams were deployed to affluent residential areas where they would encounter few people at this time of night, unhoused or otherwise. Some were traversing parts of downtown lined with tents. The area our team had been assigned occupied more of a middle ground. We scoured emergency rooms and MARTA stations; we trekked through Grant Park, covering most of its 131-acre expanse; and we searched DeKalb Avenue and Cabbagetown Park and the streets surrounding Krog Street Market. I was surprised to learn, at the start of the evening, that an on-duty APD officer would be joining us for protection, and at several points the cop shone his flashlight in people's faces to wake them up. A member of our team would then apologize for the intrusion and offer the person a $5 McDonald's gift card if he or she agreed to take part in the brief survey.

As the night wore on, we trudged through the moonless, frigid dark on foot, scanning the vicinity for any signs of improvised dwellings: coming across one person here, a handful of others there; waking them up, interviewing them, then going to the next location on our map. Then we arrived at Edgewood Avenue. Dubbed the "most Atlanta of Atlanta's streets" by the city's magazine, Edgewood was the gritty epicenter of Atlanta nightlife, an area whose bars, clubs, and eateries attracted revelers until the early hours. Tonight was no different. The sidewalks were packed—not only with clubgoers but with a remarkably large concentration of people experiencing homelessness. We spent more than an hour on the street. "They got McDonald's cards over here," one man announced to his acquaintances, and soon four others were waiting their turn to complete the survey.

It was close to midnight when we approached the intersection of Edgewood and Hilliard Street. Directly in front of us, idling at the curb, was an old station wagon crammed with belongings. Pillows and blankets were visible, and a bedsheet partly covered one of its rear windows. A man sat in the driver's seat, and a woman holding a wide-awake toddler was in the passenger seat. As we drew closer, the woman turned toward us. Her face showed a look of utter weariness. Then the station wagon eased away from the curb, moving up to the red light a few feet ahead. The woman craned her head to glance at us again. A minute later, the light changed, and the car proceeded through the intersection and drove off, vanishing around the corner.

"That's so sad," the retired woman on our team remarked. We continued on.

THAT NIGHT IN JANUARY, as we watched the station wagon disappear, Michelle was in her room at Efficiency Lodge. Her relief at having escaped A2B was giving way to a frantic worry that she and her kids would soon end up in similar conditions, or worse. Celeste and Nyah and the boys were languishing at Efficiency as well. Maurice and Natalia had just gotten a room at Extended Stay America after losing their apartment. Kara and her children were still sleeping in her Toyota whenever she was unable to cover a week at a hotel. Like the people in the car on Edgewood Avenue, none of these families would be counted as homeless by HUD. They would remain invisible: omitted from the census, hidden from public view, and mostly ignored by those purporting to "eradicate homelessness," as the evening's speaker had put it.

This was by design. In the 1980s, when homelessness was starting to explode in the United States, elected officials tried to deny that there was anything to be concerned about. A top HUD official in the Reagan administration went so far as to bluntly assert: "No one is living on the streets." As these efforts at gaslighting the public failed—residents of many cities only needed to look outside—there was a shift to downplaying the severity of the problem while muddying its root causes. The sight of scores of men and women sleeping on sidewalks and in cardboard boxes was a shock to many Americans. And it was recognized early on that this shock, if not properly managed, could be politically dangerous. It could lead people to conclude that there was something profoundly wrong with the neoliberal revolution—marked by large-scale privatization, massive tax cuts for the wealthy, and major reductions in social spending—that the Reagan era had ushered in. To mitigate this risk, the shock needed to be neutralized. The narrative needed to be controlled.

Discourses on poverty had already done much to denigrate the urban poor, so it was a relatively small step to present homelessness as a lifestyle choice, or the result of laziness, or the product of any number of other personal vices. But the main strategy was to link homelessness with mental illness and addiction. Federal funding for research on homelessness was limited exclusively to the National Institute of Mental Health, the National Institute on Alcohol Abuse and Alcoholism, and the National Institute on Drug Abuse. This "lopsided research agenda," as one historian of public health would later refer to it, led academics and policymakers to focus disproportionately on a small sliver of the total number of people experiencing homelessness. Then as now, nobody denied that many of the men and women most visibly suffering on the streets were struggling with alcoholism, mental health issues, or other disabilities. These conditions, however, had no more *caused* them to become homeless than a fever causes the flu. Yet a medicalized homelessness was deemed less threatening to government policies than a politicized one. Bolstered by a deluge of sensationalist media accounts, individual pathology became the dominant frame for understanding homelessness, diverting attention from structural factors like poverty or racism. Meanwhile, the fastest-growing segment of the nation's homeless population were children under the age of six.

Some researchers, journalists, and activist groups like the National Union of the Homeless or the Community for Creative Non-Violence (whose members erected a tent city near the White House and called it "Reaganville") sought to call attention to the real reason for this mounting catastrophe. In *Rachel and Her Children,* a searing depiction of life in a towering New York shelter for families, Jonathan Kozol distilled this dissenting view into a single italicized sentence. *"The cause of homelessness,"* he wrote, observing that most homeless people could be found in cities where low-rent apartments and single-room occupancy (SRO) hotels had disappeared, *"is lack of housing."* Still, the prevailing view remained intact. In 1986, *The New York Times* and CBS News polled individuals at random, asking them what they thought caused homelessness. Thirty-two percent said it was caused by alcohol or drugs or psychological problems; 20 percent said an unwillingness to work; 19 percent cited bad luck; 24 percent cited a combination of each of these; and 5 percent had no opinion. Nobody mentioned housing.

Over the next two decades, "the homeless" solidified into a discrete, readily identified social category. Homeless people were confined to particular areas of the city, such as skid rows—and when that no longer worked, the tactic often shifted to banishment and criminalization. The shock wore off; the sense of emergency waned. Homelessness was now tragic but unremarkable, a seemingly permanent fixture of the cityscape. It became the purview of charity and social work; as a field of study, it became the object of an increasingly technical and specialized jargon, isolated intellectually.

At the same time, the interests of advocates and government agencies began to converge on a definition of homelessness that was deliberately narrow and circumscribed. For advocates, this was a matter of moral urgency: ensuring that scarce resources were targeted at those considered to be in most dire need of help. For the government, it was a matter of expediency: the more contained the problem, the easier it was to tackle—or to claim that it was being tackled. By 2005, when the Point-in-Time count was established by HUD, a small but conspicuous fraction of the total homeless population had come to stand, in the public imagination, for homelessness itself.

Everyone else was written out of the story. They literally did not count.

THIS WILLFUL DISREGARD has caused incalculable harm. Britt was not the first desperate parent to learn that in order to be considered homeless, and therefore to qualify for assistance, she and her kids would need to sleep outside or move into a shelter (assuming a shelter could

even accommodate them). Celeste was not the first person to leave
Gateway Center dazed and empty-handed, locked out of vital services
because her particular form of homelessness failed to satisfy the bureau-
crats. Even her cancer did not render her "vulnerable" enough. If she
wanted help, her family would have to split up: fifteen-year-old Jalen at
a men's facility, she and Micah at one for women and children. Every
day in America, caseworkers are forced to turn homeless families away
for not being "homeless" in the right way. Staff at schools and colleges
are forced to watch students struggle, able to offer little more than a gas
card or a food bank referral or, as with Danielle's teacher, a few days at
a hotel paid out of their own pocket. In Reddit or Facebook groups,
families crowdsource tactics for navigating a cruel and arbitrary system.
Starting a GoFundMe is the most common suggestion.

But our approach to counting and defining homelessness is not just
robbing people of support. It also distorts our understanding of the
problem. Narrow the lens, and perhaps we can persuade ourselves, as
did those respondents to the CBS/*New York Times* poll four decades
ago, that homelessness is a unique condition afflicting a particular type
of person. Widen the lens, adjust the focus, and homelessness begins to
look very different.

For years, those seeking to challenge the undercounting and misrep-
resentation of homelessness in America had few tools at their disposal.
It seemed clear that a sizable segment of the nation's homeless population, especially families with children, were being ignored by the official reporting metrics. But quantifying this omission, putting a number
on it, proved difficult.

New data and methods are changing that. In 2016, after years of trying to convince city officials that homelessness was not confined to people living in shelters or on the street, researchers at the Chicago Coalition
for the Homeless (CCH) decided to take matters into their own hands.
They formed the Homelessness Data Project and began conducting a
more expansive count, broadening it beyond the Point-in-Time census
to include those doubled up with others. They knew that such transient, often precarious arrangements were how most families in Chi-

cago experienced homelessness. Still, when the final tally came in, they were stunned. More than 64,000 residents were living doubled-up in the city, a figure that dwarfed the Point-in-Time count's total of 5,889. Local media began to amplify these findings, and soon the city's political leadership was forced to reckon with them as well. This led to a 2024 ballot measure, Bring Chicago Home, aimed at raising an estimated $100 million annually to address the full spectrum of homelessness in the city. Though this referendum, backed by Mayor Brandon Johnson, was ultimately voted down, it gained national attention, and a broad-based coalition of supporters vowed to continue fighting.

"The idea that these people aren't 'actually' homeless because they're not in shelters is absurd," Julie Dworkin, the director of policy at CCH, told me. "Oftentimes the shelters are full, or parents are afraid their kids will be taken away, or there simply are no family shelters—in which case, all these people are essentially abandoned by the system." Like many experts on family homelessness, she rejects the idea that families living doubled-up are somehow better off than those residing in shelters. Numerous studies show that children in these situations are frequently exposed to "toxic stress" that can adversely affect long-term cognitive and emotional development.

The Chicago researchers recently collaborated with colleagues at Vanderbilt University and the Heartland Alliance Social IMPACT Research Center to offer the first measure of doubled-up homelessness nationwide. What they discovered was striking: those experiencing this form of homelessness exceeded the HUD-administered total for the country's entire homeless population by a factor of six. In Georgia, approximately 118,000 residents, the majority of them families, experienced doubled-up homelessness in 2022. That same year, the Point-in-Time count total for Georgia—purporting to represent *everyone* currently homeless in the state—was 10,700. If all the men, women, and children overlooked by this official census gathered at Truist Park, the stadium where the Braves play, they could fill it nearly three times over.

The doubled-up figures alone are staggering. But what about the scores of families and individuals at extended-stay hotels? They, too, have been left out of HUD's statistics. Each year, however, the U.S. Department of Education requires school districts to submit data on student homelessness, and this reporting explicitly encompasses hotels and motels. During the 2021–22 school year, 106,621 children enrolled in the nation's public schools were identified as living at a hotel or motel—an increase of more than 20 percent from two years earlier. But the real number, advocates suggest, is almost certainly higher, since obtaining this information is dependent on schools actively seeking it out and parents or students self-reporting their circumstances. (One in-depth investigation revealed that roughly 300,000 additional students experiencing homelessness had slipped through the cracks.) And this figure includes only school-age children and youth. It doesn't include their parents or other household members.

When we put all this together, extrapolating from these disparate data sources, the evidence is clear: homelessness is an exponentially bigger and more pervasive phenomenon than we have been led to believe. A conservative estimate of the actual number of people deprived of housing in the United States—those living in vehicles or hotel rooms, or staying temporarily with others, along with people in shelters or on the street—would be well over *four million.*

These numbers matter—if they didn't, there wouldn't be an attempt to systematically deflate them. An accurate accounting of homelessness in America produces an entirely different narrative: a different sense of who in this country is becoming homeless and why. It changes our understanding of the breadth, character, and urgency of the problem. An accurate appraisal tells us that, as a country, we are in the throes of a crisis of unprecedented proportions.

THE CRISIS SHOWS no signs of abating. Housing is now unaffordable for an astonishing half of all U.S. renters, according to Harvard University's Joint Center for Housing Studies—the highest number on record. At the heart of this trend is the growing gulf between people's wages and the amount of money they are compelled to pay to keep their homes. Renters at all income levels are feeling brutalized by a merciless housing market, as more and more of their monthly earnings go directly to landlords. Housing insecurity has become an ever-widening sinkhole, swallowing up not only the poor and working class but vast portions of the downwardly mobile middle class as well. The boundary separating the housed from the unhoused is more permeable than ever. But it's those near the bottom of the income scale, people like the families in this book, who are particularly at risk.

Commentators have struggled to account for how plummeting unemployment and a booming economy could be accompanied by such widespread insecurity. Perhaps the pandemic is to blame? It's a tempting explanation, but this calamity was in the making long before Covid. The pandemic merely amplified it. Temporary relief programs— emergency rental assistance, the CDC eviction moratorium, stimulus payments, an expanded child tax credit—helped stall the effects of the deepening housing precarity. When these measures ended, the floodgates opened.

In America today, there are just thirty-four affordable and available rental homes for every one hundred extremely low-income households who need them. This amounts to a shortage of 7.3 million low-rent apartments—a colossal deficit, and the single greatest reason why so many people are continuing to become homeless. Yet, far from addressing this disaster, some of the nation's most powerful financial institutions are actively exacerbating and exploiting it. Giant private equity firms, institutional investors, and corporate landlords have been buying up properties en masse and then jacking up rents beyond the rate of inflation, "re-tenanting" buildings (replacing poorer tenants with wealthier ones), and neglecting basic maintenance because they know that if one household moves out, another will quickly take its place. In Atlanta, bulk buyers have used billions of dollars in cash to accumulate and rent out more than sixty-five thousand homes; the two largest out-of-state companies now own more than ten thousand apiece. During a twelve-month stretch starting in July 2021, investors bought one out of every three homes for sale in Atlanta.

Last year, the Justice Department accused the country's largest property managers of colluding to artificially increase rents by way of a price-setting algorithm. The scheme allegedly encompassed 70 percent of multifamily apartment buildings nationwide and sixteen million units. Yet this is merely an exaggerated form of the rent gouging that is now part and parcel of our "normal" market. Landlords of all types and sizes regularly push up rents—not because they have to, but because they rightly discern that families have few alternatives. "Where are people going to go?" the owner of Monarch Investment and Management Group, the fastest-growing landlord in the Midwest, said of the substantial rent hikes imposed by his company. "They can't go anywhere."

There's another insidious twist, as Maurice and Natalia experienced firsthand. Wall Street firms like Blackstone and Starwood Capital are not only profiting off people's desperation to remain housed. They are also, increasingly, taking over the markets and industries designed to extract revenue from those who have already lost their homes. Rooming houses and extended-stays, cosigning companies and subprime lending, storage facilities and credit repair: a whole host of enterprises have sprung up to capitalize on the nation's housing woes. Homelessness has become big business.

IT DOESN'T HAVE TO be this way. Ours doesn't have to be a society where people clocking sixty hours a week aren't paid enough to meet their basic needs; or where parents have to sell their plasma or food stamps or go without electricity in order to keep their children housed; or where your ability to afford an apartment is contingent on winning a voucher "lottery" and spending years on a waitlist, only to then lose the voucher when no landlord will accept it. In the richest country on earth, *nobody*—whether they work or have a disability or struggle with addiction or mental health challenges—should be deprived of stable shelter. Mass homelessness arose recently, within our lifetimes. It's worth reminding ourselves of this fact, because if it hasn't always been like this, then a different kind of future is possible.

How do we get there? For years we have opted for piecemeal, better-than-nothing initiatives that tweak the existing system rather than substantially alter it. We have taken it for granted that housing is a commodity, a vehicle for accumulating wealth, and that the few who own it will invariably profit at the expense of the many who need it. Looking to the private market to fix a debacle created by that very market, we have settled for incremental remedies: a few "affordable" apartments at 80 percent AMI here, a handful of supportive housing units there. If this approach to tackling the crisis seems small and unambitious, that's partly because its nature and severity have been obscured. A distorted view of the problem generates inadequate solutions.

But there's another possibility, one that invites us to envision a world where living in a safe, affordable home is not a luxury but a guaranteed right for everybody. Housing, in this view, is too precious and important to be left to the whims of the market: it is a cornerstone of both human dignity and societal well-being. In other words, housing is an essential public good—something that benefits society as a whole and contributes to the overall flourishing of communities. There are lots of things we consider public goods and fund accordingly: K-12 education, Social Security, clean water, parks, libraries, roads and highways, and other infrastructure. How have we allowed something as fundamental as shelter to be excluded from this list?

The idea of a right to housing has a long and distinguished pedigree. It has been a core principle for countless social movements, and it's enshrined in law by many of America's peer countries. "The right of every family to a decent home" even featured prominently in FDR's proposed Second Bill of Rights of 1944. Four years later, housing was included—alongside food, clothing, and medical care—in Article 25 of the Universal Declaration of Human Rights.

The time for tentative half measures is long past. If we are serious about ending this country's epidemic of homelessness and housing insecurity, then we must confront it head-on and commit to a guiding principle: everybody in America should and can have a home. It won't happen overnight, but it's the foundation on which our solutions must be built. "The housing market is a catastrophic failure, and the conditions tenants are experiencing today cannot continue," Tara Raghuveer, founding director of KC Tenants and the Tenant Union Federation, told me. "Something's got to give."

ONE IMMEDIATE WAY to relieve this misery is to keep people in the homes they already have. Every minute in the United States, there are, on average, seven evictions filed—a total of roughly 3.6 million eviction filings in a typical year, according to Princeton University's Eviction Lab. Ensuring that poor tenants have access to free legal representation, just as there's a right to counsel in criminal cases, would help to drastically reduce this number. Other tools include direct cash assistance for vulnerable renters and laws mandating basic habitability standards. Closing the qualified contract loophole for LIHTC properties (or, better, extending affordability requirements beyond thirty years) would have kept Britt in her apartment; enacting "just cause" eviction laws—designed to shield tenants from arbitrary or retaliatory evictions and, crucially, limit the reasons a landlord can refuse to renew a lease—would have kept Maurice and Natalia in theirs. Then there's rent control, among the most potent weapons against housing instability. Homeowners already enjoy de facto rent control in the form of the thirty-year fixed-rate mortgage. Why shouldn't renter households be similarly secure in knowing what they'll be paying from one year to the next?

Real estate lobbyists and the politicians they fund vigorously oppose nearly all of these measures, which is why tenant organizing and tenant unions are so important. Large-scale transformation typically begins not at the top, in the halls of power, but with concerted pressure from below—and often the groundwork is laid by those who stand to lose the most.

In 2022, a year and a half after Efficiency Lodge hired guards to forcibly remove families at gunpoint, a group of residents sued the hotel for illegally evicting them. Represented by the Atlanta Legal Aid Society and supported in an amicus brief by Housing Justice League, the Southern Poverty Law Center, and the Atlanta Volunteer Lawyers Foundation, the residents sought to prove what Natalie McLaughlin had argued to the police lieutenant immediately following the lockouts: that after years at the hotel they should have been covered by landlord-tenant law, and that management had circumvented this law by pushing them out without due process. At trial, the judge sided with the residents; when attorney and former governor Roy Barnes, the brother of Efficiency's owner, appealed the verdict, the Georgia Court of Appeals upheld it. This ruling set a precedent for other extended-stays in Georgia, granting their residents the status of "tenants" instead of "guests." What they won was the right to a court-ordered eviction rather than a summary lockout—not the dramatic victory they'd hoped for, but the seeds of more profound change, as one HJL member pointed out, were planted.

Preventing families from becoming homeless is an urgent task. Getting them into housing they don't yet have is just as critical. A range of practical interventions would ease their burden: Banning extortionate application fees, capping security deposits, outlawing biased tenant screening practices, prohibiting discrimination against voucher holders (and enforcing those rules)—these are but a few ideas. Expanding HUD's definition of *homeless* is another. But the biggest challenge by far is the housing itself: there's not enough of it, certainly not the kind that's affordable for millions of low-income renters. Restrictive land use policies have contributed to this mess. With an estimated 75 percent of land in the nation's major cities zoned exclusively for single-family homes, it's no surprise that the supply of housing has failed to keep pace with demand.

Yet simply deregulating private development is insufficient, because the market, on its own, will never be incentivized to build and maintain truly affordable housing for those in need of it. Recognizing this fact, there is a growing consensus that, as in other times of national emergency, all levels of government—federal, state, local—must intervene directly.

These interventions can take many forms, but the most promising is a model known as "social housing." Commonly described as a public option for housing, this model takes housing permanently off the private market, beyond the reach of speculators and profiteers: it can be owned and operated by nonprofits or municipal governments, or, as with limited-equity cooperatives or land trusts, residents can own a stake in their homes at subsidized rates. In recent years, Finland has made international headlines for virtually ending homelessness. Their secret? Building tens of thousands of social housing units on government-owned land, ensuring that even the most economically marginalized have access to safe, affordable homes. But it's in Vienna, where a whopping two-thirds of city residents live in high-quality, publicly owned apartments and spend about 22 percent of their post-tax income on rent and utilities, that social housing has particularly thrived.

"If people don't have to struggle all day long to survive," a Vienna resident who has lived in the city's social housing for several decades told journalist Francesca Mari, "you can use your energy for much more important things." Imagine if America's public housing—those "bright cheerful buildings" that first arose in downtown Atlanta a century ago and then spread to the rest of the nation—hadn't been set up to fail. Imagine if public housing hadn't been drastically underfunded and fallen into decrepitude; if it hadn't been treated as an option of last resort, concentrating poverty and becoming stigmatized as a result. What if, today, public housing were appealing enough that people across income levels would want to live there, not only because of the quality of the apartments but because rents would never exceed a quarter of their earnings? *That's* social housing, and combined with other complementary policies—such as raising the federal minimum wage and significantly expanding labor protections—it could be our best hope of guaranteeing, finally, that every family in this country has a roof over their heads.

Our cities are on a perilous path, with extreme and mounting wealth on one side, loss and deprivation on the other, and a credo of *hard work will be rewarded* somehow persisting despite it all. But this new American homelessness is a choice—one we have collectively made as a society—and it comes at a cost: Grace consoling her baby brother as they pass the night in a Walmart parking lot; Kyrie and Desiree moving from one living room floor to another, never knowing where they'll be staying next; DJ and his siblings sleeping in a filthy, freezing storage room. Such suffering is so unnecessary, so utterly preventable. We have the solutions. We have the resources. What we need now is the will to act.

| ACKNOWLEDGMENTS |

I am profoundly grateful to the families who welcomed me into their lives and entrusted me with their stories. Witnessing their courage, dignity, and steadfastness has been a transformative experience, and their generosity and openness have been a gift beyond measure. I am humbled and privileged to know them.

I owe an immense debt of gratitude to LaQuana "LA Pink" Alexander, whose radiant presence and unwavering commitment taught me what it looks like to show up for others. My heartfelt thanks also go to Carla Wells, whose insights about housing and homelessness were invaluable; the former residents at Efficiency Lodge and Gladstone Apartments, for graciously allowing me to be among them for long stretches of time; the members of Housing Justice League, especially Natalie McLaughlin, Quinn Mulholland, and Dani Aiello; Kamau Franklin of Community Movement Builders; Anita Beaty; Dan Immergluck; Julie Dworkin; Barbara Duffield; Molly Richard; Danny Iverson; Larry Corker; Stacey Hopkins; Jimmy Hill; Miriam Gutman; Sharon Thompson and Julie Graves at New Beginnings; and Marshall Rancifer, a fierce advocate for the unhoused who passed away in 2022. He is sorely missed.

My phenomenal editor, Amanda Cook, has been an indispensable ally in bringing this book into existence. Her passion and rigor, vision and empathy have guided every step of this journey, while her meticulous attention to detail and genuine care for the work elevated it in countless ways. Thank you, Amanda, for your incisive reads and tremendous dedication. It has been a true blessing to work with you. I am also grateful to Katie Berry, whose astute line edits did much to improve the manuscript, and to the rest of the stellar team at Crown: Penny Simon, Mary Moates, Mason Eng, Julie Cepler, Anna Kochman, Aubrey Khan, Heather Williamson, Terry Deal, Elisabeth Magnus, Dan Novack, Annsley Rosner, Gillian Blake, and David Drake. Huge thanks to my exacting and fastidious fact-checker, Julie Tate.

Adam Eaglin, my agent, believed in this book from its inception and offered wise counsel and encouragement throughout the entire process. He is simply the best, and I count myself very fortunate to have had his support. Thanks also to Elyse Cheney, Alice Whitwham, Isabel Mendia, and Beniamino Ambrosi at The Cheney Agency.

This book grew out of two magazine articles. The first, "The New American Homeless," was published in *The New Republic*. I am forever indebted to Emily Cooke, my brilliant editor, for making that story possible. My enormous gratitude also goes to Cokethia Goodman and her children, as well as to those who helped bring attention to their plight. A special thanks to Soledad O'Brien and Carrie Beehan for organizing a fundraising campaign for the family. The other article, "3 Kids. 2 Paychecks. No Home," appeared in *The California Sunday Magazine* and was edited by the amazing Raha Naddaf. My time in Salinas with Candido, Brenda, Frankie, Josephat, and Adelene left an indelible mark on me, and I appreciate their willingness to open their lives to me.

I am grateful to Charles Piot, Anne Allison, Stanley Hauerwas, Ian Baucom, and the late Diane Nelson—extraordinary mentors whose guidance during my graduate studies at Duke University deeply shaped my work and thinking. I hope their influence is reflected in these pages. I would also like to thank the Society of Fellows in the Humanities at Columbia University, particularly Eileen Gillooly and Christopher Brown; the Justice-in-Education Initiative, through which I had the great privilege of teaching at Sing Sing prison; the Luce/ACLS Fellowship in Religion, Journalism & International Affairs; and New America, especially Awista Ayub and Sarah Baline.

Over the course of this project, I was sustained by the kindness and solidarity of many people. For their invaluable feedback and encouragement, I am grateful to Jamie Alcorn, Anne Allison, Stephen Asante, Roxanna Asgarian, Rachel Aviv, Jessica Backman-Levy, Paul Backman-Levy, Max Blau, Jonathan Blitzer, Christy Burkett, Natalie Carnes, Liz Clasen-Kelly, Fred Clasen-Kelly, Gareth Cook, Emily Cooke, Zeliha Durace, Fatih Durace, Mya Frazier, David Goodman, Katie Goodman, Nikhil Goyal, Allie Gross, Gokce Gunel, Greg Harris, Rebecca Zaragoza Jackson, Katie Jentleson, Lizzie Johnson, Jaime Keiter, Hoon Kim, Cathelijn Kuis, Nathan Kuntz, Jason Lankow, Thomas Lake, Henry Lear, Yi-Ling Liu, Francesca Mari, Rachel Nolan, Casey Parks, Charles Piot, Hugh Raffles, Shaun Raviv, Tracy Rosenthal, David Russell, China Scherz, Matthew Shaer, Joshua Sharpe, Christine Smallwood, Stephannie Stokes, Nathan Suhr-Sytsma, Emily Taggart, Carole Taylor, Steven Thrasher, Lars Van De Fliert, Sonam Vashi, Dan Walsh, Matthew Whalen, Wyatt Williams, and Erin Yerby.

I could not have written this book without the unceasing support of my parents, Michael and Debra Goldstone; my sister and brother-in-law, Shawna and Scott Anderson; and my father- and mother-in-law, Jerry and Gail Brown. To Emil and Eliot: thank you for the hugs, the long hikes, the constant joy. It's an unbelievable honor and delight to be your dad.

And to Elaine, to whom this book is dedicated: thank you for *everything*. Your love, your example, your wisdom and compassion—there are no words for what you mean to me. I am overwhelmed with gratitude for all that you have given to this work, and to our life together.

| NOTES |

SOURCES AND METHODS

Most of the research and reporting for this book was conducted between late 2019 and early 2022. Scenes that occurred before this period were reconstructed through primary source materials—such as diaries and journal entries, legal records, photographs, text messages, social media posts, and audio and video recordings—in addition to repeated interviews with as many people as possible to corroborate the facts. When a person is described as having "thought" something, it is based on their direct account to me. There are no conflated scenes or composite characters in the book. To better understand the world of homeless services and the intersecting systems affecting the lives of the book's protagonists, I conducted dozens of interviews, some on "background" or off the record, with various individuals not featured in this book, including social workers, city officials, teachers, legal aid attorneys, landlords, property managers, academic researchers, shelter employees, and activists.

Early in my conversations with the families, I was asked what the reporting process would entail. "Basically," I said, "spending as much time with you as possible." This approach owed much to my training as an anthropologist, which had taught me the significance of open-ended, immersive engagement with a social world—a methodology aimed at capturing the depth and texture, the ebbs and flows, of people's lives. In practice, this involved spending long stretches of time at Efficiency Lodge, Gladstone Apartments, Extended Stay America, the West Side rooming house, and the myriad other motels, shelters, and apartments the families cycled through. I accompanied them to Gateway Center and DFCS offices, waiting with them for hours on end, and I followed them to their jobs, family gatherings, and meetings with caseworkers and service providers. As trust solidified, the reporting became more collaborative, and we improvised ways to document their experiences even when I was unable to be with them in person. The families, along with Pink, used audio and video recordings to capture events that transpired in my absence, supplementing the hundreds of recordings I had gathered myself.

As a rule, I never paid anyone for their story or for an interview, and while following the families, to maintain the integrity of the reporting, I did not provide financial support, apart from the occasional meal or tank of gas or grocery gift card. Once I transitioned from reporting to writing, however, and it became clear that assisting in more substantial ways—financial and otherwise—would have no bearing on the events recounted in this book, I allowed myself greater leeway in helping Celeste, Britt, Maurice, Natalia, Michelle, Kara, and their children with their ongoing needs.

Before publication, I met individually with each of the families to review their respective chapters. This was done not only to ensure factual accuracy and address issues of representation but also to guarantee that no material would be included in the published text without their knowledge and consent. In the end, there were no requests for changes.

INTRODUCTION

xvi   **article for *The New Republic*:** Brian Goldstone, "The New American Homeless," *The New Republic,* August 21, 2019.

xvi   **As I continued to research and write:** Brian Goldstone, "3 Kids. 2 Paychecks. No Home," *The California Sunday Magazine,* November 26, 2019.

xvi   **"safe parking lots":** Soumya Karlamangla and Rukmini Callimachi, "In California, Safe Parking Lots Offer a Haven for the 'Mobile Homeless,'" *The New York*

Times, October 19, 2023; Rick Paulas, "Americans Living in Their Cars Are Finding Refuge in 'Safe Parking Lots,'" *The Guardian,* January 5, 2024.

xvi · **employed in low-wage jobs:** This figure, given to me by the late Dennis Bowman of Nicholas House in Atlanta, is consistent with national statistics on the link between homelessness and low-wage work. Using U.S. Census data, a recent study by scholars from the University of Chicago, Yale University, and the University of Pennsylvania offers the most comprehensive portrait to date on income and employment among Americans experiencing homelessness. The study found that "a substantial share of the homeless population is drawn from the ranks of the working poor: about half of those in shelters and 40 percent of those at unsheltered locations had formal employment." Bruce D. Meyer, Angela Wyse, Gillian Meyer, Alexa Grunwaldt, and Derek Wu, "Homelessness and the Persistence of Deprivation: Income, Employment, and Safety Net Participation," University of Chicago, Becker Friedman Institute for Economics Working Paper No. 2024-48, April 2024, https://papers.ssrn.com/sol3/papers.cfm?abstract_id=4801800.

xvi · **a woman in her late forties:** The woman's name was Melanie, and we kept in intermittent touch over the coming months. The last time I spoke to her was in June 2019. She was still working and struggling to secure housing. A couple of weeks later, when I called, her phone was disconnected. I went to the encampment but found that it had been torn down by the city. In the notes from my first conversation with Melanie, I underlined two quotes. "We're always talking about how many of us have been working our whole lives," and "There's so much temporariness out here. You have to let things go."

xvii · **"unconnected to the world of work":** Peter H. Rossi, *Down and Out in America: The Origins of Homelessness* (Chicago: University of Chicago Press, 1989), 8.

xvii · **Today there isn't a single state, metropolitan area, or county:** Andrew Aurand, Mackenzie Pish, Ikra Rafi, and Diane Yentel, "Out of Reach: The High Cost of Housing," National Low Income Housing Coalition, 2023, https://progov21.org/Home/Document/V91J56.

xvii · **in the nation's richest, most rapidly developing cities:** Noah Buhayar and Esme E. Deprez, "The Homeless Crisis Is Getting Worse in America's Richest Cities," *Businessweek,* November 20, 2018.

xvii · **New York, whose economy soared:** "Basic Facts About Homelessness: New York City," Coalition for the Homeless, February 2023.

xvii · **Washington, D.C., boasts:** Emmie Martin, "This Is the No. 1 Highest-Earning Region in the US, and It Isn't in New York or California," CNBC, March 20, 2019.

xvii · **one of the greatest per capita homeless rates:** "Estimated Rate of Homelessness in the United States in 2022, by State," Statista, June 2023.

xvii · **Seattle is close behind:** Spencer Pauley, "Report: Seattle-King County Region Has Third Most Homeless People in the U.S.," The Center Square, Talk Radio KVI, December 19, 2023.

xvii · **In Austin and Phoenix:** Sarah Chaney Cambon and Danny Dougherty, "Sunbelt Cities Nashville and Austin Are Nation's Hottest Job Markets," *The Wall Street Journal,* April 1, 2023; Ron Serven, "Second-Tier Cities Thrive in the

Post-pandemic World," National Association for Industrial and Office Parks (NAIOP), Fall 2021; Myelle Lansat, "The 35 Cities in the US with the Biggest Influx of People," Business Insider, August 12, 2018.

xviii **Atlanta, the third-fastest-growing**: Kenny Murry, "Metro Atlanta Moves Up to Sixth-Largest in US, Counties Outside City See Major Increases," WABE TV, March 14, 2024.

xviii **the "Silicon Valley of the South"**: Madeline Coggins, "Georgia's Booming Tech and Startup Scene Is Helping Atlanta Become the 'Silicon Valley of the South,'" Fox Business, March 12, 2024.

xviii **Then there's the entertainment industry**: Cassam Looch, "How Georgia Overtook Hollywood to Become the Film Capital of the World," Culture Trip, August 28, 2018.

xviii **The area's population surge**: Moshe Haspel, "Atlanta's Population Growth, 1990–2020," Atlanta Regional Commission, *33n* (blog), November 4, 2021; "Metro Atlanta Population to Reach 7.9 Million by 2050, ARC Forecasts Show," Atlanta Regional Commission, February 14, 2024.

xviii **Atlanta typified the "poor in the core" phenomenon**: Dan Immergluck, *Red Hot City: Housing, Race, and Exclusion in Twenty-First-Century Atlanta* (Oakland: University of California Press, 2022).

xviii **This began to change**: Immergluck, *Red Hot City*.

xviii **The place was shinier**: "Median Household Income in Georgia in the United States from 1990–2022," Statista, November 3, 2023.

xviii **The ultimate signifier**: Kaid Benfield, "The Country's Most Ambitious Smart Growth Project," *The Atlantic*, July 26, 2011; Richard Fausset, "A Glorified Sidewalk, and the Path to Transform Atlanta," *The New York Times*, September 11, 2016.

xix **In mayoral speeches**: Kasim Reed, "2017 Annual State of the City Address," City of Atlanta Government, February 2, 2017; "Beltlining: Gentrification, Broken Promises and Hope on Atlanta's Southside," Housing Justice League and Research Action Cooperative, October 2017.

xix **Between 2010 and 2023**: Josh Green, "This Decade, Atlanta's Cost of Renting, Owning Went Through the Roof," Curbed Atlanta, December 17, 2019; Hanna Zakharenko, Abha Bhattarai, and Janice Kai Chen, "Rent Is Finally Cooling. See How Much Prices Have Changed in Your Area," *The Washington Post*, July 31, 2023.

xix **metro area lost a staggering sixty thousand**: J. D. Capelouto, "Regional Study: Metro Atlanta Lost 60K Affordable Rental Units from 2014–2019," *The Atlanta Journal-Constitution*, March 2, 2022.

xix **Over the past decade**: Josh Green, "Report: Almost All New Atlanta Apartments Qualify as 'Luxury,'" Urbanize Atlanta, July 19, 2022.

xix **A city that was 67 percent Black**: Quick Facts, Atlanta City, Georgia, U.S. Census, 2023.

xix **According to the most recent studies**: "Worst Case Housing Needs: 2023 Report to Congress," U.S. Department of Housing and Urban Development, Office of Policy Development and Research.

xix   **a kind of dystopian rejoinder to the claim:** Richard Florida, *The Rise of the Creative Class: And How It's Transforming Work, Leisure, Community and Everyday Life* (New York: Basic Books, 2002).

xx   **But since 1985, rent prices nationwide:** Testimony by Matthew Desmond, United States Senate Committee on Banking, Housing and Urban Affairs, August 2, 2022, https://www.banking.senate.gov/imo/media/doc/Desmond%20Testimony% 208-2-22%20.pdf; U.S. Census Bureau, American Community Survey, 1985–2022; U.S. Department of Housing and Urban Development, Fair Market Rents (40th Percentile Rents), 1985–2022.

xx   **Some fifty-three million Americans:** Martha Ross and Nicole Bateman, "Low-Wage Work Is More Pervasive Than You Think and There Aren't Enough 'Good Jobs' to Go Around," Brookings, November 21, 2019. Recent years have seen renewed calls for a federal job guarantee as a powerful tool to combat economic inequality and racial disparities. Proponents argue that such a program would empower workers, establish a wage floor, and eliminate the threat of unemployment— directly addressing the conditions that drive "working homelessness." See Darrick Hamilton, "The Federal Job Guarantee: A Step Toward Racial Justice," Dissent, November 9, 2015, https://www.dissentmagazine.org/online_articles/federal-job -guarantee-racial-justice-darrick-hamilton/; Mark Paul, William Darity Jr., Darrick Hamilton, and Khaing Zaw, "A Path to Ending Poverty by Way of Ending Unemployment: A Federal Job Guarantee," RSF: The Russell Sage Foundation Journal of the Social Sciences, 4(3) 2018, https://socialequity.duke.edu/wp-content/ uploads/2019/10/A-Path-to-Ending-Poverty.pdf.

xx   **In Atlanta, the "housing wage":** Aurand et al., "Out of Reach" 2023, 71–72.

xx   **Georgia's minimum wage:** "Your 2024 Guide to Every State's Minimum Wage," Paycom, December 21, 2023.

xx   **In Boston, a tenant:** Andrew Aurand, Mackenzie Pish, Ikra Rafi, and Diane Yentel, "Out of Reach: The High Cost of Housing," National Low Income Housing Coalition, 2024. I'm using the Point-in-Time numbers on family homelessness here: Partners for Home, "2023 Point-in-Time Count: City of Atlanta," 10, https:// partnersforhome.org/wp-content/uploads/2020/07/2023-PIT.pdf.

xx   **Counting the homeless has always been politically charged:** Marian Moser Jones, "Creating a Science of Homelessness During the Reagan Era," *Milbank Quarterly* 93, no. 1 (2004): 139–78; James D. Wright and Joel A. Devine, "Counting the Homeless: The Census Bureau's 'S-Night' in Five U.S. Cities," *Evaluation Review* 16, no. 4 (1992): 355–64. For a critical overview of this "numbers controversy," see Christopher Jencks, "The Homeless," *The New York Review of Books,* April 21, 1994.

xx   **denied vital assistance:** Testimony of Barbara Duffield, executive director of SchoolHouse Connection, *Legislative Review of H.R. 1511, the "Homeless Children and Youth Act of 2017,"* Hearing Before the Subcommittee on Housing and Insurance, Committee on Financial Services, U.S. House of Representatives, 115th Cong., 2nd sess., June 6, 2018, https://democrats-financialservices.house.gov/ uploadedfiles/06.06.2018_barbara_duffield_testimony.pdf; Evie Blad, " 'Hidden

Homeless': A Key Measure of Homelessness Excludes Most Students," *Education Week*, April 3, 2023; Katie LaGrone, "Defining Homeless: How It Determines Which Homeless Families Get HUD Help," ABC Action News, March 21, 2022.

xx **as bad as the official numbers are:** Jon Kamp and Shannon Najmabadi, "U.S. Homeless Count Surges 12% to Highest-Recorded Level," *The Wall Street Journal*, December 15, 2023; "2023 Annual Homeless Assessment Report: Part 1—PIT Estimates of Homelessness in the U.S.," U.S. Department of Housing and Urban Development, https://www.huduser.gov/portal/datasets/ahar/2023-ahar-part-1-pit-estimates-of-homelessness-in-the-us.html.

xx **Recent research reveals:** On the new data and methods allowing a more accurate homeless count, see "Approach: Homelessness Data Project," Chicago Coalition for the Homeless, accessed June 22, 2024, https://chicagohomeless.org/our-work/data-research/; Molly K. Richard, Julie Dworkin, Katherine Grace Rule, Suniya Farooqui, Zachary Glendening, and Sam Carlson, "Quantifying Doubled-Up Homelessness: Presenting a New Measure Using U.S. Census Microdata," *Housing Policy Debate* 34, no. 1 (2024): 3–24.

xxi **And all are Black—as are 93 percent of homeless families in Atlanta:** Partners for HOME, "2023 Point-in-Time Count: City of Atlanta," 10, https://partnersforhome.org/wp-content/uploads/2020/07/2023-PIT.pdf.

CHAPTER 1

5 **But this was before the Fair Housing Act:** Danyelle Solomon, Connor Maxwell, and Abril Castro, "Systemic Inequality: Displacement, Exclusion, and Segregation," Center for American Progress, August 7, 2019.

5 **A century of housing discrimination:** Douglas S. Massey and Nancy A. Denton, *American Apartheid: Segregation and the Making of the Underclass* (Cambridge, Mass.: Harvard University Press, 1993); Richard Rothstein, *The Color of Law: A Forgotten History of How Our Government Segregated America* (New York: Liveright, 2017); Beryl Satter, *Family Properties: Race, Real Estate, and the Exploitation of Black Urban America* (New York: Metropolitan Books, 2009).

5 **In the public imagination:** Katie Marages Schank, "What's in a Name? East Lake Meadows and Little Vietnam," *Atlanta Studies*, March 16, 2017.

5 **where people managed to forge a community:** Josh Green, "New Doc Chronicles the Downfall, Communal Resolve of Atlanta's Notorious 'Little Vietnam,'" Curbed Atlanta, March 24, 2020.

5 **Atlanta real estate titan Tom Cousins:** Max Blau, "I'll Take You There," The Bitter Southerner, March 24, 2020, https://bittersoutherner.com/ill-take-you-there-east-lake-meadows.

6 **The neighborhood's rapid change:** "Atlanta Neighborhood 'Tore Down Hell, Built Heaven,'" *Chicago Tribune*, April 13, 2020; "Case Study: East Lake Atlanta," 2012,

The Bridgespan Group; David C. Lewis, "How Golf Transformed a Blighted Neighborhood," NBC News, April 17, 2008.

6   **not everyone benefited from it:** Jennifer Robinson, "East Lake Meadows: A Public Housing Story," KPBS, March 23, 2020.

7   **the nation's primary means of offering housing support:** Eva Rosen, *The Voucher Promise: "Section 8" and the Fate of an American Neighborhood* (Princeton, N.J.: Princeton University Press, 2020); Rafael E. Cestero, "Opinion: Universal Housing Vouchers Are Key to Ending a National Crisis," *City Limits,* December 14, 2023.

7   **Roughly fourteen million:** Ed Gramlich, "Housing Choice Vouchers," National Low Income Housing Coalition, 2024.

7   **For these lucky few:** Ingrid Gould Ellen, "What Do We Know About Housing Choice Vouchers?," *Regional Science and Urban Economics* 80 (January 2020): 103380.

7   **On the radio and local news shows:** "Section 8 Waiting List Opens Tuesday," 11 Alive, January 6, 2015; Affordable Housing Online 2014, "Atlanta Housing Authority Section 8 Waiting List Hangout," YouTube, December 17, 2014.

7   **like they'd won the lottery:** Jake Blumgart, "What an Affordable Housing Moonshot Would Look Like," Slate, July 1, 2016.

7   **In 2010, a crowd of thirty thousand:** Dianne Mathiowetz, "30,000 Wait in Scorching Heat for Housing Vouchers," *Workers World,* August 19, 2010.

8   **the small municipality:** Isabel Hardman, "Thousands Mob Housing Officials in the US," *Inside Housing,* August 18, 2010.

8   **several people were trampled:** "Thousands Line Up, Stampede to Get on Wait List for Housing Vouchers in Dallas County," *Dallas Morning News,* July 14, 2011; Marie Diamond, "5,000 Poor Dallas Residents Stampede Each Other in Race for Scarce Housing Vouchers," Think Progress, July 16, 2011.

8   **When the application window closed:** "MTW Annual Report," Atlanta Housing Authority, June 30, 2015, https://www.hud.gov/sites/dfiles/PIH/documents/Atlanta FY15Report.pdf.

9   **In larger cities:** Aaron Schrank, "It's a Long Wait for Section 8 Housing in U.S. Cities," Marketplace, January 3, 2018.

9   **The ambient bustle:** "Hartsfield-Jackson Retains Top Spot at Busiest Airport in the World," Fox5 Atlanta, July 19, 2023.

10 **The median rent for a one-bedroom unit:** Myrydd Wells, "Commentary: Atlanta Needs More Affordable Housing, but the City's Plan Is Short on Dollars and Details," *Atlanta Magazine,* July 11, 2019.

10 **this despite a building frenzy:** John Yelling, "Atlanta Leads U.S. In Intown Apartment Development," *Atlanta Agent Magazine,* September 14, 2022.

12 **Like many of the sixty-three thousand:** Khushbu Shah, "City in a City: The 63,000 People Who Run the World's Busiest Airport," *The Guardian,* October 26, 2018; Kelly Yamanouchi, "Hartsfield-Jackson Cleaners Get Raise After 13-Year Push," *The Atlanta Journal-Constitution,* March 30, 2022.

CHAPTER 2

13   **the inpatient ward of Grady's psychiatric unit:** Mike King, "Georgia's Broken
      Mental-Health System," *Creative Loafing,* June 9, 2016; "Former First Lady Rosa-
      lynn Carter to Open Grady's New Mental Health Center," PR Newswire, May 11,
      2010; Max Blau, "Proposed Fulton Cuts Could Leave Thousands Without Grady's
      Mental-Health Services," *Creative Loafing,* January 15, 2014.

13   **Her first impression:** "Fleeing Man Shot at Atlanta Hospital," CNN, August 3,
      1999; Mike King, "Georgia's Broken Mental-Health System," *Creative Loafing,*
      June 9, 2016.

14   **A decade earlier:** Max Blau, "How Grady Memorial Hospital Skirted Death," *Cre-
      ative Loafing,* February 28, 2013.

16   **a recently passed law:** Georgia State Senate Research Office, "2005 Legislative Ses-
      sion Highlights."

16   **medical risks associated with abortion:** "Conceptions of Choice: Coming to Terms
      with the End of Roe," Georgia State University Library, online exhibit, accessed
      July 19, 2024, https://exhibits.library.gsu.edu/conceptions/medical-concerns/#:~:text
      =May%2010%2C%202005%20Women's%20Right,medical%20risks%20of%20
      the%20chosen; Priscilla Greear, "Passage of 'Right to Know' Bill Called Historic
      Step," *The Georgia Bulletin,* March 10, 2005.

18   **a series of scathing government audits:** "Job Corps Could Not Demonstrate Benefi-
      cial Job Training Outcomes," Department of Labor, Office of the Inspector Gen-
      eral, March 30, 2018.

19   **born at Atlanta Medical Center:** In October 2022, Wellstar Health System an-
      nounced that it was closing Atlanta Medical Center because the hospital was los-
      ing money. Like Grady, Atlanta Medical Center served a patient population that
      included many low-income residents without insurance. Donovan J. Thomas,
      "After Weeks of Drama, Disappointment, Atlanta Medical Center to Close," *The
      Atlanta Journal-Constitution,* October 31, 2022.

CHAPTER 3

25   **Everything they knew about the city:** Jeffrey Ogbar, "Atlanta's Remarkable Trans-
      formation from Heart of the Confederacy to Black Mecca," *Next Big Idea Club
      Magazine,* December 11, 2023.

25   **the "Black Mecca" they had envisioned:** For a powerfully argued critique of At-
      lanta's self-fashioning as the nation's Black Mecca, see Maurice J. Hobson, *The
      Legend of the Black Mecca: Politics and Class in the Making of Modern Atlanta* (Cha-
      pel Hill: University of North Carolina Press, 2017).

25   **they'd thought they were putting down roots:** Karen Pooley, "Segregation's New
      Geography: The Atlanta Metro Region, Race, and the Declining Prospects for
      Upward Mobility," *Southern Spaces,* April 15, 2015; John Ruch, "How Race and

Racism Shaped Growth and Cityhood in North Metro Atlanta," Rough Draft Atlanta, July 3, 2020.

25   **a six-million-person expanse of suburbs:** "Atlanta Metro Area Now 6th Largest in the U.S.," Metro Atlanta Chamber, March 14, 2024.

25   **Born of white flight in the 1960s:** Kevin Kruse, *White Flight: Atlanta and the Making of Modern Conservatism* (Princeton, N.J.: Princeton University Press, 2007); Sam Rosen, "Atlanta's Controversial 'Cityhood' Movement," *The Atlantic,* April 26, 2017.

25   **"build up a city separate from Atlanta and your Negroes":** Kruse, *White Flight,* 247–48.

26   **"a politics of suburban secession":** Susan Eaton, "How a 'New Secessionist' Movement Is Threatening to Worsen School Segregation and Widen Inequalities," *The Nation,* May 15, 2014; Emily Badger, "How Atlanta's Politics Overtook the Suburbs, Too," *The New York Times,* December 9, 2020.

26   **places like Sandy Springs:** Dan Immergluck, *Red Hot City: Housing, Race, and Exclusion in Twenty-First-Century Atlanta* (Oakland: University of California Press, 2022), 176–215; Fiza Pirani, "How Diverse Is Your Georgia City?," *The Atlanta Journal-Constitution,* April 11, 2019.

26   **were evolving in subtle ways:** Jay Caspian Kang, "Everything You Think You Know About the Suburbs Is Wrong," *The New York Times,* November 18, 2021; William H. Frey, "Today's Suburbs Are Symbolic of America's Rising Diversity: A 2020 Census Portrait," Brookings Institution, June 15, 2022; Willow S. Lung-Amam, *The Right to Suburbia: Combating Gentrification on the Urban Edge* (Oakland: University of California Press, 2024).

26   **why the area was attracting so many people:** Lauren Finney Harden, "A Local's Guide to the 12 Best Suburbs in Atlanta, Georgia," *Landing,* November 4, 2022.

27   **public transportation was notoriously limited:** Darin Givens, "Anti-transit Design in the Atlanta Suburbs: Aiming for Exclusion, and Failing," Medium, January 30, 2017; Sean Richard Kennan, "Atlanta Ranked Among Worst U.S. Cities to Commute by Public Transit, Car," Curbed Atlanta, May 3, 2019.

CHAPTER 5

35   **the nickname "Buckhead":** Margaret Newkirk, "Richest Atlanta District Inches Closer to Seceding from City," Bloomberg News, February 28, 2023.

36   **a notorious three-and-a-half-mile stretch of Candler Road:** Alan Judd, "Life, Death, and Gangs in South DeKalb," *The Atlanta Journal-Constitution,* November 29, 2015.

37   **charged with murder after a shooting near the hotel:** Preezy Brown, "Yung Mal Charged in Murder of Atlanta Man," *Vibe,* July 13, 2021.

37   **Like much of DeKalb County:** Emily Badger, "This Can't Happen by Accident," *The Washington Post,* May 2, 2016; Dan Immergluck, *Red Hot City: Housing, Race,*

>25

and Exclusion in Twenty-First-Century Atlanta (Oakland: University of California Press, 2022), 135–75.

37 **there were two kinds of poor Black neighborhoods:** Stephannie Stokes and Geoff Hing, "As Property Values Rise in Atlanta, So Does the Exploitation of Black Homeowners," WABE, September 14, 2020; Jaclynn Ashly, "The Black Residents Fighting Atlanta to Stay in Their Homes," *Al Jazeera,* November 30, 2020.

37 **These spaces, hollowed out:** Ruth Wilson Gilmore, *Abolition Geography: Essays Toward Liberation* (London: Verso, 2022), 301–7; see also Ananya Roy, "Grammars of Dispossession: Racial Banishment in the American Metropolis," in *Grammars of the Urban Ground,* ed. Ash Amin and Michele Lancione (Durham, N.C.: Duke University Press, 2022), 41–57.

37 **Although they appeared worlds apart:** Neil Smith, "Gentrification and Uneven Development," *Economic Geography* 58, no. 2 (1982): 139–55; Tom Slater, *Shaking Up the City: Ignorance, Inequality, and the Urban Question* (Oakland: University of California Press, 2021); Desiree Fields and Elora Lee Raymond, "Racialized Geographies of Housing Financialization," *Progress in Human Geography* 45, no. 6 (2021): 1625–45.

43 **The stain on her rental history:** Matthew Goldstein, "The Stigma of a Scarlet E," *The New York Times,* August 9, 2021; Kathryn Sabbath, "Erasing the 'Scarlet E' of Eviction Records," *The Appeal,* April 12, 2021.

44 **She was dead:** Ty Tagami and Alexis Stevens, "Mother of Pregnant 14-Year-Old Killed: 'They Took Away Two Lives from Me,'" *The Atlanta Journal-Constitution,* November 20, 2018.

44 **although Souleymane would later be arrested:** Yamil Berard, "Suspect with Criminal Record Arrested in Shooting Death of 14-Year-Old," *The Atlanta Journal-Constitution,* November 22, 2018.

47 **the school system classified students living at hotels and motels as homeless:** "The McKinney-Vento Definition of Homeless," National Center for Homeless Education, accessed July 19, 2024, https://nche.ed.gov/mckinney-vento-definition/.

CHAPTER 6

51 **Although the "30 percent rule":** Megan Leonhardt, "Use the 30% and 28/36 Rules to Figure Out How Much You Should Be Spending on Housing," CNBC, July 14, 2021.

52 **the vast majority of low-income tenants in Atlanta:** "The Gap: A Shortage of Affordable Homes," National Low Income Housing Coalition annual report, 2019, https://nlihc.org/sites/default/files/gap/Gap-Report_2019.pdf; Dan Immergluck, "Commentary: Atlanta Needs More Affordable Housing, but the City's Plan Is Short on Dollars and Details," *Atlanta Magazine,* July 11, 2019; Jeff Stein, "In Expensive Cities, Rents Fall for the Rich—but Rise for the Poor," *The Washington Post,* August 6, 2018.

53   **ten times more likely to experience homelessness:** Katherine Beckett, "Homelessness and Housing Insecurity Among Former Prisoners," *RSF: The Russell Sage Foundation Journal of the Social Sciences* 6, no. 2 (2020): 1–35; Alexi Jones, "Nowhere to Go: Homelessness Among Formerly Incarcerated People," Prison Policy Initiative, February 2021.

54   **scrolling through Zillow:** Sonam Vashi, "Why Aren't Atlanta Landlords Renting to Section 8 Tenants?" SaportaReport, January 14, 2019; Eva Rosen, *The Voucher Promise: "Section 8" and the Fate of an American Neighborhood* (Princeton, N.J.: Princeton University Press, 2020).

55   **the tail end of a golden era:** "Public Housing History," National Low Income Housing Coalition, October 17, 2019.

55   **Techwood Homes, the nation's first public housing project:** "Techwood Homes," Georgia Historical Society, historical marker erected 2022, https://www .georgiahistory.com/ghmi_marker_updated/techwood-homes/#:~:text=In %201933%2C%20the%20PWA%20funded,Housing%20Authority's%20creation %20in%201938.

55   **the project was a shining example:** Frank Ruechel, "New Deal Public Housing, Urban Poverty, and Jim Crow: Techwood and University Homes in Atlanta," *The Georgia Historical Quarterly* 81, no. 7 (Winter 1997): 915–37. On the early history of public housing in the United States, see Gail Radford, *Modern Housing for America: Policy Struggles in the New Deal Era* (Chicago: University of Chicago Press, 1996); Edward G. Goetz, *New Deal Ruins: Race, Economic Justice, and Public Housing Policy* (Ithaca, N.Y.: Cornell University Press, 2013); Lawrence J. Vale, *From the Puritans to the Projects: Public Housing and Public Neighbors* (Cambridge, Mass.: Harvard University Press, 2000).

55   **"We have met here today" :** Lawrence Vale, *Purging the Poorest: Public Housing and the Design Politics of Twice-Cleared Communities* (Chicago: University of Chicago Press, 2013).

55   **The plan was not without its adversaries:** Mark B. Lapping, "The Emergence of Federal Public Housing: Atlanta's Techwood Project," *American Journal of Economics and Sociology* 32, no. 4 (1973): 379–85.

55   **it was generally considered a godsend:** John Lear, "Uncle Sam Uses Atlanta as His Housing Laboratory," *The Atlanta Journal-Constitution,* August 28, 1938.

56   **Yet these "bright, cheerful buildings":** Franklin D. Roosevelt, "Address at Atlanta, Georgia," November 29, 1935, https://www.presidency.ucsb.edu/documents/ address-atlanta-georgia.

56   **Despite government rhetoric:** Vale, *Purging the Poorest*.

56   **A separate project:** Irene V. Holliman, "Techwood Homes," New Georgia Encyclopedia, last edited August 26, 2020, https://www.georgiaencyclopedia.org/articles/ arts-culture/techwood-homes/.

56   **Those accepted into public housing:** Vale, *Purging the Poorest*.

56   **The high quality of life:** https://tile.loc.gov/storage-services/master/pnp/habshaer/ ga/ga0600/ga0662/data/ga0662data.pdf.

56   **As late as 1968:** Vale, *Purging the Poorest.*

56   **Over the previous two decades:** La-Brina Almeida, "A History of Racist Federal Housing Policies," August 6, 2021, Massachusetts Budget and Policy Center.

56   **when whites-only projects were finally desegregated:** Vale, *Purging the Poorest,* 18.

56   **This, combined with growing pressure:** Vale, *Purging the Poorest.*

57   **It was at this point:** Richard Rothstein, "Race and Public Housing," Economic Policy Institute, December 17, 2012.

57   **"We're getting out of the housing business":** *The Crisis in Homelessness: Effects on Children and Families: Hearing Before the Select Committee on Children, Youth, and Families, House of Representatives,* 100th Cong., 1st sess., 1987 (Washington, D.C.: U.S. Government Printing Office, 1987), 160.

57   **the "failure" of public housing:** On the orchestrated demise of public housing in America and the public-private model that replaced it, see Ben Austen, *High-Risers: Cabrini-Green and the Fate of American Public Housing* (New York: Harper, 2018); Catherine Fennell, *Last Project Standing: Civics and Sympathy in Post-welfare Chicago* (Minneapolis: University of Minnesota Press, 2015); Edward Goetz, "The History of American Public Housing Shows It Didn't Have to Decline," *Jacobin,* January 2023.

57   **In 1994, the year Britt was born:** Harvey K. Newman, "The Atlanta Housing Authority's Olympic Legacy Program: Public Housing Projects to Mixed Income Communities," Research Atlanta, Inc., April 2002.

57   **The city had been selected:** Bill Torpy, "Legacy of the Olympic Games in Atlanta Endures," *The Atlanta Journal-Constitution,* September 11, 2010.

57   **a particular embarrassment and liability:** Lawrence Vale and Annemarie Gray, "The Displacement Decathlon," *Places Journal,* April 2013.

57   **called it a "cesspool":** Vale and Gray, "Displacement Decathlon."

57   **"infested with crack dealers":** Laura Parker, "Neighboring Housing Project Tarnishes Atlanta's Dream Site for Olympic Gold," *The Washington Post,* July 6, 1991.

57   **the spectacle of "Olympic Games meet Southern Slum":** "Poor Area Indulges in the Olympic Dream," *Chicago Tribune,* August 25, 1991.

57   **Atlanta Housing Authority embarked:** Howard Husock, "Atlanta's Public-Housing Revolution," *City Journal,* Autumn 2010.

57   **Under her leadership:** Vale, *Purging the Poorest.*

57   **where a remarkable 13 percent of the city's population:** Renée Glover, "The Atlanta Blueprint: Transforming Public Housing Citywide," in *From Despair to Hope: HOPE VI and the New Promise of Public Housing in America's Cities,* eds. Henry Cisneros and Lora Engdahl (Washington, D.C.: Brookings Institution Press, 2009), 146.

57   **Rather, the agency rebranded itself:** Atlanta Housing Authority, "CATALYST Implementation Plan and Appendices (Fiscal Year Ending 2010), Board Approved," https://www.hud.gov/sites/dfiles/PIH/documents/AtlantaFY10Plan.pdf.

57   **giving eligible families vouchers:** Maya Dukmasova, "Tricknology 101," *Jacobin,* October 2014.

58   **But AHA's innovations didn't stop there:** Husock, "Atlanta's Public-Housing Revolution."

58   **These measures, declared an admiring column:** Husock, "Atlanta's Public-Housing Revolution."

58   **When Glover described her approach:** *Living in America: Is Our Public Housing System Up to the Challenges of the 21st Century? Hearing Before the Subcommittee on Federalism and the Census of the Committee on Government Reform, House of Representatives,* 109th Cong., 2nd sess., February 15, 2006, https://www.govinfo.gov/content/pkg/CHRG-109hhrg27282/pdf/CHRG-109hhrg27282.pdf.

58   **The Atlanta Model, as it came to be known:** Edward G. Goetz, *New Deal Ruins: Race, Economic Justice, and Public Housing Policy* (Ithaca, N.Y.: Cornell University Press, 2013), 12.

58   **For more than thirty years, business leaders:** Vale, *Purging the Poorest.*

58   **Together with an aggressive effort:** "Olympics—Atlanta Cleanup Includes One-Way Tickets for Homeless," Associated Press, March 22, 1996.

58   **Glover proudly pointed:** Vale, *Purging the Poorest.*

58   **At Centennial Place:** Vale, *Purging the Poorest.*

58   **In the winter of 2011:** Stephanie Garlock, "By 2011, Atlanta Had Demolished All of Its Public Housing Projects. Where Did All Those People Go?," Bloomberg News, May 8, 2014.

58   **AHA's well-funded public relations machine:** Vale, *Purging the Poorest.*

59   **The first city in the country:** Deirdre Oakley, Chandra Ward, Lesley Reid, and Erin Ruel, "The Poverty Deconcentration Imperative and Public Housing Transformation," *Sociology Compass* 5, no. 9 (2011): 824–33.

62   **Vouchers were supposed to deconcentrate poverty:** Jacqueline Rabe Thomas, "How Wealthy Towns Keep People with Housing Vouchers Out," ProPublica, January 9, 2020.

62   **In reality, families with vouchers:** On the predicament facing voucher holders in America's cities, see Eva Rosen, *The Voucher Promise: "Section 8" and the Fate of an American Neighborhood* (Princeton, N.J.: Princeton University Press, 2020); Lawrence J. Vale and Yonah Freemark, "From Public Housing to Public-Private Housing: 75 Years of Social Experimentation," December 5, 2012, https://www.tandfonline.com/doi/abs/10.1080/01944363.2012.737985; : *Stephanie Wykstra, "Vouchers Can Help the Poor Find Homes. But Landlords Often Won't Accept Them," Vox, December 10, 2019.*

63   **The "hotter" the local rental market:** Kristal Dixon, "Atlanta Wants More Landlords to Accept Section 8 Vouchers," Axios, November 30, 2022; Andy Peters and Stephen Dee, "Atlanta to Make All Landlords Accept Housing Vouchers," *The Atlanta Journal-Constitution,* February 17, 2020.

63   **She wasn't alone: that year:** City of Atlanta, Georgia, Ordinance 20-O-1155, https://atlantacityga.iqm2.com/Citizens/Detail_LegiFile.aspx?Frame=SplitView&MeetingID=3089&MediaPosition=&ID=20913&CssClass=. Nationally, according to a major study, approximately 40 percent of Housing Choice Voucher recipients end up losing their voucher because they are unable to find a landlord who will accept it. Ingrid Gould Ellen, Katherine O'Regan, and Sarah Strochak, "Using HUD Administrative Data to Estimate Success Rates and Search Durations for

New Voucher Recipients," U.S. Department of Housing and Urban Development, December 2021.

CHAPTER 7

64   **"Mr. Dejene, this is Ms. Thompson again":** Attempts were made to contact Dejene for comment via phone and email, but he did not respond.

66   **Georgia, among the most landlord-friendly states:** "'Safe at Home Act' House Bill 404 for Tenants' Rights," Georgia Appleseed Center for Law and Justice, March 21, 2024.

66   **these were endemic in complexes:** Willoughby Mariano and Alan Judd, "Dangerous Dwellings," part 1, *The Atlanta Journal-Constitution,* June 9, 2022.

66   **But nothing prevented landlords:** A law banning retaliatory evictions passed in Georgia the following year, after the events in this chapter took place. Nevertheless, significant gaps remain in its enforcement. See Nicole Hammett, "An Eye for an Eye and a Tooth for a Tooth: An Analysis of Georgia's Landlord Retaliation Law," *Georgia Law Review* 55, no. 3 (2021): 1327–54; "New Ga. Law to Prevent Landlord Retaliation," FOX5 Atlanta, August 13, 2019.

67   **as in the overwhelming majority of eviction hearings:** Sandra Park and John Pollock, "Tenants' Right to Counsel Is Critical to Fight Mass Evictions and Advance Race Equity During the Pandemic and Beyond," American Civil Liberties Union, January 12, 2021; Matthew Desmond, "Eviction and the Reproduction of Urban Poverty," *American Journal of Sociology* 118, no. 1 (2012): 88–133; Susanna Blankley, "Right to Counsel: The Nationwide Movement to Fight the Eviction Crisis," Stout, October 14, 2019, https://www.stout.com/en/insights/article/right-to-counsel -nationwide-movement-fight-eviction-crisis.

75   **ordinances that made sleeping and living in your car risky:** "Is It Illegal to Sleep in Your Car?," Insurify, updated June 15, 2022, https://insurify.com/car-insurance/ driver/driving-record/is-it-illegal-to-sleep-in-car/#:~:text=While%20no%20 federal%20law%20bans,can%20sleep%20in%20your%20car; Soumya Karlamangla and Rukmini Callimachi, "In California, Safe Parking Lots Offer a Haven for the 'Mobile Homeless,'" *The New York Times,* October 19, 2023, https://www.nytimes .com/2023/10/19/us/homeless-parking-lots.html.

75   **approximately 20 percent of child removals:** Cited in Stephannie Stokes, "When Families Need Housing, Georgia Will Pay for Foster Care Rather Than Provide Assistance," ProPublica, January 18, 2024, https://www.propublica.org/article /georgia-housing-assistance-foster-care; see also National Data Archive on Child Abuse and Neglect, https://www.acf.hhs.gov/sites/default/files/documents/cb/afcars -tar-ga-2021.pdf. For searing narrative accounts of the long-term impact of child removals, see Andrea Elliot, *Invisible Child: Poverty, Hope, and Survival in an American City* (New York: Random House, 2021), and Roxanna Asgarian, *When We Were Once a Family: A Story of Love, Death, and Child Removal in America* (New York: Farrar, Straus and Giroux, 2023).

CHAPTER 8

78   **Like many patients on Medicaid:** Patricia Pittman and Candice Chen, "The Doctor Won't See You," MedPage Today, August 14, 2023.

80   **She considered applying for SSI:** Kathleen Romig, "Policymakers Should Expand and Simplify Supplemental Security Income," Center on Budget and Policy Priorities, July 20, 2021.

80   **Disability benefits that didn't begin:** Rebecca Vallas, "New Bipartisan Bill Would Update Outdated SSI Income Limits," Spotlight on Poverty and Opportunity, September 13, 2023.

82   **It was a business model:** Mya Frazier, "When No Landlord Will Rent to You, Where Do You Go?," *The New York Times Magazine,* May 20, 2021; Anne Kniggendorf, "Kansas City's Housing Crisis Forced This Couple into an Extended Stay Hotel. And It's Only Getting Worse," KCUR, June 29, 2021; Samantha M. Shapiro, "A Motel Is Not a Home," *The New York Times,* February 21, 2024.

82   **As more and more people found themselves:** Michael E. Kanell, "Many Norcross Families Working but Trapped in Extended-Stay Hotels," *The Atlanta Journal-Constitution,* March 24, 2020.

82   **Gateway Center, located in downtown Atlanta:** Eric Celeste, "Solving Downtown's Homeless Problem Begins with Taking the Red Pill," *Creative Loafing,* November 3, 2011.

82   **The surrounding blocks were crammed:** Brian Goldstone, "The New American Homeless," *The New Republic,* August 21, 2019.

84   **"coordinated entry" system:** On the emergence and uses of the coordinated entry system, see chap. 3 ("High-Tech Homelessness in the City of Angels") in Virginia Eubanks, *Automating Inequality: How High-Tech Tools Profile, Police, and Punish the Poor* (New York: St. Martin's Press, 2018); see also Shane Phillips, "The Hunger Games of Homeless Services: How Coordinated Entry Is Failing Unhoused People," *Shelterforce,* June 30, 2021.

85   **or the VI-SPDAT:** Numerous criticisms of VI-SPDAT have arisen in recent years. Marissa J. Lang, "Homeless Vulnerability Scores Don't Help People Find Housing. D.C. Wants to Change That," *The Washington Post,* May 18, 2022; Abigail Stark, "New Research on the Reliability and Validity of the VI-SPDAT: Implications for Coordinated Assessment," *The Homeless Hub Blog,* October 14, 2021.

86   **the criteria for "literal homelessness":** "Criteria and Recordkeeping Requirements for Definition of Homelessness," HUD Exchange, January 2012.

86   **Advocacy groups had been fighting to expand the definition:** Cara Baldari, "Policy Brief: Child, Youth, and Family Homelessness in the United States: Undercounted & Misunderstood," Campaign for Children, November 22, 2021; Rachel M. Cohen, "How Should HUD Count Homeless Families?," Bloomberg, July 19, 2018.

86   **refuting the myth:** Catherine G. Coughlin, Megan Sandel, and Amanda M. Stewart, "Homelessness, Children, and COVID-19: A Looming Crisis," *Pediatrics* 146,

no. 2 (August 2020): e20201408; Lara Burt, "How Does Homelessness Impact Child Health and Developmental Outcomes?," National League of Cities, January 30, 2024; testimony of Barbara Duffield, executive director, SchoolHouse Connection, *Legislative Review of H.R. 1511, the "Homeless Children and Youth Act of 2017," Hearing Before the Subcommittee on Housing and Insurance Committee on Financial Services, U.S. House of Representatives,* 115th Cong., 2nd sess., June 6, 2018, https://democrats-financialservices.house.gov/uploadedfiles/06.06.2018_barbara _duffield_testimony.pdf.

86   **the U.S. Department of Education counted as homeless:** "Children and Youth Experiencing Homelessness: An Introduction to the Issues," National Center for Homeless Education, October 2018.

86   **35,538 homeless children and youth:** "Georgia State Profile," National Center for Homeless Education, 2020, https://profiles.nche.seiservices.com/StateProfile.aspx ?StateID=13.

86   **the state's HUD-administered total:** "Point in Time Homeless Count," Georgia Department of Community Affairs, 2019, https://www.huduser.gov/portal/sites/ default/files/pdf/2019-AHAR-Part-1.pdf.

CHAPTER 9

93   **D.C. was changing before their eyes:** Brandi Thompson Summers, *Black in Place: The Spatial Aesthetics of Race in a Post-Chocolate City* (Chapel Hill: University of North Carolina Press, 2019); Uzodinma Iweala, "The Gentrification of Washington DC: How My City Changed Its Colours," *The Guardian,* September 12, 2016; Mike Myers Asch and George Derek Musgrove, *Chocolate City: A History of Race and Democracy in the Nation's Capital* (Chapel Hill: University of North Carolina Press, 2017).

93   **D.C. saw a staggering 202 percent increase:** Jason Richardson, Bruce Mitchell, and Juan Franco, "Shifting Neighborhoods," National Community Reinvestment Coalition, March 19, 2019.

93   **the very states their grandparents had fled:** Isabel Wilkerson, *The Warmth of Other Suns: The Epic Story of America's Great Migration* (New York: Random House, 2010).

93   **It was a new Great Migration:** Charles M. Blow, "We Need a Second Great Migration," *The New York Times,* January 8, 2021; William H. Frey, "A 'New Great Migration' Is Bringing Black Americans Back to the South," Brookings Institution, September 12, 2022.

94   **It was all perfectly legal:** Annie Howard, "Fighting No-Fault Evictions with a Just Cause Ordinance," *Shelterforce,* December 11, 2020.

95   **suburbs such as Sandy Springs:** Elisa Lanari, "Envisioning a New City Center: Time, Displacement, and Atlanta's Suburban Futures," *City and Society* 31, no. 3 (2019): 365–91.

95   **"displace-and-replace suburban redevelopment":** Dan Immergluck, *Red Hot City:*

Housing, Race, and Exclusion in Twenty-First-Century Atlanta (Oakland: University of California Press, 2022), p. 203.

96   **exorbitant application and "administrative" fees:** Eric Dunn, "The Case Against Rental Application Fees," *Georgetown Journal on Poverty Law and Policy* 30, no. 1 (2022): 21–47; Ariel Nelson, April Kuehnhoff, Chi Chi Wu, and Steve Sharpe, "Too Damn High: How Junk Fees Add to Skyrocketing Rents," National Consumer Law Center, March 2023.

96   **Atlanta's underfunded mass transit system:** Josh Green, "Analysis: Atlanta Clunks as Bottom Five U.S. Commuter City. Ouch!," Urbanize Atlanta, October 4, 2023; Doug Monroe, "Where It All Went Wrong," *Atlanta Magazine,* August 1, 2012.

98   **America's credit scoring system:** National Consumer Law Center, "Past Imperfect: How Credit Scores and Other Analytics 'Bake In' and Perpetuate Past Discrimination," May 2016; Will Douglas Heaven, "Bias Isn't the Only Problem with Credit Scores—and No, AI Can't Help," *MIT Technology Review,* January 17, 2021; Caroline Ratcliffe and Steven Brown, "Credit Scores Perpetuate Racial Disparities, Even in America's Most Prosperous Cities," Urban Institute, November 20, 2017.

98   **a three-digit number:** Mya Frazier, "When No Landlord Will Rent to You, Where Do You Go?," *The New York Times Magazine,* May 20, 2021; "Digital Denials: How Abuse, Bias and Lack of Transparency in Tenant Screening Harm Renters," National Consumer Law Center, September 2023.

98   **"cosigning companies" that had sprung up:** "What Is a Cosigning Company & Do I Need One? Apartment Guarantors 101," *Dwellsy Blog,* January 2024; John Triplett, "A Passion for Helping Tenants with Poor Credit Get Apartments and Homes," *Rental Housing Journal,* December 6, 2023.

CHAPTER 10

108   **"Name a problem the community faces":** Joshua Sharpe, "Hope at Last for Notorious South DeKalb Strip," *The Atlanta Journal-Constitution,* November 24, 2015.

108   **In a lawsuit, Almond's family:** Joshua Sharpe, "Family: DeKalb Hotel Employees Did Nothing as Man Bled to Death," *The Atlanta Journal-Constitution,* August 24, 2016.

CHAPTER 11

115   **Chosewood Park, like other historically Black communities:** Alissa Walker, "Urbanism Hasn't Worked for Everyone," Curbed, July 16, 2020.

115   **investors targeted older residents:** Willoughby Mariano, " 'We Buy Houses': Investors Target Seniors with Below Market Offers," *The Atlanta Journal-Constitution,* November 22, 2019; Stephannie Stokes, "Equity Theft: The Exploitation of Atlanta's Low-Income Homeowners," WABE, September 14, 2020.

115   **In Oakland City, on the West Side:** Michael E. Kanell, "The Most-Dramatic Surge in Atlanta Home Prices? South of I-20," *The Atlanta Journal-Constitution,* December 11, 2019.

116   **In 1990, 27 percent of residents:** Dan Immergluck, "Gentrification and the Subsidizing City," *Atlanta Studies,* September 28, 2022.

116   **the central city's median income now exceeded the suburbs':** Immergluck, "Gentrification and the Subsidizing City."

116   **gentrification in the sense defined by the LA Tenants Union:** Tracy Rosenthal, "101 Notes on the LA Tenants Union," *Commune Magazine,* Winter 2020.

116   **Atlanta was the fourth-fastest gentrifying city:** Christopher Quinn, "Atlanta Ranked Fourth-Fastest Gentrifying City," *The Atlanta Journal-Constitution,* July 18, 2019.

116   **Gentrification is purposeful and produced:** Neil Smith, *The New Urban Frontier: Gentrification and the Revanchist City* (New York: Routledge, 1996); Loretta Lees, Tom Slater, and Elvin Wyly, *Gentrification* (New York: Routledge, 2008); David Harvey, "The Right to the City," *International Journal of Urban and Regional Research* 27, no. 4 (2003): 939–41; Jason Hackworth, *The Neoliberal City: Governance, Ideology, and Development in American Urbanism* (Ithaca, N.Y.: Cornell University Press, 2006).

117   **the intertwined interests of real estate capital and urban policy:** Samuel Stein, *Capital City: Gentrification and the Real Estate State* (London: Verso, 2019).

117   **The wider the rent gap:** Neil Smith, "Gentrification and the Rent Gap," *Annals of the Association of American Geographers* 77, no. 3 (September 1987): 462–65; see also Tom Slater, "Planetary Rent Gaps," *Antipode* 49, no. 1 (September 22, 2015): 114–37.

117   **Urban planners—increasingly concerned with growth:** Nikil Saval, "The Plight of the Urban Planner," *The New Yorker,* November 20, 2019.

118   **originally called Wellswood Apartments:** Thanks to Paul C. McMurray for providing me with the information and supporting documents regarding this history.

119   **As plants and factories disappeared:** "Financing Closes on Englewood Senior, Part of Planned Mixed-Use Development," What Now Atlanta, April 24, 2024.

120   **Earlier in the week, Tyler Perry:** "Tyler Perry Pays Off $400K Worth of Layaways at Georgia Walmarts," Associated Press, December 7, 2018.

CHAPTER 12

123   **Such wait times for mental health treatment:** Ching-Fang Sun, Christoph U. Correll, Robert L. Trestman, Yezhe Lin, Hui Xie, Maria Stack Hankey, Raymond Paglinawan Uymatiao, et al., "Low Availability, Long Wait Times, and High Geographic Disparity of Psychiatric Outpatient Care in the US," *General Hospital Psychiatry* 84 (September 2023): 12–17.

126   **Based in Nashville:** Kali Persall, "Covenant Capital Group Raises Its Largest Investment Vehicle to Date," Institutional Real Estate, January 4, 2023.

126   **In Indianapolis, an investigation:** "Indianapolis Evictions: Biggest Corporate Landlords File for . . . ," *Indy Star,* August 26, 2022.

126 **very much in keeping with that of the newer, larger corporate landlords:** Edwin Rios, "Four Corporate US Landlords Deceived and Evicted Thousands During Covid, Report Reveals," *The Guardian,* August 4, 2022; Elora Raymond, Richard Duckworth, Ben Miller, Michael Lucas, and Shiraj Pokharel, "Corporate Landlords, Institutional Investors, and Displacement: Eviction Rates in Single-Family Rentals," Federal Reserve Bank of Atlanta, December 21, 2016; "Do Large Landlords' Eviction Practices Differ from Small Landlords?," Urban Institute, February 1, 2023.

126 **a "private equity strike zone":** Dan Immergluck, "Atlanta as a Private Equity 'Strike Zone' in Wall Street's Single-Family Rental Boom," *Nonprofit Quarterly,* September 28, 2022.

126 **evictions were becoming increasingly automated:** Mya Frazier, "The Eviction Experts," *Harper's,* April 2024; Desiree Fields, "Automated Landlord: Digital Technologies and Post-crisis Financial Accumulation," *Environment and Planning A: Economy and Space* 54, no. 1 (2019).

CHAPTER 13

132 **She also began selling her plasma:** Kathleen McLaughlin, *Blood Money: The Story of Life, Death, and Profit Inside America's Blood Industry* (New York: Simon and Schuster, 2023).

134 **some were paid to guard these properties:** Francesca Mari, "Using the Homeless to Guard Empty Houses," *The New Yorker,* November 30, 2020.

137 **Extensive research showed that most women:** Matthew Desmond, "Americans Want to Believe Jobs Are the Solution to Poverty. They're Not," *The New York Times Magazine,* September 11, 2018.

137 **But in 1996, when President Bill Clinton:** "The 1996 Personal Responsibility and Work Opportunity Reconciliation Act in the US," Centre for Public Impact, October 30, 2017.

137 **By 2020, a mere twenty-one out of every one hundred:** Dylan Matthews, "Welfare Reform Took People Off the Rolls. It Might Have Also Shortened Their Lives," *The Washington Post,* June 18, 2013.

137 **That was on a *national* level:** Alex Camardelle, "Modernizing Cash Aid for Thousands of Georgia Children in Deep Poverty: Bill Analysis: HB 91," Georgia Budget Policy Institute, February 10, 2021.

137 **only 10 percent of Georgia's TANF funds:** Ife Finch Floyd, "Georgia Can Afford to Begin to Modernize TANF and Move Past Its Racist Legacy," Georgia Budget and Policy Institute, December 10, 2021.

138 **Nationwide, less than 17 percent:** "The Need for Child Care Funding," StateOf ChildCare.org, accessed July 20, 2024, https://stateofchildcare.org/map.html.

139 ***There is an inherent dignity in work:*** Hannah Hilligoss, "The 'Dignity of Work,' Its Racist Roots, and How It's Threatening Reform," *OnLabor* (blog), May 26, 2021.

139 **Many women didn't have access:** Gina Adams and Monica Rohacek, "Child Care and Welfare Reform," Brookings Institution, February 2002.

CHAPTER 14

147 **only some people were being asked to assume such risk:** Steven W. Thrasher, *The Viral Underclass: The Human Toll When Inequality and Disease Collide* (New York: Celadon Books, 2022); Julia Raifman, Alexandra Skinner, and Aaron Sojourner, "The Unequal Toll of COVID-19 on Workers," Economic Policy Institute, February 7, 2022; Oliver Laughland, "'Death by Structural Poverty': US South Struggles Against Covid-19," *The Guardian,* August 5, 2020.

147 **Across the country, the ranks of the newly jobless:** Heather Long, "U.S. Now Has 22 Million Unemployed, Wiping Out a Decade of Job Gains," *The Washington Post,* April 16, 2020.

148 **Of course many people:** H.R. 748—CARES Act, 2020, Congress.gov.

148 **Georgia's unemployment system:** Thomas Wheatley, "Georgia Left Thousands Waiting for COVID Unemployment Aid," Axios, May 7, 2002; H.R. 748—CARES Act, Congress.gov.

148 **In February 2020, the state's labor department:** Greg Griffin, State Auditor, and Leslie McGuire, "GDOL's Unemployment Insurance Pandemic Response: Many Factors Contributed to Payment Delays," February 2022, Report No. 20-15, Georgia Department of Audits and Accounts.

148 **Soon it climbed to 1.3 million:** Griffin and McGuire, "GDOL's Unemployment Insurance Response."

150 **a taskmaster unlike any she'd encountered:** Alex N. Press, "Food Delivery Workers' Labor Conditions Are Abysmal," *Jacobin,* April 28, 2023; Saru Jayaraman, "What It's Really Like to Work for Postmates and DoorDash," Eater, December 16, 2021.

151 **classified its drivers not as employees:** Veena Dubal, "The New Racial Wage Code," *Harvard Law and Policy Review* 15 (2022): 511–49; Katie J. Wells, Kafui Attoh, and Declan Cullen, *Disrupting D.C.: The Rise of Uber and the Fall of a City* (Princeton, N.J.: Princeton University Press, 2023); Rachel M. Cohen, "The Coming Fight over the Gig Economy, Explained," Vox, October 12, 2022.

CHAPTER 15

166 **It is widely assumed:** "Did You Know There Are Four Types of Homelessness?" CaringWorks, accessed July 21, 2024, https://www.caringworksinc.org/did-you-know-there-are-four-types-of-homelessness/#:~:text=Episodic%20homelessness,from%20health%20issues%20or%20addiction.

167 **While those with direct deposit:** Katie Lobosco, "Millions of Low-Income Americans Are at Risk of Missing Out on Stimulus Payments," CNN, April 8, 2020.

167   **There were media reports:** Lisa Rein, "IRS to Begin Issuing $1,200 Coronavirus Payments April 9, but Some Americans Won't Receive Checks Until September, Agency Plan Says," *The Washington Post,* April 2, 2020.

CHAPTER 16

170   **in 2018, an article had appeared:** Jamiles Lartey, "Nowhere for People to Go: Who Will Survive the Gentrification of Atlanta?," *The Guardian,* October 23, 2018.

171   **a "tax credit" complex:** All documentation pertaining to Gladstone's LIHTC status was obtained via a series of open records requests from the Georgia Department of Community Affairs, the government agency that oversees and administers the LIHTC program in the state. Many thanks to Sonam Vashi for her extensive research assistance with the material in this chapter.

171   **LIHTC introduced a model:** The process of creating a LIHTC unit begins at the federal level, with the U.S. Treasury Department allocating tax credits to state housing agencies, which then distribute the credits to developers willing to set aside a certain number of apartments in a given project for people earning less than 50 or 60 percent AMI. In order to generate start-up capital for a project, developers typically sell their credits to the highest outside bidder. Cash from these investors helps reduce the amount of money a developer has to borrow and pay interest on, thus offsetting the revenue lost by charging below-market rents. Most of these investors are corporations. They benefit from LIHTC not only by receiving a dollar-for-dollar reduction in federal taxes owed on other income but also by their ability to write off the depreciation of the property in question. Ed Gramlich, "Low Income Housing Tax Credits," National Low Income Housing Coalition, 2015 Advocates' Guide.

172   **It gained bipartisan approval:** Raphael Bostic, "Message from the Assistant Secretary: The LIHTC Program," U.S. Department of Housing and Urban Development, HUD User Home, February 28, 2012; Miriam Axel-Lute, "LIHTC: How It Started, How It's Going," *Shelterforce,* November 15, 2023.

172   **the affordability is temporary:** "This is one of the most urgent problems with Affordable Housing: It expires. Almost a half a million Affordable Housing covenants will expire in the next eight years. . . . Lawmakers have orchestrated multiple scramble sessions on the topic, yet none have fully prepared for the fallout nor challenged the absurdity of continuing to legislate like tomorrow will never come." Tracy Rosenthal, "The Enduring Fiction of Affordable Housing," *The New Republic,* April 2, 2021.

172   **Federal law stipulates:** Gramlich, "Low Income Housing Tax Credits."

172   **Affordable housing in America, already in perilously short supply:** "Balancing Priorities: Preservation and Neighborhood Opportunity in the Low-Income Housing Tax Credit Program Beyond Year 30," National Low Income Housing Coalition, report, October 2018.

172   **A monthly rent of $600 is the maximum:** Josh Silver, "The Racial History of Plan-
ning in Atlanta Sounds Alarm Bells for CRA Reform Efforts," National Community Reinvestment Coalition, February 24, 2023; "Atlanta Declared a Renter's
State of Emergency," Housing Justice League, July 13, 2016.

172   **The report recommended "interventions":** "Supplement to the 2030 Strategic Implementation Plan," Atlanta BeltLine Integrated Action Plan for Economic,
Housing and Real Estate, December 2015.

173   **He was the first victim:** Neima Abdulahi, "When Her Teen Was Killed in 1979 She
Was Heartbroken, but Didn't Know He Would Be the First of Dozens," 11 Alive,
April 12, 2019. The "Atlanta Child Murders" have received a great deal of attention over the years, including at least two podcast series and an HBO documen-
tary, but a neglected book on the subject is James Baldwin's *The Evidence of Things
Not Seen* (New York: Holt, Rinehart and Winston, 1985), which delves into the
larger racial and social implications of the case.

CHAPTER 17

180   **Across the country, in more than 140 cities:** "Cities on Edge as Fires Burn Near
White House," *The New York Times,* May 31, 2020.

180   **State leaders deployed:** Anita Snow, "AP Tally: Arrests at Widespread US Protests
Hit 10,000," Associated Press, June 4, 2020.

181   **What got her were his words:** Eric Levenson, "How Minneapolis Police First Described the Murder of George Floyd, and What We Know Now," CNN, April 21,
2021.

181   **And then, three days earlier:** Shelia M. Poole, "Pence Joins Others in Paying Trib-
ute to Evangelist Ravi Zacharias," *The Atlanta Journal-Constitution,* May 29, 2020.

182   **a galvanizing report:** "Beltlining: Gentrification, Broken Promises, and Hope on
Atlanta's Southside," Housing Justice League and Research Action Cooperative,
October 2017.

184   **When Kara called the hotline:** During the early months of the pandemic, I volunteered with the Housing Justice League emergency hotline, and Kara's call was
my first encounter with her. Later, after I followed up with her to see if she had
received the assistance she needed, Kara and I continued to communicate and,
finding a rapport, she allowed me to report on her family's struggle to secure stable
housing.

188   **rapid rehousing was intended:** "Rapid Re-housing," National Alliance to End
Homelessness, 2022.

189   **the "homeless industrial complex":** Tracy Rosenthal, "Inside LA's Homeless Industrial Complex," *The New Republic,* May 19, 2022.

189   **"Not everything that can be faced can be changed":** James Baldwin, "As Much
Truth as One Can Bear," *The New York Times Book Review,* January 14, 1962.

CHAPTER 18

198 **The city's police chief had resigned:** Aimee Ortiz, "What to Know About the Death of Rayshard Brooks," *The New York Times,* November 21, 2022.

198 **Brooks had been married:** Helena Oliviero and Christian Brooks, "Rayshard Brooks Leaves Four Young Children Behind," *The Atlanta Journal-Constitution,* June 14, 2020.

200 **"We're going to survive":** Donesha Aldridge, "Rep. John Lewis Inspired by People Standing Against Injustice: 'We're Going to Make It,'" 11 Alive, June 4, 2020.

202 **Penned by lawyer:** James Weldon Johnson, "Lift Every Voice and Sing," Poetry Foundation.

202 **The hymn's marching tempo:** "Lift Ev'ry Voice and Sing: A Powerful Anthem with an 120-Year History," National WWII Museum, June 19, 2021.

203 **She learned that the promise:** "Juneteenth and the Broken Promise of '40 Acres and a Mule,'" National Farmers Union, June 19, 2020. As the historian Keri Leigh Merritt writes, "When judged comparatively with other nations' emancipatory histories, the Reconstruction experience in the United States is unique. While African Americans were the only freed slaves to be granted political rights so soon after emancipation, those rights were limited for a people without capital or job prospects. Land *would* have served as the primary source for reparations. . . . [It] is the legacy of the Reconstruction—particularly the failure of land redistribution— that so closely coupled poverty and race in the US." "Land and the Roots of African-American Poverty," *Aeon,* March 11, 2016. See also Keri Leigh Merritt, *Masterless Men: Poor Whites and Slavery in the Antebellum South* (Cambridge, UK: Cambridge University Press, 2017).

203 **strict "Black Codes":** Theodore Brantner Wilson, *The Black Codes of the South* (Tuscaloosa: University of Alabama Press, 1965); "Black Codes (1865)," National Constitution Center.

203 **Sharecropping and debt peonage:** Isabel Wilkerson, *The Warmth of Other Suns: The Epic Story of America's Great Migration* (New York: Random House, 2010); Steven Hahn, *A Nation Under Our Feet: Black Political Struggles in the Rural South from Slavery to the Great Migration* (Cambridge, Mass.: Harvard University Press, 2003); Nadra Kareem Nittle, "How the Black Codes Limited African American Progress After the Civil War," History.com, August 4, 2023.

203 **the Thirteenth Amendment's slavery loophole:** Douglas A. Blackmon, *Slavery by Another Name: The Re-enslavement of Black Americans from the Civil War to World War II* (New York: Anchor Books, 2009); Khalil Gibran Muhammad, *The Condemnation of Blackness: Race, Crime, and the Making of Modern Urban America* (Cambridge, Mass.: Harvard University Press, 2010).

204 **a magazine article:** Ta-Nehisi Coates, "The Case for Reparations," *The Atlantic,* June 2014.

206 **The elaborate spectacle:** Tyler Estep, "DeKalb Judge Dismisses Attempt to Restore Decatur Confederate Monument," *The Atlanta Journal-Constitution,* October 22, 2021.

206   **there, in 1960:** "Ku Klux Klan Rally on Courthouse Steps," Getty Images, May 28, 1960.

206   **At close to midnight:** Raisa Habersham, Vanessa McCray, and Kristal Dixon, "Juneteenth 2020: How Atlanta Is Marking the Holiday Devoted to the End of Slavery," *The Atlanta Journal-Constitution,* June 19, 2020.

CHAPTER 19

210   **According to an *Atlanta Journal-Constitution* investigation:** Alan Judd and Willoughby Mariano, "At Violent Apartment Complexes, Business Model Thrives on Housing Shortage, Government Inaction," *The Atlanta Journal-Constitution,* June 9, 2022.

CHAPTER 20

225   **The older woman mentioned her fear of Covid:** Cecelia Smith-Schoenwalder, "States Pull Back Reopenings amid Virus Surge," *U.S. News & World Report*, June 29, 2020.

CHAPTER 21

241   **Soon Blackstone, the private-equity behemoth:** "Blackstone and Starwood Capital Group Complete Acquisition of Extended Stay America," Global Newswire, June 16, 2021.

241   **followed by the purchase of a portfolio:** TRD Staff, "Blackstone, Starwood to Pay $1.5B for WoodSpring Suites Properties," The Real Deal, January 21, 2022.

241   **"To be sort of flip":** Cameron Sperance, "Economy Extended Stay Is Strongest of the Weak U.S. Hotel Sector in March," Yahoo Life, April 7, 2020.

241   **Today, of the 5.6 million hotel rooms:** Mya Frazier, "When No Landlord Will Rent to You, Where Do You Go?," *The New York Times Magazine,* May 20, 2021.

241   **New construction of extended-stay hotels:** Matthew Rothstein, "Can Extended-Stay Hotels Be Both a Key Safeguard Against Homelessness and a Hot Investment Target?" Bisnow, May 11, 2023.

242   **a "tailwind" for his company:** Sean O'Neill, "Why Every Hotel Company Wants an Extended Stay Brand Now," Skift, May 15, 2023.

242   **a 2018 survey of extended-stay guests in Gwinnett County:** Kathleen Allen, Aixa Pascual, Lejla Prljaca, and Malik Watkins, "When Extended-Stay Becomes Home," Live Norcross, May 2019.

242   **A more recent analysis by the Southern Poverty Law Center:** Rachel Garbus, "After Moving to Atlanta with Jobs, Savings, and a Plan, This Family Still Ended Up in an Extended-Stay Motel," Atlanta Civic Circle, May 18, 2023. Data cited are from

Efficiency Lodge v. Neason et al., brief of Amicus Curiae Housing Justice League, the Atlanta Volunteers Lawyers Foundation, the Southern Poverty Law Center, Daniella Aiello, PhD, Taylor Shelton, PhD, and Brian Goldstone, PhD, in support of plaintiffs-appellees, August 12, 2021, https://www.splcenter.org/sites/default/files/a21a1263_-_brief-amicus_curiae.pdf.

242 **"It's a reinforcing cycle":** quoted in Rothstein, "Can Extended-Stay Hotels Be Both."

244 **The "Liberty Guarantee," as the company had dubbed it:** "If a resident breaches their contract with the property, the property just needs to take affirmative steps to evict the tenant. Once the property is 'rent ready' or back on the market 'for rent' Liberty will make the property whole on all lost rents from the guaranteed resident. Liberty will make a property whole until the unit is rented, or six months, whichever comes first." John Triplett, "A Passion for Helping Tenants with Poor Credit Get Apartments and Homes," *Rental Housing Journal,* December 6, 2023.

CHAPTER 22

252 **a searchable online database:** Moiz Syed and Derek Willis, "Tracking PPP: Search Every Company Approved for Federal Loans," ProPublica, July 7, 2020, updated December 22, 2023, https://projects.propublica.org/coronavirus/bailouts/.

252 **"innkeepers' lien" laws:** "2022 Georgia Code, Title 43—Professions and Businesses, Chapter 21—Lodging Providers, Article 1—Innkeepers, Section 43-21-5—Lien," Justia, 2022.

254 **As such, an occupant was entitled:** Housing Justice League, *Eviction Defense Manual,* DeKalb County ed., 2020, https://drive.google.com/file/d/1YapYIb42xgcu9p8WvbkoO-bkjHTiIWu9/view.

256 **They were referring to the national moratorium:** "C.D.C. Eviction Moratorium Fact Sheet," National Low Income Housing Coalition, September 1, 2023.

256 **This was not hyperbolic:** Kathryn M. Leifheit, Sabriya L. Linton, Julia Raifman, Gabriel L. Schwartz, Emily A. Benfer, Frederick J. Zimmerman, and Craig Evan Pollack, "Expiring Eviction Moratoriums and COVID-19 Incidence and Mortality," *American Journal of Epidemiology* 190, no. 12 (December 2021): 2503–10.

CHAPTER 23

260 **Two complexes in the nearby Thomasville Heights:** Sean Keenan, "Mayor Finally Slates Forest Cove for Demolition, Two Years After Condemnation," Atlanta Civic Circle, January 4, 2024.

261 **not a single city or county in America:** Technical Assistance Collaborative, "Priced Out: The Affordable Housing Crisis for People with Disabilities in 2024," Technical Assistance Collaborative, April 2024.

261 **a $225-million growth-capital boost:** "Carlyle Group Provides C$225 Mln in Growth Capital Financing to Empire Communities," Reuters, May 17, 2018.

262   **an owner could request a "qualified contract":** "Qualified Contract Policy and Pro-
cedures," Novogradac, accessed July 22, 2024, https://www.novoco.com/public
-media/documents/georgia_year_15_qualified_contract_policy_and_procedures
_070815.pdf.

263   **For two decades, this loophole drew little notice:** Juliette Rihl, " 'Waste of Federal
Money': Arizona Is Losing Thousands of Affordable Rentals. Here's How," *Arizona Republic,* April 14, 2023.

263   **more than one hundred thousand affordable units would be lost prematurely:** "Pro-
tecting Long-Term Affordability by Closing the Qualified Contract Loophole,"
National Housing Trust, July 10, 2023; Donna Kimura, "Bill Seeks to Eliminate,
Modify Qualified Contract Option," Affordable Housing Finance, July 12, 2019.

263   **The IRS code specified the price:** The formula used by the IRS is meant to ensure
(among other things) that owners are compensated for their original investment
and any additional contributions, adjusted for inflation—which typically puts
the price far above market value. Affordable housing advocates have been pushing to change this formula as part of a larger effort at reforming the LIHTC
program. "26 CFR § 1.42-18—Qualified Contracts," Legal Information Institute, https://www.law.cornell.edu/cfr/text/26/1.42-18; Sandra Larson, "How to
Reform the Low-Income Housing Tax Credit Program," *Shelterforce,* November 21, 2023.

263   **Most were located in gentrifying neighborhoods:** Ed Gramlich, "Low Income
Housing Tax Credits," National Low Income Housing Coalition, 2023.

263   **For Gladstone's owner, the decision to exit LIHTC early:** All documentation pertaining to Metzger's use of the qualified contract process to exit the LIHTC program prematurely was obtained via a series of open records requests from the
Georgia Department of Community Affairs.

264   **He sold it to Empire:** These figures were obtained at the Fulton County Deeds and
Records Department on June 10, 2024. Because Metzger did not respond to phone
calls and emails seeking comment on the Empire deal, I was unable to verify that
the total sale amount did not exceed this figure. But records demonstrate that the
sale price was *at least* this amount. My thanks to Max Blau for his help in locating
this information.

264   **They did, however, note the developer's refusal:** The meeting minutes and summary of this Design Review Committee session were obtained via an open records
request to the Atlanta BeltLine, Inc. See also Douglas Sams, "Massive Southside
Trail Apartment Project will Not Offer Deeper Affordability," *Atlanta Business
Chronicle,* October 22, 2020.

265   **as did the Atlanta Regional Commission:** The ARC review noted that Empire's
project was "replacing an apartment complex that was previously affordable for
hundreds of residents. Based on historical experience with similar redevelopment
projects elsewhere in metro Atlanta, it's unlikely that the same residents will be
eligible or able to return to the same community." Nonetheless, the project was
given the go-ahead. Atlanta Regional Commission, "Regional Review Finding,"
December 7, 2020, https://documents.atlantaregional.com/Land%20Use/Reviews/

ID2074/ARC%20Final%20Report%20-%20Chosewood%20Development%20 DRI%203206.pdf.

266 **Like most of the construction happening:** Jarred Schenke, "Opportunity Zone Investors Focusing on Atlanta's 'Low-Hanging Fruit,'" Bisnow, August 5, 2019.

269 **She was surprised to see Yateshia:** Neima Abdulahi, "Residents Worry, Fear Gentrification as Atlanta Apartment Complex near BeltLine Faces Demolition," 11 Alive, September 28, 2020.

269 **There was a reference to the development:** Dyana Bagby, "Developer Seeks to Construct More Than 1,100 Residential Units near Southside Trail," *Atlanta Business Chronicle,* September 17, 2020.

269 **The clip ended with the reporter:** Abdulahi, "Residents Worry."

CHAPTER 24

276 **former Georgia governor Roy Barnes:** Shade Elam and Stephanie Ramage, "Barnes' Growing Business," *Atlanta Business Chronicle,* September 21, 1998.

276 **Although Barnes, whose financial disclosures:** Angie Thompson, "Barnes Net Worth: $16.6 Million," *The Tifton Gazette,* May 5, 2010.

277 **His brother, Ray Barnes, remained Efficiency's owner:** J. D. Capelouto, "Ex-governor Responds to Lawsuit, Complaints Against Brother's Motel Chain," *The Atlanta Journal-Constitution,* October 9, 2020.

277 **"You'll always have undesirables":** Elam and Ramage, "Barnes' Growing Business."

279 **A vibrant new tenants' rights movement:** For a masterful analysis of tenant organizing and the growing movement for housing justice during the pandemic, see Keeanga-Yamahtta Taylor, "Cancel the Rent," *The New Yorker,* May 12, 2020.

279 **Homes Guarantee campaign:** "Homes Guarantee," People's Action, https://homes guarantee.com/; Jessica Klein, "This Radical Plan Would See the U.S. Build 12 Million New Units of Social Housing," *Fast Company,* September 6, 2019.

279 **In California, unhoused Black and Latino families:** Rick Paulas, "Homeless People Are Taking Over Vacant Homes to Escape the Coronavirus," Vice News, June 19, 2020.

279 **LA Tenants Union saw its membership double:** Hannah Black, "Tenant Unions for the Future," *Dissent,* August 13, 2020.

279 **the Southern Towers apartment complex:** Eliza Tebo, "'No Job? No Rent': Residents at an Alexandria Apartment Complex Prepare to Strike," WAMU, April 8, 2020.

279 **Members of KC Tenants:** Allison Kite and Robert A. Cronkleton, "Kansas City Tenants Blockade County Courthouse, Shut Down Much of Eviction Docket," *Kansas City Star,* October 16, 2020.

279 **Seventeen members of the Philadelphia Tenants Union:** Claudia Lauer, "Protesters Demand Philadelphia Halt Evictions; 17 People Arrested," WHYY, September 3, 2020.

280   **The Atlanta Legal Aid Society had just filed a lawsuit:** Zachary Hansen, "Court: Evictions Were Illegal at Extended Stay Motel with Ties to Former Governor," *The Atlanta Journal-Constitution,* March 9, 2022.

280   **"We have an obligation":** Zachary Hansen and J. D. Capelouto, "Extended Stay Motel with Ties to Former Governor Facing Lawsuit from Residents," *The Atlanta Journal-Constitution,* October 7, 2020.

281   **Eventually the story would be picked up:** Sudhin Thanawala, "For Many Motel Dwellers, Eviction Ban Provides No Relief," Associated Press, March 27, 2021.

281   **A headline in *The New York Times*:** Matthew Goldstein, "Falling Behind on Weekly Rent and Afraid of Being Evicted," *The New York Times,* December 17, 2020.

282   **They would enlarge the photos:** Jon Styf, "See Inside Former Gov. Roy Barnes Christmas Home," *Cobb Life Magazine,* November 30, 2021.

284   **Aside from a brief chuckle:** David Brand, "Queens Man Evicted," *Queens Daily Eagle,* November 7, 2020.

CHAPTER 25

287   **"the poor get fucked over and out":** Busta Rhymes, "There's Only One Year Left!!! (Intro)," in *Extinction Level Event: The Final World Front,* Elektra Records, 1998, https://www.songlyrics.com/busta-rhymes/there-s-only-one-year-left!!!-intro -lyrics/.

290   **as overwhelmed as everyone else:** Alec MacGillis, "The Students Left Behind by Remote Learning," ProPublica, September 28, 2020.

CHAPTER 26

303   **Like extended-stay hotels, rooming houses were proliferating:** Ann Larson, "The Dark Reality of the Modern-Day Rooming House," *Fast Company,* May 5, 2023. For a more optimistic view of the rooming-house boom, see Nicholas Kristof, "The Old Way to Provide Cheap Housing," *The New York Times,* December 9, 2023.

303   **Rooming houses are notorious for attracting slumlords:** The Atlanta-based company PadSplit, which was founded in 2017 and describes itself as "the largest coliving marketplace in the U.S.," has been the subject of multiple exposés revealing a range of predatory practices. Nevertheless, the company continues to grow: PadSplit has received $35 million in venture capital funding, and as of mid-2024, it encompassed more than eleven thousand rooming-house units in eighteen cities. According to the company, 40 percent of its "members" have experienced homelessness; 83 percent are people of color. See Larson, "Dark Reality"; Rebecca Burns, "Like Airbnb, but for Flophouses," *The New Republic,* June 23, 2021; Nicole Carr, "Tenants Report Dangerous Living Conditions from Affordable Housing Startup Now Facing Legal Trouble," WSB-TV, October 12, 2020.

304 **Before she was discharged:** Matt Broaddud and Leighton Ku, "Out-of-Pocket Medical Expenses for Medicaid Beneficiaries Are Substantial and Growing," Center on Budget and Policy Priorities, May 31, 2005.

305 **It was shared and reshared:** Celeste asked me to share the link to her GoFundMe campaign on my Twitter and Facebook accounts, which I gladly did.

CHAPTER 27

308 **Natalia spotted a new post:** Like excessive application and administrative fees, nonrefundable "risk fees" for tenants with low credit scores, previous debt, or limited rental history have been denounced by advocacy groups. In 2022, the National Consumer Law Center and the National Housing Law Project submitted comments to the Consumer Financial Protection Bureau urging the agency to "investigate and prevent the imposition of junk fees" on renters. "NCLC & NHLP Comments to the Consumer Financial Protection Bureau Regarding Fees Imposed by Providers of Consumer Financial Products or Services," National Consumer Law Center, April 2022.

310 **he added up the amount of money:** America's affordable housing crisis has been a boon to the multibillion-dollar self-storage industry—indeed, there are now more self-storage units in the United States than in all other countries combined. Mike Kuhlenbeck, "The Costs Lurking in Self Storage," *The Progressive Magazine,* October 24, 2022.

312 **the grim statistics:** Brenda Richardson, "More Americans Own Their Homes, but the Black-White Homeownership Rate Gap Is the Biggest in a Decade, Survey Finds," *Forbes,* March 4, 2023.

312 **the country's owner-renter divide was a key driver of its racial wealth gap:** Liz Mineo, "Racial Wealth Gap May Be a Key to Other Inequities," *Harvard Gazette,* June 3, 2021.

CHAPTER 28

322 **It turned out he *was* capable:** Ashley Crockett, "LRPD Searching for a Suspect Who Police Say Killed His Girlfriend," ABC 7, April 11, 2022.

CHAPTER 29

327 **an annual rate of 26.84 percent:** Ryan Felton, "The Big Business of Bad Car Loans," *Consumer Reports*, January 22, 2022.

327 **its practices "put car buyers in economic danger":** "AG Healey Secures $5.5 Million for Consumers, State in Subprime Auto Loan Settlement," Mass.gov, April 8, 2019, https://www.mass.gov/news/ag-healey-secures-55-million-for-consumers

-state-in-subprime-auto-loan-settlement#:~:text=%E2%80%9CThis%20company's %20loans%20put%20Massachusetts,securitizers%2C%20and%20protect%20 consumers.%E2%80%9D.

327   **Meanwhile, as of 2023, an astounding 30 percent:** Paige Smith, Scott Carpenter, and Rachael Dottle, "Wall Street Is Making Millions Pushing Subprime Car Loans to People Who Can't Afford Them," Bloomberg, November 13, 2023.

334   **a memoir by:** Cicely Tyson, *Just as I Am: A Memoir,* with Michelle Burford (New York: HarperCollins, 2021).

336   **Investment capital had continued to pour into the area:** Josh Green, "Southside Development 'Blowing Up' Beltline's Chosewood Park," Urbanize Atlanta, May 19, 2022.

336   **surge of development dollars into Chosewood Park:** Savannah Sicurella, "Southside Trail Residential Boom Raises Concerns over 'Responsible Development,'" *Atlanta Business Chronicle,* November 19, 2021.

CHAPTER 30

339   **rent-to-own stores were infamously predatory:** Chico Harlan, "Rental America: Why the Poor Pay $4,150 for a $1,500 Sofa," *The Washington Post,* October 16, 2014; National Consumer Law Center, "The Rent-to-Own Racket," National Consumer Law Center, February 5, 2019, https://www.nclc.org/resources/report -the-rent-to-own-racket/.

348   **the resources to offer such assistance:** Stephannie Stokes, "When Families Need Housing, Georgia Will Pay for Foster Care Rather Than Provide Assistance," ProPublica, January 18, 2024.

349   **Medicaid's "coverage gap":** "The Medicaid Coverage Gap in Georgia," Center on Budget and Policy Priorities, fact sheet, July 8, 2021.

349   **subsidized "family planning services":** "Planning for Healthy Babies (P4HB) Fact Sheet," Georgia Department of Community Health, 2023.

EPILOGUE

352   **Dubbed the "most Atlanta of Atlanta's streets":** Floyd Hall and Austin L. Ray, "What's the Most Atlanta Street?," *Atlanta Magazine,* September 14, 2022.

353   **none of these families would be counted:** "Don't Count on It: How HUD's Point-in-Time Count Underestimates the Homelessness Crisis in America," National Law Center on Poverty and Homelessness, report, 2017; "The Pitfalls of HUD's Point-in-Time Count for Children, Youth, and Families," SchoolHouse Connection, December 2023.

353   **"No one is living on the streets":** This statement is attributed to Philip Abrams, deputy assistant director for housing for HUD, on June 16, 1982. Quoted in Jon Erickson and Charles Wilhem, *Housing the Homeless* (New Brunswick, N.J.: Rutgers University Press, 1986), 315.

354   **the neoliberal revolution:** George Monbiot and Peter Hutchison, *Invisible Doctrine: The Secret History of Neoliberalism* (New York: Crown, 2024); Gary Gerstle, *The Rise and Fall of the Neoliberal Order: America and the World in the Free Market Era* (New York: Oxford University Press, 2022).

354   **the shock needed to be neutralized:** Much of this section is indebted to Peter Marcuse's incisive work, in particular his essay "Neutralizing Homelessness," *Socialist Review,* no. 1 (1988): 69–97.

354   **as a lifestyle choice:** President Ronald Reagan popularized this view when, during a televised interview that aired in January 1984, a reporter asked him about criticism that his policies benefited the rich at the expense of low-income Americans. Reagan responded by referring to "the people who are sleeping on the grates, the homeless who are homeless, you might say, *by choice.*" Quoted in William Raspberry, "Homeless by Choice," *The Washington Post,* February 2, 1984. A transcript of the full interview, "Interview with David Hartman of ABC News on the 1984 Presidential Election," January 30, 1984, can be found at National Archives, Ronald Reagan Presidential Library & Museum.

354   **Federal funding for research on homelessness:** Marian Moser Jones, "Creating a Science of Homelessness During the Reagan Era," *Milbank Quarterly* 93, no. 1 (2004): 139–78. For a discussion of how the Reagan administration explicitly delineated the acceptable parameters of social research, see Constance Holden, "Reagan Versus the Social Sciences," *Science* 226, no. 4678 (1984): 1052–54.

354   **"lopsided research agenda":** Jones, "Creating a Science," 142. Jones notes: "Far less attention has been paid to homelessness among people without serious mental illness or other disabling conditions. This pattern is consistent with trends begun during the first generation of homelessness research. In a 1990 article, two leading investigators of family homelessness alleged that 'researchers seeking federal dollars to study homelessness are steered away from concerns about housing or poverty or racism, and toward the differential diagnosis of mental disorders among homeless people'" (165). The 1990 article is Marybeth Shinn and Beth C. Weitzman, "Research on Homelessness: An Introduction," *Social Issues* 46, no. 4 (1990): 1–11.

354   **had no more *caused* them to become homeless:** In their book *Homelessness Is a Housing Problem: How Structural Patterns Explain U.S. Factors* (Oakland: University of California Press, 2022), Cregg Colburn and Clayton Page Aldern draw on national homelessness data to rebut the claim that drug abuse and mental illness are the fundamental causes of homelessness. If mental health issues or substance use were major drivers of homelessness, Colburn and Aldern argue, then areas of the United States with higher rates of these problems would see higher rates of homelessness. But that's not the case. States like Utah, Alabama, Kentucky, West Virginia, and Wisconsin have some of the highest rates of mental illness and drug use in the country, but modest levels of homelessness. High housing costs and low vacancy rates, they conclude, are the two key variables determining higher homelessness rates in a particular area.

354   **a medicalized homelessness was deemed less threatening:** Arline Mathieu, "The

Medicalization of Homelessness and the Theater of Repression," *Medical Anthropology Quarterly* 7, no. 2 (1993): 170–84. As sociologist Loïc Wacquant argues, the medicalization of homelessness became "a conduit to criminalization at the bottom of the class structure as it introduced a logic of individual treatment." Loïc Wacquant, *Punishing the Poor: The Neoliberal Government of Social Insecurity* (Durham, N.C.: Duke University Press, 2009), xxii. See also the chapter "From Pathology to Population" in Craig Willse, *The Value of Homelessness: Managing Surplus Life in the United States* (Minneapolis: University of Minnesota Press, 2015), 81–108.

354   **the fastest-growing segment of the nation's homeless population:** Debra J. Rog, C. Scott Holupka, and Lisa C. Patton, "Characteristics and Dynamics of Homeless Families with Children," Office of the Assistant Secretary for Planning and Evaluation Office of Human Services Policy, U.S. Department of Health and Human Services, Fall 2007.

354   **erected a tent city near the White House:** " 'Reaganville' Camp Erected to Protest Plight of the Poor," *The New York Times,* November 27, 1981.

354   **a searing depiction:** Jonathan Kozol, *Rachel and Her Children: Homeless Families in America* (New York: Crown, 1988).

355   **polled individuals at random:** E. R. Shipp, "Do More for Homeless, Say Half of Those Polled," *The New York Times,* February 3, 1986.

355   **an increasingly technical and specialized jargon:** A dominant theory pertaining to homelessness in the 1980s and 1990s was the "disaffiliation" thesis. Its most well-known formulation: "Homelessness is a condition of detachment from society characterized by the absence or attenuation of the affiliative bonds that link settled persons to a network of interconnected social structures." Quoted in Ella Howard, *Homeless: Poverty and Place in Urban America* (Philadelphia: University of Pennsylvania Press, 2013), 148.

355   **deliberately narrow and circumscribed:** Jones, "Creating a Science," 154; see also "Hidden Homelessness in the U.S.: Why Congress Must Change HUD's Definition of Homelessness to Align with Other Federal Agencies," SchoolHouse Connection, December 19, 2023.

355   **For advocates, this was a matter of moral urgency:** Sam Tsemberis, *Housing First: The Pathways Model to End Homelessness for People with Mental Illness and Addiction* (Center City, Minn.: Hazelden, 2010); Jill Khadduri and Marybeth Shinn, *In the Midst of Plenty: Homelessness and What to Do About It* (New York: Wiley-Blackwell, 2020) and Deborah Padgett, Benjamin Henwood, and Sam Tsemberis, *Housing First: Ending Homelessness, Transforming Systems, and Changing Lives* (New York: Oxford University Press, 2015); Nan Roman, *The Ethics of Housing: The Case for the Housing First Approach* (Washington, D.C.: National Alliance to End Homelessness, 2018).

356   **Staff at schools and colleges:** Brian Goldstone, "3 Kids. 2 Paychecks. No Home," *The California Sunday Magazine,* November 26, 2019; "The Education of Children and Youth Experiencing Homelessness: Current Trends, Challenges, and Needs," fact sheet, SchoolHouse Connection, March 2024.

357 **More than 64,000 residents were living doubled-up:** "2016 Estimate of Homeless People in Chicago," Chicago Coalition for the Homeless.

357 **Bring Chicago Home:** Becky Vevea, "Election Results Show Chicago Voters Reject Ballot Measure Aimed at Helping Homeless," Chalkbeat, March 19, 2024; Kari Lydersen, "The Fight to Bring Chicago Home Isn't Over," *In These Times,* May 2, 2024.

357 **"The idea that these people aren't 'actually' homeless":** Quoted in Brian Goldstone, "The New American Homeless," *The New Republic,* August 21, 2019.

357 **frequently exposed to "toxic stress":** Jack P. Shonkoff, Andrew S. Garner, Benjamin S. Siegel, Mary I. Dobbins, Marian F. Earls, Laura McGuinn, John Pascoe, and David L. Wood, "The Lifelong Effects of Early Childhood Adversity and Toxic Stress," *Pediatrics* 129, no. 1 (January 2012): e232–e246; "Impact of Trauma on Children Experiencing Homelessness," Horizons for Homeless Children, 2023.

357 **What they discovered was striking:** The study used American Community Survey microdata from the U.S. Census to measure doubled-up homelessness nationwide. The researchers note: "This estimate represents a subset of people living in poor or near poor households who meet specific criteria suggesting they are likely doubling up due to economic hardship—also referred to as doubled-up homelessness. We define doubled-up homeless individuals as poor or near poor individuals (at or below 125% of a housing-cost adjusted poverty threshold) in a poor or near poor household who are either: a relative that the household head does not customarily take responsibility for (based on age and relationship); or a non-relative who is not a partner and not formally sharing in household costs (not listed as roommates). Single adult children and relatives over 65 may be seen as a householder's responsibility, so such cases are only included if the household is overcrowded (more than 2 people per bedroom)—an arrangement suggesting economic hardship." Molly K. Richard, Julie Dworkin, Katherine Grace Rule, Suniya Farooqui, Zachary Glendening, and Sam Carlson, "Quantifying Doubled-Up Homelessness: Presenting a New Measure Using U.S. Census Microdata," *Housing Policy Debate* 34, no. 1 (2024): 3–24.

357 **In Georgia, approximately 118,000 residents:** The estimated figure for 2022 was 117,943. Many thanks to Molly K. Richard for providing me with this estimate, drawing on 2022 ACS one-year data. "Analysis of American Community Survey 1-Year (2022) Microdata," downloaded from IPUMS USA: Version 15.0 [dataset] (Minneapolis, MN: IPUMS, 2024), https://doi.org/10.18128/D010.V15.0.

357 **the Point-in-Time count total for Georgia:** "2022 Georgia Statewide Point in Time Count Report," Georgia Department of Community Affairs, 2022, https://www.dca.ga.gov/sites/default/files/2022_georgia_dca_statewide_point_in_time_count_homeless_report.pdf.

358 **children enrolled in the nation's public schools:** "Student Homelessness in America: School Years 2019–20 to 2021–22," brief, National Center for Homeless Education, 2023, 9.

358 **One in-depth investigation:** Amy DiPierro, "Hidden Toll: Thousands of Schools Fail to Count Homeless Students," Chalkbeat, November 15, 2022.

358 **well over *four million*:** This estimate draws on the 2023 Point-in-Time count results (653,100), the most up-to-date (school year 2021–22) Department of Education data on homeless students residing in hotels and motels nationwide (106,621),
and the national estimate of doubled-up homelessness as of 2022 (approximately
3.3 million). There is, of course, a degree of duplication among these data sources,
but given the widely acknowledged undercounting that attends the Point-in-
Time and Department of Education reporting, such an estimate can indeed be
described as conservative.

358 **an astonishing half of all U.S. renters:** "America's Rental Housing 2024," Joint Cen-
ter for Housing Studies of Harvard University, 2024; Jennifer Ludden, "Housing
Is Now Unaffordable for a Record Half of All U.S. Renters, Study Finds," NPR,
January 25, 2024.

359 **Temporary relief programs:** Matthew Desmond, "Tools to End the Poverty Pandemic," *The New York Review of Books,* January 18, 2024.

359 **thirty-four affordable and available rental homes:** "Latest Gap Report Reveals Only
34 Affordable and Available Homes Exist for Every 100 Extremely Low-Income
Renters," National Low Income Housing Coalition, March 2024.

359 **a shortage of 7.3 million low-rent apartments:** "The Gap: A Shortage of Affordable
Homes 2023," National Low Income Housing Coalition, March 2023.

359 **Giant private equity firms:** Heather Vogell, "When Private Equity Becomes Your
Landlord," ProPublica, February 7, 2022; Francesca Mari, "A $60 Billion Housing
Grab by Wall Street," *The New York Times Magazine,* March 4, 2020; Roshan
Abraham, "People Are Organizing to Fight the Private Equity Firms Who Own
Their Homes," Vice, May 16, 2023.

359 **bulk buyers have used billions of dollars in cash:** Brian Eason and John Perry,
"American Dream for Rent: Investors Elbow Out Individual Home Buyers," *The
Atlanta Journal-Constitution,* February 9, 2023.

359 **the two largest out-of-state companies:** Eason and Perry, "American Dream for
Rent." See also Sean Keenan, "Study: Three Corporate Landlords Anonymously
Own Outsize Chunk of Metro Atlanta's Rental Homes," Atlanta Civic Circle,
March 5, 2024.

359 **investors bought one out of every three homes for sale:** Eason and Perry, "American
Dream for Rent."

360 **colluding to artificially increase rents:** Heather Vogell, "Pressure Grows on Real
Estate Tech Company Accused of Colluding with Landlords to Jack Up Apartment Rents," ProPublica, November 14, 2022.

360 **sixteen million units:** Matt Stoller, "Monopoly Round-Up: FBI Raids Big Corporate Landlords," *The Big Newsletter,* June 3, 2024.

360 **"Where are people going to go?":** Quoted in Kriston Capps and Sarah Holder,
"Wolf of Main Street," Bloomberg, March 3, 2022.

361 **Looking to the private market:** Tracy Rosenthal, "The Enduring Fiction of Affordable Housing," *The New Republic,* April 2, 2021.

361 **a guaranteed right for everybody:** David Madden and Peter Marcuse, *In Defense of*

Housing: The Politics of Crisis (London: Verso, 2016); Keeanga-Yamahtta Taylor, "Cancel the Rent," *The New Yorker,* May 12, 2022.

361   **The idea of a right to housing:** Rachel G. Bratt, Michael E. Stone, and Chester Hartman, *The Human Right to Housing* (New York: Routledge, 2006); David Madden and Peter Marcuse, *In Defense of Housing: The Politics of Crisis* (Verso, 2016); Mariana Mazzucato and Leilani Farha, "The Right to Housing: A Mission-oriented and Human Rights–based Approach," working paper (2023), https://make-the-shift.org/wp-content/uploads/2023/06/Right-to-Housing-Missions-Final-DIGITAL.pdf.

361   **proposed Second Bill of Rights of 1944:** Franklin D. Roosevelt, "State of the Union Message to Congress," January 11, 1944, Franklin D. Roosevelt Presidential Library & Museum.

361   **Article 25:** United Nations General Assembly, "Universal Declaration of Human Rights," Article 25, December 10, 1948.

362   **roughly 3.6 million eviction filings in a typical year:** Eviction Lab homepage, accessed July 26, 2024, https://evictionlab.org/; Michael Casey and R. J. Rico, "Eviction Filings Soar over 50% Above Pre-pandemic Levels in Some Cities as Rents Increase," *PBS NewsHour,* June 17, 2023.

362   **access to free legal representation:** Vamsi A. Damerla, "The Right to Counsel in Eviction Proceedings: A Fundamental Rights Approach," *Columbia Human Rights Law Review,* May 5, 2022; Heidi Schultheis and Caitlin Rooney, "A Right to Counsel Is a Right to a Fighting Chance," Center for American Progress, October 2, 2019.

362   **direct cash assistance:** Rachel M. Cohen, "The Federal Government's New Plan to (Maybe) Give Renters Straight Cash," Vox, June 13, 2024.

362   **Closing the qualified contract loophole:** "Protecting Long-Term Affordability by Closing the Qualified Contract Loophole," National Housing Trust, July 10, 2023; Donna Kimura, "Bill Seeks to Eliminate, Modify Qualified Contract Option," Affordable Housing Finance, July 12, 2019.

362   **"just cause" eviction laws:** Jade Vazquez and Sarah Gallagher, "Promoting Housing Stability Through Just Cause Eviction Legislation," National Low Income Housing Coalition, May 18, 2022; Greg David, "How N.Y.'s 'Good Cause Eviction' Bill Breaks from Other States' Laws," *The City,* February 28, 2024.

362   **rent control, among the most potent weapons:** Mark Paul, "Economists Hate Rent Control. Here's Why They're Wrong," *The American Prospect,* May 16, 2023; Charlie Dulick, "Rent Control Now!," *The New Republic,* May 24, 2024.

362   **Real estate lobbyists:** Brendan O'Brien, "Big Real Estate Says Regulations Caused Housing Crisis, but They Wrote the Rules," Truthout, September 9, 2023; Americans for Financial Reform, "Report Exposes How Real Estate Industry Maintains Housing Crisis," Americans for Financial Reform, news release, June 6, 2024.

362   **why tenant organizing and tenant unions are so important:** Tracy Rosenthal and Leonardo Vilchis, *Abolish Rent: How Tenants Can End the Housing Crisis* (Chicago: Haymarket Books, 2024). See, for example, Jamila Michener and Mallory SoRelle, "Power, Politics, and Precarity: How Tenant Organizations Transform

Local Political Life," *Interest Groups & Advocacy* 11 (2022): 209–236, https://link
.springer.com/article/10.1057/s41309-021-00148-7; Tressie McMillan Cottom,
"What's Happening in Louisville Could Solve a Housing Crisis," *The New York
Times,* August 6, 2024.

363   **a group of residents sued the hotel:** In August 2021, I (along with two academic
researchers) signed on to an amicus brief in support of the lawsuit against Efficiency Lodge. Zachary Hansen, "Court: Evictions Were Illegal at Extended Stay
Motel with Ties to Former Governor," *The Atlanta Journal-Constitution,* March 9,
2022; Kayla Pfeifer, "From Transient to Tenant OverNite: The Georgia Court of
Appeals Leaves Room for Improvement in the Rights of Extended-Stay Motel
Residents," *Mercer Law Review* 74, no. 2 (2023): 767–82.

363   **Banning extortionate application fees:** David Dayen, "The Junk Fee Fight Spreads
to Rental Housing," *The American Prospect,* July 25, 2023.

363   **prohibiting discrimination against voucher holders:** Alison Bell and Barbara Sard,
"Prohibiting Discrimination Against Renters Using Housing Vouchers Improves
Results," Center on Budget and Policy Priorities, December 20, 2018.

363   **Expanding HUD's definition of** *homeless***:** Teresa Wiltz, "Redefining Homelessness
Could Help Families on the Edge, Advocates Say," *Wisconsin Examiner,* Novem-
ber 27, 2019; Rachel M. Cohen, "How Should HUD Count Homeless Families?,"
Bloomberg, July 19, 2018.

363   **Restrictive land use policies:** Jerusalem Demsas, *On the Housing Crisis: Land, Devel-
opment, Democracy* (New York: Zando/Atlantic Editions, 2024); Sonia A. Hirt,
Zoned in the USA: The Origins and Implications of American Land-Use Regulation
(Ithaca, N.Y.: Cornell University Press, 2014).

363   **75 percent of land in the nation's major cities:** Emily Badger and Quoctrung Bui,
"Cities Start to Question an American Ideal: A House with a Yard on Every Lot,"
The New York Times, June 18, 2019.

364   **a model known as "social housing":** Saoirse Gowan and Ryan Cooper, "Social
Housing in the United States," People's Policy Project, April 2018; Amee Chew,
"Social Housing Is Public Housing," *Jacobin,* April 6, 2024.

364   **Finland has made international headlines:** Ella Hancock, "Helsinki Is Still Leading
the Way in Ending Homelessness—but How Are They Doing It?," World Habi-
tat, April 5, 2023; Tahiat Mahboob, "Housing Is a Human Right: How Finland Is
Eradicating Homelessness," CBC Radio, January 24, 2020.

364   **social housing has particularly thrived:** Francesca Mari, "Lessons from a Renter's
Utopia," *The New York Times Magazine,* May 23, 2023.

364   **a Vienna resident:** Mari, "Lessons from a Renter's Utopia."

364   **set up to fail:** Gail Radford, *Modern Housing for America: Policy Struggles in the New
Deal Era* (Chicago: University of Chicago Press, 1996); Edward G. Goetz, *New
Deal Ruins: Race, Economic Justice, and Public Housing Policy* (Ithaca, N.Y.: Cor-
nell University Press, 2013).

364   **raising the federal minimum wage:** Steven Greenhouse, "'The Success Is Inspirational': The Fight for $15 Movement 10 Years On," *The Guardian,* November 23,

2022; Matthew Desmond, "The $15 Minimum Wage Doesn't Just Improve Lives. It Saves Them," *The New York Times Magazine,* February 21, 2019.

364   **significantly expanding labor protections:** Hamilton Nolan, *The Hammer: Power, Inequality, and the Struggle for the Soul of Labor* (New York: Hachette Books, 2024); Kim Kelly, *Fight Like Hell: The Untold History of American Labor* (New York: One Signal, 2022); Steven Greenhouse, *Beaten Down, Worked Up: The Past, Present, and Future of American Labor* (New York: Knopf, 2019); Jane F. McAlevey, *No Shortcuts: Organizing for Power in the New Gilded Age* (New York: Oxford University Press, 2016).

INDEX

| ABOUT THE AUTHOR |

Brian Goldstone is a journalist whose long-form reporting and essays have appeared in *Harper's Magazine, The New Republic, The California Sunday Magazine,* and *Jacobin,* among other publications. He has a PhD in anthropology from Duke University and was a Mellon Research Fellow at Columbia University. In 2021, he was a National Fellow at New America. He lives in Atlanta with his family.

BRIANGOLDSTONE.NET

X: BRIAN_GOLDSTONE